TRANSFORMATION IN TIMES OF CRISIS

Eight Principles for Creating Opportunities and Value in the Post-Pandemic World

Nitin Rakesh and Jerry Wind

notionpress.com

INDIA • SINGAPORE • MALAYSIA

Notion Press

No. 8, 3rd Cross Street,
CIT Colony, Mylapore,
Chennai, Tamil Nadu – 600 004

First Published by Notion Press 2020
Copyright © Nitin Rakesh and Jerry Wind 2020
All Rights Reserved.

ISBN 978-1-63714-755-9

We dedicate this book to the COVID heroes of frontline workers – doctors, healthcare workers and essential staff, including technology staff – who made possible the seamless transition to a virtual economy at scale.

I (Jerry Wind) dedicate this book to my partner Barbara Eberlein for her inspiration and love, which sustained me while working on this book and will continue to do so long after its publication.

Contents

Some Early Reactions

1. From profoundly philosophical to immeasurably practical, the authors offer a solid playbook that businesses can use during times of disruption and global economic volatility. This is a must-read primer for businesses, entrepreneurs, students, and philanthropists alike, as well as those with a keen interest in identifying the tectonic shifts of our times. It will help readers understand how to build high-impact organizations that consistently deliver the best results to customers.

   – Mukesh Aghi, President and CEO,
   US-India Strategic Partnership Forum

2. Congratulations to Nitin Rakesh and Jerry Wind for completing a wonderful book at an absolutely appropriate time. It will guide all decision makers how to think about navigating through the current crisis successfully. This is a playbook that can be applied at all times, including the current crisis.

   – Raamdeo Agrawal,
   Co-Founder and Joint Managing Director,
   Motilal Oswal Financial Services Ltd

3.   The COVID-19 crisis this year struck a body blow to many retailers who were forced to close their stores with little warning. It pushed some over the edge. At Williams-Sonoma, we embraced the crisis as a challenge. Our digital-first strategy combined with our omni-channel approach and commitment to sustainability have been a powerful source of differentiation and competitive advantage – and they have worked wonders. We have seen record growth in earnings and e-commerce during the past two quarters. These are the very strategies that Jerry Wind and Nitin Rakesh emphasize in their timely book. All retailers should heed their lessons.

– Laura Alber,
President and Chief Executive Officer,
Williams-Sonoma

4.   Timely and provocative, Jerry Wind and Nitin Rakesh will challenge you to lean into the crisis and use it to disrupt your business to emerge even stronger. The interdependent chapters are sequenced in a way that offers leaders a roadmap to turn the ideas into real change.

– Paul Bascobert,
Investor/advisor, former CEO,
Gannett Inc.

5.   In this short and terrific book, the authors make a compelling case that COVID-19 is both a crisis on its own as well as an experiment at scale of the impact of disruption. Companies must evidently fix the now, but the best ones are already looking at the after-COVID world, building new ways to sweat assets, building competencies, and creating new ways to compete – with a 360 degrees renewal. The eight principles

form an excellent cookbook to speed up the change and succeed.

**– Jacques Bughin, Portulans Institute,
P.E. advisor at Fortino, former Senior
Partner at McKinsey and
Director of McKinsey Global Institute**

6. If you are a decision-maker in an arts education or performing arts institution, Transformation in Times of Crisis provides a timely and powerful approach to confidently adapt to, innovate from, and lead amidst the permanent effects that the pandemic is having on our field. While the book is written for all fields of business, arts organizations in particular are struggling to overcome this once-in-a-lifetime upheaval and have no roadmap to do so. With this book, which I wholeheartedly recommend, Rakesh and Wind detail useful strategies for us to emerge from the crisis with the courage to try new and untested ways to enact our artistic and educational missions.

    **– Roberto Diaz, President and CEO,
    Curtis Institute of Music**

7. Rakesh and Wind waste no time combatting the most significant inflection point in our lifetimes. They give you a once-in-an-era chance to make changes you never thought possible, or never even realized you needed to make. They delve into the cut-throat opportunities being presented by this massive shift to a purely digital environment and the mindset business and IT leaders must adopt if they are going to stand a chance of thriving in this environment. Most importantly they focus on the mental shift we have to confront head-on with how we approach our talent, our technology and our careers. A definite must-read for any business

leader needing validation and inspiration as an uncertain, but opportunistic, future unravels.

– Phil Fersht, CEO and Founder,
HFS Research

8. We are aware of collateral damage from catastrophes of all kinds, but there is also collateral benefit when societies or businesses adapt to circumstances imposed on them by external forces – natural, political, behavioral or technological. In this book, Wind and Rakesh have created a playbook for just such adaptation, and for conceptualizing your organization in anticipation of external forces to come. It is written with astonishing clarity and argued with rich histories of reinvention. This book is the Mother of all Mothers of Invention.

– Bob Garfield, Co-host, WNYC Studios'
"On the Media"; Host,
"The Genius Dialogues" on Audible;
Co-founder and president,
The Purple Project for Democracy

9. This book is essential reading in 2020 and beyond. This current crisis has catalyzed and accelerated the digital transformation journeys already underway for businesses and in turn, created tremendous new opportunities for the industry. These opportunities have compelled us to redraft the playbook for the IT industry with talent, trust and innovation as key pillars of success in a hyper-digital, largely contactless world. Technology is a moving goalpost and without digital mastery over technology that has largely become democratized, we will lose our competitive edge to compete on the world stage. The eight principles in this book form a great framework to change our mindset and focus on the right implementation strategy to survive and succeed in the

next normal. This is our moment and we cannot afford to lose it. Kudos to Nitin and Jerry for bringing this to us.

– Debjani Ghosh, President, NASSCOM

10. During my 44 years as Founder, CEO and Chairman of the fastest growing and largest background check company in the world, crises have lived in my blood. There was never a moment in my career that I had not been required to change what we fundamentally did. I prided myself by saying my business card should say "Agent of Change" not CEO. I have a sign on my desk that says "If it ain't broken, fix it anyway." For a period of time, one of the job requirements in our firm was to wear sneakers because you could not run fast enough with shoes. We also believed that making mistakes was core to our culture. I even paid people a dollar for each mistake at one point in my career. What Nitin Rakesh and Jerry Wind have written strikes at the core of my beliefs on how to run a business. Having known Mr. Rakesh for almost two decades, I admire his and Prof.   Wind's instincts and abilities to transcend today's issues and historical framework and transform them into the needs of a post-pandemic economy.

**– William Greenblatt, Founder,
Ex-Chairman and CEO, Sterling Talent Solutions**

11. I believe we should view the global pandemic, social unrest and economic crisis not as problems but as opportunities. These are helping us speed up long overdue changes to test new programs, partnerships, business models and approaches to set the stage for the continued transformation of TIME. For example, we are streamlining our B2B approach, accelerating data collection and recurring revenue streams, and launching fresh services focused on health care and kids. This is consistent with the

approach that Rakesh and Wind recommend, which is why I am sure other leaders will find their book as relevant as I did.

– Keith A. Grossman,
President, Time Magazine

12. Companies as well as countries are trying to grapple with the global pandemic. At such a time, Transformation in Times of Crisis is one of the most insightful, timely and relevant books to be written. Its core message – that every crisis presents opportunities disguised as challenges – needs to be heard widely. While the book is not aimed at government officials, it makes a compelling case why public policy must work hand in hand with private enterprise to find innovative solutions to the global crisis.

– Lady Barbara Thomas Judge,
Senior Advisor, Athene Capital

13. This book is the one that needed to be written. Many books cover one or a few of these principles in depth. This book spells out all eight major principles that can help your company navigate through recovery, normalization, and growth. Don't rely on only a few principles. All eight principles interact and need your full understanding and action.

– Philip Kotler, S.C. Johnson &
Son Distinguished Professor of International
Marketing, Kellogg School of Management,
Northwestern University (emeritus)

14. Read this necessary book. It is indispensable knowledge for today's climate and in general for those interested in building sustainable businesses and brands. The pandemic has accelerated

an impending change and led to very large and complex problems for many companies that many could not and did not anticipate. Wind and Rakesh, however, have been able to distill the complexity, uncertainty and change, and they provide optimism and wisdom. This book delivers very compelling actions of a new mindset leaders and organizations need to thrive in a world of change. Read the sections on "Challenge your mental models" and "Innovate and then experiment" immediately.

– Laurent Larguinat, Sr. Director,
Mars Consumer and Market Insights

15. During periods of change and disruption, leaders must recognize the importance of transforming while maintaining a long-term perspective. As Rakesh and Wind skillfully illustrate in their topical, timely, well-argued book, companies can only survive and emerge stronger after crises by doing the right thing and serving the interests of all of their stakeholders.

– William P. Lauder, Executive Chairman,
The Estée Lauder Companies and Lecturer,
The Wharton School, University of Pennsylvania

16. In a world marked by global uncertainty and incredible dynamism, the authors' prescient eight principles are truly a breath of fresh air, providing a solid framework for businesses new and old to redefine themselves in this era of unprecedented disruption. I cannot recommend it more highly.

– David K.P Li, Chairman and
Chief Executive of Bank of East Asia

17. Leaders do not have the luxury of choosing when a crisis will occur, but their response and actions often have lasting

implications. The authors of Transformation in Times of Crisis provide a smart, tangible approach to help companies emerge from crises, not only intact but stronger.

– Manny Maceda,
Worldwide Managing Partner, Bain & Co.

18. This book delivers real-world strategies to play offense and disrupt rather than be disrupted. It's a primer for navigating the dangers and seizing the opportunities of today's once-in-a-lifetime triple whammy of crises.

– David Morey, Chairman, DMG Global and
best-selling author of Creating Business
Magic and Innovating Innovation

19. Nitin Rakesh and Jerry Wind are a rare combination of a successful tech CEO and an American business guru. Their complementary skill sets have resulted in a timely book that provides useful insights to millions of businesses struggling to grapple with the post-COVID world."

– Saurabh Mukherjea, Founder and
Chief Investment Officer,
Marcellus Investment Managers

20. In the midst of the worldwide pandemic, leaders of institutions and companies have to make immediate choices. What is still relevant? What is to be discarded? In this timely guide to transformation, Nitin Rakesh and Jerry Wind use their lifetime of executive coaching experience to set forth immediate action steps for all leaders to meet the new needs of the people they serve, whether in private markets or in public and non-profit service. They adapt classic organization change models with the

lessons of the post 2000 period to provide an essential manual on how to experiment and succeed in an accelerating world.

– Ralph Muller, CEO (retired)
University of Pennsylvania Health System

21. The COVID crisis has dramatically accelerated the trends of digital disruption that were already underway. Businesses either need to seize the opportunities created by that disruption, or risk being left behind. Rakesh and Wind provide a smart guide to the first option.

– Alan Murray, CEO, Fortune

22. This book carefully assembles a framework for guiding businesses in thinking through their recovery after the destruction wrought by the pandemic. It is argued with exceptional clarity and dotted with several illuminating examples of success.

– P. Jayendra Nayak, Former Chairman &
CEO, Axis Bank, India

23. In the more than 25 years that I have known Jerry Wind, his ability not only to see the future but to understand clearly what to do about it has not only impressed but inspired me. In this book, Jerry and Nitin have outlined a timely and critical guide for thriving through and beyond the crisis that we all face. The advice and processes laid out in Transformation in Times of Crisis is essential reading for anyone leading an enterprise who is trying to make it to the time when things get back to normal – simply because that normal of years past will never return.

– Ben Nelson, Founder, Chairman and
CEO, Minerva Project

24.   One of the clear impacts of the COVID-19 pandemic is that it brought to a standstill many business-related activities: travelling, meetings, working in factories or offices, logistics, etc. We believe that the reaction to this period of stoppage will be an increase in the speed of business as companies try to recover lost ground. The work of Nitin Rakesh and Jerry Wind is the first approach I have seen to create a management structure for this increase of speed in order to facilitate how to control business operations and manage them better. Nitin and Jerry explain very well the fact that the new environment after controlling the pandemic requires a new strategy or at least some changes in strategy. The work of Nitin Rakesh and Jerry Wind can be of extraordinary help for enthusiastic managers who want to transform the Covid-19 pandemic into an opportunity to gain leadership in their sector through a faster speed than their competitors.

– Pedro Nueno, Professor IESE,
Honorary President CEIBS

25.   As is stated in Jerry Wind's and Nitin Rakesh's new book, "Winston Churchill is believed to have said that one should never let a good crisis go to waste." In their timely book on managing during a crisis they have compiled what Sir Winston tried to say in one sentence. All organizations must adapt their approach to a crisis in a different manner and if they do not, they might find themselves damaging or destroying themselves. Leaders must become even more active in their style, and they must take charge in a manner that perhaps was not the approach in better times. Often that new style needs to be "do it and do it now." Even in good times you should sit down and imagine what type of crisis could be cast upon you at some future date and determine what the approach might be if it comes around the corner. Those who deny that strong action must be taken in times of crisis

are doomed to even greater difficulties. The "old way" probably won't work. Jerry and Nitin have encapsulated the problems and how to address them in this excellent "eight principles" book.

– Russ Palmer, Chairman & CEO,
The Palmer Group; former Dean, The Wharton
School of the University of Pennsylvania

26. Wow, we finally have a playbook for the new world. It's well-informed, surprising, provocative and as current as today's New York Times. I'm really glad I got to read it before everyone else does.

– Chuck Porter, Chairman,
Crispin Porter and Bogusky

27. Rakesh and Wind see the impact of the pandemic: a decade of trends compressed into a single year, delivering high failure rates and unplanned demand. Some leaders will surf the tsunami, others will drown. This book is the surfboard every CEO needs to turn challenges into triumph.

– Donald H. Putnam, Managing Partner,
Grail Partners LLC

28. John D. Rockefeller famously said "I always try to turn every disaster into an opportunity." Jerry Wind and Nitin Rakesh are providing a handbook for any CEO to make an opportunity of the COVID-19 crisis by transforming their business into a dynamic and successful enterprise. This book draws on the authors' cumulative years of experience advising and teaching CEOs of companies in consulting assignments and as part of Wharton Executive Education. It offers eight integrated principles which I, as CEO of QS, a leading

enterprise in higher education rankings and data analytics, can immediately seize upon and start to implement to transform our organisation. Transformation in Times of Crisis is practical, easy to understand and designed to be implemented in a structured fashion. Of the eight integrated principles, I have long since learned from Jerry to constantly challenge my mental models. I can also say that QS in 2020 is in the process of "speeding up our digital transformation and personalising user experience, reinventing our talent strategy and embracing a multi-stakeholder approach, whilst planning a portfolio of innovation initiatives over multiple time horizons." But after reading this book, I realise we need to consider "open innovation, deploying idealized design and above all else... to experiment more." I am excited to see where this journey takes us.

– Nunzio Quacquarelli, CEO,
QS Quacquarelli Symonds

29. To best navigate through a time of crisis and disruption, leaders need a crystal clear and practical roadmap – and we are fortunate that Nitin Rakesh and Jerry Wind have written just such a book. Their eight principles to create opportunities in times of crisis and disruption set the foundation for an actionable strategy, and their implementation framework provides leaders and their institutions with indispensable tools to assure that the strategy becomes reality. All in all, Transformation in Times of Crisis: Eight Principles for Creating Opportunities and Value in the Post Pandemic World is an invaluable and indispensable guide for leaders of organizations of all types in an extraordinary time.

– Glenn W. Reed, ex Managing Director,
The Vanguard Group, Inc.

30. Nitin Rakesh is the Jack Welch of our time. A multi-faceted leader who has that rare ability to distill ideas, concepts and business challenges into their most basic building blocks and then mobilize and motivate teams to execute massive transformational change across organizations. This book is the must-read primer for CEOs, boards, and aspiring leaders to refresh their innovation and agility skills and leverage a design and tech mindset to help them navigate in an ever increasingly changing world.

– Geeta Sankappanavar, Co-Founder, President,
Grafton Asset Management,
Chair of Board, University of Calgary

31. In Transformation in Times of Crisis, Nitin Rakesh and Jerry Wind offer important, useful, tested insights that are uniquely timely – and timeless. Crises tend either to unite an organization or to divide it. They challenge the organization to see the need for conservatism, and the opportunity for invention and reinvention, not as opposites but as complements. Through structured frameworks, and thoughtful examples chosen from the current crisis and past crises, the authors do more than illuminate how crises unfold. They challenge organizations to act in accord with a dynamic, complex, yet malleable environment; and to offer the optimism that it is possible to do so effectively.

– David Schmittlein, John C Head III
Dean and Professor of Marketing,
MIT Sloan School of Management

32. As a nonprofit museum leader navigating the concurrent disruptions generated by the global pandemic, Transformation in Times of Crisis has challenged and empowered me to boldly

reframe the situation at hand. It helped me pivot from triage mode to proactively harnessing this moment to rebuild, reimage, and reinvent our organization at a pace that was unimaginable before the crisis.

– Gary Garrido Schneider,
Executive Director, Grounds For Sculpture

33. This new release may be the best business book of the year. In his characteristically well researched yet plain spoken manner, Jerry Wind and Nitin Rakesh dissect the global pandemic crisis of 2020, and then with conviction, determine that this unprecedented time can lead to unparalleled opportunities for inventive business leaders. After acknowledging the conditions of our vastly altered marketplace, Wind and Rakesh then build a most compelling case for why now is precisely the time to conceive and implement transformational ideas. They buttress strategic principles with a comprehensive support package, including tools to ensure readers can and will implement their ideas. I urge all leaders to buy the book and use it to optimize opportunities in today's significantly altered marketplace.

– Meg Touborg, Business Development Strategist and
Co-Founder, The Leaders of Design Council

34. Though COVID19 has closed so many doors at so many firms, at the same time it has opened radically new ways of doing business – if rightly appreciated and properly led. In Transformation in Times of Crisis, Nitin Rakesh and Jerry Wind give us eight timely principles and plenty of examples for doing so, moving us beyond the calamity by accelerating, digitizing, personalizing, and reinventing our enterprise now, a ready roadmap for all who would seize it.

– Michael Useem,
Professor of Management at the Wharton School,
University of Pennsylvania, and author of The Leadership
Moment and co-author of Mastering Catastrophic Risk

35. Jerry Wind and Nitin Rakesh have created an excellent and important book for the times we are living in. The recent crisis has cast us all to the wind, leaving transformation as our only tool to go forward. Yet, until now, leaders have lacked the steps to help us move forward in this new paradigm.

– John Winsor,
Founder and CEO, Open Assembly

36. When the COVD-19 pandemic struck in the spring of 2020, it was more than a healthcare crisis. It also struck a crippling blow at educational institutions – which were forced to shut down almost overnight and send millions of students home. Still, as this book, Transformation in Times of Crisis, shows, catastrophe often is the mother of invention. Universities that use the current crisis as a spur to reinvent their pedagogical models will enhance their digital footprints and emerge stronger after the crisis has passed. That is one of this book's most important messages – and one of many reasons why it belongs on the bookshelf of every leader in education and other fields.

– Rebecca Winthrop,
Co-director – Center for Universal Education,
Senior Fellow – Global Economy and Development,
Brookings Institution

37. The need for this book is urgent – Nitin and Jerry's eight key principles forming a highly adaptive framework underscores the importance of being customer-centric, especially at a time

of crisis. With a coordinated response from central banks and economies reopening, recovery for the global economy will depend heavily on consumer spending, specifically on services. The answer to how businesses should monetize these new opportunities in the service of consumers to unleash new areas of growth lies in this seminal book.

> – **Arshad R. Zakaria,**
> **Chief Executive and Founder,**
> **New Vernon Capital**

Foreword by Philip Kotler

I wish that I had written this book! I am so impressed with its content and ideas. If your company or organization could only read and work with one book to help you survive during this brutal Covid nightmare, it's this book.

Jerry Wind and Nitin Rakesh wrote *Transformation in Times of Crisis* out of an overwhelming wish to be at your side and supply the questions, the information, the strategies and implementation stops that you need to save your business. They give you eight principles to guide your actions, each fully described in a separate chapter. But you can't save your company with just one principle. You need to weave all eight together to secure your future.

The authors are also gifted storytellers. They illustrate the principles with companies that disrupted whole industries; legacy companies that failed to react fast enough; fantastically successful companies that spotted a need and filled in quickly.

The authors make a strong case for understanding your customers even on a one-to-one basis so that you can personalize your offerings and your messages.

In the last chapter they supply ten tools for moving forward. I like very much their discussion about how to generate creative options through morphologic analysis, benchmarking, and SCAMPER (substitute, combine, adapt, modify, put in another use, eliminate, reverse).

At the end of each chapter is always a full set of questions to make you think about your company in relation to the companies they discussed. I kept feeling that they were playing the role of a doctor analyzing your aches and pains and showing you the right medicine for what ails you and your business.

Their proposed transformation system is primarily cast in terms of how to deal with the coronavirus pandemic. But they show that their transformation model is appropriate for responding to other crises that will undoubtedly occur, such as climate change, another recession, and the entry of a new disruptor.

If I ran a business school, I would make *Transformation in Times of Crisis* a required reading. Business students would gain important information, stories, and tools for competing. They will tour the changes that are challenging such important industries as hospitality, automobiles, health care and travel, among others.

In essence, this book really presents a roadmap on how to think about changes, challenges and crises that come your way. My compliments go to the authors of this wonderful package of principles, tools and stories that will help us handle any crisis with hope and insight.

Philip Kotler has been called the father of modern marketing. He taught at Northwestern University's Kellogg School of Management for more than five decades. He is the author of Marketing Management *and several other books. Kotler's textbooks are among the most widely read in the world and have sold more than 3 million copies in 58 countries.*

Foreword by Harish Manwani

Charles Dickens might have said, these are "the best of times [and] the worst of times." On the one hand, technology has enabled the world to be connected like never before. On the other, we see challenges to globalization, the rise of protectionism, the return of "tribalism" and an increasing push for localization of workforce and markets.

These changes were upon us well before the current crisis hit. The pandemic has merely precipitated many of the socio-economic mega trends and disruptions that were already playing out at a rapid pace. The world was grappling with rising inequality, the challenges of a resource-stressed world, the effects of climate change and, importantly, the double-edged sword of technology which was positively changing everyday life and leisure but was also beginning to disrupt the nature of work itself. None of that has changed.

In this emerging new world, expectations from business were also changing. Corporates realised that they needed to be a part of the solution to this new reality and their focus had to shift from just serving the needs of the shareholders to also serving the communities in which they operate. Growth and profits are still vital but responsible growth is key to success over the long term.

As businesses were coming to terms with this new reality, we were struck by a pandemic that has literally pressed a pause button to the world and created an unprecedented existential crisis for communities and corporates. A statement that is sometimes attributed to Vladimir Illych Lenin in the context of the Russian Revolution of 1917 notes that there are decades when nothing happens, and there are weeks when decades happen. We are clearly experiencing that phenomenon, but the silver lining is that, like everything else, this too shall pass, albeit with a new normal.

Many letters of the alphabet have been used to describe the timing and shape of the post pandemic economic recovery – from V-shaped to K-shaped. The more immediate job for the government and corporates alike is to first cope with the crisis. But the more important job is to prepare for the post-COVID world.

So, how should businesses go about doing this? The important question is not just about what needs to be done but how to do it. That is where this book, *Transformation in Times of Crisis*, written by Nitin Rakesh and Jerry Wind, could not have been more timely. The authors have focused on digital transformation as a tool for value creation both during and after the current crisis.

In today's world, every company is in the business of technology either as a creator of technology or an enabler of technology or a user of technology. Hence, the "eight principles for digital transformation" is a powerful framework and widely relevant across sectors. Nitin, as a sitting CEO of a global IT services company and Jerry, as a distinguished academic and consultant, combine extremely well to make this book both insightful and a pragmatic guide to help you future-proof your business even as you manage the here-and-now challenges of the current crisis.

Harish Manwani is a senior operating partner at Blackstone, a private equity firm with $564 billion in assets under management. Before joining the firm in 2015, he was chief operating officer of Unilever. Mr. Manwani serves on the board of directors of Gilead Sciences, Qualcomm, Whirlpool, the Indian School of Business (Chair), and Tata Sons, among other international boards.

Introduction

It is one of the best-known scenes in William Shakespeare's *Julius Caesar*. The emperor, on his way to the Theatre of Pompey, encounters a soothsayer who cautions him to "beware the Ides of March." Caesar shrugs off the fortune teller's warning about dire events that lie ahead. Soon—as everyone who is familiar with the tragedy knows—the outcome is fatal. A band of conspirators, including Caesar's friend Brutus, assassinates the emperor. As Brutus plunges in the knife, Caesar cries out, "Et tu, Brute? Then fall, Caesar." Little wonder that the Ides of March have long been associated with calamitous misfortune. And seldom has the tragedy been as deep, dark and deadly as in March this year.

The coronavirus crisis, which began in China in late 2019 but emerged as a full-blown pandemic in March 2020, has plunged the world into a health crisis and an economic downturn combined with a shutdown of normal life. Because it affects every country, the pandemic is far more pervasive than any other crisis we have experienced in our lifetimes. According to the World Health Organization (WHO), by mid-April people in more than 200 countries, areas and territories had tested positive for

> **The coronavirus pandemic has not just created a new normal; it has brought into being a new reality.**

COVID-19. The only comparable tragedy in terms of magnitude, possibly, is the Black Death plague pandemic of 1346, which led to the death of an estimated 100 million people in Europe and Asia.

At times like this, it is easy to overlook what John D. Rockefeller said about every disaster containing the seeds of an opportunity. Winston Churchill is believed to have said that one should "never let a good crisis go to waste" (See exhibit 1).

EXHIBIT 1

COVID-19 Has Accelerated the Pace of Disruption and the Need for Digital Transformation

Credit: (c) Tom Fishburne, www.marketoonist.com. Used by permission. © marketoonist.com

The COVID-19 crisis magnifies deep disruptions that were already underway: The changing relationship between empowered, skeptical customers and enterprises; the dramatic transformation due to technology (rise of the world wide web, mobile and social networks, cloud and cognitive computing, the growth of AI); new business models (by disruptors such as Uber, Airbnb); the growth of globalization (the rise of China, India and other so-called emerging markets); deepening social divisions (the ideological and income divide in the U.S., U.K. and other countries; racial discrimination as highlighted by the killing of African-American George Floyd by a white police officer in the U.S. in May 2020, the subsequent massive social unrest and the resurgence of the Black Lives Matters movement); the redefinition of major industries such as retailing (the explosive impact of Amazon, the shift of nearly every retailer to omnichannel marketing), automobiles (the shift to electric cars embodied by Tesla, the emergence of autonomous driving) and several others. The interplay of all these forces has led to mighty upheavals in the way the world – and business – works. The global business landscape was going through changes that had been building for more than 20 years. As consumers pivoted away from brands, relationships between major brands and their customers were slowly but steadily being shredded and customers redefined their connection to these enterprises.

Consider, for example, giant financial institutions such as Citibank or Bank of America. These banks had moved money for their customers for decades. But often, most of their customers were older people who are now gradually fading from the scene. Ask the children or grandchildren of these customers – the rising Millennial or Gen Z generations – how they prefer to move money. They hardly ever think about banks when they want to share costs after a meal or a drink; they simply "Venmo" the cash or send it via PayPal over their cell phones. In the process, their relationship with big banks is not just non-existent; for many of them, it is almost irrelevant.

> **The business landscape was going through changes that had been building for some 20 years.**

Empowered by technology, these customers are loyal not to an institution's brand but rather to their own experience. If a newborn startup makes life easier – whether it is for transferring money, ordering food, or getting a ride – these customers will move swiftly from one brand to the next. It is immaterial how long an established enterprise may have dominated its industry. If it fails to engage with this emerging customer base, it topples from its perch. These disruptions help explain why just half the companies that were on the *Fortune* 500 list in 2000 are still part of the rankings today.

The coronavirus contagion arrived even as these changes were disrupting global enterprises. What the crisis has done is to accelerate the pace of disruption– and dramatically so. It is pushing companies and industries – where change has long been overdue – to transform themselves. For anyone who has grown dependent on the predictable patterns of the past, the choice is simple: Transform yourself or be destroyed.

Fortunately, destruction is hardly the only option. The truth is that every crisis, while deeply unsettling, contains the seeds of opportunity. When we face the kind of dramatic crisis we do today, we need to consider three questions:

1. How do we cope with this crisis now? This question is uppermost in people's minds – as it should be – and it also tends to dominate the news.

2. What opportunities does this crisis create?

3. What can be done to anticipate crises in the future and prepare for them? Even if it isn't possible to pre-empt a future crisis, what can be done to respond rapidly and effectively?

How a New Reality Impacts Ongoing Disruption

Most people focus just on the first question, which has to do with immediate survival. In this book, we will discuss how to create opportunities in times of disruption by offering eight principles to help organizations and individuals do that effectively. Keep in mind that a crisis is the ultimate disruptor and everything we suggest that can help identify opportunities in times of crisis can also help defend against disruptors or help become a disruptor.

Before we do that, though, recognize that the coronavirus pandemic has not just created a new normal; it has brought into being a new reality. Let us explore some of its dimensions:

- As several countries went into lockdown or instituted shelter-in-place rules, companies asked most employees to work from home. According to *The New York Times*, in early April some 4 billion people had been asked to stay home[1]. Hard as it may be to imagine, that is more than half the population of the planet.

- Universities discontinued traditional classroom instruction and switched to online learning. In April, classrooms for 90% of the world's students were closed, noted *The New York Times*.[2]

- Retail establishments other than supermarkets, pharmacies and gas stations were closed.

- Social distancing was the norm, limiting most human contact to digital communications and relationships. While digital communications were already on the rise, forced lockdowns have made them mandatory rather than optional in several countries. This was hardly conceivable even six months before the crisis struck. Social communication among family and friends also moved online, with virtual dinner parties being organized over Zoom, Skype, WebEx, FaceTime and other platforms.

---

[1] "Coronavirus in America: A Highlight Reel," The New York Times, April 4, 2020

[2] "Coronavirus in America: A Highlight Reel," The New York Times, April 4, 2020

- Air travel was largely suspended and restrictions were placed on land travel. Businesses had to switch to audio, video and web conferencing as dominant modes of communication.

- Global supply chains have been disrupted.

- Massive unemployment replaced a tight labor market in a matter of weeks. In the U.S. alone, jobless workers filed more than 3 million claims in a single week in March, the highest in the country's history. This was followed by more than 6 million people applying for unemployment benefits in the beginning of April. By the middle of the month, the total number applying for benefits since March rose to more than 22 million, according to the *Financial Times*.[3] By the end of May, this number went up to more than 40 million.[4] *The New York Times* reported at the end of July that the U.S. GDP, a measure of goods and services, had shrunk by 9.5% in the second quarter, wiping out "five years of growth."[5]

- Cultural institutions such as museums and theaters have closed. Public gatherings and even weddings have either been postponed or moved online.

While pondering the unprecedented impact of the coronavirus pandemic, make no mistake. This might be a new reality but that does not mean we should surrender to it. We can transform any crisis into opportunities if we apply these eight principles and an analytical framework to our own unique situation.

---

[3] "Another 5.2 million Americans file jobless claims as virus' toll spreads," Financial Times, April 16, 2020

[4] "'Still Catching Up': Jobless Numbers May Not Tell Full Story," The New York Times, June 9, 2020. https://www.nytimes.com/2020/05/28/business/economy/coronavirus-unemployment-claims.html

[5] "A Collapse That Wiped Out Five Years of Growth, With No Bounce in Sight," The New York Times, July 30, 2020. https://www.nytimes.com/2020/07/30/business/economy/q2-gdp-coronavirus-economy.html

To help you do that is the primary purpose of this book.

For an example of a company whose fortunes have soared despite – or, perhaps, because of – the pandemic, consider Zoom, the videoconferencing platform. As millions of workers are forced to work remotely, usage of Zoom's teleconferencing software has exploded. An estimate by J.P. Morgan reckons that daily usage increased more than 300% after the onset of the crisis. The company offers a free basic service, but several experts believe that demand for its premium offerings is rising as well. Some users now design custom background screens[6] for use during work sessions to conceal the clutter of their homes. As Zoom's popularity increased, so did its stock price – which went up some 50% in March – though later the stock fell after users raised concerns about privacy and security. The company's market capitalization that month exceeded $44 billion, higher than the combined value of airlines such as Delta, United and American. Even before the crisis, videoconferencing was growing in popularity. Platforms such as WebEx, Skype, Teams, Google Meet and Slack have also seen steady increases in usage. For all these platforms, the crisis significantly stepped up the pace of adoption and change.

> **For some companies, the crisis continues to provide new opportunities for growth.**

Netflix, the media streaming company, is another case in point. Before the pandemic, as increasing numbers of users consumed media over streaming services, the company's customer base had grown to more than 167 million. This happened despite growing competition from rival platforms including Amazon Prime, Apple TV, and Google's YouTube. Industry observers estimate that Netflix has a 65% share of video streaming customers. After the start of

---

6   "How to Hide Your Messy Room for a Zoom video conference," The Verge, March 11, 2020. https://www.theverge.com/2020/3/11/21173608/zoom-video-conference-how-to-virtual-background-greenscreen

the pandemic, as more and more people were forced into social distancing and movie theaters shut down, demand for streaming media went up by more than 60% at Netflix and other services, according to Nielsen.[7] Again, the trend toward streaming was already disrupting other forms of media consumption. The crisis significantly amplified it.

Zoom and Netflix are not isolated cases of companies that are thriving during the COVID-19 crisis. As the *Financial Times* recently wrote in a feature titled, "Prospering in the Pandemic: The Top 100 Companies,"[8] companies around the world have found silver linings amid the thunder clouds of the downturn and changed the way they work to seize these opportunities.

> **Solutions that worked before the crisis may fail to do so during and after the crisis.**

At the forefront, notes the report, are companies in the pharmaceutical sector such as AbbVie and Roche, whose fortunes have improved as the race for a vaccine to beat the virus heats up. The technology giant Amazon, which demonstrated its e-commerce prowess during the lockdown, has seen its stock soar and added more than $400 billion to its market capitalization as of July 31. Other winners include Microsoft, whose technology helped remote workers connect with one another more easily during the months of social distancing.

In addition to the *Financial Times* ranking, *Advertising Age* published a list of America's Hottest Brands for 2020. It highlights companies whose performance and image have improved during the pandemic. Among them were some expected names such as Clorox, whose cleaning products were in much higher demand. The

---

[7]   "Nielsen explains how COVID-19 could impact media usage across the U.S." TechCrunch, March 17, 2020 https://techcrunch.com/2020/03/17/nielsen-explains-how-covid-19-could-impact-media-usage-across-the-u-s/

[8]   "Prospering in the Pandemic: the top 100 companies," Financial Times, June 19, 2020. https://www.ft.com/content/844ed28c-8074-4856-bde0-20f3bf4cd8f0

ranking also included surprising names such as Chewy, an online retailer of pet food, whose sales went up in response to a marketing campaign showing that pets could help prevent loneliness during the lockdown.

Large companies are hardly the only ones that have been able to grab new opportunities. The U.S. Chamber of Commerce has reported[9] that small firms in sectors such as cleaning services, delivery services, and grocery stores also made huge strides forward. And we do not mean to suggest that the ability to thrive during a crisis is limited to the present pandemic. A 2014 report[10] in *Forbes* highlighted "amazing companies" that were launched during the financial crisis of 2008. The report noted that of the 100 companies named in the magazine's annual list of America's most promising firms, "around a third were forged in the doom and gloom years of the global financial crisis." In other words, many companies and their leadership teams, large and small, have been able to create opportunities in times of crisis – and so can you.

> **We will show you what needs to be done and how you can do it.**

Eight Principles to Create Opportunities in Times of Crisis and Disruption

The coronavirus pandemic is the kind of unpredictable, global catastrophe of staggering proportions that comes along not just every few years but perhaps once in a hundred years, if not every few centuries. It has brought about unparalleled disruption in almost every aspect of the social and business lives of millions of people around the planet. And yet, despite the widespread distress, the

---

[9]   "15 Small Businesses Thriving During Coronavirus," https://www.uschamber. com/co/start/strategy/coronavirus-successful-businesses

[10] "20 Amazing Companies Founded During the Financial Crisis," Forbes, January 22, 2014. https://www.forbes.com/sites/hollieslade/2014/01/22/20-amazing-companies-founded-during-the-financial-crisis/#3224d3fb7377

picture is more complex than it might seem. For some companies, the crisis has – and continues to – provide opportunities for new growth. In the pages that follow, we will show you *what* needs to be done to create opportunities for digital transformation and value creation during and after the crisis. Just as important, we will discuss *how* you can do it.

What we have for you in this book includes:

1. Eight principles to create opportunities in a crisis, and to defend against disruptors or become one.

2. A framework to develop your implementation strategy.

3. To help you utilize the principles, we offer 10 tools that can help you with the implementation process. The tools will help you decide what to do as well as how to implement your strategy.

4. As another part of the package, we plan to provide a dashboard that will allow you to monitor in real-time the progress you and your organization are making in implementing your strategy.

5. In the future, we will develop an app that provides you with a strategy worksheet. Once it is ready, you can work on it as an individual or with your team and use it as a collaborative platform that can help you reflect the eight principles as they can be applied to your strategy.

The principles are discussed in separate chapters. The framework and tools are discussed in the final chapter. These, along with the app and the dashboard – as soon as they are ready – will allow us to continue our interaction through a community website. These will empower you to join a support network of peers and other readers. We hope that together we can build a thriving community where we can share experiences and challenges with one another.

These eight principles reflect the best practices of numerous companies and are also consistent with the recommendations of many top consulting firms. (A few are listed in the notes at the end of this book.) They are best-in-class and well-established. However, what makes our approach different – even unique – is the combination of the principles and their interdependence with the framework and tools we have developed to help you implement them. Keep in mind that these are not standalone principles. In order to defend yourself against any crisis and disruption and become a disruptor yourself, you must work on *all* eight. While customizing and prioritizing the principles and the experiments to implement them should reflect the unique conditions and aspirations of your organization, it is imperative that you address all of them. Further, prioritization is not only for closing the gap between where you are at present and the ideal, but for leveraging areas of strength to capture opportunities at the earliest. These principles apply to all organizations – large and small, B2B and B2C, U.S. and non-U.S., for profit and nonprofit (See Exhibit 2).

Our eight principles offer guidelines for developing and experimenting with creative strategies.

Every chapter discussing a principle includes examples of companies that illustrate that principle. These examples are for you to understand what others are doing and what you can do. You don't necessarily have to do the same things. (As companies like Uber, Airbnb and others have discovered, disrupting existing industries and taking on incumbents can be a hazardous game, rife with legal and regulatory challenges.)

EXHIBIT 2

Eight Principles to Create Opportunities in Times of Crisis and Disruption

Principle 1: Challenge Your Mental Models and Always Stay Ahead

Principle 2: Reimagine and Reinvent Your Approach to Customers and Stakeholders

Principle 3: Speed up Digital Transformation and Design for Personalization at Scale

Principle 4: Reinvent Your Talent Strategy and Embrace Open Innovation and Open Talent

Principle 5: Seize the Need for Speed and Design for Agility, Adjacencies and Adaptability

Principle 6: Innovate Then Experiment, Experiment, Experiment

Principle 7: Redraw Your Timelines and Build a Portfolio of Initiatives Across all Innovation Horizons

Principle 8: Deploy Idealized Design, Recreate Your Organizational Architecture and Network Orchestration

Ask yourself what you can learn from the various examples. See what applies to you and what does not. Also, several companies have undergone significant changes; some have grown exponentially, others have been acquired and a few have shut down. All this goes to show how dynamic the business environment is. Further, given the new reality being created by the magnitude of the impact of the current crisis on whole industries and on all our lives, there is no assurance that what worked before the crisis will work during or after the crisis. We are confident, however, that our eight principles offer sound guidelines for developing creative strategies and experimenting with them.

We will begin by previewing the eight principles. As you go through each of them, you will see that these can help prepare you for any kind of turbulence, whether it is the COVID-19 pandemic, systemic racial discrimination raising its ugly head, the impending climate change, the 9/11 terrorist attack in 2001, the SARS coronavirus in 2002, the financial crisis of 2008 or the ongoing tech disruptions. More importantly, they can help you discover new opportunities and ways to build long-term value beyond the crisis.

Principle 1: Challenge Your Mental Models and Always Stay Ahead

Your mental models represent the way you view and interpret the world. While they help you function steadily during normal times, in a crisis they can hold you back unless you challenge your ideas and change the way you think. Instead

> **We should ask how to use the current situation to speed up long overdue changes.**

of viewing the present situation as a short-term necessary evil that we should try to leave behind as soon as possible and return to a comfortable pre-crisis past, we should ask how to use the current situation to speed up long-overdue changes. Let us examine two examples of industries where digital transformation was overdue – and which are being forced to change their mental models because of the crisis.

First, consider universities. Many institutions have been tinkering around the edges for years with online learning initiatives. While some progress was made in recent years with massive open online courses (or MOOCs), the universities' dominant pedagogical model remained unchanged. Movement toward online learning was not only very slow, but it was also detached from the institutions' mainstream efforts. Educators knew that traditional teaching methods were ineffective, but it was almost impossible to get them to change. Elite universities, especially, were complacent because of the perceived strength of their brands, which kept attracting profitable streams of overseas students. When your old ways keep generating cash, that reinforces the resistance to change. Breaking down those barriers requires a powerful force.

Then the coronavirus crisis struck. Almost overnight, universities were forced to close, students were sent home, and faculty were asked to conduct classes online. At one stroke, almost in a baptism by fire, universities were pushed into offering *all* their programs via online learning platforms. What a jolt to their entrenched mental models! Hopefully, these changes will continue after the crisis has passed and lead to long-term transformation. Institutions that view the crisis as an opportunity to innovate around online learning will be well-positioned to succeed in the post-pandemic world.

Universities will need to focus on three types of innovations. The most immediate changes – which can and must be done now—involve improvements in online instruction and engagement. Second, after the crisis, faculty will need to change their pedagogical approach and offer students a creative blend of online and in-class instruction. This will involve dynamic versions of the so-called flipped classroom, in which lectures are viewed online at home while classroom exercises focus on deliberation and discussion and implementation of the material studied online. And third, universities will have to rethink their business and revenue models. In the U.S., this factor has been highlighted by Democratic presidential candidates who have been drawing attention to the country's massive burden of student loans. According to the Federal Reserve of New York, in 2019 student debt stood at $1.48 trillion.[11] As calls to relieve this debt burden and provide affordable or free education grow louder, this presents educational institutions with opportunities to design innovative business and revenue models to deal with this issue.

> **When your old ways keep generating cash, that reinforces the resistance to change.**

---

[11] "Quarterly Report on Household Debt and Credit," Federal Reserve Bank of New York, August 2019. https://www.newyorkfed.org/medialibrary/interactives/householdcredit/data/pdf/hhdc_2019q2.pdf

Next, consider art museums. Like universities, they have long been aware that they needed to move away from traditional ways of engaging with their audiences. They know all too well that they needed to shed their singular focus on galleries and augment their offerings with digital material. Yet, traditional curators feel much more comfortable focusing only on the galleries and printed catalog of exhibitions. The closing of museums to the public because of COVID-19 is now compelling curators to expand their role. They have no choice but to curate both physical and digital exhibitions for the gallery spaces in the museums. They have an enormous opportunity to offer digital displays of their exhibitions for millions of people around the world and not just limit their services to a few local visitors who can visit the museums in person.

Consider two examples of museums that already were moving toward improving their digital offerings. In New York City, the Metropolitan Museum of Art created an open-access network of more than 400,000 images of public-domain works from its collection—which are available to anyone with an Internet connection. In Philadelphia, the Barnes Foundation offers free talks and tours of its famed collection on its website. In addition, those who are interested can sign up for online classes on topics ranging from the art of French impressionist Edouard Manet to the paintings of Florentine artist Giotto di Bondone. Such changes open up the museums to a broader audience base in addition to tourists in these cities, and in the process, these expand the museums' audience and generate more revenue opportunities. While these museums were already expanding their online offerings, the coronavirus pandemic and the shutdown of their physical locations compelled them to focus on their online offerings with greater urgency.

> **Ask yourself, which mental models have kept you for too long in your comfort zone?**

Every company in every industry can find its opportunity in this crisis if its executives view these times as an opportunity to reexamine, and if needed change, their mental models. Ask yourself, which mental models have kept you for too long in your comfort zone? How can you rethink your mental models to see opportunities you may have missed in the past and position yourself for growth in the future?

Principle 2: Reimagine and Reinvent Your Approach to Customers and Stakeholders

While being customer-centric is always important, never does it matter more than during and after a crisis. How you relate to and meaningfully engage your customers during a crisis will define your role in their lives long after the crisis. While there is a lull in business activities, you can map out and push toward a customer-centric digital transformation of your organization. You can adopt a customer-first digital architecture. Create an "intelligent" intermediary layer that connects the front-end of your organization with the back-end systems and processes, thereby insulating the customer experience from past legacy. Some of these terms might seem confusing, but bear with us, we will explain as we go along.

> **How you relate to customers during a crisis will define your role after the crisis.**

Companies have been speaking for a long time about the importance of focusing on their customers. While this trend has been visible long before the coronavirus crisis arrived, it will intensify and become a necessity as a result of the crisis. Companies are becoming proactive about communicating with their customers, but they must do this in a sensitive fashion.

As companies slim down and shed staff, paradoxically they will have to become even more highly focused on the employees that remain. They will need to deal with their employees as people, and not only in their narrow role as employees but as human beings.

Companies will also have to shift their attention from serving just their shareholders to other stakeholders and society.

Millennials and Gen Z want to work for companies that are changing the world. They prefer to buy products and services from companies that have a positive social impact. That is why switching to a stakeholder focus is increasingly important. At the end of March, in an unprecedented move, the U.S. government approved a $2.2 trillion coronavirus rescue plan. We will see a rethinking of the relationship between the private and public sectors. Companies will have to learn to interact more effectively with the public sector and the not-for-profit sector as part of the broader stakeholder orientation.

To build long-term value after the crisis, it is critical to understand the changing business environment, and reimagine and reinvent our approach to customers and stakeholders. Ask yourself, are we paying attention to our consumers' frustrations, needs and aspirations, even those of which they themselves are not aware? Do we view our consumers as human beings in their broader roles as consumers, customers, employees, vendors, partners, spouses, parents, and citizens? Do we keep in mind how technology is empowering them? Have we aligned the objectives and strategies of our company with those of all stakeholders including society? Have we begun to co-create with them? Do we have a 'win-win' strategy for all stakeholders?

> **Ask yourself, do you have a win-win strategy for all stakeholders?**

Principle 3: Speed Up Digital Transformation and Design for Personalization at Scale

The shutdown of the physical world and the shift to the digital world is transforming not just universities and museums but also organizations in other fields. Think about what is happening at retail stores, orchestras and theaters. All these require a strong digital infrastructure. The fact that brick-and-mortar channels are closed is forcing organizations to speed up their digital transformation.

For example, the National Theatre in London, unable to perform plays in an auditorium during the lockdown, announced that it would stream its performances for free on YouTube.[12] The extension of its digital capabilities—along with the goodwill generated among a global rather than local audience – should continue to serve it well long after the crisis has passed. Every play is unlikely to interest every member of the audience. Drama fans will choose which plays to watch, and that self-selection process can allow the development of individual data profiles, much as Amazon does for books or Netflix for movies and TV shows. While many theaters that cater to local markets may not have needed to use recommendation engines in the past, with a global audience they could begin to do so. Organizations that use the lockdown to enhance their digital capabilities and capitalize on existing trends will be able to get closer to offering real-time, personalized experiences.

> **The fact that brick-and-mortar channels are closed is speeding up digital transformation.**

As a case in point from a different field, consider how the crisis is expanding the role of telemedicine in health care organizations. The remote delivery of health services, enabled by technology, was already growing in different parts of the world and disrupting the age-old relationship of in-person consultations between patients and doctors. Given the speed at which the pandemic spread, several health providers introduced video visits. In part, this was to protect doctors from patients who might be infected by COVID-19 virus – and it was also aimed at curbing the virus's spread. Doctors point out that while telemedicine is not necessarily "a solution to the current crisis, it will be one of its lasting consequences."

---

12 "National Theatre to Broadcast Shows Online on Thursdays," The Guardian, March 26, 2020. https://www.theguardian.com/stage/2020/mar/26/national-theatre-to-broadcast-shows-online-on-thursdays

Customers expect high levels of personalization. They have started to drive not just what they want, but also when they want it, where they want it and how they want it delivered. As providers of products and services, one central point to keep in mind is that understanding and predicting your customer's desires and needs, and offering relevant products, services and experiences is non-negotiable. You need to be able to offer this at scale. You can achieve this by having an integrated data strategy and using big data and cognitive technologies and leveraging technologies such as geo-fencing, facial, voice and emotional recognition, virtual reality, augmented reality and social media.

Ask yourself, have we sped up our digital transformation and do we have an integrated data strategy, and are we using big and smart data, predictive AI and cognitive technologies as the foundation of our firm's strategy to design for personalization at scale? Does our data strategy empower the entire company to have the same holistic view of our customers? Are we leveraging technologies such as geo-fencing, facial, voice and emotional recognition, virtual reality, augmented reality and social media to deliver personalization in real-time? Have we been able to coordinate among and bridge the silos within our firm?

Principle 4: Reinvent Your Talent Strategy and Embrace Open Innovation and Open Talent

In a crisis, it is more critical than ever to have the best possible talent. A good team comprising the right internal and external talent can steer the firm successfully through the turbulence. Many companies have on their staff non-productive employees who do not have the competencies needed to succeed in the 21ˢᵗ century. During a crisis, when organizations have no choice but to become leaner, companies can restructure their employee pool with

> A team with the right talent can steer your firm through turbulence.

more relevant and productive talent. Often companies find it difficult to let go of people, but in the long run it is best for everyone including for the remaining employees who resent having non-productive employees around. We do not mean to suggest that companies should heartlessly lay people off or blame them for being unproductive. The approach we advocate is that companies should provide all employees with an environment in which they can keep learning and adding to their skills and to own their careers.

It is possible to build a new talent strategy around a small core of full-time employees (mostly designers, integrators and leaders) and augment it with the talent of open innovation. Such a fluid organizational structure, which combines the talent, capabilities and agility of employees with networks of independent contractors, can help navigate even the toughest of times and reap rich dividends. Research across more than 1,000 cases shows that open innovation can be more than four times faster and eight times less expensive than relying on internal talent alone. Internal talent must be used for critical and core in-house functions like implementing strategies and leading the change.

> **During a crisis, companies can restructure their employee pool with more relevant and productive talent.**

Incorporating open innovation is always the right solution for companies that want to adopt a smart talent strategy. Ask yourself, do we have the right mix of internal and external talent? Have we opened our innovation process and strategies and harnessed the wisdom and power of the crowd? Have we tapped global markets to gain access to the talent we need? Are we paying for efforts or for results? Are we leveraging our internal talent to implement strategies and lead change? Are we doing all we can to innovate better, faster and cheaper to fulfill our customers' expectations?

Principle 5: Seize the Need for Speed and Design for Agility, Adjacencies and Adaptability

During a crisis, your regular business may slow down or even come to a complete halt. You need to be able to quickly respond to the changing situation, adapt to the new reality, and spot and create new opportunities for survival and growth. Put on the thinking cap of a startup: most successful startups have gone through a number of pivots from their original concept.

> **One way to spot new opportunities is to creatively address uncertainties, fear and lack of trust.**

One way to spot new opportunities is to creatively address people's fears, uncertainties and lack of trust. For example, as demand has overwhelmed supply, enormous shortages of hospital beds, especially in intensive care units or ICUs, for COVID-19 treatment have emerged worldwide. In response, Italian architects Carlo Ratti and Italo Rota have designed "an intensive care pod within a shipping container" for hospitals. Named CURA, which stands for Connected Units for Respiratory Ailments, these pods are meant to help hospitals add to their ICU capacity. The first prototypes were tested in Milan, a city in Italy that the coronavirus has devastated. In India, food delivery platforms like Swiggy and Zomato expanded their services to deliver groceries during the pandemic-related national lockdown. This enabled these firms to not only utilize their delivery fleet effectively and keep their business running, but also to cater to the essential needs of their customers and build a strong relationship with them.

Prepare yourself to introduce new and better products, services, solutions and experiences; continuously analyze results and evaluate strategy; promptly identify and understand new developments; and swiftly change tracks as required. At the same time, be stable and consistent. Alongside, look for adjacencies. An adjacency could mean introducing a new offering to your current market, expanding your current offering to a new segment, using your current distribution to reach new segments or make new offerings, or reaching either your current or new segments via new distribution systems. More importantly, along with products, markets, and distribution areas that are new to you, look at areas that have not yet been discovered. In a dynamically changing environment, ensure you can adapt fast. Build the capability to quickly mold yourself to flourish in any environment.

Ask yourself, do we promptly identify and understand new developments and swiftly change tracks as required? As we prepare to introduce new and better products, services, solutions and experiences, are we continuously analyzing and re-evaluating our strategy? More importantly, along with products, markets, and distribution areas that are new to us, have we looked at areas that have not yet been discovered? In a dynamically changing environment, have we seized the need for speed, and designed for agility, adjacencies and adaptability?

Principle 6: Innovate Then Experiment, Experiment, Experiment

A crisis is a great opportunity to learn from natural experiments. There are numerous new opportunities that come up for us to explore. Further, given the magnitude of changes a crisis brings, we cannot assume that strategies that worked before the crisis will continue to work during or after it has passed. We cannot, therefore, plan to go back to the same strategies we had before the crisis. Experimentation and innovation are a must in today's environment. We must innovate in everything we do, not only in our products but also with respect to areas such organizational architecture. Still, you cannot do everything at once. Given the uncertainties during a crisis, the only way to learn is to continuously improve what you are doing. This can be achieved through continuous experimentation.

> **A crisis offers an opportunity to learn from natural experiments.**

Our recommendation is to speed up the innovation process and make sure that innovation is done by everyone and not just by a separate unit. Everyone should be thinking about how things can be done better. Experiments should be designed to deal with short-term challenges as well as longer-term issues. Also think about where the next crisis could come from, what you can do to prevent it from happening or to protect yourself if it occurs. Given the turbulent times we live in, we need to learn from the natural experiments that occur around us.

One way to make innovation cost-effective and continuous is by using adaptive experimentation. Most agile companies use this approach to test ideas about everything from budget allocation to advertising campaigns. Adaptive experimentation involves rapid deployment of variations, learning what works and what does not, and then moving on to a different variation. A critical aspect is a mindset that views failure as an integral and valuable part of the process, since each failure provides information. Companies like Google, Facebook, Amazon and Uber constantly conduct thousands of experiments to test their ideas.

> **Make sure that innovation involves everyone and not just a separate unit.**

Given the speed and complexity of the changes of the business environment, the way to assess the causal impact of our innovative strategies is through constant experimentation. Ask yourself, have we made adaptive experimentation part of our management philosophy? Have we developed a portfolio of experiments to understand the link between what we do and the outcome? What lessons have we learned from our experiments? How have we applied these lessons to create a sustainable advantage and build long-term value?

Principle 7: Redraw Your Timelines and Build a Portfolio of Initiatives Across All Innovation Horizons

In times of crisis, cash is always king. The question is, how can you generate cash? Traditionally, companies have tried to save on costs by firing or laying off people. Based on research over the years, we are convinced that companies must first ask themselves, "Are we doing the right things right?" If they do that, they can save at least 20% of their budgets. If you look across departments and business units, you will find that very often efforts are duplicated. There is a huge opportunity for cost savings by reexamining all aspects of operations, by reexamining business models and by reexamining the revenue models.

Even as you are addressing the current needs during a crisis, you also need to create opportunities it offers, and prepare for the next crisis. The same holds true in regular times also. We must continuously and concurrently plan for the future, even as we manage our current day-to-day business. This means addressing the needs of the present as well as planning for the medium and the long-term by way of experiments and initiatives that can help you offer new valuable experiences and address new markets. Importantly, we need to proactively allocate resources to enable this.

Alongside, we must regularly and systematically review all operations and discard all activities that do not contribute value. Keep in mind that the horizons are dynamic, they are different for different companies and they are unique for you. So, allocate resources for activities across the different horizons based on the unique situation of your company. Whatever is the allocation you are comfortable with, have the courage to quickly do what is untried and untested. That is where the future is. And the future is now.

> **In times of crisis, cash is always king.**

We can't predict the future but to remain successful in the long term, we need to prepare for it now. Ask yourself, have we evaluated the efficiency and effectiveness of current activities and resource allocation? Can we shift resources from ineffective initiatives to new innovative initiatives? Can we plan concurrently across all horizons—current operations, medium-term and long-term—for initiatives that can help offer new experiences and address new markets?

Principle 8: Deploy Idealized Design, Recreate Your Organizational Architecture and Network Orchestration

Crises often offer opportunities to acquire at bargain prices companies that may be in trouble or talent that has been laid off. While such opportunities are often tempting, it is smart to be selective and have a grand vision and master strategy that guides these acquisitions. When such moves are combined with an idealized design process, they can help move the organization toward mergers and acquisitions and strategic alliances that build long-term value. The idealized design process is a powerful tool, which involves imagining what the future could be and then working backward to the present to create that reality.

> **Imagine the future and then work backward to the present to create that reality.**

It is critical for companies to ensure that the organization is agile, adaptable and resilient. To do this, we must reexamine the organizational architecture. This includes organizational culture as well as competencies, performance measures, incentives and reward systems as well as infrastructure, processes, technology and facilities. Only agile and adaptable organizations will be able to survive after the crisis. It is equally important to find creative and effective ways to bridge or eliminate organizational silos. The reason is that consumers increasingly judge organizations based on their own customer experience – and this often requires seamless and consistent delivery of products and services across silos. Companies that succeed in bridging silos will operate more effectively during and after the crisis.

A critical aspect of redesigning the organizational architecture is to expand the boundaries of the organization. Innovative companies don't view themselves as isolated entities but as part of a network – an ecosystem that is geared toward creating value. For instance, one could create a network like the Apple Developer network, Facebook network, Uber network of drivers and customers, etc. or design the ideal ecosystem that will enable the firm to achieve its vision and objectives by joining various networks. Companies have been talking for a long time about moving toward a network orchestrator model. It is obvious in today's environment—and this was true before the crisis—that you cannot succeed by competing company-against-company. You must focus on network-against-network competition. A study on the network imperative[13] found that companies that leveraged their networks had a market value of eight times their revenues. In contrast, manufacturing companies had a multiple of one to two. These data are probably obsolete because of the crisis, but the reality is that the benefit of networks will be more important than ever now.

We must speed up the shift toward network orientation and orchestration. Managing network communications in a thoughtful, respectful manner requires a different kind of leadership model. Many companies these days send messages about COVID-19 to customers with whom they have done business. Would it not be better for such companies to encourage their customers to share experiences, problems and solutions with one another, rather than flooding their customers with coronavirus emails and social media posts?

> **You cannot succeed by competing company-against-company. Focus on network-against-network competition.**

To implement the eight principles and their associated strategy, it is critical to have the right talent and organizational architecture and

---

13 Barry Libert, Megan Beck and Yoram Wind, The Network Imperative: How to Survive and Grow in the Age of Digital Business Models, Harvard Business Review Press, June 2016.

network orchestration. Ask yourself, have we examined every component of our organizational architecture? What changes are required to implement our new strategy and to achieve the objectives? How could we redesign our organizational architecture and network orchestration in a manner that they can support our disruptive strategies?

Developing an Implementation Strategy and Framework

As mentioned earlier, these eight principles are interrelated. They will be most effective when you work on all of them together (See Exhibit 3).

EXHIBIT 3

Eight Inter-related Principles to Guide Your Actions

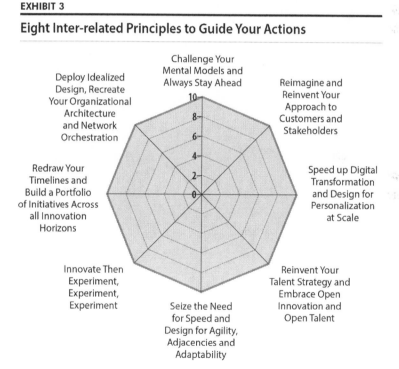

Use this spider diagram to assess the degree to which you are applying our principles at present. Zero indicates that you are not applying a principle at all and 10 indicates that you are applying it effectively. The distance between your current rating and 10 indicates the areas that require further action.

We believe you can develop a winning strategy by using the principles we have outlined above. But having a great strategy is not enough; the key is how we implement it. Remember, *execution is king* (See exhibit 4). Assume the following matrix:

EXHIBIT 4

Implementation Strategy

		STRATEGY	
		Excellent	**Poor**
EXECUTION	**Excellent**	1	2
	Poor	3	4

Obviously, we all want to be in cell 1 and avoid cell 4. But who do you think will be more successful — firms in cell 2 or cell 3? The answer is cell 2. Great executors will manage to flip and change and succeed even with poor strategy. *So how do we master execution? Well, it takes as much effort as developing the plan. It is critical that we pay as much attention to implementation as we do to developing the strategy.*

The first step in developing strategy is to begin with the customer. With customers as the starting point, we explore their current and evolving needs. Based on those, we come up with products and services that will meet those needs, and then we bring together the processes, resources, technologies, talent and incentives that will allow us to create those products and services.

Even the best strategy has no chance of success unless it is implemented well. The starting point in implementation is to focus on the people and organizational units responsible for implementation. Their needs, objectives and their likely resistance to implementation need to be understood and considered. Creative ways must be found to address these needs and objectives. The implementation strategy also needs to be iterated – in the sense that effective solutions may evolve over time rather than being put in place all at once. Possible solutions might involve offering people incentives for implementing the strategy, and if these are unlikely to work, to change the people responsible for implementation and bring in fresh talent. While bringing together the processes and resources required for implementation, companies can look within their organizations as well as to the broader network ecosystem. Here is our 10-step implementation framework: (See Exhibit 5)

EXHIBIT 5

Implementation Model

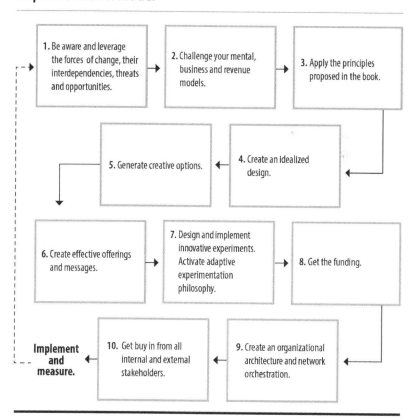

Tools to Deal with Disruption and Build Resilience

In addition to the eight principles and the implementation framework, this book will give you access to 10 tools to translate these principles and framework into action.

There are two self-assessment tools which will help you evaluate:

1. Your awareness of the changing forces of change and their interdependencies and how ready and willing you are to address their threats and take advantage of the opportunities they offer.

2. Whether you are challenging your mental, business and revenue models.

The remaining tools will help you to:

3. Apply the principles we have proposed in the book.

4. Create an idealized design.

5. Generate creative options.

6. Create effective offerings and messages.

7. Design and implement effective and innovative experiments and an adaptive experimentation philosophy.

8. Get the needed funding.

9. Create an organizational design and network orchestration that facilitates the implementation of the disruptive strategies.

10. Get the needed buy-in from all relevant internal and external stakeholders.

Preparing for Future Crises

So far, we have dealt with eight principles to survive and find opportunities in crises. The next question involves preparing for crises that might arise in the future. How can companies do that?

The answer is first to have an intelligent early warning system (radar) to monitor and forecast the changing business environment. This often involves the use of data to flag potential problems that might emerge while they are still nascent and before they manifest in full force. Once the warning signs are apparent, companies need to be organizationally agile and adaptable so that they can pivot to deal with the changing situation.

If a crisis is on the horizon, ask yourself: Can we pre-empt it? If not, how can we prepare ourselves for a fast and effective response? If we suffer damage because of the crisis, how can we plan for our recovery? What steps should we take today to build organizational resilience so that we can emerge stronger tomorrow?

The Need for Bold Leadership

Discovering new opportunities in a crisis, transforming the way you think and work, building long-term value after the crisis has passed and preparing for future crises requires bold leadership. Understanding what needs to be done is of little use unless you have the courage

> **Understanding what should be done is of no use unless you have the courage to do it.**

to do it. Have the courage to do whatever it takes, as long as it is ethical and legal, to stay ahead. Have the courage to do what has not been done before —the untried and the untested.

In July 2020, Albert Bourla, CEO of pharmaceutical giant Pfizer, announced that the company would start manufacturing its proposed vaccine for the coronavirus even before it got approval from the Food and Drug Administration (FDA). Bourla said that the company's early-stage trial results of its vaccine were promising. and it was willing to bet big by investing $2 billion in the venture. Bourla's reasoning was that time is of the essence, given the scale of the COVID-19 crisis. If their vaccine got FDA approval, Pfizer would not have to wait before beginning to produce it. The flip side, of course, is that if the vaccine does not get FDA approval, the entire investment would have to be written off. This is a first for Pfizer. The company has never before manufactured a drug before the FDA has approved it.. But, as Bourla said in his interview to *Time magazine*[14], these are unusual times. When millions of lives and the world economy are at stake, one has to look beyond conventional thinking about return on investment.

We believe that Bourla's decision is a superb example of courageous leadership. The decision might turn either way, but the issue here is not whether it is right or wrong. It is about having the courage to make a tough, risky and potentially expensive decision when the circumstances demand it. Many executives lack the courage to make difficult decisions and prefer to play it safe. That can hardly be called leadership, let alone bold leadership.

In times of crisis—and even after they have passed—we need leaders who are willing to acknowledge uncertainties. We need leaders who recognize the urgency of the situation and are willing to act swiftly and decisively. Leaders must have the courage to forge ahead in the face of resistance from within and outside their organization. Above all, we need leaders

> **Above all, we need leaders who are compassionate.**

who are compassionate. Compassion is important because as you move toward a network organization, you need much more collaboration. We need leaders who believe in a win-win approach as the model for their activities.

At a time when fear is pervasive, it is tempting either to be in denial or to succumb to panic. At such moments, level-headed leaders, who are compassionate, calm and driven by empathy, often rise to the top. They inspire trust because they view turbulence as a teacher that can help them become better pilots in the future.

---

[14] "Pfizer CEO Bourla Raises Expectations That the Pharma Giant Can Deliver a COVID-19 Vaccine By Fall," Time, July 12, 2020. https://time.com/5864690/pfizer-vaccine-coronavirus/

Several studies have shown that the reputations of leaders as well as organizations are shaped by their actions during crises. Selfish actions are not easily forgotten, and compassionate behavior is remembered long after the crisis. In addition to the eight principles, we believe that a commitment to compassionate leadership will make you more effective during these challenging times.

When we speak about leadership, we don't mean just CEOs; we mean leaders of business units as well. In small companies you have CEOs who lead the companies, but in large companies you have huge business units or brands. Every president of a business unit or a brand is like a mini CEO. They are the ones who are more likely to move quickly. We hope everyone has the courage to become a leader who can leverage these principles to find opportunities in the current crisis.

> **The reputations of leaders and organizations are shaped by their actions during crises.**

If that happens, we can move beyond the Ides of March to a brighter, more successful tomorrow. Now it is time to see how to get there and begin our exploration together.

Call to Action

COVID-19 has changed the world. Even before the pandemic, exponential advances in science and technology, empowered and skeptical consumers, and other forces of change were disrupting every industry. The COVID-19 global pandemic has accelerated these forces of change and their impact. If companies and their leaders don't equip themselves for the new reality, they risk becoming irrelevant.

Meghna is bored. Her city has been in lockdown for the past few weeks because of the COVID-19 pandemic and she cannot move out. Every evening, after completing her office work-from-home, she looks forward to watching movies and shows on her regular streaming platform. But some of the shows Meghna wants to watch are not available with them. She is wondering whether to switch to other streaming services and starts checking them out on a search-engine. Suddenly she gets a message from her streaming service. It says that they have noticed that some of the programs she has been searching for on their platform are not available with them. As a way of showing their appreciation for being their valued customer, they would like to offer Meghna access to some of other popular streaming

> **Even before the pandemic, forces of change were disrupting every industry.**

platforms—*free of charge—till the lockdown is lifted. That's not all. They are compiling a list of shows she might enjoy and they will soon be adding those to their platform. They also offer her a discount to their annual membership. Meghna is thrilled.*

John is at the airport after a hectic day at work. He has a flight to catch for an important business meeting the next day. He is looking forward to reaching his destination on time, checking into his hotel, relaxing, and waking up fresh for the morning appointment. But, instead of a boarding announcement, John is informed that his flight has been delayed by a couple of hours. That very instant, he gets a message on his mobile phone from the airline apologizing for the delay and the inconvenience. The message also offers John, a frequent flyer, a coupon with a generous discount for a leading sports store. John is an avid tennis player and has, in fact, been browsing online for a new racket. The message brings a smile to his face.

Yegya is sitting with his travel agent. The holiday season is approaching, and he wants to plan a vacation for his family after travel restrictions imposed during the pandemic are lifted. Even as Yegya is discussing various options, he gets a message on his mobile phone from his bank offering him a vacation loan on attractive terms. The message includes a list of airlines and hotels the bank partners with, where he can get exclusive deals. Yegya has been a long-standing customer of the bank. The bank knows him well and the offers are pre-approved. Yegya is delighted.

Jane is at a shopping mall with her friends. She gets a message on her mobile phone from a brand store she had visited the previous week. Jane had gone there to buy a pair of jeans but the color she wanted was not

available. The message says that it was now at the store. And not just that; to make up for the disappointment of the previous visit, Jane is offered two T-shirts of her choice from a select collection, free of cost. Jane is thrilled.

★ ★ ★

Li, a consumer goods retailer, wants to get the best bang for his social media advertising buck. His new-age advertising agency tells him that using a proprietary artificial intelligence (AI) algorithm, they can capture and analyze millions of posts on social media and predict what conversations would be most popular in a given period. Then, by combining their creative expertise with predictive AI, they can make ads for Li's brands in line with the trending conversations. They would then place these ads on different social media platforms in a timely manner to ensure maximum impact. Li is elated.

★ ★ ★

These scenarios are not all science fiction. These experiences could be made possible today; most legacy companies, however, are not offering them. But customers, and indeed all stakeholders, increasingly expect this hyper-personalized level of service. And now, in the post-pandemic world, where they are financially and emotionally bruised and battered—some of them may still be in lockdown—they also expect companies to be compassionate and understanding about their challenges, fears and uncertainties. They expect companies to communicate with them and address their needs in a relevant and urgent manner.

> Most customers and all stakeholders expect [a] hyper-personalized level of service.

What does that mean for you and your company? Simply this: Having the right data and predictive analytics, understanding and predicting your customers' and stakeholders' desires and needs, and offering relevant and timely products, services and experiences is not optional. If you want to stay in the battle and continue to win, these are must-have weapons in your armory. You don't have to look far to understand why. The need to focus on customer-centricity is all around us. It is in the changes, both obvious and subtle, that are redefining every aspect of our personal and professional lives.

Forces of Change That Are Impacting Businesses

The COVID-19 crisis has changed our world. COVID-19 started in China in December 2019 and was declared a pandemic by the World Health Organization in March 2020. Across the

> The need to focus on customer-centricity is all around us.

globe, it has hit us where it hurts most—our health and our economy. People in more than 200 countries, areas and territories have tested positive for COVID-19 and with half of the world population forced into a lockdown, economic activity has come to a near halt *(See Exhibit 1)*. At the time of writing, the world is in the grip of deep turbulence and uncertainty. As a business, you need to prepare for different scenarios— most optimistic, most pessimistic, and the most likely ones *(See Exhibit 2)*.

EXHIBIT 1

COVID-19 Diffusion Worldwide

An interactive, web-based dashboard to track the global diffusion of COVID-19 in real time has been developed by the Center for Systems Science and Engineering (CSSE) at Johns Hopkins University (JHU). The size of the circles indicates the relative scale of diffusion by region. The snapshot shown here is from 5/2/2020 at 4:32 pm.

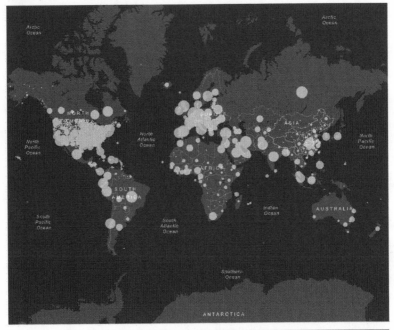

EXHIBIT 2

COVID-19-related Scenarios

Here are possible scenarios to consider with respect to the duration of the pandemic and the speed of economic recovery. As a business, you will want to prepare for the key scenarios depicted here. It's really a case for preparing for the worst and hoping for the best.

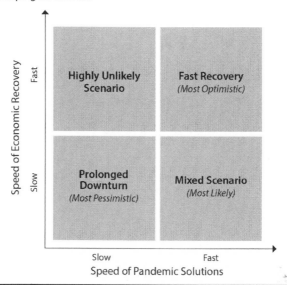

The way we see it (and as also expressed by authors Yoram (Jerry) Wind and Catharine Findiesen Hays in their 2016 book *Beyond Advertising: Creating Value Through All Customer Touchpoints*),[15] even before the COVID-19 crisis, five major forces of change were impacting businesses. The coronavirus crisis has further accelerated the pace of disruption.

1. Disruptive advances in science and technology: Be it the cloud, Internet of Things (IoT), connected communities, wearable computing, 3-D printing, AI, robotics, Blockchain, personalized

---

15 Yoram (Jerry) Wind and Catharine Findiesen Hays, Beyond Advertising: Creating Value Through All Customer Touchpoints,, Wiley, 2016.

medicine, gene therapy, flying cars, quantum computing, physiological computing, neuro-technology, new materials, and many other scientific discoveries—all these are changing the art and science of what is possible, measurable, understandable and actionable in every facet of our lives *(See Exhibit 3)*.

EXHIBIT 3

Top Disruptive Technologies

Top technologies such as the ones listed here are impacting everything from computing and communications to health care and finance. Individually and collectively they are transforming how we conduct our lives and our business, today and in the future.

1. 3-D Printing
2. 5G
3. Advanced Materials
4. Advanced Oil and Gas Exploration and Recovery
5. Advanced Robotics
6. Artificial Intelligence
7. Autonomous and Near-autonomous Vehicles
8. Automation of Knowledge Work
9. Biotechnology
10. Blockchain
11. Cloud
12. Cyber Security
13. Digital Money
14. Energy Storage
15. Hyper-personalized Medicine
16. Internet of Things
17. Mobile Internet
18. Next-generation Genomics
19. Quantum Computing
20. Renewable Energy
21. Robotic Process Automation
22. Voice & Facial Recognition

According to International Data Corporation, 336.5 million wearable devices were shipped worldwide in 2019—an 89% increase over 2018. At Alphabet's experimental X, (The Moonshot Factory), whose mission is to "create radical new technologies to solve some of the world's hardest problems," six "moonshot" projects have been spun off as independent businesses within Alphabet. These are Waymo (self-driving cars), Chronicle (cybersecurity), Verily (life sciences), Dandelion (geothermal energy), Loon (Internet balloons) and Wing (delivery drones). June 2018 saw the launch of Summit, the world's most powerful and smartest AI supercomputer—at least for now. Built by IBM for the U.S. Department of Energy, Summit can perform 200 quadrillion calculations per second and uses a new architecture to leverage huge amounts of data and AI. According to an IBM statement made during the launch, the Summit can help in areas such as cancer research, understanding certain factors leading to opioid addiction, and exploring the origins of the universe.

> **You need to prepare for different scenarios – most optimistic, most pessimistic, and the most likely ones.**

In March 2020, the U.S. Department of Energy deployed Summit in the fight against the coronavirus pandemic. In just two days, performing simulations with unprecedented speed, Summit was able to deliver data which would otherwise have taken months. While the result thrown up by Summit is not a cure for COVID-19, it is expected that these computational findings will be helpful for further investigations.

And here's the thing: Earlier, technology was more of an "enabler" for businesses to get things done. But now, a fundamental shift is taking place. With smartphones and other new devices becoming ubiquitous and the primary modes of interaction, there is unprecedented access to customer data. Deep, actionable insights can now be derived from analyzing it. From being an enabler, technology can now become a strong differentiator, depending on how well it is used. According to a 2019 report titled *Navigating the World of Disruption* by the McKinsey Global Institute, "Companies that are digital leaders in their sectors have faster revenue growth and higher productivity than their less-digitized peers. They improve profit margins three times more rapidly than average and are often the fastest innovators and disruptors of their sectors."[16]

In tandem with these advances in technology, scientific progress is transforming our understanding of fields ranging from biology to climate change. As a case in point, consider personalized medicine. With insights gained from the mapping of the human genome, new drugs are being launched that can provide unique treatments for patients, depending on their genetic makeup. This will lead to massive disruptions in the way health care is delivered in the future. Equally radical changes have arisen because our scientific understanding of climate change has deepened, notwithstanding the political backlash this has provoked. Protests by millions of people around the world have drawn attention to the need for companies to move away from operations that generate greenhouse gases. At the same time, global investment in green energy continues to grow rapidly. According to the United Nations, in the decade from 2010 to 2019, global investment in renewable energy crossed $2.5 trillion. [17]

> **From being an enabler, technology can become a differentiator, depending on how well it is used.**

2. Dramatic changes in the media landscape: New connected platforms have completely changed the way people communicate.

---

16 Navigating the World of Disruption, McKinsey Global Institute, 2019. https://www.mckinsey.com/featured-insights/innovation-and-growth/navigating-a-world-of-disruption

17 Global Trends in Renewable Energy Investment, United Nations Environment, Frankfurt School, 2019. https://wedocs.unep.org/bitstream/handle/20.500.11822/29752/GTR2019.pdf?sequence=1&isAllowed=y

Unlike the earlier static, one-way, stationary, passive, unidimensional experience, today media is a mobile, two-way, dynamic, multisensory and immersive experience. According to the *Global Digital Report 2018* prepared jointly by We Are Social, a social media marketing and communications agency, and Hootsuite, a social media management platform, more than 4 billion people around the world use the Internet. Of these, more than 3 billion use social media like Facebook, YouTube, WhatsApp, WeChat, Twitter, and Instagram, each month. Nine out of 10 of these users access these platforms via mobile devices. The report says that "the number of people using the top social platform in each country has increased by almost 1 million new users every day during the past 12 months – that's more than 11 new users every second."[18] We Are Social's 2019 report titled *Think Forward* lists putting brand values into practice on social, the importance of crowdsourcing, the rise of synthetic influencers, hyperlocal targeting, and democratization of data as some of the key trends shaping social communication in 2019. The drivers behind these trends, the report says, are basic human needs like the need for safety and control, the need to interact with others, the need to feel part of a community, the need for validation in society, the need to grow, learn and develop, and the need to help.[19]

> **New connected platforms have completely changed the way people communicate.**

Market research firm GlobalWebIndex's 2019 report on consumer trends in online commerce, points out that social networks are the "second-most prominent channel for product research after search

---

[18] Digital in 2018, Essential Insights into Internet, Social Media, and Ecommerce Use Around the World, We Are Social, Hootsuite. https://digitalreport. wearesocial.com/

[19] Think Forward: Trends Shaping Social in 2019, We Are Social. https:// wearesocialit.s3.amazonaws.com/think-forward-report-2019/WAS_ ThinkForward_2019_spread.pdf

engines." The report notes that social has "come to the fore in the purchase journey" because "social behaviors are now less focused on sharing personal information and more purpose-driven." The report adds that social platforms also provide important brand-consumer touchpoints. According to this report, "37% of Internet users follow their favorite brands on social media, with 25% following brands they are thinking of buying something from."[20]

The pandemic and the resulting lockdown in many parts of the world has been an amazing catalyst to speed the adoption of communication technology. There is increased use of video and web conference facilities, collaboration platforms, online education by universities, and online digital engagement of audiences by all cultural institutions and most businesses, and so on. Social media and streaming services have also seen a huge rise *(see Exhibit 4)*. According to Statista, an online portal for statistics, as of March 2020, social media usage increased globally by 21%, messaging services usage increased by 22% and video streaming services usage increased by 27%. We expect that the current switch to digital and the consumer environment may lead to permanent changes in consumers' use of media.[21]

The switch to digital may lead to permanent changes in consumers' use of media.

---

[20] The Ecommerce Trends to Know, Global Web Index, 2019. https://www.globalwebindex.com/reports/commerce

[21] Media Consumption Increase Due to the Coronavirus Worldwide 2020, by Country, Amy Watson, Statista. https://www.statista.com/statistics/1106766/media-consumption-growth-coronavirus-worldwide-by-country/

EXHIBIT 4

Global Coverage of Social Media Platforms

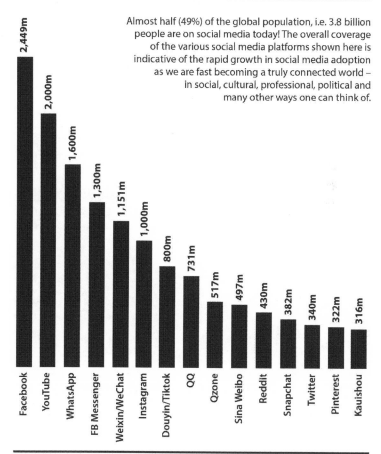

Almost half (49%) of the global population, i.e. 3.8 billion people are on social media today! The overall coverage of the various social media platforms shown here is indicative of the rapid growth in social media adoption as we are fast becoming a truly connected world – in social, cultural, professional, political and many other ways one can think of.

Platform	Value
Facebook	2,449m
YouTube	2,000m
WhatsApp	1,600m
FB Messenger	1,300m
Weixin/WeChat	1,151m
Instagram	1,000m
Douyin/Tiktok	800m
QQ	731m
Qzone	517m
Sina Weibo	497m
Reddit	430m
Snapchat	382m
Twitter	340m
Pinterest	322m
Kauishou	316m

The data are from January 2020 and based on multiple sources including company data and social media platforms' self-serving advertising tools.

As communication over social media platforms continues to grow in volume, conversations seem to be getting more acrimonious and polarized at the same time. This reflects to some degree the deepening rifts that have been fracturing social and political life across the world. As a result, the sense of a commonly-shared belief and objective, scientific truth seems to be getting lost amid the storms of partisan opinions on issues ranging from climate change to immigration policies. The backlash that some social media platforms have been facing from advertisers is yet another sign of these tensions, which have become more acute in the aftermath of the COVID-19 crisis *(See Exhibit 5).*

EXHIBIT 5

Massive Increase in Social Media Influence

Social media platforms have deployed artificial intelligence (AI) technologies to significantly influence the many decisions we make in almost every walk of life, including who we connect with, what content we consume, what things we buy, who we marry, and who we vote into power. Most of this can be attributed to marketers of products and services who pay these social media platforms to influence their audiences in a highly targeted manner.

How AI within Social Media Platforms Is Influencing Our Life Decisions	
Connections	Algorithms suggest who we connect with based on various vectors of relationships, interests, location and more.
Engagement	News feeds and what content or posts we see are driven by algorithms and thus influence what and whom we engage with.
Relationships	Algorithms in dating apps influence who we meet, date, have a relationship with or marry.
Travel	Travel recommendation engines and travel posts influence where we go, stay, etc.
Entertainment	Algorithms present entertainment content and events, that may interest us, based on our profile and usage behavior, and also based on what our friends are watching.
Shopping	Recommendation engines use algorithms such as collaborative filtering to influence what products we buy.
Elections	Opinion shaping algorithms including 'fake news' target us based on our profiles to influence who we vote into power.

---

3. Empowered and skeptical consumers: Many consumers today are way ahead of most companies when it comes to adopting new technologies. (Here and elsewhere in this book, when we refer to consumers and customers, we are in fact referring to the individuals in their myriad roles—as consumers, customers, employees, vendors, spouses, parents, citizens and so on.) This access to technology and vast amounts of information is making them powerful and in control. They can now effortlessly find what is available, compare different options and choose what suits them best. They want better value for every penny they spend, and they want better tools to help them make better choices. They also want a seamless, omnichannel experience. Yes, they pretty much want it all.

One of the most significant implications of this empowerment is the dramatic transformation of consumer behavior. This is reflected in the differences in values, expectations and behavior across generations; in the deep cultural divisions that are evident in the U.S., Britain, Israel and other countries; and the deepening income and digital divide, among other changes.

> **Access to technology and vast amounts of information is making consumers powerful and in control.**

Signs that changing values are leading to dramatic shifts in consumer behavior are visible everywhere. You can see them in the attitudes that young consumers have toward transportation (they would rather take an Uber or a Lyft than buy a car); toward clothing (they are comfortable renting clothes rather than buying them); toward travel (they would rather stay in an Airbnb property than a hotel). Even the spending habits of younger consumers are changing – they would prefer to pay for experiences rather than products. Disruptors who have challenged the status quo have driven many of these changes in consumer behavior.

At the same time, consumers are becoming increasingly skeptical. For instance, they want to know how information about them is being used and protected. They are also questioning the motives and actions of companies. And why shouldn't they? They are now well informed and aware of some actions taken by companies that they once trusted, such as financial institutions creating fake accounts. Little wonder that trust and confidence in business, in government and other institutions have sunk to new lows.

The COVID-19 pandemic has also significantly impacted consumer behavior and sentiments. The pace and the severity of the pandemic has resulted in uncertainty about the future, apprehensions about reduction or even loss of income, and decrease in overall spending, particularly discretionary spending. The crisis is leading consumers to fear for their lives and economic viability and increasingly to reflect on the purpose of life. We expect that the ongoing trend of focusing on experiences as against buying and owning products is likely to grow stronger after the pandemic.

4. Disruptive cultural, social, economic and geo-political environments: Every aspect of life around the world is in the throes of change. There are changes in the population, and in the global economy, as a result of the rise of China and India and potentially Africa. There is a crisis in education. Citizens of countries around the world are demonstrating to get their governments to act on climate change. Income inequality is growing, leading to a widening economic divide as well as a deepening digital divide. Incidents of terrorism are increasing, and recent years have witnessed the rise of nationalistic right-wing governments all over the world.

> The trend of focusing on experiences rather than owning products may grow stronger after the pandemic.

In the U.S., in May 2020, George Floyd, a 46-year-old African-American man was killed in Minnesota when a white police officer knelt on his neck for more than eight minutes. Though the officer responsible has been charged with murder, Floyd's killing sparked mass protests in cities around the U.S. as well as in other parts of the world. Importantly, unlike previous protests, times the Black Lives Matter movement attracted thousands of young people from a wide range of ethnicities.

Discrimination is an issue that is facing every society and every business organization. We believe that no company can afford to ignore it. There can be no place for racism or indeed any kind of discrimination in any organization. Every company needs to state it upfront and embrace social justice and inclusion as part of its DNA. Every organization has to visibly demonstrate its commitment and show by its actions that it truly believes that every life matters. In subsequent chapters we have suggested some solutions, in connection with mental models, talent policies and value systems, which we believe could help deal with this social cancer.

There are other shifting dynamics. For instance, China, which in recent years has helped drive the global economy, is now showing signs of slowdown. For the year 2019, China's economic growth, hit in part by the trade war with the U.S., slowed to a record low of 6.1%. In the first quarter of 2020, devastated by COVID-19, China's GDP *fell* by 6.8% year-on-year – the first contraction in the country in more than 40 years. (According to a *Financial Times* report, while the Chinese government has been reporting quarterly economic growth estimates only from 1992, it was in 1976 that it last officially acknowledged a year-on-year fall in output.)[22]

At the time of writing in mid-2020, the full impact of the pandemic on globalization, the economy, political and social order is yet to unfold, but some changes that we can expect include economic recession, disruption of all global supply chains leading to new supply chains, a sharp reduction in travel because of the shift to a digital way of life, and increased global collaboration especially in finding solutions to the health crisis.

> **There can be no place for racism or any form of discrimination in any organization.**

---

[22] "China's Economy Shrinks for the First Time in Four Decades," Financial Times, April 17, 2020. https://www.ft.com/content/8f941520-67ad-471a-815a-d6ba649d22ed

5. New business and revenue models: Even prior to the pandemic, as a result of the different forces of change, businesses were coming up with new and disruptive business models in an attempt to address them. For instance, on-demand transportation services like Uber, Lyft, Didi Chuxing and Ola Cabs, and accommodation providers like Airbnb, HomeAway, and FlipKey, don't own any vehicles or properties respectively. They simply connect suppliers and users through a technology platform. In addition, on-demand video streaming services like Netflix and Amazon Prime Video allow access to unlimited viewing against fixed plans *(See Exhibit 6).*

EXHIBIT 6

Disruptors Across Industries

Modern, exponential disruptors such as the ones shown here, reinvent industries so they can leave all of its leading companies behind. They are asset light, using new business models that do not require large capital investments like the traditional players, and are digitally well positioned to compete directly for the whole market.

FACEBOOK World's largest media company owns no content	**AIRBNB** World's largest hotel chain owns no property
ALIBABA World's largest merchant owns no inventory	**UBER** World's largest taxi company owns no cars
GOOGLE World's largest software vendor doesn't write most apps	**NETFLIX** World's largest movie house owns no theaters

SKYPE   ZOOM
World's largest telecommunication companies
own no telecom infrastructure

A crisis forces one to further reexamine the business and revenue models of the past. What worked earlier may not necessarily work in the new reality. Instead of viewing the crisis as a short-term forced pause in our activities, we should use it as an opportunity to explore and adopt new ways of thinking and working.

We will examine the manifestations of all these forces of change in detail later in this chapter and also, as we go along the book, but for now let's grasp one hard-hitting truth: In these times of unprecedented disruption, only one thing is certain for every organization: *Its ability to relate to the customer, augmented with organizational and network capabilities, to deliver a relevant, real-time value and experience will define and decide its future.* Continuing to do the same things in a dramatically changing environment will not work. If you are not able to change your mental models to respond to the changing environment and if you don't align your business model to give your customers the experience they want, when and the way they want it, you risk becoming irrelevant to them.

> **Do not view the crisis as a short-term pause; use it to explore new ideas.**

It is also critical to recognize the interdependencies that exist among the elements we describe here as well as among the forces of change. The increase in speed, complexity and uncertainties of change are a consequence of these interdependencies. Importantly, the changes brought about by the pandemic are going to impact all the forces of change and further accelerate their pace of change. This is the new reality. The old pre-crisis world is not coming back. We need to accept and address this. Scenario planning (*refer to exhibit 2*) is extremely important to synthesize our understanding of the various forces of change, their likelihood of occurrence and their impact.

The first of the 10 tools that we have for you in the final chapter will help you assess your awareness of the crisis and forces of change, their interdependencies, and how ready and willing you are to address their threats and take advantage of the opportunities they offer.

Current vs. Earlier Disruptions: What's Different?

One may argue that a company's relationship with its customers has always been important. Sure, it has. But then, as mentioned above, times have changed dramatically and, as a result, today's customers are fundamentally different. One may then point out that disruptions have happened earlier too, so what is so dramatically different about the current environment? One factor is of course the impact of the unprecedented pandemic crisis, but even if we were to look at the disruptions in recent years prior to this crisis, possibly the closest comparison that we can make with earlier disruptions is with the industrial revolutions of the 19th

> The magnitude, speed, and scope of disruption we see today has never been seen earlier.

and 20th centuries. The fundamental difference between what happened then and what is happening today is that the kind of convergence, the interdependency among the different components, the exponential nature, and the sheer magnitude, speed and scope of disruption that we are seeing today has never ever been seen earlier. All this is resulting in far more dramatic changes all around us.

We are often not able to gage the full impact of these changes. Take the exponential growth in the processing power of microchips, which has impacted many of the changes in the technology space. In 1965, Gordon Moore, co-founder of Intel, predicted that the amount of processing power on a single computing chip would double every 18 months to two years. In 2015, at the 50th anniversary celebration of Moore's law, Intel's then CEO Brian Krzanich explained what this means in layman's terms.[23] A rough calculation by Intel engineers shows that if a 1971 VW Beetle had improved at the same rate as microchips did under Moore's Law, the car would be able to travel at 300,000 miles per hour and run for two million miles per gallon of fuel, at a cost of just four cents!

---

[23] "Moore's Law Turns 50," The New York Times, May 13, 2015. https://www.nytimes.com/2015/05/13/opinion/thomas-friedman-moores-law-turns-50.html

Here are some more numbers that reflect the pace of change. It took 75 years for the telephone, which was introduced in the 1870s, to reach 50 million users. The Internet, which went public in 1991, took just four years to reach the same number. Facebook, launched in 2004, took two years. YouTube, started in 2005, took 10 months. The augmented reality game Pokemon Go which was released in 2016 took just 19 days. Some Facebook videos that went viral have hit 50 million views in only 24 hours *(See Exhibit 7)*.

EXHIBIT 7

Pace of Innovation Is Increasing

The time taken to diffuse innovation across the world has shrunk rapidly over the years. It now takes only a few days for a product to be adopted by 50 million users. And it just takes hours for a piece of viral content to get, say, 50 million views!

TELEPHONE	AUTOMOBILES	ELECTRICITY	RADIO	TELEVISION	INTERNET	FACEBOOK	INSTAGRAM	YOU TUBE	TWITTER	ANGRY BIRDS	POKEMAN GO	AAROGYA SETU (Covid-19 Health App for India)
75 years	62 years	42 years	38 years	13 years	4 years	2 years	19 months	10 months	9 months	35 days	19 days	13 days
1876	1885	1759	1895	1927	1960	2004	2010	2005	2006	2009	2016	2020

Time to reach 50 million customers

The Third Industrial Revolution

Jeremy Rifkin, economist, social theorist, political advisor and author, describes the current era as the "third industrial revolution." In his book *The Third Industrial Revolution: How Lateral Power Is Transforming Energy, the Economy, and the World,* published in 2011, Rifkin says that history shows that great economic revolutions occur when there is a convergence of three forces—new communication technologies, new sources of energy and new modes of transportation. In the 19th century, the coming together of steam-powered printing, cheap and abundant coal, and railways resulted in the first industrial revolution. In the 20th Century, the telephone (followed by the radio and television), cheap oil, and internal combustion vehicles gave rise to the second industrial revolution. And now, Rifkin says, the digitized communication Internet is converging with a digitized renewable energy Internet and a digitized automated transportation and logistics Internet to create a super IoT infrastructure resulting in the third industrial revolution.

> Jeremy Rifkin describes the current era as the "third industrial revolution."

According to Rifkin, the infrastructure of the third industrial revolution comprises five key pillars. These are: "(1) shifting to renewable energy (2) transforming the building stock of every continent into micro-power plants to collect renewable energies on-site (3) deploying hydrogen and other storage technologies in every building and throughout the infrastructure to store intermittent energies (4) using Internet technology to transform the power grid of every continent into an energy-sharing intergrid that acts just like the Internet (when millions of buildings are generating a small amount of energy locally, on-site, they can sell surplus back to the grid and share electricity with their continental neighbors) and (5) transitioning the transport fleet to electric plug-in and fuel cell vehicles that can buy and sell electricity on a smart, continental, interactive power grid."

These five pillars, Rifkin says, are only components and they must be put in place simultaneously for the system to function efficiently. According to him, "it's when these pillars are connected that we create the synergies that transform them into a seamless new infrastructure for a new economic paradigm for the 21st century."[24] In his 2019 book *The Green New Deal*, Rifkin shares his vision to confront global climate change and create a green post-fossil fuel culture.

Rifkin's proposition has been resonating well across the world. The European Union and China, for instance, have adopted his paradigm as their platform for economic growth. Rifkin has been an advisor to the leadership of the European Union since 2000. In February 2017, Maros Sefcovic, vice president of the European Commission, Markku Markkula, president of the Committee of the Regions, and Rifkin announced the Smart Europe third industrial revolution long-term economic development plan. Rifkin's website says he is "currently advising the European Commission on the deployment of the Smart Europe initiative and will be working with the 350 formal regions of the European Union in the creation of road maps to

> The pandemic, while cruel, can serve as an important lesson for mankind.

deploy the new economic narrative and vision across Europe." Rifkin is also advising the leadership of the People's Republic of China on the build-out and scale-up of China's Internet Plus third industrial revolution infrastructure.

In a video interview with *Handelszeitung*, a German-language Swiss weekly newspaper in April 2020, Rifkin said that the COVID-19 pandemic, while cruel, should serve as an important lesson for mankind and he hoped it would lead to a huge shift in awareness. He pointed out that even before the pandemic, most

---

[24] Jeremy Rifkin, The Third Industrial Revolution: How Lateral Power is Transforming Energy, The Economy and the World,, Palgrave Macmillan,2011. https://www.foet.org/books/the-third-industrial-revolution/

companies realized that a world based on fossil fuels was not sustainable. This view is now being accepted more widely. Rifkin believes that, the "the Green New Deal is the only way we can go after this crisis."

What Rifkin calls the third industrial revolution, Klaus Schwab, founder and executive chairman, World Economic Forum Geneva, describes as the "fourth industrial revolution." In a December 2015 article titled *The Fourth Industrial Revolution,* Schwab notes: "There are three reasons why today's transformations represent not merely a prolongation of the Third Industrial Revolution but rather the arrival of a Fourth and distinct one: velocity, scope, and systems impact. The speed of current breakthroughs has no historical precedent. When compared with previous industrial revolutions, the Fourth is evolving at an exponential rather than a linear pace. Moreover, it is disrupting almost every industry in every country. And the breadth and depth of these changes herald the transformation of entire systems of production, management, and governance."[25]

Even before the pandemic, a world based on fossil fuels was unsustainable.

Sanjeev Khagram, director-general and dean at the Thunderbird School of Global Management, believes that the pandemic will accelerate the fourth industrial revolution. In an article titled *Why coronavirus will accelerate the fourth Industrial Revolution,* Khagram says the COVID-19 crisis is pushing us toward more reliance on breakthrough technologies—be it digital, biological or physical. It is also making us more innovative in using these technologies and creating value in new ways. Khagram sees "several" silver linings in the pandemic. One of them is the "chance to experiment with technologies and co-operative approaches across

---

[25] "The Fourth Industrial Revolution: What it Means and How to Respond," Foreign Affairs, December 12, 2015. https://www.foreignaffairs.com/articles/2015-12-12/fourth-industrial-revolution

borders that could lead to safer, more sustainable and more inclusive global futures."[26]

The pandemic has, of course, brought its own unexpected devastation. Some of the hardest hit industries include travel and tourism, airlines, hotels, restaurants, retail, consumer durables, apparel and automotive. In April 2020, the International Air Transport Association for instance, estimated that passenger revenues for 2020 would drop by 55% as compared to 2019, A March 2020 statement by the World Travel and Tourism Council said 75 million jobs globally were at "immediate risk." It also projected a global loss of $2.1 trillion in revenue in 2020 for the sector.

Transform or Perish

What this means for organizations is that they have to constantly reinvent themselves to remain relevant. Staying at the status quo is not a viable option. While the disruption caused by COVID-19 has accentuated this manifold, for non-believers the numbers below should be an eye-opener.

In their 2014 book *Exponential Organizations*, Salim Ismail, Michael S. Malone and Yuri Van Gheest note that the average half-life of a business competency dropped from 30 years in

> **Organizations must constantly reinvent themselves to remain relevant.**

1984 to five years in 2014 and 89% of Fortune 500 companies from 1955 were not on the list in 2014. Ismail, Malone and Van Gheest define an "exponential organization" (ExO) as "one whose impact (or output) is disproportionately large—at least 10x larger—compared to its peers because of the use of new organizational techniques that leverage exponential technologies." They note that while the

---

[26] "Why Coronavirus Will Accelerate the Fourth Industrial Revolution," The Economist Intelligence Unit Perspectives, April 24, 2020. https://eiuperspectives. economist.com/financial-services/why-coronavirus-will-accelerate-fourth-industrial-revolution

information age is "now moving exponentially," the organizational structures, especially of larger and older organizations, "are still very linear." According to them, our organizational structures have evolved mainly to "manage scarcity of people, money, and assets/resources." And while the "concept of ownership works well for scarcity," they believe that in an "abundant information-based world, accessing or sharing works better." The authors list companies like Uber, Airbnb, Netflix, Google, Waze (community-based traffic and navigation app), Tesla (electric vehicles), Snapchat (messaging app) and Quirky (community-led invention platform) as some of the best ExOs.[27]

> **While the information age is moving exponentially, organizational structures are still linear.**

According to the *2018 Corporate Longevity Forecast: Creative Destruction is Accelerating* by consulting firm Innosight, the average tenure of companies on the S&P 500 narrowed from 33 years in 1964 to 24 years in 2016.[28] Innosight's *2019 Corporate Longevity Update: Creative Destruction Rides High,* forecasts "a steady decline in tenure over the next decade." The longevity rate is expected to drop to a 12-year average lifespan by 2027[29] *(See Exhibits 8 and 9).*

---

[27] Salim Ismail, Michael S. Malone, and Yuri Van Geest, "Exponential Organizations: Why New Organizations are Ten Times Better, Faster, and Cheaper than yours (and what to do about it)",, Diversion Books, 2014. https://www.maybank-ke.com/media/490246/exponential-organizations.pdf

[28] 2018 Corporate Longevity Forecast: Creative Destruction is Accelerating, Innosight.
https://www.innosight.com/insight/creative-destruction/

[29] Corporate Longevity Update: Creative Destruction Rides High, Innosight, 2019.
https://www.innosight.com/insight/corporate-longevity-update-creative-destruction-rides-high/

EXHIBIT 8

Most Valuable Public Companies

Companies are clearly setting themselves up for obsolescence, if they fail to innovate. As you can see below, many of the top Fortune companies have vanished from or lost their dominant position in the Fortune 500 list over the years. Nothing could be a starker evidence of disruption.

1917	1967	2017	2019
U.S. Steel ($46.4 B)	International Business Machines ($258.6 B)	Apple ($898.0 B)	Apple ($961.3 B)
American Telephone & Telegraph ($14.1 B)	American Telephone & Telegraph ($200.5 B)	Alphabet ($719.0 B)	Microsoft ($946.5 B)
Standard Oil of N.J. ($10.7 B)	Eastman Kodak ($177 B)	Microsoft ($644.0 B)	Amazon.com ($916.1 B)
Bethlehem Steel ($7.1 B)	General Motors ($171.2 B)	Amazon $543.0 B)	Alphabet ($863.2 B)
Armour & Co. ($5.8 B)	Standard Oil of N.J. ($106.5 B)	Facebook ($518.0 B)	Berkshire Hathaway ($561.4 B)
Swift & Co. ($5.7 B)	Texaco ($82.3 B)	Berkshire Hathaway ($452 B)	Facebook ($512.0 B)
International Harvester ($4.9 B)	Sears Roebuck ($64.6 B)	Johnson & Johnson ($374 B)	Alibaba ($448.0 B)
E.I. du Pont de Nemours ($4.9 B)	General Electric ($63.9 B)	Exxon Mobil ($350.0 B)	Tencent Holdings ($472.1 B)
Midvale Steel & Ordinance ($4.8 B)	Polaroid $58.0 B)	JP Morgan Chase ($340.0 B)	JP Morgan Chase ($368.5 B)
U.S. Rubber ($4.6 B)	Gulf Oil ($58.0 B)	Wells Fargo & Co. ($266.0 B)	Johnson & Johnson ($366.2 B)

Source: Data from respective companies listed here, June 2020.

EXHIBIT 9

Average Lifespan of S&P 500 Companies

As you can see from this exhibit, the average lifespan of S&P 500 companies has steadily shrunk over the years. For continued relevance and success, and to avoid getting disrupted, companies need to continuously innovate and deliver products and services that are in tune with the times and also be prepared to survive through any crisis.

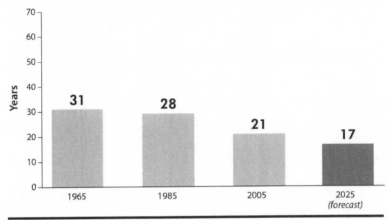

Source: Data: INNOSIGHT/Richard N. Foster/Standard & Poor's

Later in this chapter we will examine some companies that lost out because they failed to anticipate change and did not take the necessary steps, but it's also important to keep in mind that it's not only legacy firms that are under threat. Given the unprecedented pace of change, the complexities and uncertainties of our times, and the disruption caused by COVID-19, new economy firms are equally vulnerable. Some of them realize this and are continuously reinventing themselves. Think about this. Are you reading the signals of change? Are you reinventing yourself?

Social networking site Facebook's turnaround is an interesting example of a company reinventing itself for the world of mobile computing. In 2012, Facebook was struggling with mobile advertising. So much so, that in a U.S. Security and Exchange Commission (SEC) filing[30] it cautioned investors about its limitations in the mobile market. Cut to 2018. With 2.20 billion monthly active users and 1.45 billion daily active users, in the first-quarter results the company reported that its mobile advertising revenue had crossed the 90% mark. In that quarter, 91% of its advertising revenue came from mobile advertising. In the second quarter of 2019, with 2.41 billion monthly active users and 1.59 billion daily active users, this number went to approximately 94%.

How did Facebook do this? How did it become a successful mobile-first company? Facebook founder, chairman and CEO Mark Zuckerberg had this to say in the company's January 2016 earnings call: ".... we realized mobile was growing faster than desktop and people were shifting their usage. It was [more important] for people's consumer experience. That's when we made the shift. Not in our business first, but in how we developed the products .... We prioritized making the experience good before putting ads in."

Another pillar of Facebook's strategy is acquisitions. Since its inception in 2004, the company has made more than 65 acquisitions in areas such as photo management and sharing, file hosting and sharing, mobile advertising, group messaging, customer loyalty, travel recommendations, and so on. The mega-deals include WhatsApp, the mobile messaging app for a whopping $22 billion in 2014; Oculus VR, the virtual reality technology for $2 billion in 2014; and photo-sharing app Instagram for $1 billion in 2012.

Are you reading the signals of change? Are you reinventing yourself?

In March 2020, in the midst of the pandemic, Facebook paid $5.7 billion to acquire 9.9% stake in Jio Platforms, a subsidiary of Reliance Industries, India's leading conglomerate and the country's

---

[30] Facebook, amendment No. 6 to form S-1 registration statement, Securities and Exchange Commission, May 9, 2012. https://www.sec.gov/Archives/edgar/data/1326801/000119312512222368/d287954ds1a.htm

Acquisitions seem to be a popular move with new economy firms.

largest mobile telecom provider. Jio Platforms houses all of Reliance's digital and tech capabilities including mobile and broadband services. This is the largest single investment by Facebook in another company aside from its acquisitions. This is also touted as the largest investment for a minority stake by a technology company anywhere in the world. The deal will provide Facebook direct access to Jio's 388 million subscribers and a strong foothold into India's booming mobile market and e-commerce market. In December 2019, Jio soft-launched an e-commerce platform called JioMart with plans to soon take it national. India is the largest market for Facebook-owned WhatsApp with more than 400 million users. WhatsApp is waiting for government approval to roll out its payments service in India. A major focus of the new partnership with Jio is to bring together India's small businesses and consumers on JioMart using WhatsApp and providing them a seamless digital retail experience. In May 2020, Facebook launched a new feature in the U.S. called Facebook Shops which enables sellers to set up online stores on Facebook and Instagram.

Acquisitions seem to be a popular move with other new economy firms too as they strive to strengthen their digital and other capabilities and stay on top of their game *(See Exhibit 10)*. Collectively, Facebook, Amazon, Microsoft, Google and Apple have made around 29 $1 billion-plus acquisitions as of March 2020. Microsoft leads this list with 11 $1 billion-plus acquisitions, followed by Google (8), Facebook (4) and Amazon (4). Microsoft's $26 billion acquisition of LinkedIn is the largest, followed by Facebook's acquisition of WhatsApp at $22 billion and Amazon's acquisition of Whole Foods at $13.7 billion.

EXHIBIT 10

Illustrative Tech Giants Billion Dollar Acquisitions

The big tech giants - Facebook, Apple, Microsoft, Google and Amazon - have continued to acquire companies as part of their various strategies to accelerate their foray into new markets or expansions in existing markets. Most of these acquisitions are fueled by a competitive motivation to dominate the markets they operate in, and these companies, as shown here, are willing to pay significant sums for the acquisitions.

Time Period	Facebook	Apple	Microsoft	Google	Amazon
2000–2005			Visio ($1.4B), Microsoft Dynamics NAV ($1.3B)		
2006–2010			DoubleClick ($3.1B) Fast ($1.2B)	YouTube ($1.7B) aQuantive ($6.3B)	Zappos ($1.2B)
2011–2015	Instagram ($1.0B) WhatsApp ($22.0B) Oculus ($2.0B)	Beats ($3.0B)	Skype ($8.5B) Yammer ($1.2B) Nokia ($7.2B)	Motorola ($12.5B) Waze ($1.2B) Nest ($3.2B)	
2016–2020	CTRL-Labs ($1.0B)	Intel's Modem Operations ($1.0B)	Mojang ($2.5B) LinkedIn ($26.2B) GitHub ($7.5B) Affirmed ($1.4B)	HTC ($1.18) Looker ($2.6B) Fitbit ($2.1B)	Whole Foods ($13.7) Ring ($1.2B) Pill Pack ($1.0B)

Source: https://www.cbinsights.com/research/tech-giants-billion-dollar-acquisitions-infographic. May 5, 2020.

One sector that has stood out in mergers and acquisitions activity is payment technology. An August 2019 article in the *Financial Times* reported a boom in mergers and acquisitions in the payments sector, with 2019 becoming the "third successive year of record-breaking deal volumes." The article said that "a structural shift" toward e-payments led to higher valuations and companies wanted to combine to achieve better scale and reach.[31]

According to the *2019 Annual Fintech Almanac* released in February 2020 by Financial Technology Partners, 2019 saw 221 M&A deals worth $127.4 billion in the global payments industry.[32] The coronavirus crisis will most likely see a huge increase in M&A across sectors; many companies in trouble will have to merge or be acquired.

Just look around you. Practically every business and every organization can benefit from enhancing its operations with digital capabilities. In fact, we strongly believe that *every business today is a digital business*. Those who don't know it yet will realize it sooner rather than later.

The Success Mantra

Keep the Customer at the Center

> Every business today is a digital business.

Being customer-centric has always been true and it is even more critical at times of crisis. This is an opportunity for smart organizations to strengthen their ties with their customers and increase their engagement and loyalty. It is also a competitive opportunity to capture customers of competitors who ignored their customers.

When we look at industries that have been disrupted in recent times, we can see a common thread: Any industry that has a consumer element is the first to get disrupted. Examples are aplenty—retail with Amazon, payments with PayPal and Square,

---

[31] "KKR Wins Race to Buy German Payments Group for €600m", Financial Times, August 4, 2019. https://www.ft.com/content/65a1b036-b698-11e9-8a88-aa6628ac896c

[32] 2019 Annual Fintech Almanac: Global Financing and M&A Statistics, Financial Technology Partners, 2020. https://ftpartners.docsend.com/view/5bfsfn5

retail lending with LendingTree and SoFi. The reason is that traditionally companies ran their businesses based on what their core systems could support. For instance, if you were an insurance company, you had an underwriting system, a claims system and a policy admin system. These systems determine how you run your business. But over the last 10 years, there have been huge and rapid advances in consumer-facing technology. Now customers have started to drive what kind of service they want, when they want it and how they want it delivered.

Consider Oscar Health. Started in 2012 by Mario Schlosser (CEO), Josh Kushner and Kevin Nazemi, this New York-based health insurance company's mission is to make buying health insurance easier and more transparent and to provide better customer service. In an interview with *CNBC* in May 2018, Schlosser said: "We pay claims in an average of three days. Next year, it will be close to real-time. That's a big shift toward the way the [health care] system should be working." According to Schlosser, 41% of Oscar Health's members use its app and website to manage their health every month. Members can use the app to find physicians, talk to doctors for free, see their lab reports and prescriptions, interact with a dedicated six-member concierge team (which includes a nurse), track their deductibles, and so on. For businesses, Oscar Health has features such as customizable plans for different levels of employees or different health conditions and an online portal which allows for easily adding or removing employees and making payments. The company's website claims to have 250,000 members across New York, New Jersey, Ohio, Tennessee, Texas, California, Arizona, Michigan, and Florida.

> **Any industry that has a consumer element is the first to get disrupted.**

A March 2019 report in news portal *TECHregister* says that the health insurer has "officially cracked $1 billion in gross premium revenue in 2018" and that the 2018 financials show its operations are improving. "The company said it has managed to get medical costs under control, spending about 80.5% of the premium revenue it takes in from its members on medical care, down from about 95% the year before. That resulted in a net underwriting profit of $141 million in 2018, up from $10 million in 2017." Oscar Health's investors include Goldman Sachs, Fidelity, and Google Ventures. It has attracted more than $1.2 billion in investments.[33]

Uber has transformed the way people commute in more than 600 cities across 78 countries.

Let us now look at Uber and Airbnb. While both these firms have taken a severe beating during the COVID-19 pandemic because of restrictions on movement and travel and their future is now uncertain, these are well-known examples of disrupters and worth revisiting for the huge impact they have had on transforming consumer behavior and expectations and consequently on their respective industries and even beyond. In his book, *The Zero Marginal Cost Society*, where Rifkin describes the power of the network and how you can leverage that to scale with zero marginal cost, Rifkin says that companies like Uber and Airbnb can grow indefinitely without incurring a major increase in costs.[34]

A taxi-hailing app, Uber started in San Francisco in 2009 with a simple premise: What if you could hail a cab from your phone? Since then, it has transformed the way people commute in more than 600 cities across 78 countries. Instead of having to wait endlessly at the curbside for a taxi, customers can now use the Uber app and get a ride

---

[33] "Oscar Health Full Year 2018 Financial Results From Obamacare", TECHregister, March 1, 2019. https://www.techregister.co.uk/oscar-health-full-year-2018-financial-results-from-obamacare/

[34] Jeremy Rifkin, The Zero Marginal Society: The Internet of Things, The Collaborative Commons, and The Eclipse of Capitalism, S Griffin, 2014. https://thezeromarginalcostsociety.com/

within minutes, sometimes even seconds, from the comfort of their homes, or offices or shopping mall. They can share a vehicle or ask for a personal one. They don't have the hassle of giving directions to the driver to the pickup or drop point. They don't need to have cash to pay for their ride.

Even people who did not use taxis earlier regularly and instead used public transport now think of Uber as a viable option. Not just that. Uber is also impacting consumer sentiment and behavior, especially among city-dwellers,

> **Uber's goal is to make it easier for people to live without owning a car.**

regarding whether they need to own a car. Uber is simply far more convenient. The easy availability and affordability that Uber provides has another impact on consumer behavior. For instance, people may now be more willing to, say, go for a late-night show or dinner or work late at the office because they are now confident of getting a safe ride home.

Uber got its first customer in July 2010 and completed its first billionth trip on December 30, 2015. The second billion came within the next six months in June 2016. In May 2017, it completed 5 billion trips. All this and much more—and Uber doesn't own a single vehicle. Uber's success has spawned an entire on-demand ride-sharing industry across the globe. To name just a few: Lyft (U.S.) Didi Chuxing (China), Ola (India), Careem (Middle East), Grab (South-East Asia) and Easy Taxi (South and Central America).

Uber's stated goal is to make it easier for people to live without owning a personal car" and thereby improve urban life "by reducing congestion, pollution and the need for parking spaces." In a move toward this, it is now looking to bring multiple modes of transport like electric bikes and flying taxis within the Uber app. While the air-mobility service is still on the drawing board, Uber has already made headway with bikes. In 2018, Uber bought JUMP Bikes, an electric, dockless bike-sharing service. In the cities where Uber offers this service, Uber customers can book a JUMP bike from the Uber app itself. In India, Uber's biggest rival Ola is piloting a dockless bike-sharing service called Ola Pedal. And in the U.S. Lyft has signed a partnership with the city-operated Baltimore Bike-Share scheme in Maryland.

Bike-sharing of course has been around for some time, but now the dockless model is gaining traction around the world. For instance, there is Mobike in China, LimeBike in the U.S. and Mobycy in India. Electric scooters are also proving to be a huge draw. Bird, the California-based electric scooter sharing startup founded in September 2017, has become the fastest ever startup to achieve unicorn status (startups with a valuation of over $1 billion); it reached the milestone in May 2018. To put this in perspective: It took Uber, the poster-child of disrupters, four years to become a unicorn. This is how dockless sharing, in which riders can pick up and drop off the bicycles/scooters anywhere, typically works: you open a bike-sharing app on your phone and locate the company's GPS-enabled bicycles closest to you. Once you reach the bicycle, you tap the unlock button on the app and scan the QR code to unlock it. After you are at your destination, you need to park it legally and manually lock it. This automatically ends the trip. The pricing and the payment happens through the same app. The dockless bike/scooter sharing model is not without its own challenges, of course. For instance, it requires a large number of vehicles to be available across a city. This means large upfront costs, issues around maintenance and also the danger of these vehicles being littered across the cities. It remains to be seen how this model will actually pan out.

> **Bike sharing has been around for some time, but now the dockless model is gaining traction.**

But see how these new-age companies are impacting the entire mobility sector. For instance, with customers increasingly moving away from ownership to experience and wanting to pay only for what they use, auto majors are being compelled to adopt this model and are introducing car-sharing services. The way the service works is similar to bike-sharing: Users can locate and unlock vehicles from the relevant app on their mobile phones and after using the vehicles, they can leave them in any legal parking space within the operating area. The pricing and the payment is done through the same app. Look at Daimler and BMW and their joint car-sharing service Share Now. What's even more interesting is that Daimler and BMW had initially introduced their own car-sharing services called Car2Go and ReachNow respectively. But even as the two auto giants remain competitors in their core business, in March 2018 they entered into a partnership to merge their mobility sharing business units and Car2Go and ReachNow became part of the Share Now initiative. What's more, apart from car-sharing, the Daimler-BMW partnership is looking to offer ride-hailing, parking, charging, and multimodality services. What Daimler and BMW are planning to build together is more than just a joint venture. It's an entire ecosystem. Would you have thought it possible even a few years ago that two strong competitors would join forces to defend themselves against disruptors? Is this something that you would be open to doing?

What Uber is doing to the transportation industry, Airbnb is doing to hospitality. Founded in 2008, Airbnb connects travelers looking for accommodation with homeowners who are willing to play host for a suitable price. For customers this means that they no longer have to depend only on hotels

> **Would you think it possible that two competitors would join forces to defend themselves against disruptors?**

for accommodation. They have many more options in terms of the place and the experience they want *and* at the price they want it. Over the years, what was considered a niche service has become mainstream, including business travelers, and along with other new-age companies is posing a strong threat to established hotel chains *(See Exhibit 11)*.

EXHIBIT 11

Hotel Industry Disruption

The hotel industry has been disrupted by new-age companies that are leveraging technology to improve every aspect of the hospitality experience. The new-age consumer is increasingly opting for best-of-breed, personalized experiences at lower costs.

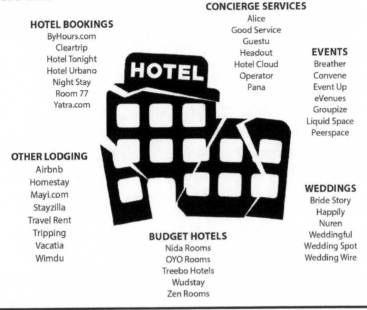

CONCIERGE SERVICES
Alice
Good Service
Guestu
Headout
Hotel Cloud
Operator
Pana

HOTEL BOOKINGS
ByHours.com
Cleartrip
Hotel Tonight
Hotel Urbano
Night Stay
Room 77
Yatra.com

EVENTS
Breather
Convene
Event Up
eVenues
Groupize
Liquid Space
Peerspace

OTHER LODGING
Airbnb
Homestay
Mayi.com
Stayzilla
Travel Rent
Tripping
Vacatia
Wimdu

WEDDINGS
Bride Story
Happily
Nuren
Weddingful
Wedding Spot
Wedding Wire

BUDGET HOTELS
Nida Rooms
OYO Rooms
Treebo Hotels
Wudstay
Zen Rooms

Source: CB Insights;. June 16, 2016.

Since it started, Airbnb has expanded to more than 5 million listings in some 80,000 cities across 190 plus countries. In 2016, Airbnb went a step further offering unique local experiences to its guests through hosts who are intimately familiar with the city. In February 2018, Airbnb launched a new high-end service called 'Airbnb Plus' in which the homes are "verified for quality" and offer a standard set of amenities similar to a hotel. Airbnb describes these as a "selection of high-quality, well-equipped homes."

In a bid to counter the threat from Airbnb and its clones, established hotel chains are being forced to expand their offerings.

Hilton is a case in point. In 2016, it launched a new franchise-only mid-scale brand called 'TRU by Hilton.' TRU has rooms that are smaller and cheaper than Hilton's core brand but has large and inviting social and workspaces. In October 2018, Hilton announced a new micro-hotel brand called Motto. These hotels will be centrally located, have rooms even smaller and cheaper than the TRU brand and, instead of a consistent "Hilton" experience, will offer local experiences with local partners for food and beverages. The first Motto hotel is expected to be launched in 2020. Tripp McLaughlin, global head, Motto by Hilton, claims that with Motto, Hilton has "deconstructed the traditional hospitality experience to create something truly fresh and exciting." Are you open to moving away from the traditional notion of your industry? Are you thinking of new ways to excite and engage your customers?

Are you thinking of new ways to excite and engage your customers?

Similar rethinking is underway at Marriott, which is weighing a foray into the home-sharing segment. In April 2018, Marriott introduced a pilot program with Hostmaker, a London-based home rental management firm, to launch Tribute Portfolio Homes in a few European cities. Armed with insights from its pilot—for instance, nearly 90% of guests who stayed at the Tribute Portfolio Homes were members of its loyalty program Marriott Bonvoy, over three-quarters were traveling for leisure, the average guest stay was more than triple the typical hotel stay—in May 2019, Marriott expanded this pilot and launched it as a global offering called Homes & Villas by Marriott International. This home rental initiative from Marriott comprises 2,000 premium and luxury homes located in more than 100 destinations across the United States, Europe, the Caribbean and Latin America. Marriott has launched the selected properties in partnership with property management companies that are already managing these homes. In a company statement,

Stephanie Linnartz, global chief commercial officer at Marriott International, said: "The launch of Homes & Villas by Marriott International reflects our ongoing commitment to innovation as consumer travel needs evolve."

Beware: Competition Can Come from Anywhere

In these complex and uncertain times, another big challenge companies need to prepare for is that competition can come from anywhere. The crisis has now accentuated it. For example, by shifting people's behavior to the digital sphere, in some ways the crisis has been a huge catalyst for globalization. Consider a local art museum that prior to the crisis relied on local audiences and some tourists. During the crisis, when all cultural institutions had to close their doors, the audience interested in art had the option of online tours of all the great museums of the world. Sotheby's sent emails to its customers encouraging them to visit online the great museums of the world. Sophisticated museums such as the Metropolitan Museum of Art (MET) in New York, the Barnes in Philadelphia, and the Getty in Los Angeles are intensifying efforts to engage with their current audiences and attract and engage new global audiences. In contrast, the museums that were waiting for the good old days to return are losing their audiences.

> Another challenge that companies need to prepare for is competition can come from anywhere.

But the competition for museums is not limited to art museums. They compete for the time, attention and engagement of the consumers. This includes competition from all cultural institutions be it theaters, orchestras, dance groups, opera, and even other activities such as going to dinner with friends, going for a walk, watching or going to a sports event and so on. While this was true even earlier, it will now be intensified since all the performance art institutions are switching to digital and increasing their presence in the consideration set of consumers.

That traditional industry boundaries are fast becoming irrelevant is reflected in Apple CEO Tim Cook's comment in January 2019 that he believed that Apple's biggest contribution to mankind would be in health care.[35] Looking at Apple's success in other areas, Cook's comment should raise a red flag for current players in health care. Think about the implications of Apple's vision on your future and what you need to do.

Disruption is also sweeping through banking and financial services. Telecom firms, financial technology firms (fintechs) and big-tech firms like Google, Apple, Facebook and Amazon (collectively called GAFA) are shaking up this industry *(See Exhibit 12)*. *The World FinTech Report 2018* produced by Capgemini and LinkedIn, in collaboration with the European Financial Management Association (EFMA), notes that "the financial services industry is being reshaped by expanding customer expectations for convenience and personalization–driven by the bar set by big-tech firms such as GAFA —combined with fintechs meeting these expectations with agility and an improved customer journey." Pointing out that the four tech giants enjoy "first-in" status when it comes to consumers' digital lives, the report says: "What consumer does not have a GAFA relationship these days? If financial services become the next boundary that big-techs unconditionally cross, the long-term impact could be momentous."

> **Traditional industry boundaries are fast becoming irrelevant.**

---

[35] "Tim Cook: Apple's Greatest Contribution Will be 'About Health'", CNBC, August, 9, 2019.
https://www.cnbc.com/2019/01/08/tim-cook-teases-new-apple-services-tied-to-health-care.html

EXHIBIT 12

Disrupting the Traditional Bank

Traditional banks are under attack from a number of emerging specialist startups. Here are some fintech startups disrupting banking.

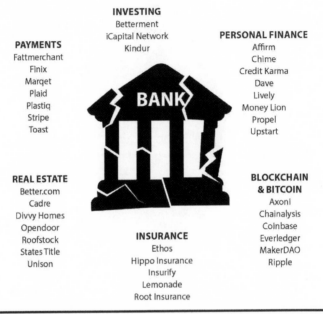

INVESTING
Betterment
iCapital Network
Kindur

PAYMENTS
Fattmerchant
Finix
Marqet
Plaid
Plastiq
Stripe
Toast

PERSONAL FINANCE
Affirm
Chime
Credit Karma
Dave
Lively
Money Lion
Propel
Upstart

REAL ESTATE
Better.com
Cadre
Divvy Homes
Opendoor
Roofstock
States Title
Unison

INSURANCE
Ethos
Hippo Insurance
Insurify
Lemonade
Root Insurance

BLOCKCHAIN & BITCOIN
Axoni
Chainalysis
Coinbase
Everledger
MakerDAO
Ripple

Source: https://www.forbes.com/fintech/2020/#26094f244acd. February 12, 2020.

The *World FinTech Report 2018* adds: "GAFA and GAFA wannabes have grown exponentially in terms of active users and time spent with users. Built on a digital platform, big-techs are efficient and have the know-how to reduce operational costs. With a strong focus on research and development, these firms have huge volumes of customer data to help them understand and predict behavior as well as vast cash reserves for new ventures." (As of the second quarter of 2019, the financial reserves of these companies were: Google parent company Alphabet: $117 billion, Apple: $102 billion, Facebook: $48 billion and Amazon: $41 billion.)[36]

---

[36] World Fintech Report 2018, Capgemini, LinkedIn. https://www.capgemini.com/wp-content/uploads/2018/02/world-fintech-report-wftr-2018.pdf

GAFA has already entered the payment space with Google Pay, Apple Pay, Facebook Messenger and Amazon Pay. In 2018, Facebook subsidiary WhatsApp piloted its payment feature in India, its largest market globally with more than 200 million active users. WhatsApp is the most popular messaging app in India and is expected to drive large volumes on peer-to-peer payments in the country and also become a popular platform for merchant payments. In China, the Alipay mobile payments app from the e-commerce and technology giant Alibaba Group is estimated to own over 50% of the country's mobile payments.

> Among the tech giants that are moving into financial services, "Amazon is the most formidable."

There's more. Google is collaborating with LendingClub, the leading peer-to-peer lender, to provide low-interest financing to its partners. Amazon, which launched Amazon Lending in 2011 to offer short-term loans ranging from $1000 to $750,000 to its partners, has a partnership with Bank of America Merrill Lynch to provide loans to merchants. According to media reports, Amazon is also in discussion with leading banks like J.P. Morgan Chase and Capital One for building an Amazon-branded checking-account like product for its customers.[37] In 2017 February, Alex Rampell, a general partner at venture capital firm Andreessen Horowitz, suggested that of all the tech giants that could make a major move in financial services, "Amazon is the most formidable." Rampell said: "If Amazon can get you lower-debt payments or give you a bank account, you'll buy more stuff on Amazon." In June 2020, Amazon entered into a partnership with Goldman Sachs to enable small and medium businesses on its platform to get loans up to $1 million from the financial services firm.

---

[37] "Amazon Reportedly Looks to Offer Checking Accounts for Customers via JP Morgan, Other Banks", CNBC, March 5, 2018. https://www.cnbc.com/2018/03/05/amazon-in-talks-with-jp-morgan-other-banks-about-branded-checking-account-wsj.html

While earlier too Amazon was giving loans to sellers on its platform, the loan value was not so high and was controlled by the etailer. This partnership will allow Goldman Sachs to leverage data shared by the sellers on Amazon's platform and offer loans directly to them.[38]

Look at this illustration below based on a CB Insights report titled *Everything You Need To Know About What Amazon Is Doing In Financial Services* (See Exhibit 13).

EXHIBIT 13

Amazon's Financial Services

From payments to lending to insurance to checking accounts, Amazon is attacking financial services from every angle without applying to be a conventional bank.

Amazon

Credit Cards
Amazon Prime VISA
Amazon.com
Store Card

Checking Accounts
Amazon Cash
Cash Amazon.in

Payment Solutions
Amazon Go
Amazon Pay Code
Amazon Pay
Pay Amazon

Insurance
Amazon Protect

Merchant Services
Reload

Prepaid Cards
Amazon Rechargable
Amazon Allowance
Reload

Business Checking
Amazon Cash
Cash Amazon.in

Business Credit Cards
Amazon Prime
Amazon Revolving
Credit Line

Business Lending
Amazon Lending

Line of Credit/Loans
Amazon Lending

Source: CB Insights Research Report titled "Everything You Need To Know About What Amazon Is Doing In Financial Services" Link: https://www.cbinsights.com/research/report/amazon-across-financial-services-fintech; December 4, 2019.

Some legacy banks do understand the looming threat and are making moves to counter it. Banco Bilbao Vizcaya Argentaria, S.A. (BBVA), one of the largest banks in Spain with 698.6 billion euros in

---

[38] "Here's Why This Top VC Says Amazon Is Set to Rule the Fintech Game", Fortune, February, 15, 2017.
https://fortune.com/2017/02/14/andreessen-horowitz-fintech-alex-rampell-amazon/

total assets in 2019, was founded in 1857. It is investing in fintechs. BBVA has its own data analytics firm and has also made some of its application programming interfaces (API) commercially available to startups and developers, allowing them to build new products and services by accessing and integrating the banking data of BBVA's customers—with their permission—into their applications. In a statement in 2017, Derek White, the then global head of customer solutions at BBVA, said that by opening its data and services commercially, BBVA is "turning 'open banking'—a model that is going to speed up the transformation of the financial industry— into a reality. Not only are we adapting to EU standard PSD2 [the second payment services directive], which aims to boost competition in the industry, but are actually aiming to become the best platform on which to build new digital experiences. This is a customer-led business opportunity."

In June 2019, BBVA launched a new logo. An article on its website says that "the change in logo – as well as unifying the bank's brand names across its ten countries – were part of BBVA's digital transformation program." According to this article: "The change underscores BBVA's aim to deploy a unique value proposition

> **Some legacy banks do understand the looming threat and are making moves to counter it.**

and a consistent customer experience, similar to what people have come to expect from digital companies across the world. The Group aims to have global products and services as a result of BBVA´s one-time development process, which allows for worldwide collaboration, resource prioritization, faster speed to market and customization for specific market dynamics."

In Russia, Sberbank, one of its largest and oldest banks— Sberbank is the historical successor of the Russian Imperial Savings Associations established in 1841. Its total assets in 2019 were 27.7 trillion rubles (approximately $437 billion)—has its eye firmly on leveraging new technologies and enhancing customer convenience and experience. For instance, in April 2015, it launched a new digital platform and merged 83 standalone regional sites into one single digital experience. In a press release, Nikita Volkov, the then senior vice president of Sberbank (Volkov became deputy head of the technology block for Sberbank projects in August 2018), said: "The new platform makes the interaction with the site for our customers much more convenient. And by providing personalized offers that may interest users, we can improve the efficiency of our digital cross-and-up-sell campaigns."[39] In its 2017 annual report, Sberbank said that it was "actively developing its channels for interacting with clients through a unique physical and digital infrastructure, creating an IT system based on modern innovative technologies (artificial intelligence, machine learning, Blockchain, robotics, and others)."[40] In December 2017, presenting the bank's strategy for 2018-2020, CEO and chairman Herman Gref said: "Our clients' needs go far beyond the financial sector, and we will work on offering them digital non-financial products and services to help them save one of the most valuable resources—their time."[41] Sberbank's moves are getting recognized and rewarded. For instance, in August 2018 it was named the most innovative digital bank among consumer banks of Central and Eastern Europe by *Global Finance*,

> Sberbank was named the most innovative digital bank among consumer banks of Central and Eastern Europe.

---

[39] "Sberbank Launches New Digital Platform Based on Backbase CXP," BackBase, April, 21, 2015.
https://www.backbase.com/press/2090/sberbank-backbase-cxp/

[40] 2017 Annual Report, Sberbank. https://ircenter.handelsblatt.com/download/companies/sberbank/Annual%20Reports/US80585Y3080-JA-2017-EQ-E-01.pdf

[41] "Sberbank Presents its 2020 Strategy," Sberbank, December, 14, 2017. https://www.sberbank.ru/en/press_center/all/article?newsID=fd683cff-c781-4fd8-bb30-c308b47121a0&blockID=1539&regionID=50&lang=en

a U.S.-based financial magazine. This award measures how actively financial organizations use cutting-edge technology for servicing customers. Sberbank was also awarded the best in social media marketing and services, and best SMS/text banking. [42]

At J. P. Morgan, after rolling out Amazon's voice-activated assistant Alexa for its investment banking clients and mobile apps for its trading business in early 2018, efforts are on to develop an AI-powered virtual assistant for its treasury services business. While virtual assistants are already available in retail banking in banks like Bank of America and Wells Fargo, this move by J. P. Morgan for its treasury services is among the first of its kind for corporate payments. In an interview with *CNBC* in June 2018, Jason Tiede, innovation head for treasury services at J. P. Morgan, said: "Based on your behavior each time, it will start to learn what you ask for. We think there's a huge opportunity to suggest creative and insightful recommendations to clients. When you log in, it can say, 'Looks like you have sent 100 US dollar wires to Singapore. Do you know you could send a foreign-exchange ACH payment instead? Click here to sign up.'"[43]

> Some legacy companies have been trying to keep pace with the changing times.

Fighting Back with New Capabilities

In other sectors too some legacy companies have been trying to keep pace with the changing times. The entertainment giant, Walt Disney Co., for instance, is using digital technologies to remove

---

[42] "Sberbank Recognized as Most Innovative Digital Bank in CEE", Sberbank, August, 14, 2018.
https://www.sberbank.at/press-releases/sberbank-recognized-most-innovative-digital-bank-cee

[43] "JP Morgan is Unleashing Artificial Intelligence on a Business That Moves $5 Trillion For Corporations Every Day", CNBC, June 20, 2018. https://www.cnbc.com/2018/06/20/jp-morgan-is-unleashing-artificial-intelligence-on-treasury-services.html

typical pain points like long queues at its theme parks and ensure that visitors have a hassle-free experience. Disney's MyMagic+ digital service includes a personalized wristband with accompanying website and mobile applications. It works as a theme park ticket, a digital wallet, a FastPass that allows visitors to skip long queues, as a PhotoPass that lets guests view, purchase and share pictures, a hotel room key, and so on. The mobile app provides information like character-greeting locations and show timings and helps visitors plan their itinerary. All this not only provides a superior customer experience, it helps the company to improve its operations further and also identify new and more targeted marketing opportunities because it is able to track and analyze customer behavior and activities.

However, while this is a brilliant strategy for good times, Disney as a company was not prepared for the pandemic crisis that closed all its theme parks, hotels and cruise boats. It has had to postpone many of its studio releases and its television segment which includes the sports channel ESPN has also been hit. While Disney's streaming services ESPN+ and Disney+ are expected to grow (given that viewership of streaming services has increased during the pandemic lockdown), they cannot compensate for the loss in all the other businesses. What Disney, and indeed all companies, need is a more balanced portfolio instead of a one that depends so much on personal visits. Disney could have perhaps avoided this huge damage to its business if it had considered scenarios that would have required social distancing. The big question now is what have they learned from the pandemic and how will they change their portfolio given that the next global disaster may involve climate change that can also lead to restrictions on travel and visits to physical places.

> **Disney needs a more balanced portfolio rather than one that depends heavily on personal visits.**

At the Swedish automobile firm Volvo Cars (owned by China's Zhejiang Geely Holding), one of the stated targets is to make one-third of its vehicles self-driving by 2025. In a move to gain access to new technologies and capabilities like AI, autonomous driving and digital mobility services, the company set up a

> Companies like Netflix have pivoted their business models to become successful disruptors.

tech fund in 2018. The fund made its first investment in June in Luminar, a California-based startup in the development of advanced sensor technology for use in autonomous vehicles. Earlier, in April 2018, the automaker tied up with Amazon for an in-car delivery service to customers of Amazon and Volvo Cars in the United States. In a press statement, Atif Rafiq, the then-chief digital officer at Volvo Cars, said: "Simplifying the customer experience is central to Volvo's digital vision. Receiving a package securely and reliably in your car, without you having to be there, is something we think many people will appreciate. This mix of car and commerce is starting the next wave of innovation and we intend to be at the forefront."[44]

Some companies, like Netflix, have pivoted their business models to become successful disruptors. Netflix, which started as an American DVD-by-mail service in 1998, has transformed the way people watch movies and television shows across the world. The company introduced online streaming of videos in 2007 in the U.S. and as of December 2019 it had 167 million subscribers in more than 190 countries. Netflix members can watch as much as they want, anytime, and anywhere on various Internet-connected devices like personal computers, tablets and smartphones and can even move from one device to another seamlessly. Netflix uses analytics to understand the

---

[44] "Volvo Cars adds in-car delivery by Amazon Key to its expanding range of connected services," Volvo Global Newsroom, April 24, 2018. https://www.media.volvocars.com/global/en-gb/media/pressreleases/227845/volvo-cars-adds-in-car-delivery-by-amazon-key-to-its-expanding-range-of-connected-services8

preferences of its customers and uses these insights to create original content. In 2013, it became the first Internet streaming network to be nominated for the primetime Emmy awards, further challenging the established television networks. Netflix also disrupts the movie studios. Its content series have made "binge-watching" of its shows a reality and it is able to make massive amounts of investments in producing original content. In a first for streaming services, Netflix in 2020 won 23 nominations for the Academy Awards, compared to 22 for Disney, according to a CNBC report.[45] Demand for Netflix's streaming services exploded in the wake of the COVID-19 pandemic.

> **We will have to challenge and potentially change our mental, business and revenue models.**

In a move to fight back competition from streaming giants like Netflix and tech giants like Amazon and its Prime Video, in June 2018 the American communications, media and entertainment giant AT&T acquired the media and entertainment group Time Warner (comprising Warner Bros., HBO and Turner). According to Randall Stephenson, chairman and CEO of AT&T Inc., combining the strengths of Time Warner (in content and creative) and AT&T (direct-to-consumer distribution across television, mobile and broadband) will allow them to "offer customers a differentiated, high-quality, mobile-first entertainment experience." Stephenson believes that AT&T's direct customer relationships provide unique insights which will enable it to offer "addressable advertising and better tailor content." In July 2019, WarnerMedia—AT&T created this when it bought Time Warner—announced a new online streaming service called "HBO Max." This was launched in May 2020. According to an AT&T media statement, HBO Max will

---

[45] "Netflix leads Oscar nominations with 24 nods—a first for a streaming service," CNBC, January 30, 2020.
https://www.cnbc.com/2020/01/13/oscars-2020-netflix-leads-oscar-nominations-with-24-nods.html

include "an extensive collection of exclusive original programming (Max Originals) and the best-of-the-best from WarnerMedia's enormous portfolio…"[46] More such deals are likely to take place as legacy firms try to transform themselves for the new age.

The pandemic crisis that is bringing a new reality to our lives and business requires a fundamental examination of everything we think and do. Just going back to what we did before the crisis is not going to work. We will have to challenge and potentially change our mental, business and revenue model and mode of operations. An important lesson from the crisis is that to survive in times of turbulence, it is critical to develop the following capabilities:

> **Most legacy companies don't have the managerial vision, competence, and the courage to change themselves.**

agility, speed of response, a cash and revenue model that assures a continuous stream of cash, asset-light strategies, having a diversified portfolio of businesses, the ability to collaborate, and most important of all, courageous leadership. You can do all of this by adopting the eight principles we propose in this book.

The Blinkered and Failed

Unfortunately, most legacy companies don't have the managerial vision and competence and, most importantly, the courage to change themselves. The result: they are no longer in the game.

Kodak is a prime example. The company, which was founded in 1884 and a leader in photography, filed for bankruptcy in 2012. The top management at Kodak failed to see digital photography as a disruptive force. It simply failed to keep pace with its customers' readiness to adopt this new technology. And the irony is that Kodak

---

[46] "WarnerMedia Names Upcoming Direct-to-Consumer Service HBO Max," WarnerMedia, July 09, 2019.
   https://www.warnermediagroup.com/newsroom/press-releases/2019/07/09/warnermedia-names-upcoming-direct-consumer-service-hbo-max

was in fact the first to come up with the technology for digital cameras. Apparently, when Steven J. Sasson, an electrical engineer who invented the first digital camera at Eastman Kodak in the 1970s showed it to the management, their reaction was: "That's cute—but don't tell anyone about it."[47]

> The music industry offers a vivid example of failure to keep pace with customers' changing aspirations.

Kodak's existing and very successful business was rooted around film and paper and the company didn't have the foresight or the courage to cannibalize it for something new. When customers started moving away from the film-based 'click and print' photography to filmless digital photography that allowed them to easily store, share, and even enhance their pictures, Kodak fell by the wayside.

The music industry is another vivid example of failure to keep pace with customers' changing aspirations. While the music companies were more concerned about protecting their intellectual property, customers were looking for easy and convenient ways to access and share music. In their book, *The Power of Impossible Thinking*, published in 2005, authors Yoram (Jerry) Wind and Colin Crook with Robert Gunther point to a 2002 study by consulting firm KPMG which found that only 43% of media companies made *some* of their content available in digital form; the rest made no attempt to respond to consumers. The authors say that these companies "were held back by their own mental models."[48]

---

47 "At Kodak, Some Old Things Are New Again," The New York Times, May 2, 2008.
https://www.nytimes.com/2008/05/02/technology/02kodak.html

48 Yoram (Jerry) Wind, Colin Crook, The Power of Impossible Thinking: Transform the Business of Your Life and the Life of Your Business, Wharton School Publishing, 2004.
https://wsp.wharton.upenn.edu/book/power-impossible-thinking/

The business world is full of examples like Blockbuster (video rental chain), HMV (music retailer), RadioShack (electronics retailer), Polaroid (instant photography), BlackBerry (phone), Digital Equipment (computers) and many others who lost out because they did not keep pace with the changing times and the new technologies and did not anticipate the aspirations and demands of their highly empowered customers.

Fraudulent Firms Are Eroding Customer Confidence

Earlier in the chapter we spoke briefly about how a large number of consumers today are also becoming increasingly skeptical. With easy access to information, they are seeing how across industries, some company or the other is betraying their trust and taking advantage of them. Let's look more into it now.

The series of fraudulent activities at Wells Fargo, the third-largest bank in the U.S. in terms of assets, is a prime example. It turns out that for years employees had been creating fake accounts, forcing services and products like auto insurance on customers without their knowledge or consent, overcharging veterans on refinancing loans, levying wrong charges on home mortgage customers, and so on. Apparently, the employees did all this to meet their sales deadlines and claim bonuses. In April 2018, in one of the largest such penalties imposed by government agencies, Wells Fargo was slammed with a fine of $1 billion. In February 2020, Wells Fargo reached a $3 billion settlement with U.S. regulators to settle the investigation. A new management, headed by CEO Charlie Scharf, is now trying to turn the bank around and rebuild its reputation, with client trust at the center of the turnaround strategy.

> Consumers are seeing how companies are betraying their trust and taking advantage of them.

Or, take the German automobile maker Volkswagen. Engineers at Volkswagen were intentionally manipulating emission testing norms for vehicles. When the cheating came to light in 2015, apparently it had been going on for 10 years. In October 2017, in an interview with *Knowledge@Wharton*, the business journal of the Wharton School, Jack Ewing, author of the book *Faster, Higher, Farther: The Volkswagen Scandal*, points out that not only did Volkswagen manipulate the emission tests, it also advertised heavily to convince customers that this was clean diesel. "You had a lot of people who were environmentally conscious who thought they were driving a clean car. I'm not sure it's even possible for Volkswagen to get those people back," says Ewing.[49]

> **To defend against disruptors or to become one, companies must gain the trust of consumers.**

Customers of Cuisinart, a home appliance brand owned by U.S. firm Conair Corporation, found that the company had released a defective, and potentially dangerous, product in the market. In December 2016, Conair recalled some 8 million Cuisinart food processors saying that the blades were defective and could crack and cause injuries. A 2016 *New York Times* article says that the company had in fact been alerted about the defect many years before it recalled the product.[50] According to the United States Consumer Product Safety Commission website Conair had "received 69 reports of consumers finding broken pieces of the blade in processed food, including 30 reports of mouth lacerations or tooth injuries."

To defend against disruptors or to become one and to capture the opportunities in times of crisis, it is critical to gain the trust of

---

49 "Can Volkswagen Rebuild Its Brand," Knowledge@Wharton, October 23, 2017. https://knowledge.wharton.upenn.edu/article/can-volkswagen-rebuild-its-brand/

50 "Cuisinart Recall 'Just Screwed Up the Holidays for a Lot of People,"The New York Times, December 15, 2016. https://www.nytimes.com/2016/12/15/dining/cuisinart-recall.html

consumers and other stakeholders and abide by both legal and ethical standards.

Is Brand Loyalty Dead? New Loyalty is to Customer Experience

Keep in mind that the increasing lack of consumer confidence in business, thanks to instances of fraud like the ones described above, is in tandem with their growing empowerment and expectations. What this in turn means is that increasingly large segments of consumers have no loyalty to brands. Loyalty seems to be moving away from being brand-driven to being convenience- and experience-driven. An October 2019 *Forbes* article notes that a study of 34,000 consumers worldwide by customer engagement company Verint Systems with Opinium Research, two-thirds of consumers surveyed said that they were more likely to switch to the competitor that provides the best customer service or experience.[51]

What is also becoming equally clear, as illustrated earlier, is that maintaining the status quo and continuing on the same path are not viable options. Changes in the external world coupled with the lack of the required competencies and mindset within companies to deal with the new environment is a huge threat to legacy firms.

Times of crisis offer a great opportunity for sophisticated companies to build brand loyalty. If companies understand their customers, engage with them effectively, are compassionate, and offer relevant solutions to their current and evolving needs, they can build deep connections with them *(See Exhibit 14).*

> **Loyalty seems to be moving away from being brand-driven to being convenience- and experience- driven.**

---

[51] "Customer Loyalty And Retention Are In Decline," Forbes, October 13, 2019. https://www.forbes.com/sites/shephyken/2019/10/13/customer-loyalty-and-retention-are-in-decline/#29bf9a5f4329

EXHIBIT 14

Rising Stars of the Pandemic Era

Many companies have found new or renewed relevance and growth in the pandemic era.

Communication	Zoom, Webex, Skype, MS Teams
Hygiene/Personal Protection	Chlorox, Lysol, Purell, Wostar gloves
Telemedicine	Most hospitals and health care providers
Online Shopping	Amazon Prime, Instacart
Streaming Media	Netflix, Amazon Prime, Hulu
Paper Products	Georgia Pacific, Kimberly-Clark
Vaccination / Testing	Gilead Sciences, Roche, Serum Institute of India
Other	Robots for disinfecting rooms using UVC light, Cusinart (Bread Machines), Advil (pain relievers), Liquor Stores

To assess how aligned you and your organization are with the ideas and examples discussed in this chapter, we would encourage you to consider the questions listed below.

Ask Yourself:

1. What is the current and future impact of the pandemic on your business?

2. What are the threats to your business from the pandemic and the interrelated forces of change?

3. What opportunities do the pandemic and other forces of change offer you and your business?

4. In planning your business strategy, what scenarios should you consider?

5. What can you learn from the current disruptors?

6.   How ready are you to transform your business?

7.   Are you truly customer-centric?

8.   Are you considering competition from not only your direct rivals but also from companies outside your industry?

9.   Do you have the needed capabilities for the new reality?

10. What can you learn from companies that failed?

11. What safeguards do you have to avoid unethical behavior by anyone in your organization and network?

Chapter 1

Principle 1: Challenge Your Mental Models and Always Stay Ahead

The world and our lives will never be the same as they were before the COVID-19 pandemic. To capture the opportunities the crisis offers, we must challenge and change our mental models. At the core of most human disruptions, new mental models have played a central role.

> To capture the opportunities the crisis offers, we must challenge and change our mental models.

Who could have ever thought that a player in the luxury sector could make something as basic as hand sanitizers? Well, Bernard Jean Étienne Arnault, chairman and chief executive of leading luxury goods company **LVMH** Moët Hennessy—Louis Vuitton SE, did. On March 15, 2020 Arnault instructed the company's perfumes and cosmetics business to temporarily discontinue the production of fragrances for its Christian Dior, Givenchy and Guerlain brands, and use the production facilities to make hand sanitizer instead. The world was in the grip of the coronavirus COVID-19 pandemic. There was an urgent requirement of hand sanitizer but it was in short supply. Arnault said the hand sanitizer produced by LVMH would be given free of charge to the French health authorities and

Assistance Publique—Hôpitaux de Paris, the largest health system in Europe, and that LVMH would honor this commitment for as long as necessary.

> **During the pandemic, the mundane hand sanitizer was a "luxury" item — it could save lives.**

Consider how Arnault thought about and responded to the crisis. Look at how he moved away from the conventional definition of luxury. Arnault realized that at this point in time, the basic and mundane hand sanitizer which was in short supply was in fact a *"luxury"* item— *it could save lives.* By using his perfume factories to produce hand sanitizer and distributing it for free, not only did Arnault respond to the need of the hour, but he was also able to keep his factories open, enable his employees to continue to come to work, and position LVMH as a responsible and caring organization. Consumers will certainly remember this long after the crisis has passed. And it will surely bring its own rewards to the company.

Challenging Established Industry Models

Let's look at another example. The year was 2008, which seems like an age ago, before the pandemic struck. It was a snowy evening in Paris. Two young men couldn't get a cab. Was this an extraordinary event? No. Not at all. This happens to people all the time, all over the world. It may have happened to you too at some point. But, from that very ordinary, one could even say an everyday occurrence, sprang an extraordinary idea. This idea has not just transformed the taxi industry globally, but is also promising to transform every aspect of mobility and beyond.

Yes, we are talking about Travis Kalanick and Garret Camp and their company **Uber.** What started as an anytime, anywhere, cab-hailing app in San Francisco in 2008 has grown to include driverless cars, on-demand electric bikes, a freight tool that connects trucking companies with shippers, food delivery (with Uber Eats, the company is not just able to cross-sell to its mobility customers, it is also attracting new customers who have never used the ride-hailing app), and much more. For instance, in October 2019, Uber announced that it was acquiring a majority stake in South American online grocery retailer Cornershop. The same month it launched an app called Uber Works in Chicago to match temporary workers with businesses. (Uber closed this in May 2020 during the pandemic crisis.) It is considering the introduction of e-flying taxis/air-mobility services with electric vertical takeoff and landing aircraft by 2023.

Why are we talking about Uber yet again? The reason is that almost all of you reading this book can probably relate to Kalanick's and Camp's experience of not getting a cab when you needed one. But—and here is the important question—how many of you came up with, or even thought of, a whole new business model centered on a cab-hailing app to solve the problem you faced?

> Disruptors come up with a mental model that challenges an industry's established way of thinking and doing.

LVMH and Uber are great examples of what we are going to discuss in this chapter: That disruptors come up with a mental model that challenges an industry's established mental model. They challenge the established way of thinking and doing. You must do the same *(See Exhibit 1)*

EXHIBIT 1

Companies that Challenged and Changed Mental Models

Try to find what is common to these brands from so many different industries. Upon reflection, you will see that all of them challenged and changed the mental model of their industry.

What do we mean by a "mental model"? It simply means our assumptions, beliefs and behaviors toward something. While all of us may see and experience the same things, what impacts and influences our subsequent actions is our "mental models." In their 2005 book *The Power of Impossible Thinking,* authors Yoram (Jerry) Wind and Colin Cook with Robert Gunther point out that "In our business and personal lives, we often fail to see the true threats and opportunities because of the limits of the way we make sense of the world."[52] As business leaders, it is critical to recognize that it's our mental model that shapes our company's business model and revenue model.

---

[52] Yoram (Jerry) Wind, Colin Crook, "The Power of Impossible Thinking: Transform the Business of Your Life and the Life of Your Business," Wharton School Publishing, 2004.

https://wsp.wharton.upenn.edu/book/power-impossible-thinking/

Take Uber. Kalanick and Camp thought differently about their problem of not getting a cab when they wanted it, i.e. they changed their mental model. They saw an opportunity to create value through providing connectivity. This led to their coming up with the idea of creating a platform to connect cab drivers and passengers in real-time, i.e. a new business model—that of a network orchestrator. And this new business model in turn led them to an entirely new revenue model: Uber gets a percentage of the fare without having to own the assets/inventory. While the Uber IPO in May 2019 was much below expectations ($82 billion valuation against an expected valuation of $100 billion to $120 billion), it's still a big IPO and an important signal of the major changes that are happening around us.

We believe that one of the biggest challenges to any business today is the mental models of its leaders about how value is created. In these complex and fast-changing times, traditional mental models are in danger of becoming outdated and leaving your business vulnerable to disruptors. This holds true for every player in every industry today. The COVID-19 pandemic has brought another aspect to the fore; it's not just human disruptors we need to worry about. There is another type of disruptor that we are rarely, if ever, ready to deal with: Mother Nature. Consider the swine flu pandemic of 2010, the Spanish flu of 1918, the black plague around 1350 or other natural disasters such as earthquakes, floods, and typhoons. The next global disaster is predicted to be around climate change, global warming and the flooding of coastal cities. We need to be prepared for such disruptions.

> It is our mental model that shapes our company's business and revenue model.

There is something else we need to guard against: not falling into the trap of the typical mental model during times of crisis. What do we mean by this? Think about how we usually console ourselves in difficult times. We tell ourselves, "These are tough times. But this will pass. Let's wait for the crisis to end and we will return to the good old days before the crisis." This is a fatally flawed mental model. A crisis changes everything, and post-crisis we have to be ready for a new reality.

Consider the tragic death of George Floyd in May 2020 in the U.S. Ask yourself how you as an individual and as a company have responded to the killing of Floyd, an African-American, by a white police officer. How have you reacted to the subsequent Black Lives Matters uprising? Have you challenged your traditional mental model? Have you reexamined your values? Have you recast your talent strategy and your organizational architecture? Have you reconsidered your responsibility to society? We believe that it is imperative for every business to draw a new blueprint for being an inclusive, fair, compassionate and socially responsible entity. How effectively you respond today to the changing environment and your ability to lead the change will have a great bearing on how you succeed going forward.

At another level, take the post-pandemic scenario. Working from home will not simply disappear. Instead, we should consider it as part of the new workplace environment, as the new, normal way of working. Some firms have already announced that some 75% of their workforce will be working from home over the next five years. This may or may not pan out. But look at the direction in which companies are thinking. Similarly, increased reliance on videoconferencing is not going to disappear. It is now part of the new normal way of communicating, negotiating, and doing business. Movie studios will be releasing their new content on digital platforms instead of in brick-and-mortar theaters. What could be the new reality in your industry? Are you gearing up for it? More importantly, can you *lead* the change?

> **Working from home will not disappear. We should consider it part of the new work environment.**

Disruptors & Innovators

Think about almost any breakthrough innovation over the years—whether it was **Starbucks,** the first mobile phones, or **Tesla**. These innovations challenged the basic premise of their industries. In CALL TO ACTION, where we spoke about the new forces of change, we listed a few companies including Uber, Lyft, Airbnb, HomeAway, Netflix and Amazon Video as those that have radically changed how their sectors work by introducing new business models. As this partial list from *CNBC's* 2020 Disruptor 50 below shows, there are many others *(See Exhibit 2)*.

EXHIBIT 2

Top Global Innovators, Disruptors (2020)

Forward-thinking startups, such as the twenty-five shown here, from the seventh annual Disruptor 50 list by CNBC, have identified unexploited niches, in the markets – from biotech and machine learning to transportation, retail and agriculture – that have the potential to become billion-dollar businesses. In fact, many of these already are billion-dollar businesses.

1.	Stripe	Unlocking the lockdown's biggest value
2.	Coupang	Beating Bezos at his own online game?
3.	Indigo Agriculture	The future of farming is carbon negative
4.	Coursera	Online ed's biggest test begins
5.	Klarna	No online sale left behind
6.	Tempus	Precision medicine for the Covid crisis
7.	Zipline	Medicine takes flight autonomously
8.	SoFi	The future of your financial future
9.	Neteera	Contactless health
10.	Gojek	Indonesia's original ridehail, growing up
11.	WeLab	Branchless banking
12.	DoorDash	The most in-demand in on-demand
13.	Heal	The next big thing in medicine: housecalls?
14.	Movandi	A network key to the 5G future
15.	Better.com	Closing the mortgage gap online
16.	Grab	Southeast Asia's super app
17.	Lemonade	A.I.-ing the end of the insurance agent
18.	Root Insurance	Replacing demographics with real driver data
19.	Healthy.io	Home-based health testing
20.	GoodRx	Technology tackling the high cost of health care
21.	Eat JUST	Just the egg, no chicken
22.	goPuff	The convenience store gets more convenient
23.	Affirm	Building new credit history
24.	Kabbage	A main street lending lifeline
25.	Chime	No-fee banking

Credit: CNBC

CNBC's 2020 Disruptor 50 list features venture-backed startups across sectors that are changing the world with their innovations. These 50 companies together were valued at more than $277 billion and raised more than $74 billion in venture capital, according to data from financial data and software company PitchBook. Many of them are billion-dollar businesses already. [53]

Here is another set of innovative companies. You will again see that most of them challenge the mental models of their industries *(See Exhibit 3).*

EXHIBIT 3

Innovators, Disruptors – Different Lists; All Breakthrough Ideas

Many of the top innovative company lists from various leading publications, (as the partial lists shown here), have the same common theme of companies disrupting their markets with breakthrough ideas – the kind of ideas that can only come about by challenging the prevalent mental models of the incumbents and coming up with truly transformative solutions.

Fortune– Future 50 List, 2019	FastCompany– The World's Most Innovative Companies, 2020	Forbes–The World's Most Innovative Companies List, 2020
Workday	Snap	ServiceNow
Square	Microsoft	Workday
ServiceNow	Tesla	Salesforce.com
Contemporary Amperex Technology	Big Hit Entertainment	Tesla
Spotify Technology	HackerOne	Amazon.com
Atlassian	White Claw	Netflix
Xiaomi	Shopify	Incyte
Ctrip.com International	Canva	Hindustan Unilever
Salesforce	Roblox	Naver
Vertex Pharmaceuticals	Zipline	Facebook

Source: Fortune–Future 50 List (https://fortune.com/future-50/), 2019; FastCompany–The World's Most Innovative Companies (https://www.fastcompany.com/most-innovative-companies/2020), June 2020; Forbes–The World's Most Innovative Companies List (https://www.forbes.com/innovative-companies/ list/#tab:rank), June 2020.

---

[53] "These are the 2020 CNBC Disruptor 50 companies," CNBC, June 16,2020. https://www.cnbc.com/2020/06/16/meet-the-2020-cnbc-disruptor-50-companies.html

Whichever industry you are in, look at the innovators and disruptors there. Look at how they are thinking differently. Look at how they are doing things differently. Look at the

> **Look out for models in other sectors that you could adopt.**

new business and revenue models they have devised. And then ask yourselves, what are the other opportunities for disruption? At the same time, identify your current mental model and the resulting business and revenue models you have been using. This can be part of a rigorous SWOT analysis. Ask yourself to what extent your current mental business and revenue model will work in the changing business environment and when disruptors enter your industry. And of course, always remember that your competition need not necessarily come from your own industry. We discussed this in CALL TO ACTION. Competition for banks and financial services players is not only from disruptors in their own industry but from big-tech firms like Amazon, Google, Facebook and Apple or from China's e-commerce giant Alibaba's Ant Financial and its mobile and payment platform Alipay. For your industry too, competition can come from anywhere.

Keep in mind that it's not just about increasing your market share. Think about what you can do in terms of increasing your share of the customers' wallet and also of increasing the lifetime value of your customers. **Nike,** for instance, acquired Zodiac Inc., a consumer data analytics company in 2018.[54] Founded in 2015 by Wharton professor Peter Fader and a team of Ph.D. statisticians and data scientists at the University of Pennsylvania, Zodiac is a predictive customer analytics platform that forecasts the behavior and lifetime value of individual customers and customer segments.

Alongside, look out for models in other sectors that you could adopt. For instance, ask yourself if you can adopt the Uber or the

---

[54] "NIKE, Inc. Acquires Data Analytics Leader Zodiac," Nike, March 22, 2018. https://news.nike.com/news/nike-data-analytics-zodiac

Airbnb model in your line of business. If you are in the business of financial services, or education, or health care, can you Uberize it? Can you create a platform that links investors and advisors, educators and students? Can you provide a doctor on demand? Or, whichever business you are in, can you, like Google, develop a model in which your end customer doesn't pay? Instead, say, the advertisers pay. Or, like Narayana Health, an Indian health care provider that we will discuss later in this chapter, can you develop a business model around frugal innovation? The possibilities are endless.

Who do you think will be the disruptors and innovators of the pandemic era? We believe that the pandemic and the disruption it has wrought have thrown up new opportunities for *every* industry. It is now up to *each of you* to spot, leverage, and create opportunities for yourselves. You could well be the disruptor and innovator of this era.

Redefine Success: Make a Difference

> Redefine your definition of success to include a positive social impact.

We believe that the writing on the wall is clear: If you want to stay in the game and retain a sustainable competitive advantage, you need to challenge your thinking and come up with new mental, business, revenue models and offerings. We would like to add one more recommendation here: In whatever you are doing, have a strong social purpose. Redefine your definition of success to include a positive social impact. Think again about LVMH and how it responded to the needs of society during the COVID-19 crisis.

Consider the *Statement on the Purpose of a Corporation* published in August 2019 by Business Roundtable, an association of CEOs of America's leading companies such as Apple, Amazon, Walmart, Coca-Cola, Ford and others. The statement, which is signed by 181 CEOs, says that the nation's largest companies have a "fundamental commitment" to all their stakeholders: customers, employees, suppliers, communities and shareholders. Also, consider the concept of 'technological social responsibility' (TSR).[55] In an article titled *Can artificial intelligence help society as much as it helps business?* in the August 2019 *McKinsey Quarterly*, authors Jacques Bughin (former director of the McKinsey Global Institute and a former senior partner in McKinsey's Brussels office)) and Eric Hazan (senior partner in McKinsey's Paris office) describe it as "a conscious alignment between short and medium-term business goals and longer-term societal ones." Bughin and Hazan write: "We believe the time has come for business leaders across sectors to embed a new imperative in their corporate strategy. We call this imperative technological social responsibility (TSR). It amounts to a conscious alignment between short- and medium-term business goals and longer-term societal ones."[56]

Here is another strong indicator of the shift of focus from shareholders to stakeholders. A 2020 Deloitte report titled *Advancing environmental, social, and governance investing: A holistic approach for investment management firms*, says that the proportion of institutional and retail investors that apply environmental, social, and governance (ESG) principles to a minimum of a quarter of their portfolios jumped to 75% in 2019 from 48% in 2017. Over the next three years, around 200 new funds with an ESG investment mandate are expected to be launched in the U.S, and by 2025, ESG-mandated assets in the U.S.

> **Every breakthrough innovation has challenged the basic premise of its industry.**

---

[55] "Business Roundtable Redefines the Purpose of a Corporation to Promote 'An Economy That Serves All Americans,'" Business Roundtable, August 19,2019. https://www.businessroundtable.org/business-roundtable-redefines-the-purpose-of-a-corporation-to-promote-an-economy-that-serves-all-americans

[56] "Can Artificial Intelligence Help Society as Much as it Helps Business," McKinsey Quarterly, August 6, 2019. https://www.mckinsey.com/business-functions/mckinsey-analytics/our-insights/can-artificial-intelligence-help-society-as-much-as-it-helps-business#

could grow almost three times as fast as non-ESG-mandated assets and comprise 50% of all professionally managed investments.[57]

> What has worked for others may not work for you. You must chart your own course.

We will now share more examples of companies that are doing things differently and those that have recrafted their mental, business and revenue models. As you examine how each is moving in a new direction or has moved out of its traditional approach, think how you can do the same with your company. Of course, what has worked for others may not necessarily work for you. You have to chart your own course. What is important is that you realize the need to change, embrace it and turn it into action.

Expanding Into Breakthrough Areas

Ford

Look at any legacy player that operates in the space that Uber has disrupted. And again, remember, we are talking not only about the taxi industry but the entire mobility space. So think of a company like Ford, for instance, that has traditionally been an automobile manufacturer. If Ford wants to survive and win in the new environment, it has no option but to move beyond its traditional thinking and traditional approach.

Ford understands this. A few years ago at a lecture at Wharton, chairman Bill Ford announced that Ford is changing its business from manufacturing cars to becoming a leader in mobility. The company now wants to make people's lives better through automotive and mobility leadership. To do this, it has to shift its business model

---

[57] "Advancing Environmental, Social, and Governance Investing: A Holistic Approach for Investment Management Firms," Deloitte Insights, 2020. https://www2.deloitte.com/content/dam/insights/us/articles/5073_Advancing-ESG-investing/DI_Advancing-ESG-investing_UK.pdf

from being an automaker to becoming a transportation facilitator through strategic reallocation. In line with this new thinking, Ford is forging new partnerships and acquisitions and entering new areas. For example, Ford is working with chipmaker and mobile technology firm Qualcomm on cellular vehicle-to-everything (C-V2X) technology that enables various technologies and applications in a city like vehicles, stoplights, signs, cyclists and pedestrian devices to speak to one another and share information. In January 2018, Ford acquired Autonomic, a transportation architecture and technology provider, as part of its initiative to develop an open, cloud-based platform for mobility services. The idea behind these initiatives—of sharing real-time mobility data among communities and between vehicles and city infrastructure—is to help optimize traffic flow, unclog streets and open up curb space.[58] Ford's acquisitions in 2019 include Journey Holding Corporation, a technology company specializing in software for intelligent transportation systems, and Quantum Signal, which works in the area of developing algorithms to help guide self-driving vehicles. Ford expects to have a fully autonomous vehicle in commercial operation by 2021.

> **Ford is changing its business from manufacturing cars to becoming a leader in mobility.**

In 2018, Marcy Klevorn, who was at that time executive vice president and president – mobility at Ford, (in April 2019 Klevorn moved as chief transformation officer at the company and then retired in October 2019) shared some interesting possibilities in her address titled *Taking Back the Streets: Using Systems Thinking to Return Our City Streets to the Community* at the Consumer Electronics Show (CES) in January 2018. For example, she pointed

---

[58] "Ford Realigns Mobility Group; Acquiring Autonomic, Transloc to Accelerate Growth," Ford, January 15,2018.
https://media.ford.com/content/fordmedia/fna/us/en/news/2018/01/25/ford-realigns-mobility-group.html

out that the solutions that Ford was working on would help to enable the city traffic system to inform a driver when a particular curbside parking space would be available and the driver could reserve it and also pay for it via a wireless transaction. Or, a vehicle in front of yours could send you an alert about a road hazard that's forcing it to make a sudden movement. This would allow you to adjust your vehicle's positioning accordingly. Or, in case of an accident, a stoplight could send alerts giving commuters time to reroute and emergency vehicles a clear path to the accident location.[59]Ford also plans to operate its own robotaxi network to transport people and goods by 2021. In 2017, the company announced an investment of $1 billion over five years in Argo AI, an AI startup, in order to compete with new-age firms such as Waymo and Uber as well as its traditional rivals such as General Motors and Toyota in developing self-driving vehicles. Ford plans to operate a network of custom-built vehicles itself, rather than sell its technology to a ride-hailing operator. It is also testing self-driving vehicles in partnerships with Walmart, Domino's and logistics company Postmates. In an interview with *Financial Times* in April 2018, James (Jim) Farley Jr., executive vice president and president— global markets at Ford, said: "One of the most important parts of the test is the business model itself." This would help assess how revenue could be split and at what price the service would be useful to consumers and customers such as logistics firms. Ford also plans to open its network to local businesses for transporting goods. This will mean that Ford will be competing against local

> **Ford plans to operate its own robo-taxi network to transport people and goods by 2021.**

59 "Ford at CES: Taking Back the Streets – Using Systems Thinking to Return our City Streets to the Community." Ford, January 9, 2018.
https://media.ford.com/content/fordmedia/fna/us/en/news/2018/01/09/taking-back-the-streets-using-systems-thinking.html

courier services. [60] According to Klevorn (as reported in her CES address mentioned earlier), Ford isn't interested in developing self-driving vehicles to "operate simply as isolated nodes in a massive transportation environment, because that likely won't deliver on the potential the technology can bring about. Inside an efficient, connected and optimized transportation system, this technology holds the promise for a whole new approach to moving goods, distributing content and serving humanity."[61]

Collaborating for Success

Toyota

Like Ford, Japan's largest automaker Toyota wants to transform itself from a car manufacturing company to one that is capable of providing all types of mobility-related services. One of its strategies toward attaining this goal is strategic collaborations. In October 2018, Toyota entered into a strategic collaboration with the country's multinational conglomerate SoftBank Group to set up a new joint venture company named Monet Technologies.

> Toyota wants change from a car manufacturer to a provider of all types of mobility-related services.

Monet (which in June 2019 got five additional Japanese investors—Isuzu Motors, Suzuki Motor Corp., Subaru, Daihatsu and Mazda) will combine the capabilities of Toyota's mobility services platform and its information infrastructure for connected vehicles with SoftBank's IoT platform and will launch mobility-as-a-service and autonomous-

---

[60] "Ford Plans Driverless Network 'at Scale' by 2021," Financial Times, April, 15, 2018.
https://www.ft.com/content/2ee71d1a-3f02-11e8-b7e0-52972418fec4

[61] "Ford at CES: Taking Back the Streets – Using Systems Thinking to Return our City Streets to the Community," Ford, January 9, 2018.
https://media.ford.com/content/fordmedia/fna/us/en/news/2018/01/09/taking-back-the-streets-using-systems-thinking.html

mobility-as-a-service business. These will include demand-focused just-in-time mobility services such as transportation, logistics, meal delivery vehicles where food is prepared while on the move, hospital shuttles where onboard medical examinations can be performed, mobile offices, and so on. Toyota plans to use its dealer network across the world to roll out the new mobility services. Here is a task for you: Try and imagine what new business and revenue models can be considered here.

> **Toyota plans to use its dealer network across the world to roll out the new mobility services.**

Akio Toyoda, president of Toyota, calls this collaboration with SoftBank the third of a three-pillar strategy to create "friends and allies." This is important, he says, in order to keep pace with the changes that are sweeping across the automotive industry because of innovative technologies, also known as the connected, autonomous, shared and electric (CASE) technologies. The first pillar is to strengthen ties with group companies such as Denso and Aisin. The second pillar is strengthening alliances with other automakers like Suzuki and Mazda. For instance, in September 2017, Mazda, Denso, and Toyota set up a company called EV C.A. Spirit to identify new development methods. The third pillar, as mentioned above, is strategic alliances with companies that are providing mobility services. Apart from this new partnership with SoftBank, Toyota has alliances with companies like Uber, Grab, Didi, and Getaround.[62]

In May 2019, Toyota AI Ventures, a Silicon Valley-based venture capital firm that was set up in 2017 as a subsidiary of the Toyota Research Institute, announced Fund II, a new $100 million fund for early-stage startups working on disruptive technologies and business

---

[62] "President Akio Toyoda Speech at Joint Press Conference by Toyota Motor Corporation and SoftBank Corp," Toyota, Oct. 04, 2018. https://global.toyota/en/newsroom/corporate/24775961.html

models in the autonomous mobility and robotics markets. Fund II brings Toyota AI Ventures total assets under management to more than $200M. As of February 2020, the firm has invested in more than 25 startups. In a company statement, Jim Adler, managing director of Toyota AI Ventures, said: "Auto manufacturers must participate in the startup ecosystem to stay ahead of the rapid shift in the auto industry. Investing in startups creates long-term relationships that help Toyota explore the latest innovations in mobility."[63]

Other Partnerships

Meanwhile, Japan's Honda Motor Co. and General Motors of the U.S. have come together to develop an autonomous vehicle that can be produced in high volumes and deployed globally in ride-sharing fleets. In October 2018, Honda announced an investment of $2.75 billion in Cruise, General Motors' self-driving cars unit. Other partnerships in the automotive industry include BMW with Fiat Chrysler, Intel and Mobileye (visual recognition software); and Daimler AG with Bosch to develop autonomous taxis. Clearly, the auto industry has realized that it needs to rewire its business model and become a software and services platform. Or else, it may end up as only a supplier of commodity hardware. A Volkswagen investor presentation noted in 2017 that the auto industry has seen disruption driven by product as well as business model innovation.

The auto industry has realized that it needs to rewire its business model.

Let's pause here for a moment. Those of you who are in the automotive industry, consider how the initiatives of these auto majors

---

[63] "Toyota AI Ventures Launches New $100M Fund: Firm Continues Commitment to Discover and Invest in Early-Stage Startups in Autonomous Mobility and Robotics," Toyota, May, 2, 2019. https://global.toyota/en/newsroom/corporate/27991449.html

could impact you. Those in other industries, think about what you can learn from the approaches used by these firms and how you can apply these lessons in your own industry.

Consider also how some other organizations are embracing tech-based collaborations to equip themselves for the new age. In July 2018, the **Hong Kong Monetary Authority**, the country's de-facto central bank, announced that it is setting up a Blockchain-backed trade finance platform. This platform is expected to link around 21 banks and will be owned by the partner banks. This collaborative model using Blockchain technology is expected to reduce the time and paperwork that is typically required for routine trade finance and supply chain finance transactions. In India, in August 2018, 19 life insurance companies announced that they were planning to come together and share the medical records of their customers with one another (with the consent of the customers) via Blockchain. This real-time availability of their medical records is expected to offer a superior customer experience. It will be easier and faster for customers to buy new policies from different insurers since sharing and processing information will be smoother. It is also expected to help companies weed out fraudulent claims.

In July 2018, the Belgium-headquartered cross-border payments organization **SWIFT**, along with 10 corporates and 12 banks, announced a first-of-its-kind cross-industry collaboration for a new multi-bank standard to provide a superior cross-border payments experience for multi-banked corporates. The design for the new standard has been developed through a series of SWIFT-led co-creation workshops with pilot banks and corporates. A SWIFT press statement says that the new standard enables corporate treasurers to initiate and track global payments innovation (gpi) payments to and from multiple banks in a single format and integrate gpi flows in their

> **Think about what you can learn and how you can apply these lessons in your own industry.**

ERP and treasury management systems. The press statement lists what corporations are looking for: a faster payments' experience, real-time tracking, certainty of credit to end-beneficiaries, transparency, and predictability of payment information such as transaction fees and foreign exchange rates. This new capability is expected to enable these for corporates in a consistent and scaled fashion across multiple banks.[64]

COVID-19 has opened up opportunities for players in sectors such as say health care, in pharmaceutical and medical R&D laboratories to shift their traditional competitive mental models to accommodate global collaboration with other laboratories and governments. Ask yourself: Are you leveraging the opportunity the pandemic has thrown up?

> **Walmart, which built its empire on brick-and-mortar stores, is gearing up for an Amazon-driven omnichannel world.**

Going Omnichannel

Walmart

Consider Walmart, the world's largest retailer. As of June 2018, Walmart's revenue at $500 billion was 10 times that of Amazon, the world's largest etailer ($52.9 billion). But, on September 4, 2018, when Amazon's market capitalization touched $ 1 trillion, Walmart's market capitalization was just $279 billion. Later in this chapter, we will see how unlike traditional firms, Amazon embraced a completely new mental and business model and for years didn't focus on profits, and also how it has been continuously reinventing itself. But first, let us look at how Walmart, which has built its business empire on physical brick-and-mortar stores, is gearing up for an Amazon-driven world that is not only fast going online, but where customers are

---

[64] "Corporates Pilot to Start Testing New Multi-Bank Payments Tracking on SWIFT gpi," Business Insider, July 26, 2018. https://markets.businessinsider.com/news/stocks/corporates-pilot-to-start-testing-new-multi-bank-payments-tracking-on-swift-gpi-1027400970#

increasingly looking for a seamless, anytime, anywhere, omnichannel retail experience.

One could argue that the intense digital experience during the pandemic lockdown has significantly impacted consumer habits and the weight of digital in an omnichannel experience is likely to be higher in the immediate future. While no doubt this is true, we believe that in the long-term the trend toward omnichannel will continue. The physical stores, though, will have to intensify their efforts at offering innovative, meaningful and relevant store experience to attract customers.

We believe that in the long term the trend toward omnichannel will continue.

Getting back to Walmart's online journey, like Ford, Walmart has taken the acquisition route. An interesting move is its acquisition of Flipkart, India's largest online retailer. In May 2018, in the *biggest acquisition globally* of any e-commerce company, Walmart paid $16 billion for a 77% stake in Flipkart. India is one of the fastest-growing e-commerce markets globally and Amazon is making a serious play for it. Ever since the company entered India in June 2013, Amazon has announced investments of more than $5 billion. According to news reports Amazon too was interested in acquiring Flipkart but Walmart beat it to the deal.

Walmart has also been steadily increasing its interest in China, another big e-commerce market. Walmart entered the Chinese e-commerce market in 2012 through a 51% stake in a Chinese e-commerce firm called Yihaodian. But this didn't work out as anticipated and in August 2016 Walmart sold its stake in Yihaodian to China's second-largest e-tailer, JD.com, in exchange for a 5.9% stake in the company. In October 2016, Walmart increased its stake in JD.com to 10.8% and then to 12.1% in February 2017. A few months later, in May 2017, Walmart opened a store on JD.com. This store has more than 1,700 of

Walmart's most-purchased items from its brick-and-mortar stores in China.

Walmart's investments in India and China not only give it access to the world's fastest-growing retail markets, but they also help it gain a multichannel footprint and a deeper understanding of how online retail works. Meanwhile, in the U.S. too, Walmart has been taking over digital native firms such as plus-sized fashion retailer Eloquii (October 2018), menswear etailer Bonobos (in June 2017), women's fashion etailer ModCloth (March 2017, Moosejaw (February 2017), footwear etailer Shoebuy (December 2016) and multi-category etailer Jet.com (August 2016).

> **Walmart's investments in India and China give it access to the world's fastest-growing retail markets.**

The acquisition of Jet.com for $3.3 billion, Walmart's first major acquisition in the online space, signaled the company's intention to gain scale with speed and adopt new models. Jet.com, founded in 2014, had a portfolio of 12 million SKUs and reached a run rate of $1 billion in gross merchandise value in its first year by introducing a radical price innovation. It rewarded customers in real-time with savings on items that were bought and shipped together. For the company, this reduced the supply chain and logistics costs. Soon after this acquisition, in September 2016, Marc Lore, the founder of Jet. com, was made the president and CEO of Walmart e-Commerce U.S. Speaking at The Wharton School in October 2018, Lore said that one key goal for Walmart is "cheap and same-day delivery." The future of retail, he said, would include offering a seamless omnichannel experience, convenience of ordering through voice and text, perfect recommendations and curations for individual customers, and virtual reality.

In 2017, in another move to strengthen its understanding of the future of retail and stay ahead in the game, Walmart launched an incubator called Store No 8. This incubates startups that are developing next-generation capabilities which Walmart believes have the potential to transform the future of retail. For instance, in February 2019, Walmart acquired Aspectiva, an Israeli-based startup, which specializes in machine learning techniques and natural language processing capabilities, and made it a part of Store No. 8. Aspectiva's capabilities are expected to help Walmart further enhance the end-to-end shopping experience. Walmart is gearing up for other ways to get closer to the customer. For instance, it is expected to introduce a membership service similar to Amazon Prime in 2020.

> **Walmart changed its mental and business model and, as a result, its offerings.**

In July 2019, *CNBC* reported that Walmart was making organizational changes to integrate its physical and online operations. For instance, its U.S. online and physical supply chain teams will now be under executive vice president Greg Smith, who will report to Greg Foran, who heads Walmart's U.S. stores, and Marc Lore, head of Walmart's U.S. e-commerce business. The article noted: "The organizational changes are a continuation of a strategy to bring together physical and digital operations, assets and leaders that the retailer has deployed for several years, largely since the acquisition of Jet.com in the fall of 2016."[65]

We believe that Walmart is a great example of a legacy firm that has changed its mental and business model and, as a result, its offerings. Walmart's actions show that its leadership understands that they cannot just continue doing what they have done. They recognize the need to transform from a physical retailer to an omnichannel company and are comfortable doing whatever it takes, including going on their own shopping spree, to make this happen.

---

[65] "Walmart Announces Executive Shuffle to Further Integrate Stores and Digital," CNBC, July 19, 2019. https://www.cnbc.com/2019/07/19/walmart-announces-executive-shuffle-to-further-integrate-stores-and-digital.html

Acquisitions are in fact a popular strategy with legacy firms as they strive to compete against disruptors. An article titled *The drumbeat of digital: How winning teams play* by Jacques Bughin, Tanguy Catlin, and Laura LaBerge in the June 2019 *Mckinsey Quarterly* has some interesting data on acquisitions and digital leaders. It says: "Our survey suggests that digital leaders spend three times more on M&A (27% of annual revenue, compared with 9% spent by others) and dedicate more than 1.5 times more of their M&A activity to the acquisition of digital capabilities and digital businesses (64%, compared with 39% for their peers). Taken together, those results suggest that the leaders are pursuing digital M&A about twice as hard, on average, as everyone else."[66]

We will look at some others that have adopted this route a little later in this chapter. Meanwhile, let's consider a few other interesting things that Walmart has been doing to stay ahead in the game.

In September 2017, the retailer started offering its products on the Google Express website and app in the U.S. Google Express was a delivery service that let customers in the U.S. order products from local retailers and have them delivered to their homes. Google Express orders could also be placed on the Google Home smart speaker through voice shopping. In 2019, Google Express was integrated with Google Shopping. In a post on the company website, Walmart's Lore indicated that voice shopping could help create lists of regularly purchased items and integrating Walmart's Easy Reorder feature into Google Express would enable the company to offer its customers

> Leaders are pursuing digital M&A about twice as hard, on average, as everyone else.

---

[66] "The Drumbeat of Digital: How Winning Teams Play," McKinsey Quarterly, June 27, 2019.
https://www.mckinsey.com/business-functions/mckinsey-digital/our-insights/the-drumbeat-of-digital-how-winning-teams-play

personalized shopping recommendations based on their previous purchases.

In September 2018, the company announced a new last-mile crowdsourced delivery platform named Spark Delivery. The pilot uses an in-house platform that enables drivers to sign up for a mutually convenient time based on the grocery delivery order, provides them with navigation assistance, and so on. In a company statement, Foran indicated that Walmart was leveraging new technology to offer a seamless shopping experience and also help save their customers' time.[67]

> Walmart introduced a service that delivers items to customers within two hours of placing an order.

Responding to consumer needs during the pandemic, Walmart introduced a new service called Express Delivery which delivers items to customers within two hours of their placing an order. Walmart started piloting this service in mid-April 2020 and expanded it to more than 2,000 stores in the following weeks. Customers could use Express Delivery to order from over 160,000 items from different categories such as daily essentials, groceries, food, electronics, etc. Walmart said it realized that the pandemic has changed the way customers live, behave and shop and it, therefore, accelerated the development and launch of this service.

In October 2018, Walmart made a big move in the over the top or OTT space. Vudu, Walmart's video-on-demand service, which it acquired in 2010, entered into a partnership with MGM. The studio will create exclusive content for Vudu. This content will be licensed to Vudu for streaming in North America and will be made available on Vudu's free service, Movies On Us. Walmart is also reportedly planning

---

[67] "Walmart Tests New Last – Mile Grocery Delivery Service", Walmart, September 5, 2018. https://corporate.walmart.com/newsroom/2018/09/05/walmart-tests-new-last-mile-grocery-delivery-service

to roll out a new video ad format for Movies On Us, which will allow viewers to make purchases from Walmart.com. The company also plans to leverage its vast customer data to build a strong advertising business. At Walmart's annual investor meeting in October 2018, CEO Doug McMillon is reported to have said: "We have a tiny ad business. It could be bigger." [68]

Harnessing the Power of Networks

Microsoft

Getting back to the strategy of acquisitions by legacy firms to keep pace with the changing environment, Microsoft offers an instructive example. Consider two of its big buys— LinkedIn and GitHub. Microsoft bought LinkedIn, the world's largest professional network, for $26.2 billion in June 2016. In an email to his employees, Microsoft CEO Satya Nadella noted that Office, which started off as a set of productivity tools, had transformed to a cloud service across any platform and device. The LinkedIn deal, he said, was the next step forward for Office 365 and Dynamics (Microsoft's line of business applications). According to Nadella, the LinkedIn acquisition is "key" to the company's "ambition to reinvent productivity and business processes."

> The LinkedIn acquisition is central to Microsoft's ambition to reinvent productivity and business processes.

Nadella explained that in order to be professionally successful, one needs a vibrant network that can bring together information about an individual from across various channels such as LinkedIn, Office 365 and Dynamics. This can enable new experiences that can

---

[68] "Amazon Has a Big Advertising Business. Walmart Wants One Too: So do Target, Kroger and Other Retailers, Which Have Customer Data That Big Brands Like Coke and Pepsi can use to Tailor ads to Shoppers," Bloomberg, February 11, 2019. https://www.bloomberg.com/news/articles/2019-02-11/amazon-has-a-big-advertising-business-walmart-wants-one-too

help the individual to work more effectively. "As these experiences get more intelligent and delightful, the LinkedIn and Office 365 engagement will grow. And in turn, new opportunities will be created for monetization through individual and organization subscriptions and targeted advertising."[69]

> **The GitHub acquisition marks a huge shift in Microsoft's traditional approach.**

Microsoft's acquisition of LinkedIn needs to be seen in the context of the opportunity that they have missed; it is probably one of the biggest missed opportunities in the world of business. They have more than a billion users of their products but they never tried to convert that into a network. There could have been a powerful network of all the Windows users around the world, more powerful than even Facebook. LinkedIn brings together more than 500 million people who are linked to the network. If they can actually combine the power of LinkedIn and Microsoft, it could be huge.

Microsoft's acquisition of GitHub, the leading software development platform, is equally transformational. GitHub provides an open platform for developers across industries and is the world's most popular destination for open source projects and software innovation. Microsoft bought GitHub in June 2018 for $7.5 billion. According to a Microsoft statement, "GitHub will retain its developer-first ethos and will operate independently to provide an open platform for all developers in all industries."[70]

The GitHub acquisition marks a huge shift in Microsoft's traditional approach. In the past, the company was regarded as

---

[69] "Satya Nadella Email to Employees on Acquisition of LinkedIn," Microsoft, June 13, 2016. https://news.microsoft.com/2016/06/13/satya-nadella-email-to-employees-on-acquisition-of-linkedin/

[70] "Microsoft to Acquire GitHub for $7.5 Billion," Microsoft, June 4, 2018. https://news.microsoft.com/2018/06/04/microsoft-to-acquire-github-for-7-5-billion/

the enemy of open-source software. Even two or three years ago it would have been unthinkable for Microsoft to have been the owner of GitHub, which is the gold standard for open source software development. Clearly, Microsoft realizes that in the new world, its old approach won't work and that it is imperative to attract more developers to the Microsoft studio. Remember, firms like Apple and Google have legions of third-party developers.

The pandemic too has made organizations realize the opportunities in creating an engaged network, say of researchers, customers, and followers. Consider 21 **Cactus Communications**, a Mumbai-based global scientific communications and technology company. In April 2020, it launched a platform called covid19.researcher.life that offers researchers access to the latest research and information on COVID-19 and also allows them to collaborate. Members can share potential hypotheses and challenges with researchers from other disciplines. This platform leverages CACTUS's AI and concept extraction capabilities, its editorial team and network of subject specialists.

Reinventing the Portfolio

IBM

With the cognitive and the cloud as its core, IBM wants to reinvent itself as "the incumbent disruptor." If one looks at IBM's history, we see that it shifted its mental and business model from a hardware manufacturer—sold off its personal computer business, which was once a jewel in its portfolio—to become a consulting and services firm. It is now betting big on the cloud and its artificial intelligence platform Watson. In this journey, acquisitions have played an important role. Since the turn of the century, the tech giant has purchased more than 150 companies. The big ones in 2018 and 2017 include the $34 billion acquisition of open-source software firm Red Hat, IBM's largest acquisition ever, Oniqua

> Since the turn of the century, IBM has bought more than 150 companies.

(maintenance repair and operations (MRO) inventory optimization solutions and services), Armanta (aggregation and analytics software for financial services firms), Vivant Digital (a boutique digital agency), XCC (digital workplace hub) and Agile 3 Solutions (cybersecurity). Interestingly, in 2015, IBM bought the Weather Company's digital assets including the Weather Channel mobile app, weather.com website and the company's data and forecasting technology. While the decision seemed odd at first glance, IBM had clearly thought it through. The Weather Company's high-volume data platform and IBM's cloud and the cognitive computing capabilities of Watson could prove to be a winning combination. After the acquisition, David Kenny, chairman and CEO of the Weather Company was in charge of IBM's Watson business till his departure from IBM in November 2018. In recent years, IBM has been buying a lot of companies in the analytics space. As the company moves forward in its journey of becoming an incumbent disruptor, we will possibly see more acquisitions in many different areas.

Apple

Look at how Apple, the tech giant, is reinventing itself. So far, the company's business and revenue model has been primarily around hardware like iPhones, iPads and MacBooks. It is now trying to generate not only new but recurrent revenue streams via new subscription offerings to counter the slowing demand for its devices by tapping into its 1.4 billion user base. In March 2019, instead of announcing any new, fancy gadgets, the company announced new services such as Apple TV+ (entertainment/video streaming), Apple News + (news), Apple Arcade (gaming) and Apple Card (credit card).

> Apple is trying to generate recurrent revenue streams via new subscription offerings.

Apple offers a good example of cannibalization. The conceptual framework comes from creative destruction—consciously destroying something to create something new. In a January 2013 earnings call, Apple CEO Tim Cook explained his company's philosophy regarding cannibalization. "I see cannibalization as a huge opportunity for us. One, our base philosophy is to never fear cannibalization. If we do, somebody else will just cannibalize it, and so we never fear it. We know that iPhone has cannibalized some iPod business. It doesn't worry us that it's done that. We know that iPad will cannibalize some Macs. That doesn't worry us." Another poster child for cannibalizing its business is Intel. Every new model that Intel introduces cannibalizes the previous one. Or take Netflix. It cannibalized its DVD business by aggressively promoting its streaming service *(See Exhibit 4)*.

EXHIBIT 4

Apple & Amazon: Betting on the Future

As a blueprint, the world's biggest and most ubiquitous tech companies such as Amazon and Apple are proving that the ability to take risks is the new standard – that daring diversifications are critical not only if one wants to thrive, but even to just survive. Both firms have an ever-changing ecosystem of products and services, each one a sizeable bet on the future.

Apple			Amazon			
Prime Sense	Beats	Shazam	Living Social	Alexa	Kiva Systems	Audible
Dialog	Texture	AuthenTec	Good Reads	Twitch	IMDb	Twillo
Intel*	Next	Anobit	Zappos	Songza	Whole Foods	Elemental

Source: Apple Inc., April 20,2020; Amazon Inc., January 11, 2019.
*In 2019 Apple agreed to buy Intel's smartphone modem business for $1 billion.

Mattel

At toymaker Mattel, a new approach is taking the form of a foray into films. In September 2018, the company launched a new division, Mattel Films, which will produce films based on its iconic brands like Barbie and Hot Wheels. The reason is easy to understand. Mattel, like other toymakers in the U.S., has been hit hard by factors such as the liquidation of retailer Toys R Us, which was its biggest customer, the increasing attraction of video games and electronic toys over traditional toys among children. A September 2018 *CNBC* report notes that Mattel's rival Hasbro has "excelled in taking its properties and translating them to successful television shows, movies and online videos. Theatrical releases of its "Transformers" films alone have grossed more than $4.37 billion at the international box office." *(See Exhibit 5).*

EXHIBIT 5

Mattel: Expanding the Brand Portfolio

Mattel diversified within its toy business across different segments such as infant, preschool, girls and boys before it diversified into the entertainment and games segments. It has focused on leveraging its brands and finding transformative opportunities in adjacent industries.

Dolls	Innovation & Tech	Games
Barbie	Barbie	Mattel Games
Creatable World	Hot Wheels	DOS
American Girl	Mattel Games	Whack a Mole
DC Comics	View-Master	Tumblin' Monkeys
Polly Pocket	My Password Journal	Bounce-Off
Monster High	Imaginext	Balderdash
EnchanTimals	Bloxels	Bezzerwizzer
Ever After High	Nabi Tablet	Blink
Wellie Wishers		Blokus
Little Mommy		Bold
		Card n Go Seek
Disney	**Entertainment**	Gas Out
Cars	Thomas & Friends	Ghost Fightin' Treasure Hunters
Mickey Mouse Club	Pooparoos	Kerplunk
Toy Story	Shimmer and Shine	Lowdown
	Octonauts	Mad Grab
Vehicles	Dora and Friends	Magic 8 Ball
Barbie	HIT Entertainments	Phase 10
Hot Wheels	Bob the Builder	Pictionary
Thomas & Friends	Fireman Sam	Rock 'Em Sock 'Em
DC Comics		Skip-Bo
Matchbox	**Action Figures**	Snappy Dressers
Cars	Jurrassic Park	SnapShouts
Power Wheels	DC Comics	Spider Pete's Treasure
Ghostbusters	WWE	Squawk
	Minecraft	Turnspell
Baby & Early Childhood	Marers of the Universe	Wizards Wanted
Fisher-Price	Ghostbusters	UNO
Little People	Max Steel	Apples to Apples
Bright Beats		
	Crafts	**Outdoor**
Construction	Barbie	Hot Wheels
Mega Bloks	Monster High	Mattel Games
	Rose Art	BOOM-Co

Source: Mattel website, June 2020. https://www.mattel.com/en-us/brands-page

In a company statement, Mattel's chairman and CEO Ynon Kreiz said: "Mattel is home to one of the world's greatest portfolios of beloved franchises, and the creation of Mattel Films will allow us to unlock significant value across our IP." Kreiz's

> **Mattel Films will allow the company to unlock significant value across its IP.**

move in taking Mattel into the film business is in line with his own experience and expertise. He was chairman and CEO of Maker Studios, a creator of online short-form video content, chairman and CEO of television production company Endemol, and the co-founder, chairman and CEO of Fox Kids Europe N.V. Whether or not Kreiz can translate his earlier experience to make a success of Mattel's film business remains to be seen, but what is interesting is that he has brought new thinking at the toymaker and is steering it in a new direction.

On January 8, 2019, Mattel Films announced its first movie deal – a partnership with Warner Bros Pictures to develop a Barbie feature film. A second partnership with Warner Bros Pictures for a Hot Wheels film soon followed. Other partnerships include those with production company Blumhouse Productions for a feature film based on the fortune-telling Magic 8 Ball; with MGM for American Girl (doll) and View Master (toy); and with Sony Pictures for Master of the Universe (toys).

Disney

Let's now turn to the Disney-Fox deal. In July 2018, the Walt Disney Company won a bidding war against Comcast and acquired the bulk of Rupert Murdoch's media and entertainment empire 21st Century Fox for $71.3 billion. In one stroke, it added to its library, blockbuster content from 20th Century Fox Film and 20th Century Fox Television, along with cable properties like FX, National Geographic, Fox Regional Sports Networks, Fox Networks Group

International, Star India and online streaming service Hulu. Commenting on the deal, Robert A. Iger, Disney's chairman and CEO, said that it would enable them "to create more appealing high-quality content, expand our direct-to-consumer offerings and international presence, and deliver more personalized and compelling entertainment experiences to meet growing consumer demand around the world." [71]

Even as it was working on concluding the deal with Fox, in April 2018 Disney launched its first streaming service ESPN+ (sports-related) for $4.99 a month. Its second streaming service Disney+ was launched in November 2019. This includes Disney, Pixar, Star Wars and Marvel movies plus exclusive films and TV shows. In preparation for all this, in August 2017 Disney had increased its stake in BAMTech, a leading player in direct-to-consumer streaming technology. With the media landscape being progressively shaped by direct relationships between users and content creators, BAMTech's technology is expected to give Disney the ability to build those relationships and also the flexibility to quickly adapt to other changes in the segment[72] *(See Exhibit 6).*

> **The deal with Fox enables Disney to offer more compelling and personalized entertainment.**

---

[71] "The Walt Disney Company Signs Amended Acquisition Agreement To Acquire Twenty-First Century Fox, Inc., For $71.3 Billion In Cash And Stock," The Walt Disney Company, June 20, 2018.
https://thewaltdisneycompany.com/the-walt-disney-company-signs-amended-acquisition-agreement-to-acquire-twenty-first-century-fox-inc-for-71-3-billion-in-cash-and-stock/

[72] "The Walt Disney Company To Acquire Majority Ownership Of BAMTech," The Walt Disney Company, August 8, 2017. https://thewaltdisneycompany.com/walt-disney-company-acquire-majority-ownership-bamtech-2/

EXHIBIT 6

Disney: Strategic Diversifications

Disney has diversified into a broad and deep business portfolio, expanding from its core animation business into theme parks, live entertainment, cruise lines, resorts, planned residential communities, TV broadcasting, and retailing, etc. Its four business segments are media networks; parks, experiences and products; studio entertainment; and direct-to-consumer and international. Disney achieved this by buying or developing the strategic assets it needed along the way.

Media Networks	Studio Entertainment	Parks, Experiences and Products
Disney-ABC Television Group	**Walt Disney Motion Pictures**	Disneyland & Walt Disney World
ABC	**Walt Disney Animation Studios**	Disney Cruise Line
ABC News	**Pixar Animation Studios**	Disney.com
ABC Owned Television Station	**Touchstone Pictures**	Disney Infinity
Equity Holdings	**Marvel Studios**	Maker Studio
ABC Family	**Luca Films**	
Disney Channel	**Disney Theater Group**	**Direct-to-Consumer and International**
	Disney Theater Production	
	Disney on Ice	Disney Licensing
ESPN		Disney Publishing Worldwide
ESPN Networks	**Disney Music Group**	
ESPN.com	Walt Disney Records	Disney Store
	Hollywood Records	
	Disney Music Publishing	

Source: Wired Magazine, November 11, 2015. https://www.wired.com/2015/11/how-disney-is-making-sure-youll-never-be-able-to-escape-star-wars/

It's easy to understand Disney's thinking and its associated moves. The media and entertainment industry is changing dynamically. Disruptors like Netflix, Amazon Video, Apple and others have given consumers a taste of anytime, anywhere and personalized viewing experience and consumers are increasingly cutting the cord and moving online. This in turn means that the traditional sources of revenues for legacy media companies like licensing, ratings-based advertisements and affiliate fees from cable and satellite companies are in danger. Disney has shown that it realizes that if it wants to remain relevant it has to change and that it is willing to take the plunge. In April 2020, with the corona pandemic disrupting release of films in movie theaters, Disney announced that it would debut its new live-action feature film *Artemis Fowl* exclusively on its streaming service Disney+. In the pre-coronavirus days, studios typically waited a few months after a movie released in a theater before making it available online. With consumers now wary of going to theaters, studios will have to embrace new ways of taking their fresh releases to the audience.

Meanwhile, in terms of acquisitions, other players in the sector have also been making their moves. A July 2018 article in *New York Times* notes: "A month before Disney closed on Fox, AT&T bought Time Warner, which includes HBO and the Warner Bros. film and TV studios. CBS and Viacom have tussled over whether they should combine. Comcast is likely to make a play for something else in addition to trying to win Sky in Europe. (Comcast acquired Sky in September 2018.) And other studios and networks like Discovery, Sony Entertainment, AMC and Lionsgate are looking for opportunities. Verizon, Dish and Charter could also scout out possible mergers."[73] Commenting on the AT&T—Time Warner deal, another *New York Times* article noted that AT&T could leverage Time Warner's business to build additional revenue lines such as new forms of video for mobile devices. [74]Remember, in 2015, ATT acquired DIRECTV and became the world's largest pay-TV provider and video distribution leader across television, mobile and broadband.

> **Mergers and acquisitions are not always from within the same industry.**

As you reflect upon these and other mergers and acquisitions, do note that they are not always from within the same industry. Just

---

[73] "Disney and Fox Shareholders Approve Deal, Ending Corporate Duel," The New York Times, July 27, 2018. https://www.nytimes.com/2018/07/27/business/media/disney-fox-merger-vote.html

[74] "AT&T Closes Acquisition of Time Warner," The New York Times, June 14, 2018. https://www.nytimes.com/2018/06/14/business/media/att-time-warner-injunction.htmls

as there is a blurring of the traditional boundaries when it comes to competition, there is also blurring of boundaries when it comes to acquisitions. So, if you are thinking of acquisitions or partnerships in order to offer a better customer experience and to shore up your competitiveness, you need to also think about companies from industries other than yours. This is true irrespective of how big or small you are. Also keep in mind that the opportunities in open innovation allow every company, whatever your size, to augment your capabilities significantly. We will be talking more about open innovation in Chapter 4.

On the Subscription Track

Look at how startups as well as established businesses are leveraging the subscription business model—one in which customers are charged a recurring fee—typically monthly or yearly—to access a product or service. This model enables businesses to offer features such as convenience, variety and personalization. In turn, they get advantages such as growing their customer base, strengthening their customer relationship, regular and predictable revenue, and so on.

Aiways

Shanghai-based automobile startup Aiways wants to make a breakthrough in Europe in 2020 with its all-electric sport-utility. This may be the first Chinese-brand electric car in a market that is dominated by combustion engine cars produced by Germans, French, Korean, Japanese and American manufacturers. In order to be competitive, Aiways plans to offer its vehicles only through leasing. This is because if Aiways were to take the traditional way of going via dealerships, it would increase its costs and make it difficult to compete with internal combustion engine vehicles.

> The subscription model enables businesses to offer features such as convenience, variety, and personalization.

A *Financial Times* article notes that according to Vehiculum, a German startup offering online leasing, with which Aiways is looking to partner, carmakers can save 15% to 20% of profit margins by moving the purchase online. Taking the subscription route offers Aiways another advantage. By eliminating big upfront costs for consumers, it reduces their apprehensions toward Aiways' Chinese background. Buyers also don't need to worry about the resale value of the Aiways car.[75]

Rent the Runway

> Consumers can choose from a huge, fancy selection of clothes that earlier were beyond their reach.

Rent the Runway, the New York City-based clothes rental company co-founded by Jennifer Hyman and Jennifer Fleiss in 2009, describes itself as a 'Closet in the Cloud'—a dream closet filled with an infinite selection of designer styles for work, for weekends, for special occasions like engagements and weddings, maternity wear and so on. The company has a subscription model and, as the name suggests, members can rent designer clothes and accessories. For consumers, this offers a tremendous opportunity to fulfill their aspirations; they can choose from a huge and fancy selection of clothes that earlier were beyond their reach. They can wear what they want and when they want without paying the huge amounts they would have to spend to *buy* the same pieces. With the flexibility that Rent the Runway provides, customers can also try out new trends easily. And all this by simply ordering online or walking into one of the company stores. After the due date, members need to return the items to the company in a pre-labeled and prepaid envelope.

---

[75] "Chinese Electric Car Start-Up to Debut in Europe, "Financial Times, May 27, 2019. https://www.ft.com/content/4ef14592-7d4d-11e9-81d2-f785092ab560

In 2018, Rent the Runway was named as the 9th most disruptive company by *CNBC*. [76]It was estimated to have more than 9 million members, revenues to the tune of $100 million and a valuation of $700 million. In 2019, it was named as the 5th most disruptive company by *CNBC*.[77] It is estimated to have more than 11 million members, and a valuation of $1 billion. In March 2019, Rent the Runway expanded into home goods. The company entered into a partnership with West Elm to make its home accessories available for rent. In Chapter 5 we will discuss why moving into adjacencies, like Rent the Runway has done with home accessories, is a smart move, but for now see how the company is cleverly increasing its customer share of wallet.

Gwynnie Bee & Caastle

Gwynnie Bee, a New York-headquartered subscription-based clothing service set up in 2011 which helps women to rent clothes from more than 150 brands, views its use of technology as a key differentiator. For instance, it uses data science to develop algorithms that help customers find the most appropriate styles and sizes based on their previous purchases. In 2018, Gwynnie Bee introduced a new line of business, a technology platform called CaaStle—meaning 'clothing-as-a-service'—which takes care of all aspects of a clothing subscription business be it the website, databases and logistics and so on.

> Gwynnie Bee's algorithms help customers find styles and sizes based on previous purchases.

Gwynnie Bee co-founder and CEO Christine Hunsicker says CaaStle was on the cards from the very beginning. In an interview with *TechCrunch*, Hunsicker said that before taking it to the retail

---

[76] "Meet the 2018 CNBC Disruptor 50 companies," CNBC, May 22, 2018. https://www.cnbc.com/2018/05/22/meet-the-2018-cnbc-disruptor-50-companies.html

[77] "2019 Disruptor 50 Full Coverage: 5. Rent the Runway," CNBC, May 15, 2019. https://www.cnbc.com/2019/05/14/rent-the-runway-2019-disruptor-50.html

world, they wanted to prove conclusively that this model with this platform and technology could work. So, they started with Gwynnie Bee as the first service.[78]

Legacy firms can leverage the clothing rental trend to defend their business against disruptors.

For traditional retailers, using a service like CaaStle helps to acquire new customers and grow the top line; gets existing customers to spend more money and increase their share of wallet along with getting a predictable and recurring revenue stream; optimize inventory monetization, and gets them higher margins. CaaStle's clients include Anne Taylor Express, New York & Company, Express, Vince, Rebecca and American Eagle and also Gwynnie Bee, which is now a subsidiary of CaaStle. In 2019, CaaStle made it to *Fast Company's* list of most innovative companies.

Urban Outfitters

Here's a move that shows that the clothing rental trend is not just for disruptors and that legacy firms can also leverage it to defend their business. In May 2019, the five-decade old apparel retailer Urban Outfitters launched its own clothing rental program called Nuuly. Under this, customers can borrow six clothing items a month from both Urban Outfitters' own portfolio as well as items from third-party labels like Reebok, Gal Meets Glam, and Fila, for a monthly fee of $88. Christine Hunsiker, founder of Gwynnie Bee and CaaStle, sees this as a validation of the subscription model in the fashion industry. In a conversation with *CNBC*, Hunsiker said that Urban Outfitters' move to build the logistics infrastructure "signals

---

[78] "Gywnnie Bee is Bringing Subscription Clothing Rental to Traditional Retailers With Launch of 'CaaStle,'" TechCrunch, March 22, 2018. https://techcrunch.com/2018/03/22/gwynnie-bee-is-bringing-subscription-clothing-rental-to-traditional-retailers-with-launch-of-caastle/

a strong belief that rental is here to stay" and that "it's strategic to their business."[79]

The subscription model for clothes has an added benefit during the crisis: the consumer does not have to worry about cleaning their clothes; they receive fresh clothes and return the used ones. Given that most cleaners have been closed during the pandemic, this is a major benefit that is likely to speed the adoption of the rental model for apparel, which will benefit companies like CaaStle.

Redefining Spaces

Changi Airport

Aviation is one of the worst-hit industries in the pandemic. Airlines, airports and related sectors such as tourism have been decimated by the COVID-19 crisis. As a case in point, consider Singapore's Changi Airport. Before the crisis, Skytrax consistently voted it the world's best airport for eight years from 2013 to 2020. Changi Airport steadily redefined the traditional notion

> **Changi Airport has almost become a destination in itself.**

of an airport – the idea that an airport is a place where passengers enter or exit from or to another city or country. Instead, Changi not only positioned itself as an entry point for all of Asia, it almost became a destination in itself.

Changi had restaurants, entertainment hubs, shopping hubs, relaxation hubs, spa services, and concierge services, among others. It had more than 400 retail stores and some 170 food and beverages outlets. There was a rooftop pool and a rooftop garden. There was

---

[79] "Urban Outfitters' new clothing rental program signals rental is here to stay: CaaStle CEO," CNBC, May 22, 2019.
https://www.cnbc.com/video/2019/05/22/urban-outfitters-new-clothing-rental-program-signals-rental-is-here-to-stay-caastle-ceo.html

a butterfly garden with some 1,000 tropical butterflies, a sunflower garden and an orchid garden. There was a curated collection of art installations. There was a movie theater and an entertainment deck. And yes, for the business traveler there was also a place to work. The company's website describes the "Changi Experience" as "personalized, stress-free and positively surprising." It goes on to say that providing this experience to meet the growing expectations of customers "involves rethinking, redesigning and realigning airport processes."

> **The Jewel is open to passengers at Changi as well as anyone in Singapore.**

To further enhance the Changi Experience and increase its appeal as a stopover destination among global travelers, in April 2019 Changi launched 'Jewel', a 10-storied mixed-use development with attractions such as the world's tallest indoor waterfall, a walking net suspended 25 meters above ground, a mirror maze set in a garden, walking trails and gardens, retail and dining outlets, hotels, aviation facilities such as passenger lounges and check-in counters and so on. The Jewel is seamlessly connected with Changi's Terminal 1, and through air-conditioned pedestrian linkways with Terminals 2 and 3. It is also connected to the rest of Singapore via the Mass Rapid Transit (MRT) station. The Jewel is open to passengers at Changi as well as anyone in Singapore. It attracts many non-travelers from Singapore for day-shopping and entertainment *(See Exhibit 7)*.

EXHIBIT 7

Changi Airport: Continuous Innovation

Butterfly Garden

Swimming Pool

Movie Theater

Koi Pond

Sunflower Garden

Playground

Waterfall

Are these what you would expect in an airport? Changi Airport in Singapore, which is rated the #1 airport in the world, is a great example of an organization that is constantly reimagining customer experience through continuous innovation. They invest significantly in experimenting, testing and curating new technologies to help introduce new experiences and improve existing facilities on an ongoing basis.

Source: Changi Airport, July 2020.

Changi has been working on ambitious plans to keep building on its strong track record. Terminal 5, scheduled to open around 2030, is expected to be Changi's largest terminal with a capacity to handle 50 million passengers a year; as of 2019, Changi has the capacity to handle 80 million passengers across its four terminals. Terminal 5 is expected to be almost completely automated. The Changi authorities had already started testing if an airport can function primarily with bots. In Terminal 4, which opened in October 2017, Changi was testing out automation extensively at various steps like when an aircraft is ready to land; positioning the aerobridge for passengers to disembark; unloading baggage and delivering it to the carousels; facial and fingerprint scans at immigration counters, and so on. Based on the results of this experiment, Changi was planning to implement it in its Terminal 5. Changi also has been deploying technologies like AI and data analytics to improve its operations. The idea behind this extensive use of technology and automation is to provide quick, efficient and seamless service to its increasing number of passengers and remain competitive vis-à-vis other airports.

And then, in early 2020, the pandemic struck, leading to unforeseen closures of international borders. This resulted in restricted movement of flights—and passenger traffic at Changi plummeted by a staggering 99% compared to pre-COVID levels. The International Air Transport Association (IATA) has estimated that airlines could lose more than US $80 billion in 2020. The Organization for Economic Co-operation and Development (OECD) reckons that international tourism could face a 60% to 80% decline in 2020.

To deal with this unprecedented crisis, the Changi leadership decided that its main strategy would involve being highly disciplined in cost management and proactively prepared for business once international travel is allowed to resume. Changi chose to defer most capital expenditure (capex) costs, putting on hold the construction of the proposed Terminal 5 by two years. To reduce operating costs, the airport's

> In response to the crisis, the Changi leadership's strategy was to be highly disciplined in managing costs.

leadership also closed two terminals (Terminal 2, which will go through an expansion and revamp in the interim, and Terminal 4), and decided to operate Terminals 1 and 3 at reduced capacity.

One of the most crucial decisions the Changi leadership made was to remain steadfast in taking care of people, "since they are the pillars to help us tide through the crisis and emerge stronger. We do not believe in simply retrenching staff as an answer to an economic crisis. We avoid retrenchment by cutting costs to save jobs. Employees' salaries have been cut, with senior management taking reductions of up to 30%," according to Liew Mun Leong, chairman of Changi Airport. "At the same time, we are collaborating closely with the Singapore government on various 'green lane' schemes to open up our borders progressively and safely. We are working hard to put in place the necessary infrastructure provisions and operational procedures to facilitate the restoration of traffic in the new normal."

While no one can predict when aviation can resume significantly, Changi Airport has been making efforts to prepare to serve passengers safely once borders are open again. This is based on the view that connectivity is crucial to the survival of Singapore's economy.

> **A crucial decision the Changi leadership made was to remain steadfast in taking care of people.**

Starbucks

Starbucks offers another creative example of adopting a new approach toward space. For Starbucks, its coffee shops are not just a place to grab a quick cup of coffee. They are "a neighborhood gathering place", a "place for conversation and a sense of community," a "third place between work and home." By positioning itself as the most important place after home and work, with its easy and comfortable environment and promise of a new lifestyle, Starbucks redefined the typical and traditional coffee shop. It transformed the simple act of consuming coffee into an experience. It redefined customer expectations and the customer experience. And this in turn allowed it to recast the price for a cup of coffee.

> Starbucks redefined the traditional coffee shop. It transformed the simple act of consuming coffee into an experience.

Starbucks has also invested significantly in digital technologies. It developed an app and expanded it into a popular mobile payment system. This helps it to gain data and insights into customer behavior and allows it to personalize its offerings, up-sell, drive customer loyalty, etc. Take its order-ahead feature. Once you enable the location service, you can order on the app, pay on the app, and then simply walk into a Starbucks outlet (based on the location, of course), and without waiting in line, ask a barista for your freshly made order at the pickup area. Starbucks also has a significant presence on social media platforms. It uses data analytics to zero in on new store locations. The list could go on.

Starbucks opened its first store in 1971 in Seattle, United States. As of December 2019, it had some 31,800 stores across the world. This is almost double the number from a decade ago. In terms of revenues, the company has grown from $10.7 billion in 2010 to $26.51 billion in 2019.

Breakthrough Advertising

Citibank

One of the most breakthrough approaches in advertising in recent years has come from Citibank. Think about their title sponsorship of New York City's bike-share system that was launched in 2013 with a fleet of 6,000 bikes. The service is operated by Motivate, the largest bike-share operator in the U.S. and is branded as Citi Bike! (Motivate was acquired by the cab-hailing firm Lyft in July 2018.) At present there are over 12,000 of these bikes— branded as Citi Bikes—in New York and as per Motivate's website, Citi Bike riders have completed more than 60 million rides since it was launched. They are an integral part of the city's transportation system.

What does this mean for Citibank? Well, these bikes are everywhere in the city. They are visible to everyone. They provide a valuable service. They reduce road congestion and the carbon footprint. And, of course, they have Citi's name and logo on them! In

> **Citi Bike riders have completed more than 60 million rides since the service was launched.**

the 2017 book *The End of Advertising: Why It Had to Die, and the Creative Resurrection to Come* by Andrew Essex, talking about Citibank's decision to sponsor New York City's bike-share system Edward Skyler, Citibank's EVP of global public affairs, said: "There is a lot of slapping one's logo on things. People don't necessarily associate you with the product. Here, we were the product."[80] Essex, co-founder of creative marketing services firm Plan A and former vice-chair and founding CEO of creative agency Droga5 and of media firm Tribeca Enterprises, writes in his book: "As a former advertising executive—one who had no role in the program—I now believe that Citi Bike has gone on to become perhaps the greatest advertising campaign of all time. Rather than squandering that eight-figure investment on increasingly ineffective traditional marketing, Citi built something additive that also reduces our carbon footprint. When a corporate behemoth expands its communication strategy from traditional ads (which in all fairness, Citibank sadly still makes) to providing bikes for six thousand New Yorkers to pedal across the Brooklyn Bridge, the time-space continuum has truly changed."[81] *(See Exhibit 8).*

---

[80] Andrew Essex, "The End of Advertising: Why It Had to Die, and the Creative Resurrection to Come," Random House Publishing Group, 2017.

[81] "How Citi Bike Started A Transportation—And Advertising – Revolution," Fast Company, June 13, 2017. https://www.fastcompany.com/40428988/how-citi-bike-started-a-transportation-and-advertising-revolution

EXHIBIT 8

Citibank: Gaining Mileage

Citi Bike is a great example of a successful campaign that delivered utility value to customers while significantly enhancing the brand. What was once a wacky advertising innovation had become a critical part of the city's infrastructure.

Source: Citi Bike Monthly Operating Reports. https://www.citibikenyc.com/system-data/operating-reports. https://www.citibikenyc.com; https://www.motivateco.com/where-we-do-it/new-york-ny publicdomainpictures.net, June 2020.

Adopting Frugal Innovation

Narayana Health

Narayana Health, a multi-specialty hospital chain in India, is a compelling example of an innovative model of health care. It has grown from a single cardiac facility with some 200 beds in Bangalore in 2001 to more than 6,000 beds across a network of 23 hospitals, seven heart centers, 19 primary care facilities across India and an international hospital in the Cayman Islands. For its founder, chairman and executive director Dr. Devi Prasad Shetty (who is a cardiac surgeon), the goal is to provide high quality and affordable health care to everyone. In their 2018 book *Reverse Innovation in Health Care*, authors Vijay Govindarajan and Ravi Ramamurti note that at Narayana hospitals, an open heart surgery costs around $2100 as against around $100,000 to $150,000 in the U.S. Metrics such as a hospital-acquired infection rate at 2.8 per 1,000 ICU days are comparable to the best hospitals in the world. Importantly, Narayana Health is a profitable venture.

In the same book, Dr. Ashustosh Raghuvanshi, who was at that time the vice-chairman, managing director and group CEO of Narayana Health, tells the authors: "Early on, we realized that the health care problem in our country was not a science problem. It was an economic problem ....Every single thing we did started from the assumption that *there is no money*. Then we started planning how to deliver what we needed to deliver." For instance, one of the first things that Shetty did when he set up the first Narayana hospital was to introduce a new compensation model for his doctors. Instead of getting paid per surgery, as is the standard practice, surgeons at Narayana hospitals take a fixed salary. Shetty doesn't pay them less than what they would get in any other hospital in India, but at Narayana they

Narayana Health's goal is to provide high quality and affordable health care to everyone.

typically perform more surgeries per day as compared to surgeons elsewhere. Since the surgeon's fee constitutes a significant portion of the cost of an operation, this model automatically reduces the cost per surgery. Shetty also has a hybrid pricing policy. While the medical facilities are the same for all patients, there is a choice of general ward, semi-private and private rooms for personal amenities. This allows him to offer concessional rates to those who can't afford the regular charges. A 2010 *Knowledge@Wharton* article on Narayana Health (at that time it was called Narayana Hrudalayala) notes that the Shetty's team "follows the unique accounting practice of studying the profit and loss account on a daily basis." The article quotes the hospital's then-chief financial officer Sreenath Reddy as saying: "By monitoring the average realization per surgery and our profitability on a daily basis, we are able to assess how much concession we can afford to give the following day without adversely impacting our profitability."[82]

Other measures at Narayana Health to rein in costs include process innovation, leveraging economies of scale, and a deep culture of frugality. For instance, instead of branded medicines, Narayana Health typically uses generic medicines. Wherever it is permitted, it re-uses surgical supplies. Instead of buying expensive equipment like MRI machines and PET-CT scanners, it typically has pay-per-use contracts with the manufacturers. The frugal culture extends to surgical procedures also. In the coronary artery bypass graft operations at Narayana the heart is usually operated on "live" without using the heart-lung bypass machine. Govindarajan and Ramamurti note: "The technique saves the hospital the cost of expensive heart-lung machines, which are standard in the U.S. heart surgeries. It also leads to fewer complications, requires shorter hospital stays, and results in a lower incidence of hospital infection. The beating heart procedure requires great surgical skill and a sizable investment in staff training, but high patient volumes and quality drivers at Narayana Health have helped an entire generation of Indian surgeons master the technique." The authors go on to add that this is proof that "quality and cost can operate in ways quite different from what is expected in Western health care models, which are often based on the assumption that high quality has to engender high costs."

> **Western health care models often assume that high quality must engender high costs.**

Narayana Health is not some low-tech medical organization. Using the latest technology is high on Shetty's priorities. For instance, Narayana Health has a cloud-based ERP system from Oracle,

---

[82] "Narayana Hrudayalaya: A Model for Accessible, Affordable Health Care?," Knowledge@Wharton, July 1, 2010. https://knowledge.wharton.upenn.edu/article/narayana-hrudayalaya-a-model-for-accessible-affordable-health-care/

cloud-based mobile health units designed by Hewlett Packard, portable ECG machines from Schiller, and its patient data systems are delivered on Apple's iPads. The hospital's ERP system connects all the Narayana Health hospitals and allows them to seamlessly share information. Shetty is also a huge believer in telemedicine. In Govindarajan and Ramamurti's book, he says: "We have been doing these things (telemedicine) for 15 years. Eventually it will become the mainstream of medicine. We are making the building blocks for that transition, which will happen first in India. Then it will move to the Western hemisphere."[83] According to a 2017 case study by The Commonwealth Fund, a New York-based private foundation that supports independent research on health care issues, Narayana Health has one of the world's largest telemedicine networks, connecting 800 centers globally.[84]

During the COVID pandemic, patients could consult with the hospital's specialists by video, which enabled the patients to continue their health consultations with their doctors during the lockdown. Narayana Health also launched a chat line on WhatsApp and SMS for addressing any COVID-related queries or concerns.

Embracing New Technologies

Charles Schwab

In Chapter 5 we will see how the San Francisco-based financial services firm Charles Schwab adopted the iterative,

> Charles Schwab adopted the iterative ready-fire-aim approach for its robo-advisory services.

---

[83] Vijay Govindarajan, Ravi Ramamurti, Reverse Innovation in Health Care: How to Make Value – Based Delivery Work, Harvard Business Press, 2018. https://books.google.co.in/books/about/Reverse_Innovation_in_Health_Care.html?id=SjEtDwAAQBAJ&source=kp_book_description&redir_esc=y

[84] "Expanding Access to Low-Cost, High-Quality Tertiary Care," The Commonwealth Fund, November 9, 2017. https://www.commonwealthfund.org/publications/case-study/2017/nov/expanding-access-low-cost-high-quality-tertiary-care

ready-fire-aim approach for its robo-advisory services. Here, let's look at how it has been changing its business model – first as a disruptor and now as a defender. Schwab started in 1971 with the traditional brokerage model of a combined package of trading activity and advisory services. But it soon introduced a completely new model. Schwab unbundled trading activity from the advisory activity and pioneered the discount brokerage industry. Riding on this new no-frills, low-cost trading services model, the firm disrupted the then brokerage industry and went on to become the largest brokerage in the country. A few years ago the erstwhile disruptor found that it was facing competition from new disruptors like Betterment and Wealthfront, which offer robo-advisory services. Of course, it also faces competition from other legacy firms like Vanguard and Fidelity which have a low-cost approach.

Instead of sitting on the sidelines, in March 2015 Schwab jumped in the game with Intelligent Portfolios, its own robo-advisory service. And, here is the twist—it went a step further than the startups that were threatening its business; while most other robo-advisory firms charge their customers low fees (thanks to the use of technology), Schwab offers this service to its customers for free. Of course, it does make money in other ways—for instance, its Intelligent Portfolios include some amount of cash that is managed by the Schwab Bank; this

> **Schwab unbundled trading activity from advisory activity and pioneered the discount brokerage industry.**

has prompted competitors like Betterment to say that this is not a transparent approach. But the important thing to note here is that the one-time disruptor that rose to become a leading player in its space, is not only defending itself against the new disruptors, it is also preparing to take the lead again with innovative thinking.

Schwab has been challenging traditional thinking in other ways. For instance, it is moving its core to the center, introducing an intelligent layer and doing the front-to-back transformation. We will discuss this in more detail in Chapter 2.

Investing in Success

Softbank

Japan's SoftBank Group started as a distributor of packaged software in 1981 and over the years has transformed itself into a technology conglomerate and one of the biggest players in the tech field

Softbank introduced a new mental model with its Vision Funds, making it a disruptor.

globally. In the mid-90s and early 2000s, SoftBank came into the limelight for its investment in Yahoo and Alibaba. In 2016, it created waves by setting up the $100 billion Vision Fund, the world's largest technology investment fund. With high-profile backers like Apple, Qualcomm, UAE-based Mubadala Investment Company, Saudi Arabia's PID public fund, Foxconn, and Foxconn-owned Sharp, the Vision Fund has come to be known for its aggressive investments in a number of companies across various sectors like e-commerce, fintech, health tech, real estate, transportation and consumer goods. Vision Fund has invested in companies such as Uber (ride-hailing), Flipkart (e-commerce), Paytm (online payments), and WeWork (co-working space).

In August 2019, SoftBank announced a $108 billion Vision Fund 2—with participants like Apple and Microsoft. This fund focuses specifically on artificial intelligence companies. An August 2019 report from Reuters reported SoftBank Group's founder and CEO Masayoshi Son saying: "Many Japanese companies are sailing using an old map. Using our new map we are looking for a new continent."[85] While SoftBank ran into its own set of problems even before the

---

[85] "Softbank Says Vision Fund 2 Could Start Investing Soon, Bags Big Gains on First," Reuters, August 7, 2019. https://www.reuters.com/article/us-softbank-group-results/softbank-says-vision-fund-2-could-start-investing-soon-bags-big-gains-on-first-idUSKCN1UX0JE

pandemic with the value of some of its tech bets seeing huge erosion, it did introduce a new mental model with its Vision Funds and we think this makes it a disruptor in its own right.

Breaking the Mold

YourStory

In India, when Shradha Sharma, a young print and television journalist, decided to set up her own online media venture to give young entrepreneurs a voice and a platform to showcase their journeys, she was met with skepticism. The constant refrain Sharma encountered from industry veterans, colleagues, investors and others was: "Who will want to read the stories of upcoming entrepreneurs? People only want to read about successful businessmen."

That was in 2008. Today, Sharma's YourStory is considered a disruptor in the media space and is one of the leading digital media platforms in the country. As of April 2020, YourStory has an annual reach of some 100 million users. It has published more than 100,000 stories of entrepreneurs and change-makers and has helped more than 50,000 entrepreneurs access networking and funding opportunities.

> YourStory is eating into the ad revenues of traditional media, forcing them to reexamine themselves.

Its business partners include big names such as IBM, Microsoft, Google, and also the Indian government. The company raised its first round of funding in 2015 and since then has raised $8.5 million from investors such as Kalaari Capital Advisors, 3One4 Capital Partners, and Qualcomm Ventures.

With YourStory becoming a leading go-to-place for all news and information related to startups, it is eating into the eyeballs and the ad revenues of traditional media in the country and is forcing them to reexamine themselves. For instance, traditional media now gives a lot of coverage to young entrepreneurs and their stories, something that they were not interested in earlier.

So what made Sharma take the plunge when everyone around her was dissuading her? Well, she was quick to read the signals of change and was open to making a bet on them. Sharma saw that young people in the country were getting on to the Internet and realized

> Sharma had no business model or revenue model in mind when she started YourStory.

that digital media sites were going to be big. She saw that there are an increasing number of entrepreneurs and each one has fascinating stories that they want to share. Sharma also sensed that Indians are hugely aspirational and many wanna-be-entrepreneurs would want to read what others are doing and pick up lessons from their journeys. But traditional media were not interested in giving them any space.

Sharma says she had no business model or revenue model in mind when she started YourStory, but she was clear that "it would make money." She had a gut feeling that the combination of leveraging the digital platform to tell the stories of entrepreneurs had great business potential. Having worked with leading print and television brands, she also knew that a media business could not be built overnight, that it needed a strong brand, trust and credibility, an extensive reach, and a "cool" quotient. And she was ready for the long haul. The first break came toward the end of 2009 when YourStory reached out to entrepreneurs and got them to enroll in a Sun Microsystems startup program.

Today, YourStory has four main revenue streams. One, it creates branded content and targeted communication for large companies and other organizations that want to reach out to startups. Two, it develops research reports on emerging fields. For instance, what startups are doing in the fields like AI, or the potential in the electric vehicle space. Three, it holds events around the startup community.

In 2019, the company forayed into the booming education industry with the launch of its online learning arm, YourStory Academy. This marked its expansion into a fourth, subscription-based, revenue model. The company turned profitable in terms of earnings before interest, tax, depreciation and amortization (EBITDA) as of April 2020.

> **During the coronavirus crisis, YourStory set up a "COVID-19 Helpdesk" on its website.**

Having gained a strong foothold with startups, Sharma is now looking to the next community that is largely ignored by traditional media – that of the small and medium businesses. She is also looking at developing strong user-generated content. We will discuss the importance of co-creating with users in Chapter 2. In addition, Sharma is looking to launch international media players in the country. "I see our businesses as content, data and community. We create content. That gives us access to a lot of data and insights. And based on content, data and insights, we create very engaged communities," says Sharma.

During the coronavirus crisis, YourStory set up a "COVID-19 Helpdesk" on its website to equip its community of startups, small and medium businesses, and ecosystem stakeholders with relevant information, resources, and support to help them not only steer their businesses through the challenging times but also prepare for life after the pandemic. The helpdesk includes articles, conversations and interactive webinars with experts on various topics like tips for startups, working effectively from home, managing salary cuts, maintaining one's mental health, and so on.

The biggest challenge for Sharma at YourStory is to ensure that the data is fresh, contextual, and real-time. "My worry is not that someone else will build another YourStory. I know that my competition can come from anywhere. My worry is how do I continue the relationship, the trust and credibility that I have built with my users. How do I get more of their time and how do I take it forward?"

New-Age Disruptors Must Continue to Innovate

So here is another important point to keep in mind: It is not just legacy firms that need to reshape their approach. Even firms that have disrupted their industries need to be on their toes and reinvent themselves for continued success.

Amazon

Look at Amazon, for instance. We spoke briefly about how it adopted a completely new mental model and business model in terms of profits. Let's examine this a little more. For years the company did not care about profits. It kept losing money. With its eye on becoming the everything store for everyone, Amazon's focus has been on continuously reinvesting in the company and increasing its customer base—even if it meant offering cut-throat pricing. But the model worked. For the quarter ended June 2018, Amazon posted record profits of $2.53 billion. And on September 4, 2018, it became the second publicly listed U.S. company to touch a market capitalization of $1 trillion. It was also the fastest to do so. It took Amazon 21 years to reach this milestone. (Apple, which reached a $1 trillion market cap on August 2, 2018, took almost 38 years.)

In fact, like Amazon, most new economy firms do not focus on the profit numbers but rather on maximizing market cap if they are publicly traded or their valuation if they are privately funded. Becoming a unicorn—being valued at more than $ 1 billion—is pretty much the first mega milestone for startups. This again is a completely new mental model which in turn allows them to have disruptive business models without having to worry about making money.

> **Even firms that have disrupted their industries must reinvent themselves for continued success.**

> Amazon began as an online bookstore and went on to redefine the retail industry.

Coming back to Amazon, it began as an online book store, transformed the way people bought and read books and redefined the retailing industry. And from there, it now wants to be everything for everyone. Over the years, it has added category after category—appliances, electronics, home products, toys, beauty, health, and sports among others. It is now going after groceries, one of the biggest categories in retail, in a big way. And it's doing this not just online but is also building a brick-and-mortar presence; in 2017, Amazon bought Texas-based grocery chain Whole Foods for $13.7 billion. What's more, it is now looking to transform the entire physical buying experience.

In January 2018, it launched Amazon Go, a first-of-its-kind cashier-less store. Customers simply have to download the Amazon Go app on their smartphones and hold it over a scanner when they enter the Amazon Go store. After this, they can pick up whatever they want from the store and simply walk out. That's right, they don't need to wait in lines or scan the products or make any payments. They can just walk out with their purchases. The payments are done via their Amazon accounts. As of February 2020, Amazon had 25 Amazon Go stores in Seattle, Chicago, San Francisco and New York. According to news reports, the company is planning to open 3,000 cashier-less stores in the next few years. It's not hard to imagine what this is likely to do to other convenience stores in the neighborhood. After all, given a choice, who wouldn't prefer the speed and convenience offered by this model? Stores that don't upgrade to this new technology will find themselves redundant. Importantly, it won't be just convenience stores that will be affected. Once consumers get used to this cashier-less experience at Amazon Go, they will expect it wherever they shop. Other retailers like 7-Eleven, Sam's Club and Giant Eagle are taking notice and exploring how to introduce cashier-less checkouts in their stores.

What about you? If you are a retailer, is this something that you are working on?

In March 2020, Amazon started selling its cashier-less technology called Just Walk Out to other retailers. Shoppers in non-Amazon stores don't need to have an Amazon account or download an Amazon app. They only need a credit card. Once they walk out from a Just Walk Out enabled store, their billing amount is charged to their credit cards. Amazon provides all the necessary technologies to enable this. The Just Walk Out platform runs on Amazon's cloud computing platform.

Amazon has been busy on many other fronts. It has invested heavily in its Prime subscription model. It offers video and music streaming services. It has developed Alexa, a voice-activated virtual assistant and introduced a range of Alexa-enabled devices and appliances like the Echo smart speakers, microwaves and wall clocks. It has an accelerator program through which it is looking to increase the bouquet of brands that can be sold exclusively on its website. It has a huge cloud computing business. It is getting into financial services. It is planning to enter health care.[86] It is growing into an advertising powerhouse. As one can see, the list is evolving. Amazon's wide array of products and services allows it to embed itself deeper and deeper into its customers' lives, get a stronger understanding of the customers, enhances their stickiness, enables it to cross-sell to them and get a bigger share of their wallet.

> **Amazon's array of products and services lets it embed itself deep into its customers' lives.**

Alipay

In China, Alipay has grown from a small third-party online payment platform to become the world's largest mobile and online payment

---

[86] "As Amazon Moves Into Health Care, Here's What We Know—And What We Suspect—About Its Plans," CNBC, March 27, 2018. https://www.cnbc.com/2018/03/27/amazons-moves-into-health-what-we-know.html

platform. It has also given rise to Ant Financial, the world's largest fintech firm (and now the parent company of Alipay). Along with Alipay, Ant Financial includes Yu'e Bao, the world's largest money market fund, Zhima Credit (also known as Sesame Credit), a private credit platform, and Mybank, an online lending firm—all of which are tightly integrated.

Alipay was set up in 2004 by China's e-commerce giant Alibaba to facilitate payments for its online marketplace Taobao. The rationale behind Alipay was simple: to build trust between the seller and the buyer. The way Alipay worked was that it would hold the buyer's money and would release it to the seller only when the buyer confirmed that they had received the product and was satisfied with it.

Alipay has grown to become the world's largest mobile and online payment platform.

The model quickly gained traction with users for its convenience and reliability. Alipay then went a step further: it used the money that its shoppers' deposited to start a money market fund. This meant that Alipay users earned interest on their money kept in Alipay, and Alipay in turn earned their goodwill and stickiness. In 2008, Alibaba set up Taobao Mall (now known as Tmall), a dedicated platform for third-party brands and retailers and Alipay could be used here also. It is also integrated with Taobao's food delivery service. (In mid-2020, Alibaba added a new payment option for the U.S.-based merchants on its B2B site Alibaba.com. Called Payment Terms, the new feature offers U.S. businesses, which meet the required criteria, higher flexibility by allowing them to place an order with any participating supplier on Alibaba.com and pay for it within 60 days.)

Over the years, Alipay grew to become widely used outside the Alibaba ecosystem. It evolved from being a digital wallet to a destination in itself and is closely integrated with its users' everyday needs. Whether it is booking a hotel, paying utility bills, hailing a taxi, buying movie tickets or air tickets, making appointments with doctors, or even buying wealth management products – all of this could be done directly through the app. Alipay is also a payment option in millions of physical stores both inside and outside China. As of 2019, it has some 520 million active users, partners with more than 200 domestic financial institutions and 250 overseas financial institutions and payment solution providers.

Facebook

Now consider Facebook. In CALL TO ACTION we spoke about how Facebook successfully transformed itself into a mobile-first company and how it has been acquiring other firms so that it can stay on top of new technologies and provide its users with new ways to connect. Is it now time for it to revamp its model? In an August 2018 *Knowledge@ Wharton* article titled *What's Behind Facebook's Slump?* James D. Cox, professor of law at Duke University said that the company's model is basically "to induce people to find a lot of psychological rewards by being on their Facebook account [often]." It then monetizes the information that those users generate by selling it to others. But privacy concerns are impacting user engagement and this in turn impacts Facebook's business and revenue model. Cox noted: "At some point, these concerns—not just in Europe and America—are going to have to lead to big changes in Facebook."[87]

> **Privacy concerns are impacting user engagement and this, in turn, impacts Facebook's business and revenue model.**

In an April 2018 *Knowledge@Wharton* opinion piece titled Should Facebook go Freemium, Ravi Bapna, professor of business analytics and information systems at the Carlson School of Management, University of Minnesota, suggested that the social media giant could solve some of its problems by introducing a two-tiered pricing model where the base service is free for consumers but they pay for an

---

[87] "What's Behind Facebook's Slump," Knowledge@Wharton, August 2, 2018. https://knowledge.wharton.upenn.edu/article/facebooks-earnings-woes/

enhanced service. According to Bapna: "Facebook needs a baseline, general data protection regulation (GDPR) level, privacy-first free version, coupled with a premium version targeted at people who have a desire for even high levels of privacy, and for other to-be-imagined features." Bapna suggests that by creating features that make it easy for people to control how the content they create is used and shared "Facebook can possibly start the long journey to win back the trust of people."[88]

But Facebook founder Mark Zuckerberg has earlier maintained that he would not opt for a paid model. Even in his Congressional testimony in April 2018 in connection with the Cambridge Analytica case, Zuckerberg said that the only way that Facebook can meet its mission of connecting every person across the globe is through an ad-supported free service. (Facebook came under fire when a whistleblower in 2018 revealed that Cambridge Analytica, a data analytics firm, had unauthorized access to more than 50 million Facebook profiles. It is alleged that this information was misused in the 2016 U.S. presidential elections to micro-target voters to benefit Donald Trump.) It will be interesting to see if Zuckerberg will be willing to change his stance with changing circumstances. There are other trends too for which Zuckerberg needs to watch out. For instance, the popular mobile messaging app WhatsApp (founded in 2009 by Jan Koum and Brian Acton) that was acquired by Facebook in 2014 for $22 billion and as of 2019 has more than one billion users, is fast facing competition from other messaging apps like Telegram (founded in 2013 by Russian brothers Nikolai and Pavel Durov) which is disrupting the messaging space with newer features. And Facebook users, especially young ones, are

> **WhatsApp, acquired by Facebook in 2014 for $22 billion, faces competition from other messaging apps.**

---

[88] "Should Facebook Go Freemium," Knowledge@Wharton, April 12, 2018. https://knowledge.wharton.upenn.edu/article/facebook-go-freemium/

reported to be moving to other social media platforms. According to the Infinite Dial 2019 study by market research firm Edison Research and Triton Digital, there were some 15 million fewer Facebook users in the 12 to 34 years age group in the U.S. in 2019 as compared to 2017. The study says that these users are moving to Facebook-owned photo-sharing app Instagram, and Snapchat and other social media platforms.[89]

Even as it grapples with these challenges, in June 2019 Facebook unveiled a new mega initiative—a Blockchain-based payment system called Libra.

Remember what we said about competition coming from anywhere. While it remains to be seen if Facebook will be able to clear all regulatory and other hurdles for the launch of Libra—in fact Facebook itself in its U.S. SEC filing for the quarter ended June 30, 2019, said "there can be no assurance that Libra or our associated products and services will be made available in a timely manner, or at all,"[90]—see how Facebook is looking to disrupt financial services. Imagine what it would mean for you if people around the world without a bank account are able to use it to make instant and nearly free international money transfers from their mobile phones.

> **See how Facebook is looking to disrupt financial services.**

Meanwhile, going back to the Cambridge Analytica case, in July 2019, the Federal Trade Commission (FTC) slapped a fine of $5 billion on Facebook on the grounds that the company had violated the privacy of its users. This is the largest-ever fine imposed by the

---

[89] "The Infinite Dial 2019," Edison Research, March 6, 2019. https://www.edisonresearch.com/infinite-dial-2019/

[90] Facebook Form 10-Q for the quarterly period ended June 30, 2019, Securities and Exchange Commission. https://d18rn0p25nwr6d.cloudfront.net/CIK-0001326801/69ea7934-e26b-499f-85ca-eb67cd2a9fc1.pdf

FTC against a tech company so far. The FTC also ordered Facebook to create an independent privacy committee on its board of directors.

Facebook's challenges around privacy and other issues are a good pointer to an important consideration all of you need to keep in mind as you challenge your current mental, business and revenue models. Remember that any innovations that you come up with either to disrupt or to defend yourself must ensure that their inherent features don't allow others to take advantage of your customers. There are perils, for instance, to encouraging oversharing of information. When users share location-based information extensively on social networking sites, they leave themselves open to their homes being robbed! A website called Pleaserobme.com shows how location-based information can be misused and how easy it is to get details of empty homes. On their website, the founders say that their intention is not to have people burgled but raise awareness of the issue. But there could well be others out there who are just waiting to prey on your vulnerabilities. So make sure that any model that you choose to adopt is as foolproof as possible.

Indeed, it is the challenges and gaps present in existing models that offer business. Spot your opportunities and grab them before it is too late.

To assess how aligned you and your organization are with the principle and the ideas and examples discussed in this chapter, we would encourage you to consider the questions listed below.

Ask Yourself:

1. **Are you exploring and creating new opportunities offered by the pandemic?**

2. **Do you challenge your mental models—your assumptions and beliefs?**

3. **Do you challenge the established norms of your industry?**

4. Have you considered using new disruptive models from other industries in your business? For instance, do examples of the emerging subscription models like that of Rent the Runway inspire you?

5. Do you think it is important to make a positive difference to society?

6. Are you expanding your business into new, breakthrough areas?

7. Are you open to collaborating with others? Are you harnessing the power of networks?

8. Do you have an omnichannel presence to reach your customers?

9. How effective are your M&As? Do they provide synergy such as Microsoft-LinkedIn deal? Do they build capabilities as some of the IBM acquisitions?

10. Are you open to reinventing your portfolio?

11. Are you adopting the latest technologies?

12. Do you believe in continuous innovation and do you follow this in your business?

Chapter 2

Principle 2: Reimagine and Reinvent Your Approach to Customers and Stakeholders

Do a customer-centric digital transformation of your organization, co-create with your consumers, and align the objectives of your company with those of all stakeholders.

These are unprecedented times. Consumers across the world are afraid as never before. They are afraid for their own health and that of their loved ones. They are afraid of the financial toll the pandemic will take on their lives, of losing their jobs, their livelihoods, and

> **How you relate to customers during the COVID-19 pandemic will redefine your relationship with them.**

of the grim uncertainty that lies ahead. Most consumers plan to cut down on purchases or postpone them. Many are even questioning the very purpose of life.

So what does this mean for you as a business? Simply this: While being customer-centric has always been important, how you relate to your customers during the COVID-19 pandemic will redefine your relationship with them and your role in their lives long after the crisis is past. A unique impact of this crisis is on consumer journeys. The lockdown, stay-at-home and work-from-home situations, the closing of most retail stores and all cultural institutions and sport events have dramatically altered the consumer journey and behavior. Any firm that tries to reach and engage the consumer has to realize this and adjust its approach accordingly.

Digital native companies are exponentially raising the bar for customer experience and resetting customer expectations.

Along with understanding and anticipating the customers' needs, companies also need to *co-create* with them. Further, they need to align their objectives with those of *all* stakeholders – customers, consumers, employees, investors, suppliers, distributors and society at large. In this time of crisis, for instance, it is important to be sensitive to the needs of the employees, have compassion and be creative in changing the work environment— be it the shift to work-from-home, digital sales calls, and so on. It is important to focus on the total human being and not only on their role as consumers.

Moreover, customer characteristics have been rapidly changing in recent years, though the pandemic has accentuated these trends. The needs, expectations and aspirations of customers are constantly being redefined. Customers are empowered and they are skeptical. They are comfortable with new concepts like that of the sharing economy. They want to play a role in building a better society and have a positive social impact. You need to recognize all these new facets of the customers and keep them in mind when you tailor new strategies to serve their needs. Also remember that all markets are heterogeneous. As such, it is important to understand what the key segments are and how they change over time.

In this chapter we will look at what customer-centric digital transformation entails. What does it mean to align your objectives with those of your stakeholders? What does co-creation mean? How can one do this successfully? What are the challenges one is likely to face? How can one safeguard against these challenges? These are critical issues for disruptors as well as those whose business is being disrupted.

The Legacy Burden

But first, let's review how legacy companies typically operate and why that leads them to disconnect from their customers.

In previous chapters, we saw how digital native companies like Facebook, Amazon, Google, Uber, Airbnb and many others are exponentially raising the bar for customer experience and resetting customer expectations. These new-age companies are able to do this because they are obsessively customer-centric. These firms succeeded in disrupting different industries because they were able to identify consumer needs that consumers did not even know they had. They identified new opportunities and came up with radically new and innovative ways of solving them. They deployed new digital technologies to understand and predict what their customers wanted and designed their back-end operations in a way that they could offer their customers relevant and timely products, services and experiences. They were not burdened by legacy issues and their customer-centric systems were built for enabling customization and hyper-personalization. They were—and still are—built for speed, agility and flexibility.

> **Legacy firms are determined by what their operations can support, not what the customer needs.**

Most established enterprises, however, are not customer-centric. They still operate back-to-front and are product- or service-centric. And what does this mean? Simply this: Legacy companies are determined by what their operations and infrastructure can support and not what the customer needs.

Look at the history of information technology over the past 50 to 60 years and how enterprises typically used technology. You took a business process or a business function and automated it using a piece of software. This, then, turned into a "system." For instance, earlier, you ran payroll manually. Over the years, you built payroll into an application and the process was automated. It became a payroll system. You earlier had a manual customer record. That became a client relationship management (CRM) system. If you are an insurance company, you had somebody keep track of the policies you sold. You had a general ledger and what was called a policy master. You automated that process and it has now evolved into a policy admin system. You also automated your internal back-office—your dealings with employees, with vendors, internal finance and accounting, etc. and you got an enterprise resource planning (ERP) system. You tried to link the various silos within your organization through enterprise systems like SAP. This was expensive and took many years.

In other words, over the years, every company has evolved a series of internal and external applications that are specific to its business and customers. A lot of intelligence and investment has gone into building these applications, and now they are the core of every large enterprise. A company's business is run through this core. Depending on the complexity of the business, the markets it operates in, the segments it services, and so on, there is a multiplicity of these core applications. Going back to the example of the insurance company, you could be operating in different parts of the globe. You could be servicing segments like commercial, large enterprises, small and medium businesses and direct-to-consumer. You would have different solutions for life, retirement, or automobiles and so on. So, you would have a portfolio of applications and systems and processes that support all these lines of business. Somehow, this spaghetti hairball mess works. And that is primarily because its growth has been evolutionary. You have been continually investing in and incrementally upgrading

> **With digital technologies and the smartphone revolution came the phase of "appification."**

this complex set of back-office systems and processes that support your business.

Undoubtedly these back-office systems do have their strengths. They are scalable: they have been built to handle a large volume of transactions. They perform well: In banks, for

> **Your enterprise must be mapped starting with the customer first.**

instance, payment systems do transactions in microseconds. They are predictable: You can define how the system will play out, both in terms of unit cost and performance. But, and here comes the rub, they are not agile. They are not flexible. They are not modular. You have to use the whole system. You can't pick and choose pieces of it. And, they definitely cannot be personalized. These systems are meant for mass-production by design, which means the system per se is standardized. It does not differentiate among customers or care too much about individual needs. Everybody who uses the system gets the same level of service. In a way, this is the Ford Model T company of today: You could get a car of any color as long as it was black because it was mass-produced.

Consider a wealth management division at a bank. Its system cannot differentiate whether you have a balance of $5 million or $50 million. That's why they put a human being in the middle, and they call it private banking. These systems also do not recognize that the same consumer often has multiple relationships with the organization and is present in many different parts of the system. For instance, a customer or prospect for life insurance could also be a customer or prospect for vehicle insurance and property insurance. But the systems do not recognize this and therefore they don't offer the consumer an integrated solution and experience. This is another huge missed opportunity.

By and large, this approach worked well for a reasonably well-run company because every large enterprise in its industry was in the same boat. Every business functioned back-office forward. No disruptors threatened their survival. Over the past five to 10 years, with the advent of digital technologies and the smartphone revolution, came what we call the phase of "appification." *Everything became an app.* Because new-age companies were sharing information and interacting through apps, a large segment of customers started expecting it from every business. So, be it a bank, utility, insurance firm or retailer, every business wanted a digital presence and introduced its own apps. But now, spurred by what they are getting from new-age companies, customers expect more from everyone. Just getting information on an app is no longer enough. They want to be able to transact on the apps.

So what is the problem here? Think about it. What do *you* believe is the reason that firms are not able to deliver on these customer expectations? Unlike the systems of the disruptors, the systems of most legacy companies are not built for interaction and transaction. They are not built for real-time dialog. And because you are forcing them to do something they are not meant to do, one of two things happens: You either start putting pressure on these back-office core systems and they start failing. Or, your real-time customer experience is very poor. We call these systems "lipstick on a pig," because all you have really done is to put a nice, good-looking front-end, without handling the mess at the back-end.

Create an intermediary layer that connects the front end with the back end.

Here is an example. Take a weather app. Its primary function is to give information about the weather. And it works fine. Now take a bank's app. If it has to only give some basic information to its users, there is no problem. But when it needs to do more than just display information, say the user wants to make a transaction, it often falls short. This is because while the bank has made a nice app at the front-end (applying the lipstick), it has not made the necessary structural changes at the back-end (the pig.) If you don't make structural changes to your back-end, you will end up with a poor customer experience.

Flip Your Model: Move Front-to-Back

What does this mean for legacy companies? We recommend flipping the back-to-front model. We believe that you can no longer afford to be the customer's servicer if you don't lead with the customer being at the center of everything you do. That is what we mean by being customer-centric.

> Knowing what programming appeals to which consumers starts the fly-wheel of a customer-centric approach.

As we said earlier, most customers now expect unique treatment because their expectations are driven by the experience they are getting from companies like Amazon, Netflix and Uber. To compete successfully with these innovative companies, your products, services and experiences have to be mapped with the customer first and not with risk management, or controls, or governance or the back-office. Also remember, most companies work in silos. The way to get over these silos is to say: Let's focus on the target consumers we want to reach and develop a platform that allows us to personalize the offering in real-time to give them a unique experience that has value for them, rather than simply offering them traditional products and services.

To understand the disconnect between what companies offer and what consumers expect, look at the retail sector. Traditional retailers still focus largely on the store experience, while what most consumers want is an omnichannel experience. The consumer expectation has moved far ahead to a seamless experience—online and in the store.

So then, what is to be done? How can legacy companies, which have so far been investing in and operating on a back-to-front model, move on to a customer-first, front-to-back digital architecture?

Many large enterprises think their problem lies in the core systems and that they need to replace these with new digital systems. But that is typically not practical or even possible. These systems have been built over decades. Even if you want to rip them out and replace them one by one, it is pretty much impossible to do that in a way that improves your customer experience. While some companies might have succeeded at doing this, we believe the odds of such an approach working are very low.

Here is an example of a company that tried to do this and failed. Executives at an insurance company in the U.K. believed that its core system was not giving its customers a good digital experience. As a result, they decided to replace the policy admin and claim systems. The company spent $250 million replacing both systems over a period of two to three years. Because these are complex systems, there were delays and cost overruns. Importantly, the customer experience worsened. The reason is the new systems ended up creating two more screens into which the brokers had to now enter data. (For this company, the broker is the customer.) More than 70% of the brokers' time was spent filling in data and because of the systems' complexity, the request-for-a-quote (RFQ) turnaround time was 72 hours. If you are a broker, and you submit a request, you ideally want the response to be in real-time. Even if you can't get a quote back in real-time because it is a complex business, it certainly shouldn't take 72 hours! The company has been losing market share. Its net promoter score is down. They are not selling enough.

Create an Intermediary Layer

Clearly, if you are a legacy company and your aim is to become customer-first then changing your core systems may not necessarily be the right way forward. An alternative route is to create an intermediary layer that connects the front-end with the back-end. This can be done faster and cheaper than replacing the entire core systems. And it also lets external developers connect with the intermediary layer and offers the benefit of open innovation. (We will discuss open innovation in more detail in Chapter 4) Let us understand how an intermediary layer works with an illustration *(See Exhibit 1).*

> Predictive analytics can help you offer services, products and experiences the end customer wants.

EXHIBIT 1

The Front-to-Back Approach to Digital Transformation

The Front-to-Back (F2B) approach is a customer-centric approach. It entails creating an intermediary layer that connects the front-end of the organization with its back-end core systems. The intermediary layer – called the intelligence layer – has various functionality and features like data and analytics, business insights, sentiment analysis and so on. The F2B approach leverages the intelligence layer and the cloud & cognitive capabilities to transform legacy environments. It empowers organizations to become customer-first and offer unique products, services and experiences to their customers.

X2C²™ Front2Back™ (F2B) Transformation

Source: https://www.mphasis.com/home/our-approach-new.html
X²C²™ and Front2Back™ (F2B) Transformation are trademarks of Mphasis Ltd., June 2020.

At one extreme you have the end-customers/stakeholders. And at the other extreme are the core systems. Two layers stand between them. The first is the engagement layer or what we call the front-end. This comprises the various ways in which a company engages with its customers—via applications, devices, social media, user interfaces, user graphics, and so on. The second is the new, intermediary layer. Let's call it the "intelligence layer". This layer intermediates between the end-customer and the core systems and brings to bear a lot of the functionality and features like data and analytics, business insights, sentiment analysis, cognitive and so on. Importantly, it has digital identities, or digital *avatars*, of customers, live at all times.

What do we mean by this? A consumer's digital avatar is the digital footprint that identifies that particular consumer's usage pattern, behavior, preferences and so on. This helps a company personalize its products and service offerings to suit or, in other words, "fit" each consumer's needs.

Consider how **Netflix** uses this approach. Netflix creates an identity for you as soon as you sign up for its service and this is reinforced each time you log in. It then tracks your preferences and, using AI algorithms, it predicts which of its contents might appeal to you. Also, when you choose a particular film or TV show, Netflix shows you, in percentage terms, how well that content matches with your profile. Over time, this knowledge of its customers' preferences becomes an input for the company's content production process. Knowing what kind of programming appeals to which segment of consumers starts the fly-wheel of a customer-centric approach *(See Exhibit 2)*.

EXHIBIT 2

The Keys to Netflix's Success

Netflix has been the poster child of combining data-driven growth with creative choices. Use big data analytics combined with machine learning algorithms to create scores and predictors of customer behavior.

1. Detailed Profiling
Build detailed customer profiles from internal and external data sources with preference, behavioral and other data. Also create analytical profiles for each product with over 100 data points for each title.

2. Advanced Analytics
Use big data analytics combined with machine learning algorithms to create scores and predictors of customer behavior.

NETFLIX

3. Personalization
Use all the relevant data and insights to deliver highly personalized recommendations for continuous engagement.

4. Content Production
Complete feedback loop by using customer behavior data to influence content design and production which in turn impacts customer experience.

5. The Data Behind Netflix's Recommendations
At its core, Netflix's big data approach has resulted in more personalized entertainment experiences for subscribers and better creative decision-making. Netflix uses hundreds of data points to make critical decisions on content production and for personalizing the experience for every customer using the service. Some examples of the data points used are ratings, watch history, rewatched programs, credit calculation, nature of show, device, search history, dates, days, times, location, who in the family watched, and browsing and scrolling behavior.

Based on information in Netflix website. May 2020.

Contrast this to a legacy business, such as banking, where digital avatars are not yet in place to help offer personalized or customized solutions at scale. Here is a personal example. Before the pandemic and its travel restrictions, as CEO of Mphasis, I [Rakesh] used to travel 200 days a year. Almost every week, several banks would reach out to me offering various kinds of credit cards, with brand affiliations to different kinds of precious metals! However, none of the offers met my needs of international travel such as favorable cross-currency rates and interchange fees, concierge-on-demand for travel needs, airport privileges or favorable ground transportation memberships. I would routinely pay 2% to 3% more on currency, have to check which of my cards have lounge access at different airports and so on. I have three of my cards linked to Uber and of course Google always knows which country I am in. The right offering could well turn out to be a Google credit card with Waymo kerbside.

> In the front-to-back model, the mid-office moves to the back-office.

Now, going back to the intelligence layer we were talking about, let us use data as the starting point of this layer. Once you are able to pool the data into a centralized data lake or hub, you can start analyzing it. You can apply artificial intelligence, machine learning and deep learning and predict what customers need at a granular level. Once you are able to do predictive analytics, you can use it to offer services, products and experiences that the end customer wants. In other words, you will be able to offer personalized products, services and experiences. Importantly, you will be able to do this in real-time *(See Exhibit 3)*.

EXHIBIT 3

Data Are Key to Personalization

Every enterprise needs to take a holistic view of data that spans multiple data sets including demographic, firmographic, psychographic, behavioral, situational, locational, devices and other contextual data sets to deliver personalized customer experiences. Besides, you also need to strike a balance with customer privacy needs and regulations.

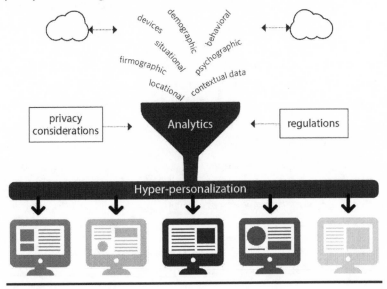

Significantly, this is not what was once called the mid-office. The mid-office used to be where risk management and controls would sit. In the front-to-back model, the mid-office moves to the back-office. The new intermediary layer—the intelligence layer as we call it—is where the core intelligence of your business resides. Your existing core systems will still be at the back as they were earlier, but you will pull data out of these core systems into the intelligence layer through microservices and application programming interfaces (APIs).

The other important feature of this model is that both layers—the engagement layer and the intelligence layer—are rooted in the cognitive and the cloud. We call this the $X2C^2$ formula –anything to cloud, powered by cognitive. The engagement layer is the point of interaction with the end-users and acts as the channel for interactions and end-user experiences through responsive, immersive as well as multimodal interfaces. The intelligence layer, on the other hand, acts as the source for all intelligence to facilitate the end-user experiences. This is made possible through AI/ML algorithms which process both historical as well as real-time data to make the end-user experience seamless and engaging. Cloud computing provides the back-end extensible compute, storage, database as well as orchestrates other external services to support the intelligence layer. This allows the organization to process, analyze, predict and personalize in real-time. We will talk more about this in Chapter 3 on how we must design for personalization at scale.

Let us go back to the insurance example. In this business, typically there is an underwriter, a claims adjuster, a broker and the end customer. The core systems are the same for all of them. But now, in this front-to-back and $X2C^2$ model, the front-end screen will change based on who is accessing it. It will change based on the user's role, their profile, their personality. It's not static. It's dynamic. In fact, soon the front-end screens may not even exist because they might disappear into voice assistants like Amazon Echo's Alexa, for example. This means you, the insurance company, may have to integrate a voice chatbot like Alexa into this intelligence layer. The simple idea is that if you are using intermediaries, they should be able to access the intelligence layer. You don't need to go back to the core for every piece of data.

> **A crisis requires every organization to speed up its digital transformation.**

A by-product of this model is that once you have the intelligence layer, you can slowly start shrinking the core systems. This can happen in various ways. One simple metric is the utilization of resources— systems and people. For instance, let us say a broker or underwriter has a query regarding the database. If the data sits in the intelligence layer, the broker or underwriter doesn't have to utilize core system resources for accessing that information. In effect, you can start to shrink the number of activities for which you use the core system. Slowly the data layer will grow into the "new core" as it will power most of the business functionality, and the "current core" will become a system of record.

Let us take another example to understand the importance of the intelligence layer. Imagine you are the head of the lending and collections division of a large global bank. Traditionally, your key result area (KRA) would be to reduce the number of delinquent loans. (Typically, the head of lending operations at a bank needs to process loans as effectively as possible. However, every loan operation also has bad debts and collections represent the post-facto recovery of loans.) One way to look at it is that given the nature of your work, the KRA is appropriate. But, look at it another way: If your organization were to have the intelligence layer, your KRA need not be to reduce the risk of delinquency. Why? Because the customer who has a loan from your division probably also has other relationships with the bank, including possibly a credit card, and/ or a mortgage, maybe a student loan or a payroll account. So, your bank already has the data for this customer in multiple systems. If your organization had the front-to-back model with the intelligence layer it would be able to

> Get a minimum viable product ready, test the waters and work on perfecting it.

see, based on the customer's spending pattern, that they may go delinquent. The system will be able to predict it. So, if you have all the data, and you have a live image, a digital avatar of the customer sitting in the cognitive layer, you will be in the business of avoiding delinquency and not in the business of collections.

Here is an example of a business that is working toward a customer-first approach. In January 2018, **CitiMortgage** integrated

LoanFx, a self-service digital mortgage platform from Digital Risk, an origination, risk, compliance, and technology services company, in all of its digital channels, including mobile and tablet interfaces. (Digital Risk is a wholly-owned subsidiary of Mphasis.) The LoanFx platform provides CitiMortgage's clients and loan officers with a single hub to manage the mortgage application through loan closing. It provides real-time updates throughout the process to CitiMortgage loan officers, their clients, and their realtors for increased transparency. What this means for CitiMortgage's clients is that now they are verifiers, instead of suppliers of information. And the entire process from application to underwriting and loan approval takes as little as 20 minutes. This also significantly reduces the cycle time of the entire mortgage process.

Start Small, Be Fast

As a legacy company you also need to see what is the timeline for your digital transformation. In times of crisis like the pandemic we are grappling with, the need for speed is even more compelling. The compulsion to shift to digital operations and the critical need for engaging with customers and other stakeholders in a sensitive, compassionate and relevant manner during a crisis requires every organization to speed up its digital transformation.

> **Be ready for creative destruction: Destroy what you have today and create something new.**

Obviously, in this fast-changing, volatile environment, a five- or even three-year time frame is not feasible. You need to accomplish the transformation in a way that starts giving you measurable benefits in as little as three months or even faster. You should start seeing benefits along the way, and not necessarily in one big bang. Rapid prototyping is one way of achieving this *(See Exhibit 4)*.

EXHIBIT 4

Rapid Prototyping for Accelerating Innovation

In this fast-moving modern-day consumer markets, companies need to develop and introduce new products faster to remain competitive. Rapid prototyping involves well-established techniques that enable companies to create, test and iterate on prototypes to take their ideas from concept to market faster.

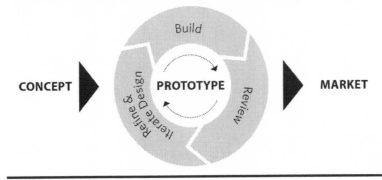

In the front-to-back and X2C^2 approach, the interface layer via the APIs and the microservices typically takes only a few weeks to develop. This allows you to start small. You can define the first set of outcomes you need, and focus on those. After that, you can define and work on the next set of outcomes, and then the next. With this iterative approach, you get to see measurable business impact every three to six months. The business impact could be the net promoter score, cross-sell, turnaround times and so on. For instance, if the target is to reduce a 72-hour RFQ to four hours, it won't go from 72 hours to four hours at one go. It will go down from 72 hours to 24 hours to eight hours and then down to four hours. Or, if the target is to introduce a new product, you don't need to have a perfect product before launching it. As against the "Ready, Aim, Fire" approach, we suggest a "Ready, Fire, Aim" approach. This does not mean that we don't have a target in mind, but that we adopt experimentation. It is an action-oriented and fail-fast approach. It ensures that we do not let perfect be the enemy of good, especially in times where we do not know the specifics of the solution. We believe that if you fire a few times, you will hit the target without wasting time or losing opportunity. The idea is to get a minimum viable product ready, test the waters and then work on perfecting it. Otherwise, by the time you take it to market it will probably be obsolete.

For instance, a large bank spent billions of dollars and a lot of time in developing a solution to upgrade their ATM machines so that these machines could capture checks when they were being deposited by the customers. But even as they were working on the solution, things changed. Smartphones came along and other banks started to introduce the facility to capture checks through phones. This particular bank too added this functionality in its mobile app. This made its upgradation of the ATMs, and the time and money spent on it, pretty much redundant.

The reference architecture-based transformation leverages technologies from previous iterations to reduce marginal cost of implementation. What does this mean? As we discussed earlier, the demand for speed has never been so acute. With changing customer requirements—whether increase in demand or decrease in demand as in crisis times, or greater customization and so on, businesses need to also be ready to deliver products, functions or features to their customers at breakneck speed. To enable this, the target state reference architecture that is drawn out becomes crucial. It forms a pathway that provides direction to the business on how to meet the demands of its stakeholders. The 'flexibility' of this architecture also determines how businesses are able to weave through the changing landscape and are not straitjacketed into one path. Businesses that are digital and are on the cloud already are reaping the benefits of being able to pilot their services or products. And based on the results of the pilot, they are able to

> **Engage your customers in co-creating solutions.**

either scale that out to all their customers or iterate their offerings toward success.

There is another aspect that you must keep in mind. To succeed in the front-to-back model, companies also need to be ready for some creative destruction: Destroy what you have today and create something new. (The theory of creative destruction was developed by the Austrian-American economist Joseph Schumpeter based on the works of Karl Marx.)

We would again encourage you to keep in mind that whenever you create something new, think of people in their many different roles and not only as consumers or customers. You can do this via the rich data you have both from internal and external sources. Alongside, think of the many stakeholders you have—employees, investors, suppliers, distributors, society and so on. Understand their evolving objectives, needs and wants and ensure that the systems that you develop address them as well. This is especially critical in times of crisis when few or any consumers are interested in or focus on any purchases other than the essentials like masks, sanitizers, disinfectants wipes, food and drinks, etc.

> The popularity of digital disruptors has been powered by users as co-creators of content.

Eight Global Truths

We have crafted what we consider to be eight global truths. And we believe that by adopting the "front-to-back" model and the "anything to cloud, powered by cognitive" approach you can achieve these eight global truths and become a customer-first organization. While we developed these eight global truths before the pandemic crisis, we believe that they are even more relevant in the crisis and post-crisis worlds. Given the manner in which the crisis has impacted all our lives, we have to make sure that we are extra sensitive to consumer moods, needs and objectives. We have to show compassion and understanding. We have to significantly increase the speed of our response and be authentic and transparent in our willingness to flip our business models and revenue models to address the changing needs of the consumers.

The eight global truths are:

1. **Respect your customers and focus on helping them achieve their objectives as part of a "win-win" value.**

2. **Improve customer experience throughout their purchase journey.**

3. **Know your customer as well as a digital business does and offer relevant, customized and unique products, services and experience.**

4. **Improve customer share of wallet using the above approach to enhance the opportunity to cross-sell.**

5. **Reduce time-to-market for new products and services, as well as turnaround time for business response like request for proposals.**

6. **Reduce cost of operations while achieving the four goals stated above.**

7. **Engage your customers in a co-creation process.**

8. **Expand these benefits to all stakeholders.**

We will discuss more of this in the chapters that follow. For now, let us look at a few of the points listed above.

Co-Create with Your Customers

So far we have seen why it is important to understand and predict your customers' needs and desires to give them what they need, when they need it and the way they need it. And we have looked at how a customer-centric, front-to-back model helps to do this. However, we believe that if you want to stay ahead in the game it is not enough to just get inputs from your customers and create solutions for them. You, as a company, need to engage with them in co-creating the solutions.

In times of lockdown and social distancing that the COVID-19 crisis has forced upon all of us, engaging your customers in digital co-creation will be doubly beneficial – not only will it bring the typical benefits of co-creation, in addition it also helps in gaining the consumer's appreciation and deeper engagement. Consider food delivery platforms, for instance. If, during the lockdown, they could add to their list of partner restaurants based on requests from customers, it could be a win-win for all concerned.

The popularity of **YouTube, Facebook, Instagram, TikTok, Snapchat** and other digital disruptors has been powered by users as co-creators of content. Think of other different roles customers can play. For instance, as co-producers (**Build-A-Bear** is the global brand with more than 400 stores worldwide where guests can create customizable furry friends), as advertisers (**Ford** used influencers to communicate their Fiesta vehicle experience with their followers) and as those who decide on the price (**Priceline.com**).

Look at what is happening in the advertising industry. Traditionally, the advertising agency would put together a small creative team to work with a client. This team worked with the clients to understand what they wanted. Based on the brief that they got from a client, the creative team suggested various options. The client shortlisted some options and after a few iterations made a final decision. Cut now to new-age advertising. **Doritos**, one of PepsiCo's best-known brands of tortilla chips, gave agencies a miss for 10 years for its Super Bowl campaigns. Every year from 2006 till 2016 it invited its users to suggest the advertising for this mega football event. The winning entry was aired by Doritos and the winner got a

> **Align your firm's objectives with those of all the players in your ecosystem.**

cash prize from the company. A blog post at Yotpo, a user-generated content marketing platform, notes: "By asking users to submit their own interpretation of what Doritos means to them, the brand got a unique look into their customers' language, personality, pain points, and wants and needs."[91]

Apart from co-creating, you need to align your firm's objectives with those of all the players in your ecosystem. What do we mean by this? It is well understood that the vision, mission,

> **Look at your firm not just by itself but as part of an ecosystem.**

objectives and strategy of any organization are dependent on its corporate culture, organizational structure, governance, processes, competencies, technologies, facilities, resources, performance measures and incentives. [We will discuss this more in Chapter 8.] But in this new age, there is another critical element. All of the above has to be embedded in a network; you need to look at your firm not just by itself, but as part of an ecosystem. In their 2016 book *The Network Imperative,* authors Barry Libert, Megan Beck and Yoram (Jerry) Wind wrote: "We are at the beginning of a rapid upending of traditional ways of creating value, and it is occurring in every industry. Firm-centric organizations that use their own resources to create and keep all the value for themselves are slowly being replaced by those that share value creation with networks of individuals connected by digital technologies."[92] We will talk about this in length in Chapter 4 where we discuss the importance of opening up one's innovation process, but for now here are some examples of how companies have adopted this approach.

---

[91] "How Doritos' Marketing Strategy Made Superbowl History," Yotpo, February 3, 2020. https://www.yotpo.com/blog/how-doritos-wins-every-super-bowl-with-ugc/

[92] Barry Libert, Megan Beck and Yoram (Jerry) Wind, The Network Imperative. Harvard Business Review Press, 2016.

Take **Apple**. When one looks at Apple, one sees beautiful designs and great advances in technology. Obviously these are key success factors for the company. But much of Apple's success also lies in its ability to provide hundreds of thousands of valuable apps through its app store. And the only way it can offer this—by way of quantity, quality, diversity, or speed—is through its developer network. Apple Developer, the company's developer program, gives its network of 23 million software developers access to its cutting-edge technologies and other resources and helps them build their apps independently. It then enables them to reach customers across the world through its app store. To ensure that the developers find it attractive to develop and market their apps on the Apple app store, the company has adopted a win-win business model. The developers get to decide the price of their apps and get a big chunk of the revenues. For every app that a developer sells on the Apple platform, Apple takes 30% and the developer gets 70%. In June 2018, Apple's CEO Tim Cook had said that the company's app store had some 500 million visitors a week and the 20 million registered Apple developers had collectively earned about $100 billion through its app store.[93] For Apple, as mentioned earlier, the big advantage is that it gets to provide a multitude of apps that it would never be able to do using only its internal resources *(See Exhibit 5)*.

> **Focus on the long-term, lifetime value of a customer.**

---

[93] "App Store Hits 20 Million Registered Developers and $100 Billion in Revenues, 500 Million Visitors Per Week," TechCrunch, June 4, 2018. https://techcrunch.com/2018/06/04/app-store-hits-20m-registered-developers-at-100b-in-revenues-500m-visitors-per-week/?guccounter=1

EXHIBIT 5

The Exploding Apps Economy

The global app ecosystem is on the cusp of rapid growth fueled by a mobile-first consumer base and significant increase in time and money spent on apps.

Number of Apps Available in Leading App Stores as of 1st Quarter 2020

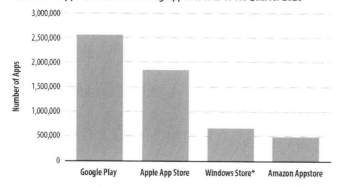

Worldwide App Gross Consumer Spend by Store as of 1st Quarter 2020

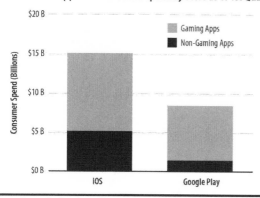

Source: Respective App Stores data, May 2020. APP ANNIE, March 2020.
"ios" in the 2nd graph above refers to Apple Store data.

Let's look at how **Mphasis,** a global IT services company, is leveraging co-creation. Mphasis has two innovation labs—NEXT Labs and Sparkle Lab. NEXT Labs co-creates solutions with the company's customers while Sparkle co-creates with startups for Mphasis customers. Jai Ganesh, senior vice president and head of NEXT Labs, explains why co-creating is important for Mphasis. "At the pace at which technology is moving, we cannot do everything on our own. We co-create with the external ecosystem on projects where we don't have the required capabilities in-house, or where the time-to-market is critical. Co-creating helps both us and our partners in developing differentiated solutions in an accelerated manner."

Jai explains how a co-creation initiative at Next Labs is different from a traditional IT services project in which the services company builds everything for the client for a fee. "Typically, co-creation projects are proof-of-value or proof-of-outcome projects. They are targeted, short-term interventions spread over a few weeks. What we take to the table is our intellectual property, our algorithms, our technology experts and our way of solving a problem. What the clients bring is their data and their domain expertise. And together we come up with the proof-of-concept." He adds that the co-creation exercise gives both parties the confidence to make the necessary investments to take it to production."

> **Working with startups has been a popular model for big firms.**

One of NEXT Labs' co-creation projects is with a leading international bank. The project involves applying artificial intelligence to resolve issues around inter-country money transfers. Let's see what this entails. All banks operating in the U.S. are governed by the Office of Foreign Assets Control (OFAC) regulations for any inter-country money transfers. Based on the U.S. foreign policy and national security goals, OFAC lists countries and entities with which it does not allow money transfers. This list gets updated based on the political and other conditions. Now, this bank has thousands of inter-country money transfers that happen daily via the U.S. The bank's risk management system automatically flags what it considers risky transactions under the OFAC regulations. Each of these flagged transactions go through 'four eyes' which means two people manually check these transactions to confirm the bank's action on them. The main challenge for the bank is that around 90% of the transactions that its system flags are false positives. Even though a particular transaction is legal, it is flagged as being illegal. This problem arises due to certain tricky issues in identifying entities. For example, if the country Cuba is a banned entity, the bank's system may stop money going to Cuba Street in Florida in the U.S. It is then checked manually by two people in the bank before being approved. This not only increases the time and the cost of transaction for the bank, it obviously makes for poor experience for the bank's end-customers who are engaged in this transaction.

NEXT Labs worked with the bank on building an AI system to resolve the flagged transactions for false positives. "We already had existing models of fraud identification with us in-house; that is our intellectual property. Our team customized these models for the client after receiving their data and inputs on their current process. The solution that we co-created with the bank helped them save cost and time by augmenting the team with an explainable AI system which accurately identifies the false positives. The AI system also brought in more consistency in decision-making," says Jai.

> **The co-creation model needs an open and inclusive mindset.**

Leverage the Strength of Startups

During the pandemic, when India was in lockdown and well-established fast-moving consumer goods firms in the country were finding it difficult to reach their end-consumers through their regular distribution and retail channels, some like food company **Britannia** and health and wellness company **Marico** found a way around by leveraging the strength of startups. Both Britannia and Marico are large, well-established companies with traditional supply chains but they are now partnering with delivery startups to ensure that their products reach the consumers during the lockdown. Britannia set up a 'Britannia Essentials' store on online delivery platform Dunzo to deliver items such as cookies, croissants, clarified butter, and dairy whitener in certain cities in India. Marico set up 'Saffola Stores' on online food ordering apps Zomato and Swiggy to deliver its Saffola brand of oats and cooking oils. The startups source the products from Britannia's and Marico's distribution centers.

Prior to the crisis too, working with startups has been a popular model for big firms. For instance, many global high-tech companies like IBM, Google, Facebook and others have established accelerators that provide mentorship, infrastructure, technical training, etc. to the startups. Some companies also announce competitions focused on specific topics in order to attract startups working in these areas.

Take **IBM's** AlphaZone accelerator program based in Israel. The company's website describes this as a "20-week professional and deep immersion program" in areas such as big data analytics, cloud, mobile, security, Internet of Things, machine learning and AI. The program description goes on to say it is looking for "industry-specific solutions that can bring innovation" to industries such as retail, health care, travel and media. At the end of the 20-week program the participating startups get an opportunity to demonstrate their solutions to different communities like angel investors, venture capitalists, IBM executives, media and industry leaders. Wherever possible, IBM also helps the startups to market their solutions. IBM started this program in 2014 and according to company information as of mid-2020, 63 startups have "graduated successfully" and "are working with IBM and with its leading customers worldwide." IBM also has programs like the SmartCamp, a global pitch competition where the winners get coaching, mentorship and opportunities to get connected with the business world.

> **Wherever possible, IBM helps startups to market their solutions.**

Mphasis Sparkle Lab

At Mphasis' Sparkle Lab, there are two models of leveraging startups. One, the Sparkle team looks for promising startups that are working on disruptive technologies. It proactively works with them to build certain solutions and then pitches these solutions to potential customers. Two, when Mphasis is working on tough problems for its clients, it looks around to see if any innovative startups have ideas that could solve them. It then works with these startups to incorporate their innovative ideas with its own solutions.

Sparkle's co-creation of a solution with the Silicon Valley-based startup NoPassword.com is case in point. NoPassword (which was acquired by Logmein in 2019) is the next generation of identity and access management solutions that substitutes passwords with human and hidden multi-factor authentication. Instead of using static passwords, NoPassword uses local biometric authentication (face, voice, fingerprint, iris and behavior) on the user's smartphone. It extracts these hidden features from the phone without interrupting the user. The idea behind NoPasswords is that the end-users can give up passwords for a more secure and much better user experience without compromising privacy. For enterprises, it offers benefits such as reduction in IT overheads, improved security and privacy compliance and better visibility into where and what their employees are accessing.

The Sparkle team came across this Silicon Valley-based startup in 2017 during a weekly pitching event at the Plug and Play global innovation platform. It saw a lot of promise and potential in what NoPassword had to offer and teamed up with it to design an innovative solution around workers' compensation. According to various studies, some 80% of worker injuries that are presented for compensation actually happen outside the workplace. By teaming up with NoPassword and its authentication software, Sparkle was able to co-develop a solution that could detect fraudulent worker compensation claims. It then pitched this solution to human resource services firms like Alight Solutions.

> **Focus on total human beings and not only on their role as consumers.**

It's a win-win situation for all parties concerned. Co-creating with startups gives Mphasis cost-effective access to innovative ideas, reduces its go-to-market time and enables it to offer quick, innovative and differentiated solutions to its clients. The startup obviously benefits by getting access to large enterprises (which it otherwise would not) and seeing early success. And the enterprises benefit by getting cutting-edge solutions from innovative startups and at the same time backed by the stability and commitment of an established company like Mphasis.

Adopt a Win-Win Approach

Co-creation has its own challenges, though. Take leadership, for instance. Traditionally, leadership has been about being in control. It has been about giving directions. It has been about looking after the interests primarily of the firm, and by and large ignoring the needs and objectives of those outside the immediate circle. The co-creation model needs a very different model of leadership. It needs an open and inclusive mindset, which recognizes that the company cannot do everything alone. In these complex times, co-creating is an essential ingredient of a winning formula. And most importantly, it requires willingness, indeed determination, to ensure that it is a win-win relationship for everyone involved in the co-creation exercise.

It is not only the mindset at the company level that needs to change. It is equally important at the customer's end. Let us say, you are an IT services company that is developing a product or service for a client. Typically, what do your clients do? They bring the problem to you and expect you to solve it and come back with a solution. So you need to educate and convince the clients that it is in fact to their advantage to work with you and co-create the solution. This is a mental obstacle that needs to be overcome, a chasm that needs to be bridged. Remember, hiring a firm is not the same as co-creating with them. Nor does co-creation simply mean doing market research to ascertain consumer preferences.

Earlier in this chapter, we spoke about respecting your customers and focusing on helping them achieve their objectives as part of a "win-win" value. How does one do this? The first step is to not think of them as targets to be taken advantage of; your business and revenue models and offering should all be guided by a "win-win" approach. The reason financial service providers are vulnerable is because their revenue model violates this principle and they win even when their customers lose. Further, be authentic and transparent. Focus on the long-term, lifetime value of a customer. And always make sure your offer is relevant and valuable to them.

Focus on All Stakeholders

Companies need to make another shift. To ensure that they are sustainable, companies now need to serve all their stakeholders and not only their shareholders. They need to look at everyone in their ecosystem – customers, employees, investors, suppliers,

> **How companies respond to the pandemic will be an acid test for stakeholder capitalism.**

distributors and society at large. And, as we pointed out earlier, it is important that the focus be on the total human being and not only on their role as consumers.

Why do we say this? Consumers, especially the millennials and Gen Z, are very socially aware and they want to contribute to making the world a better place. As part of this world view, they are more favorably disposed toward companies that have a similar philosophy. They want to work for and with companies who take care of them and are compassionate and caring toward everyone in the ecosystem. They respect companies that visibly demonstrate that they have a larger social purpose. They prefer to buy products and services from companies that have a positive social impact.

The COVID-19 crisis has brought the need for companies to play a larger role to the fore and many have stepped up to the challenge. They have acted to help their many stakeholders deal with the crisis. For instance, they have contributed to relief funds for their immediate communities and beyond; distributed cooked meals and grocery kits in their areas; taken pay cuts for the top management; increased the pay for their frontline workers; given paid leave for anyone infected with the coronavirus or requiring quarantine; moved to shorter and flexible work hours; made shopping easier for their customers, prioritized order fulfillment to the health care sector; and so on *(See Exhibit 6)*.

EXHIBIT 6

Towards a Stakeholder Orientation & Positive Social Impact

There hasn't been a more germane time for stakeholder focus and responsible capitalism than this pandemic era. Companies, large and small, are increasingly transitioning into a stakeholder-driven model of business by shifting their operations to prioritize the support and benefits for their customers, employees, partners, communities, the environment, shareholders and overall impact on society.

As Paul Polman, former CEO of Unilever and currently the chairman of the International Chambers of Commerce and vice-chair of the UN Global Compact, said in an interview with *Ethical Corporation*, how companies responded to the pandemic would be an "acid test for stakeholder capitalism."[94] In an interview with *Bloomberg* in May 2020, Unilever CEO Alan Jope said that the COVID-19 pandemic has strengthened the company's belief and practice in the multi-stakeholder approach. Pointing out that Unilever has been practicing this for around a decade now, Jope said a purpose-led business model will be more relevant than ever in the post-pandemic world.[95]

We believe it will also be a key differentiator between companies that will not only survive this turbulence but also shape the future, and those that will simply fade away.

To assess how aligned you and your organization are with the principle and the ideas and examples discussed in this chapter, we would encourage you to consider the questions listed below.

Ask Yourself:

1. **Are you focusing on your customers and all stakeholders to capture the opportunities the pandemic offers?**

2. **Do you respect your customers and focus on helping them achieve their objectives as part of a "win-win" value?**

3. **Can you understand and predict the desires and needs of your customers and offer them relevant and timely products, services and experience?**

---

[94] "Paul Polman: Coronavirus is an Acid Test for Stakeholder Capitalism," Ethical Corporation, March 20, 2020. https://www.ethicalcorp.com/paul-polman-coronavirus-acid-test-stakeholder-capitalism

[95] "Unilever CEO Sees Purpose-Led Businesses Only Gaining Relevance," Bloomberg Businessweek, May 12, 2020. https://www.bloomberg.com/news/features/2020-05-12/unilever-ceo-on-coronavirus-pandemic-purpose-led-businesses

4. Are you sensitive to the needs of the employees? Are you compassionate and creative in responding to the changing work environment?

5. Have you done a customer-centric digital transformation of your organization? Do you have a front-to-back, customer-first model?

6. Have you created an intermediary intelligence layer that connects the front-end of your organization with the back-end?

7. Do you use an iterative approach for digital transformation of your organization that helps you speed up the process? Do you get measurable benefits within as little as three months? Have you reduced your time-to-market?

8. Are you willing to adopt creative destruction? Are you open to destroying what you have today to create something new?

9. Do you co-create with your customers?

10. Do you leverage the strength of startups?

11. Have you aligned the objectives of your company with those of all stakeholders?

12. Do you view your firm as part of a larger social ecosystem?

Chapter 3

Principle 3: Speed Up Digital Transformation and Design for Personalization at Scale

Customers expect personalization, even during times of crisis. To remain relevant, you need to be able to offer this at scale. You can achieve this by having an integrated data strategy and using big data and cognitive technologies.

Let us rewind a bit. Remember Meghna, John, Yegya, Jane and Li from CALL TO ACTION? Recall how delighted they were with the personalized, real-time offerings they received. In this chapter, we will look at how you can offer such thrilling value and experiences to your customers. But first, let us recap why personalization is important.

> **To remain relevant, you must be able to offer personalization at scale.**

As we discussed, these are times of unprecedented change. The COVID-19 pandemic, disruptive advances in science and technology, dramatic changes in the media landscape, new business models largely led by digital-first startups, empowered and skeptical consumers, and fast-changing cultural, social, economic and geo-political environments are redefining the landscape around us. Consumers have in fact started to drive not just what they want, but also when they want it, where they want it and how they want it delivered. Every industry is under disruptive attack by a common theme: use of new tech and data science to enhance personalized experiences. For you, as providers of products and services, one big central point to *always* keep in mind is that understanding and predicting your customer's desires and needs, and offering *relevant* products, services and experiences is non-negotiable. Personalization in real-time increases the relevance and value of your offering for your customer. With products increasingly being viewed as commodities, it is the brand mystique (when it exists) and brand experience that allows for differentiation and increased value.

Keep in mind that personalization is *not* a luxury; it is equally important during a crisis. At such times, people are anxious and afraid of not only the current turbulence but also of the future which seems uncertain and therefore overwhelming. Any contact with them has to be relevant for them. It has to be meaningful and must address their unique needs, or else it could make you appear as uncaring and self-centered. In some categories like health care, banking, insurance, media, entertainment, and retail, the need for hyper-personalization actually goes up during a crisis. There is much to be gained by having a deep understanding of customers, especially as it relates to predicting and forecasting their needs, and actions to pre-empt them.

> **Personalization in real time increases the relevance and value of your offering for your customer.**

Personalization, at its heart, is about a deeper understanding of the customer's needs, and using that data to also do mass predictions. Further, at times of crisis, there is typically a lot of conflicting information, and so for customers, getting the correct information and service at the time they need it, is priceless. Pharmacies, for instance, could offer free and quick deliveries for senior citizens and patients with major health conditions. Retailers could offer a choice between faster deliveries or lower price.

Insurance providers could tailor new offerings. Think of how you can personalize your offerings and become more relevant to your customers in a crisis.

Traditional vs. Hyper-personalized Services

Let's look at how a traditional organization delivers a product or service compared to the way a digital company provides the same in a hyper-personalized manner. This example is from the insurance sector. Imagine that Customer X, who is traveling

> **Personalization, at its heart, is about a deeper understanding of the customer's needs.**

from Europe to the U.S., buys international travel insurance from a traditional insurance company. Another customer, Customer Y, also traveling from Europe to the U.S., buys a similar insurance from a digitally-savvy, customer-centric insurance company. Both insurers collect all kinds of data like their customer's flight information, travel itinerary, health details, vaccination details, and so on. Let's say the travel itineraries of both Customer X and Customer Y indicate they plan to visit Disneyland.

Now, imagine there is an outbreak of measles in Disneyland. Typically, in the first case, that of the traditional insurance company, there is no further interaction with the customers unless they file an insurance claim. The digitally-savvy, customer-centric insurance firm however would issue an immediate alert to Customer Y warning them about the measles outbreak. The customer could then choose whether they want to travel to Disneyland or cancel those plans. The information from the insurer would help the customer not only avoid the possibility of falling ill, but also ensure that the rest of their visit was not in jeopardy. For the insurer, this would mean that there is no claim made by Customer Y, and also that there is higher customer-satisfaction and probably higher customer stickiness. Clearly, it's a win-win situation for both.

Or consider a credit card transaction. Imagine a customer swipes their credit card at a mall. A traditional service would record the customer's transaction, check the requisite requirements and make sure the payment goes through quickly. This service is at scale and it is mass-personalized because it is personalized for a merchant or a particular type of transaction. A digital company, on the other hand, would look at not just the transaction but also the context in which it occurs. It will know that a particular customer has swiped the transaction in a mall. The customer might know that the same credit card company is offering a discount or a coupon at a different store close by. The digital firm would immediately offer the customer a 20% discount. Chances of that customer walking into the next store and making a purchase is very high. This is called contextualized service.

Two Strategies for Personalization

> Digital companies look at transactions and the context in which they occur.

Broadly speaking, companies can use two strategies for personalization. First, firms can get as much data as possible on their customers, and using predictive analytics, AI and machine learning, they can design customized offerings for segments of customers or for individual customers. For example, based on the data they have on a customer's buying history, **Amazon** uses recommendation engines to suggest that if they liked "X" item, they would probably love item "Y". Amazon also uses insights from customer feedback, or what it calls the "voice of the customer"— including reviews, rejects, exchange or customer service calls, etc.— to create private label products, which it then recommends to the customers. Similarly, **Netflix** uses a viewer's viewing history to recommend other shows they are likely to enjoy, and also to create original content. Most recent advances in personalization have been in this area.

Second, firms can create platforms that allow customers to customize their purchase. For instance, customers who want to buy computers from **Dell** can either buy a pre-configured computer or pick and choose the specific configuration they want and design their own computer. Similarly, **Nike** allows its customers to customize their shoes by choosing from a range of different materials and colors for different parts of the shoes. The key here is that companies must have a set of components or building blocks. They can then provide a platform that empowers customers to choose from these building blocks and design a complete product. The company then assembles this customized product and delivers it to the customer. In the case of Nike, for instance, it is not that the customer is building their shoe from scratch; they are designing their shoe to their personal preferences based on components that Nike provides. These include the color and/or material for the base, outsole, lining and laces. The platform approach balances the need of the individual or segment for personalized products/services with the need of the company for economies of scale. Examples of personalization – whether it is company-led, as in the case of Netflix, or consumer-driven, as in the case of Nike and Dell – can be seen on the websites of these companies.

> **A chasm often exists between the needs of innovators and those of other segments.**

A related point is that if you work with individual customers on customizing solutions, how do you ensure that other customers will respond to the same needs? This is especially important when it comes to co-creating with a customer. The danger is that if the customer you are working with is innovative and has unique requirements, your design may not apply to other segments in the market such as late adopters. A chasm often exists in the market between the needs of the innovators and those of other segments. So how can we overcome this problem? One way is to identify customers who represent different segments of the market—innovators, early adopters, late adopters and laggards—and then co-create with each of these customers. That can ensure co-creation that deals with the needs of each segment.

We will talk more about these and other examples later in this chapter. But for now, keep in mind that whichever strategy you may choose to adopt, *the ultimate goal is to offer hyper-personalized products, services and experiences to your customers in real-time (See Exhibit 1).*

EXHIBIT 1

Hyper-personalization vs Segmentation

Hyper-personalization, as compared to targeted segmentation, is an advanced, real-time personalization of offerings, content and customer experience at an individual level. Hyper-personalization leverages big data to deliver such tailor-made solutions in real-time.

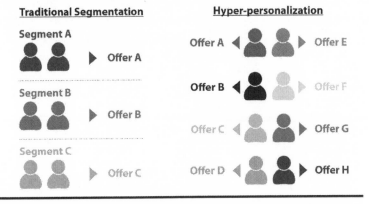

Leverage Technology to Achieve Scale

Data and Cognitive

Here is an important question: How can companies implement these strategies and design for real-time hyper-personalization *at scale*? We believe that the only way to do this is by applying technology as it has never been applied before. In order to move from mass-customization to hyper-personalization at scale, companies have to harness the power of technology, in particular big data and cognitive technologies. As we discussed in Chapter 2, the need of the hour is to do a customer-centric digital transformation using data and the cognitive layer as the new core. We called it the intelligence layer having digital identities of customers. A digital identity, as we had discussed, is the digital footprint that identifies a particular customer's usage pattern, behavior and preferences. The cognitive/intelligence layer enables companies to gauge their customers' preferences better and allows them to meet their individual requirements – including requirements that are in fact unknown to, or unarticulated by, the customer.

As we had discussed earlier, pool all the customer data into a centralized data lake or a data hub, then analyze the data, and follow this up with predicting. Apply artificial intelligence, machine learning and deep learning and play it back into offering personalized services, products and experiences. In the insurance example, the customer-centric insurer was able to offer hyper-personalized service by marrying internal information (say, the customer's travel plans and vaccination details) with external information (outbreak of measles in Florida). Armed with this contextual data, the company could provide the insight back to the customer.

Let's go back to Netflix for a minute. If you look at your Netflix screens at home, each of your family members will have different recommendations based on what they have watched. That is a great example of one-to-one

> **Pool the customer data into a centralized hub, analyze it, and follow up with predicting.**

personalization driven by data on what you actually watched rather than what you say you prefer. For Netflix to be able to do this, it needs to understand the content and the characteristics of the content and also compare and equate contents. Further, as we mentioned earlier, by aggregating the user's preferences, Netflix can create original content. For instance, seeing that a person is interested in superhero movies and also movies that have strong female lead roles, they can now create new superhero movies with female lead characters. This technology allows Netflix to create new products and also reach micro-segments that they might otherwise not be able to engage. This ability to reach micro-segments without having to have them concentrated geographically makes a huge difference for Netflix. It enables the company to satisfy unique micro-segments that may be widely dispersed.

Geo-Fencing

Look also at how companies are using geo-fencing, i.e. the use of global positioning system (GPS) or radio frequency identification (RFID) to create a virtual geographic boundary for hyper-personalization. Geo-fencing enables a company to trigger a response when a mobile device enters or leaves a particular area *(See Exhibit 2)*. For instance, when a customer (who has opted to enable location services) enters an area that has been geo-fenced, offers from companies in that area can start popping up on their mobile device.

> **Geo-fencing helps companies trigger a response when a mobile device enters or leaves an area.**

Or take **McDonald's,** which uses geo-fencing for orders placed by customers on its mobile app. This allows McDonald's outlets to ensure that food is prepared fresh and kept ready just as customers stop by to pick it up.

In March 2019, McDonald's moved another step toward personalization. In what is reportedly one of its biggest acquisitions in 20 years, McDonald's took over Dynamic Yield, a Tel Aviv and New York-based AI firm specializing in personalization and decision logic technology. With this capability, McDonald's outdoor digital Drive Thru menu displays can vary based on traffic in the restaurant, time, weather, and popular menu items. The technology can also suggest additional items based on the customer's current order. The company plans to integrate the technology into all its digital customer experience touchpoints, such as self-order kiosks and its mobile app. The Dynamic Yield acquisition is expected to help McDonald's use technology and data more effectively and create personalized experiences for its customers faster.

EXHIBIT 2

Geo-fencing Enhances Hyper-local Engagement

The confluence of beacons, geo-fencing and other location-aware technologies takes engagement within retail stores, museums and other public places to a highly interactive customer experience.

Facial and Emotional Recognition

Another cutting-edge use of technology for hyper-personalization is through leveraging facial recognition features on mobile devices. iPhone X, for instance, uses facial recognition, to help unlock your phone. Your iPhone X device identifies your face through the unique characteristics of your face. You can also use the phone facial

Concerns are growing that facial-recognition technology could invade privacy and be misused.

recognition feature for Apple Pay, App Store and iTunes purchases, and third-party apps that currently rely on Touch ID. Here's another example. A few years ago, Amsterdam-based coffee brand Douwe Egberts used facial recognition[96] to delight customers at Johannesburg's O. R. Tambo International Airport. The company put up a vending machine which dispensed a free cup of coffee to anyone who yawned in front of it.

What's more, companies can use facial recognition features to understand a customer's moods. In other words, using emotional recognition, companies can customize the user interface (UI) and also their offers to the customers based on their mood sensitivity. So the app or the offers will look different depending on whether the customer is happy or angry or sad. At the heart of this capability is AI and machine learning technology because the way you change the UI automatically generates the code that then creates the new UI. In other words, software writes the software for the new UI. This can be used by companies in practically any consumer-facing industry like retail or banking, for instance. This is because what you are doing is to gather contextual consumer data and then add that context to your messaging and offer.

Consider how **Expedia,** the travel company, uses this technology. In a microsite called 'Discover Your Aloha,' Expedia offers the ability to create personalized holiday itineraries for tourists who want to visit Hawaii. The microsite has a video showcasing the many splendors of Hawaii ranging from the beautiful beaches to adventure sports to natural and cultural attractions. Visitors to the microsite are requested to switch on their webcams when they view the video and smile at the parts they like. If the viewer consents to facial analysis, custom-built facial recognition software captures and analyzes the viewer's reactions as they

---

[96] Douwe Egberts, Bye-Bye Red Eye. https://www.youtube.com/watch?time_continue=121&v=HOTQ8z0fQHo

watch the video. It identifies which parts of the video evoke the most positive reactions. The algorithm then identifies the viewer's personal preferences and offers customized recommendations[97] *(See Exhibit 3).*

EXHIBIT 3

Personalization with Facial Recognition Technology

In another example of technology-driven personalization, the Hawaii Tourism Authority (HTA) worked with Expedia to develop an innovative, technology-forward campaign and website that integrates facial recognition technology. The visually stunning 'Discover Your Aloha' microsite features video content showcasing the beauty and spirit of Hawaii. As the video plays, if the viewer gives permission, custom-built facial recognition software analyzes their reactions to the content and creates a personalized holiday package.

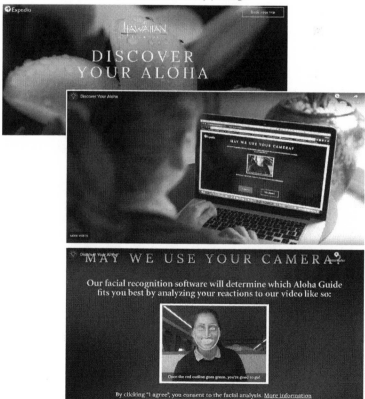

Source: Expedia Group Media Solutions, September 20, 2019.
https://www.youtube.com/watch?time_continue=16&v=bdq-hv3eHc8&feature=emb_title

---

[97] https://discoveryouraloha.expedia.com/

A word of caution here. Even as you think about *if and how* you can use facial recognition in your line of business, do keep in mind that there are growing concerns that this technology could result in invasion of privacy and also be misused. So think hard about how you can use this technology while at the same time being respectful of privacy concerns. If companies fail to do so, they might well find themselves at the receiving end of a customer backlash. Some so-called "smart city" initiatives have run into trouble because they failed to balance these issues.

Voice Recognition

Like facial recognition, voice recognition technology can also help you offer personalized experiences. Consider a company like **Beyond Verbal.** Founded by Dr. Yoram Levanon, this Israeli startup's proprietary technology provides real-time emotional analysis of vocal intonations, irrespective of language. The company's technology is able to extract various acoustic features from a speaker's voice in real-time and give insights on different aspects such as personal health conditions, well-being and emotional understanding. Let's look at some ways in which this technology can be used. In the smart home sector, for instance, a virtual private assistant (VPA) can sense that the user has had a stressful day at work and suggest a television show or music that would make them feel better. In call centers, customer service bots or agents can give appropriate responses based on the customer's mood at the time of the call. In the health and well-being sector, a VPA can recognize that the user has certain health issues and can offer personalized solutions like lifestyle changes. Or, a remote patient care bot can schedule appointments with a doctor or a therapist.

> Like facial recognition, voice recognition technology can also help you offer personalized experiences.

Beyond Verbal works with hospitals, insurance and research institutions to create a large dataset of voice recording and correlated medical records. According to the company website it has access to an extensive database of "over 150,000 patient records with over 1 million anonymized voice recordings" and its internal database has grown to include "more than tens of thousands of labeled patient records, correlated with their medical records." Using its patented AI algorithms, Beyond Verbal has come up with vocal biomarkers that can provide "non-intrusive, continuous and scalable information" into patients' health. The company's website also claims that clinical data demonstrates that by using AI, machine learning and deep learning techniques, it can predict and monitor chronic diseases. The website adds: "Having access to large patient databases with correlated (and anonymized) voice recordings of other health conditions, such as cancer, hypertension, diabetes and others, we are now busy building new vocal biomarker prediction algorithms." (In December 2019, Beyond Verbal merged with Healthymize, another early-stage Israeli AI health tech company, to create a new company called Vocalis Health.)

During the COVID-19 pandemic, the company launched an initiative to discover vocal biomarkers which could help get insights on the symptoms and early detection of the coronavirus infection. The idea was to correlate the voice of an individual with the symptoms of COVID-19 using AI. The study was conducted under the necessary government approvals required for clinical research.[98]

> **Vocal biomarkers can provide "non-intrusive, continuous and scalable information" into patients' health.**

Visual Search

Visual search technology is gaining traction with retailers. Take **FarFetch**, the London-based online luxury fashion retail platform. In December 2018, FarFetch partnered with Syte, a visual AI startup and launched a feature called "See It, Snap It, Shop It" in its app. This allows users to upload any image they like, from anywhere. The app then analyzes the image and finds and presents the same or similar items to the users from its

---

[98] COVID-19 voice study. https://www.voiceome.org/covid19/index.html

own platform comprising of items such as clothing, bags, shoes, jewelry, accessories, etc. from more than 1000 luxury brands and boutique partners like Versace, Gucci, Prada, Burberry, De Beers and others. FarFetch expects the visual search feature to improve its stickiness with customers since it gives them a superior customer experience and a compelling reason to shop on its platform. A *Business Wire* report quotes Sara Wood, Farfetch vice president – product, as saying: "Visual search is the ultimate connection between on and offline inspiration. By allowing our customers to

> **"Visual search is the ultimate connection between online and offline inspiration."**

show us what they are interested in we gain a deeper understanding of their needs, are able to inspire them with fashion based on what they are looking for, and enable a more personalized shopping experience."[99] An August 2019 article in *Forbes* notes that in the "last six years, visual search market revenue has increased 29% year-over-year, according to Statista. It's clearly a medium savvy marketers must pay attention to."[100]

Virtual Reality, Augmented Reality and Mixed Reality

Retailers have been using virtual reality (VR) and augmented reality (AR) to enhance customer experience and help with their decision-making. Shoemaker **Lacoste** has an app that allows you to try on sneakers virtually. Cosmetics firms **Charlotte Tilbury** and **Estée Lauder** have installed AR-enabled mirrors in-store. Customers can see how different styles of makeup would look on them without actually wearing any of it. *See Exhibit 4).* Footwear, clothing and accessories firm **Timberland** set up a virtual fitting room. Eyeglasses firm **Warby**

---

[99] Syte Partners With Farfetch to Power Their New 'See It, Snap It, Shop It' Feature. Business Wire press release, December 7, 2018. https://www.businesswire.com/news/home/20181207005345/en/Syte-Partners-Farfetch-Power-New-%E2%80%98See-Snap

[100] "What's Visual Search? And Why Smart Marketers Should Care," Forbes, August 14, 2019. https://www.forbes.com/sites/courtstroud/2019/08/14/whats-visual-search-and-why-smart-marketers-should-care/#4aefae7c6967

Parker has gone a step further. It uses face-mapping technology on iPhone X to map a person's face and employs that data to recommend appropriate frames for that individual. A 2018 blog on Shopify titled *How These Retailers Use Augmented Reality to Enhance the Customer Experience,* notes that "61% of consumers prefer stores that offer AR experiences — and 40% of them would pay more for your product if they have the chance to experience it through AR."[101]

EXHIBIT 4

Retail Innovation with Augmented Reality

Smart mirrors are another retail innovation that uses augmented reality to enhance customer experience. For example, Estée Lauder is enhancing the consumer experience by enabling customers to enjoy the augmented reality experience of instantly, and virtually, trying on makeup, whether visiting an Estée Lauder beauty counter, or accessing the technology from a home computer or mobile phone.

Photo courtesy of Estée Lauder

---

[101] "How These Retailers Use Augmented Reality to Enhance the Customer Experience," Shopify Retail Marketing Blog, February 21, 2018. https://www.shopify.in/retail/how-these-retailers-are-using-augmented-reality-to-enhance-the-customer-experience

There is also 'mixed reality' (MR)—a blend of physical and virtual worlds. It includes both real and computer-generated objects and combines aspects of VR and AR. The enormous advances in VR, AR, MR and the umbrella of extended reality (XR) have an increasing range of applications in all industries from live entertainment and gaming through product design and architecture to learning and life-saving medical applications. Automobile firms like **Ford** for instance are using MR to develop new concepts for vehicle designs quicker and cheaper. Designers wearing wireless headsets are able to see several digital designs as if these were already part of an actual vehicle. Say a designer wants to assess how a vehicle's side mirror aesthetics affects a driver's view. This typically takes days but with MR it can be done in minutes and even seconds. A report on the Microsoft website titled, "Make Way for Holograms: New Mixed Reality Technology Meets Car Design as Ford Tests Hololens Globally" offers some insights into how manufacturers such as Ford have been able to use new technology to transform the auto design process.

> Retailers have been using virtual reality and augmented reality to enhance customer experience.

Use Social Media

Personalization has a strong social element. While it is tempting to treat every individual as being unique, a great deal of social clustering happens based on preferences, likes and dislikes, peer groups and user profiles. Netflix is a good example of this. While its recommendation engines are hyper-personalized, the content creation is social-cluster driven.

In this new, connected age, people love to express their preferences on social media. And typically, those who use social media to express themselves like to be perceived as unique personalities. They like to be seen as distinct individuals. Leverage this mindset. Reach out to them as individuals on social media. You can be sure it will give them a positive stroke and in turn evoke a positive response toward you. Social is also a great medium to garner information about what they want from you and your industry. Real-time analysis of consumer conversations on social media is an excellent way of monitoring their preferences and their concerns. If your customers feel that you are listening to them, that you care about them and that you value their input, it will make them trust you more. This in turn will increase brand loyalty and engagement. It could also be a great risk management tool. Real-time monitoring of discussions on social networks can help you to identify potential problems. You can manage them effectively before they blow up in your face.

Take **Sephora,** the beauty chain owned by luxury French fashion house LVMH. In mid-2019, Grammy-nominated singer SZA (pronounced Sizza) tweeted that she had been racially profiled at a Sephora store in California. Sephora apologized to SZA and shut down all its U.S. stores, distribution centers and corporate offices for an hour to conduct diversity training for its employees. While skeptics questioned the effectiveness of this move from Sephora, others felt it has some value. In an article in the *Guardian*, Shaun Gabbidon, a professor of criminal justice at Pennsylvania State University –

> **Real-time monitoring of discussions on social networks can help identify potential problems.**

Harrisburg, said "There's still value in the symbolic gesture of it. It does send a message about its values." The Guardian reported Sephora as saying that the one-hour training was the start of a larger diversity initiative.[102]

Here are some suggestions on how you can use social media for personalization. On Twitter, use Twitter lists—curated groups of Twitter accounts. Target your products and services with personalized

---

[102] "Sephora Closes All US Stores for Diversity Training After Racial Profiling Allegation," The Guardian, June 5, 2019. https://www.theguardian.com/us-news/2019/jun/05/sephora-beauty-store-fashion-diversity-training

messages to people using hashtags relevant to your business. Join Twitter conversations relevant to your business. On Facebook, when people post comments on your company's or brand's page, be sure to respond. Repost their comments about you when appropriate. If a customer has had a special experience with you, request them to post a short video talking about it. See what your Facebook followers are interested in and create interactive engagements around these areas. On Instagram, you could post photographs of your customers (with their consent, of course) experiencing your products or services. Encourage them to generate content for you. Later in the chapter you will see how Italian shoe maker Sergio Rossi is using social media app WeChat to empower customers in China to design their own footwear.

Think about these and other ways in which you can use the different technologies for creating hyper-personalization in your own businesses.

Get a Single View of the Customer

Information about customers must be comprehensive, aggregated, centralized, and integrated across all products and services.

Even as you examine these strategies and how you can use different technologies for hyper-personalization, remember that if you are a company that caters to customers across multiple products and services, you must have a coordinated strategy. This requires that you must have a 'single view' of the customer. What does this mean? Simply this: Build a rich 360-degree view of customers in real-time and make sure that all departments serving a particular customer have the same holistic data about that individual. In other words, information about every customer must be comprehensive, aggregated, centralized, and integrated across all your products and services. Unless you have this single view of the customer, you can't drive hyper-personalization effectively. This is the problem with most banks, for instance. Various divisions such as consumer lending, mortgage, credit card, savings and wealth management don't talk to one another. So, while a bank may be servicing the same customer five times over, often they lack a single, comprehensive view. This silo-ed approach can hamper the bank's ability to offer the best personalized experience.

One could argue that when it comes to the B2B world, the situation with most (provider) organizations is that they are dealing with (client) organizations that themselves have multiple business units and different decision-makers in each division. That's true. And in such a scenario, silo-ed departments of the provider organization can perhaps still offer personalized solutions to the customer's different divisions. However, it will not be as ideal as the entire (provider) organization having a single view of the customer organization and an integrated approach toward the customer. And, of course, always remember that in the B2B scenario also it is imperative that you focus on your customers' customers.

> **In the B2B scenario, it is imperative to focus on your customers' customers.**

Sometimes, even in the B2C world, the decision-maker could be different from the actual buyer. For instance, in the case of gaming, the decision-maker could be a teenager, as opposed to the parent who is the actual buyer. So here again, there could be complications getting the single view of the customer. But ultimately, that is the ideal you need to strive toward. Our recommendation is that even if your company works in silos, make sure that all departments and divisions have the customer as their central focus and that the company as a whole has an integrated data strategy.

Develop An Integrated Data Strategy

Let us see what this entails. Typically, in a traditional enterprise, as we saw in the example of the bank, customer data is scattered across many different systems. What's more, these systems speak in different data forms. So the same customer in one data system—say the mortgage data system—appears differently in the retail banking data system. This problem is one of data-dialect, i.e. how will these data communicate in a way that presents a unified picture of the customer? There is also the issue of making contextual information available in real-time. Let us go back to the earlier example of a customer who swipes a credit card at a mall and is told immediately about a discounted offer from a service provider at another store in the same location. Typically, the information of a credit card swipe goes back into a data store and gets reconciled overnight. This means that by the time the information about the discounted offer gets to the customer, it is no longer relevant.

We believe that an effective way to solve these problems is through what we call the minimum viable data solution. Basically, you don't need to have all the information that you've stored over the years in multiple systems to provide contextual information. You just need the transaction information at the time it is being done, plus the contextual information that is available when the customer is actually swiping the card, i.e. the minimum set of data points needed to make it efficient right there without having to go through multiple systems. We also believe it's important to build what we call 'knowledge models.' If you have knowledge models that are good enough, even if they are not perfect, you can solve the data-dialect problem. These are two effective ways in which you can take advantage of real-time data, and solve data-related issues without having to completely overhaul your entire data program.

> **An effective way to solve problems is through the minimum viable data solution.**

Also, the traditional approach is that companies believe they need to get some good use cases out of their data. We recommend a different approach: Start with customer use cases. For instance, going back to the example of the credit card transaction, the service provider just needs to ask what kind of data it would need to make an offer to a customer while they are still shopping at the mall, and then work at getting access to just that data. This is in line with what we discussed in Chapter 2—the customer-centric, front-to-back approach, instead of the traditional back-to-front model.

In the rest of this chapter we will provide a few more examples of how companies in different industries are offering hyper-personalized experiences to their customers. As you go through each of them, see what you can learn from them and, more importantly, think about how you can go beyond these ideas and strategies to design your own.

Retail

Amazon

Earlier in the book, we saw how Amazon has been able to entrench itself deeply into a customer's life because of its wide array of products and services. This enables it to gather more and more data about each customer and thereby gain a stronger understanding of the customer's needs and wants. Through its use of AI and strong recommendation engines, it is able to personalize its offerings for each customer. Amazon has also cleverly converted Amazon Prime, its

> **Value-added services attract customers to Amazon Prime; to justify their subscription, they order more things.**

subscription service, into a personalization platform that feeds multiple products and service lines – from retail to music to video to audio books. Free shipping and value-added services attract customers into Prime, and then to justify their subscription, they end up ordering more things. In April 2019, Amazon started offering discounts to its Whole Foods customers if they were Prime members. See how all this keeps the customer locked into Amazon. Prime members tend to be more loyal and also spend more than non-Prime members. All this enables Amazon to gather more data about them and further hyper-personalize its offerings to them. In his letter to the shareholders in April 2018, for the first time CEO Jeff Bezos revealed the number of Prime members – 100 million worldwide.[103] With its smart speaker Echo and voice-activated assistant Alexa, Amazon wants to become an even more integral part of its customers' lives, add to the data it has about them, increase its level of hyper-personalization and move ahead on its vision of becoming everyone's personal everything store. In Ch. 2, we discussed Amazon Go, Amazon's first-of-its-kind cashier-less store. Think about how Amazon is using so many different ways to transform and personalize the shopping experience for its customers *(See Exhibit 5)*.

EXHIBIT 5

AI Transforms In-store Shopping Experience

Amazon Go is a new kind of store with no lines and no checkout—you just grab and go! Their checkout-free shopping experience is made possible by their "Just Walk Out" Technology, that uses a variety of technologies including computer vision, sensor fusion, and advanced machine learning. It automatically detects when products are taken from or returned to the shelves and keeps track of them in a virtual cart. After you shop and leave, Amazon charges your account and sends you a receipt. As of today there are 26 stores in operation. The first store, located in one of the company buildings, opened to employees on December 5, 2016 and to the public on January 22, 2018.

Source: Amazon Go, https://www.amazon.com/b?node=16008589011, June 2020.

---

[103] Jeff Bezos, 2017 Letter to Shareholders. https://blog.aboutamazon.com/company-news/2017-letter-to-shareholders/

eBay

At online retailer eBay, an initiative to drive hyper-personalization involves asking users directly what they are interested in, through a feature called Interests. eBay launched this feature in May 2018. The etailer recognizes that shopping through a collection of more than a billion products across various categories can be tiresome and exhausting. Through Interests, it seeks to use technology to curate its selection and personalize the customer's shopping experience based on their "passions, hobbies, and style."

> **eBay seeks to give all customers their own unique and personalized store.**

So how does this work? Through the use of data (about what people typically look for) and algorithms, eBay has created lots of different themes like apparel, electronics, sports, etc. The new personalization tool on the company's mobile app has a short questionnaire asking shoppers which themes they are interested in. The questionnaire lists various options and the customers have to only check the relevant boxes. eBay combines this information shared by the customers with data drawn from their previous searches and purchases. It then generates a customized homepage with recommendations unique to every customer. Customers can keep editing their choices on the mobile app. This allows eBay to continue to offer them relevant recommendations.

According to Bradford Shellhammer, vice president, buyer experience at eBay, with its numerous Interest combinations and getting to know its customers' preferences, eBay can give everyone their own unique and personalized store.[104]

Shellhammer explains that the strategy behind Interests is not just to throw up products that consumers are likely to buy but also to keep consumers engaged with eBay. "The new strategy is focused

---

[104] "Shop Your Interests With New Personalized eBay Experience," eBay News Team, May 17, 2018. https://www.ebayinc.com/stories/news/shop-your-interests-with-new-personalized-ebay-experience/

more on not getting it wrong, which means pulling enough of the stuff that is irrelevant out of the way so that you keep exploring, because eventually you'll fall in love with something."[105]

Walmart

Need it. Text it. Get it. That was the tagline of a personal shopping and concierge service called Jetblack, which Walmart launched in May 2018. The service was discontinued in February 2020. According to a post on the Jetblack website, its text-to-shop technology will be used by Walmart to power its conversational commerce capabilities and build new experiences for customers. The first service to be introduced from Walmart's technology incubator Store No 8, Jetblack used a combination of AI and human expertise from professional buyers. At the time of the launch Jennifer Fleiss, co-founder and CEO of Jetblack, said: "Consumers are looking for more efficient ways to shop for themselves and their families without having to compromise on product quality. With Jetblack, we have created an entirely new concept that enables consumers to get exactly what they need through the convenience of text messaging and the freedom of a nearly unlimited product catalog. We are confident this service will make shopping frictionless, more personalized and delightful." Marc Lore, president and CEO of Walmart U.S. e-commerce, believes that "powered by conversational commerce, the future of retail will bring convenience and high-touch personalization to the forefront for consumers everywhere."[106]

> **"The future of retail will bring convenience and high-touch personalization to the forefront."**

---

[105] "We Tried Out eBay's Newest Personalization Feature, And It Should Have Amazon Terrified," AOL, May 24, 2018. https://www.aol.com/article/finance/2018/05/24/ebay-personalization-amazon/23442962/

[106] Credit: Jetblack Launches in New York City for Busy Families, Delivering a Curated Shopping Experience That's One Text Away, May 31, 2018, Business Wire. Used by permission

A "members-by-invitation-only" offering priced at $50 a month, Jetblack was aimed at affluent, time-strapped shoppers, especially mothers. The service was rolled out in Manhattan and parts of Brooklyn for products across a range of categories like toiletries, household items, clothes, footwear, toys and so on. Members were on-boarded over a 10-minute phone call during which Jetblack gathered data about their likes and dislikes, favorite brands and so on. Members could also invite Jetblack employees to visit their homes and go through their cupboards to collect more information about their preferences. After this, whenever members wanted to buy anything, they needed to just text their requirements to Jetblack's AI-powered chatbot named 'J', which sent the members a short list of options to choose from. Once the member made the selection, Jetblack delivered the products to them by courier the same or next day at no additional charge. Members could also take a picture of a product that they wanted delivered or capture a screenshot from the web, and send the image to J. Anything that the member did not like could be returned. Jetblack collected feedback on every item that was retained or returned. Using this data, it fine-tuned future recommendations to sync better with the clients' preferences. The products were sourced primarily from Walmart and its subsidiary Jet.com, although where required Jetblack tapped other retailers also.

Stitch Fix

Similar to Walmart's Jetblack, San Francisco-based Stitch Fix, an online personal styling and shopping service, combines technology with human expertise to deliver a personalized and convenient shopping experience to its customers. But unlike Jetblack, Stitch Fix is open to everyone and there is no membership or subscription fee. Stitch Fix says it leverages data science to deliver personalization at scale. In a *Harvard*

> **Stitch Fix leverages data science to deliver personalization at scale.**

Business Review article in May 2018, Stitch Fix founder and CEO Katrina Lake says: "Data science isn't woven into our culture; it *is* our culture." Explaining the human element, Lake goes on to add: "A good person plus a good algorithm is far superior to the best person or the best algorithm alone. We aren't pitting people and data against each other. We need them to work together."[107]

> **"We aren't pitting people and data against each other. We need them to work together."**

And remember what we said earlier about how social can play a role in personalization? Well, Stitch Fix not only encourages its customers to give feedback on each item that they liked or disliked, but it also encourages them to add links to their Pinterest, LinkedIn, Twitter or Instagram accounts at the bottom of their Stitch Fix style profiles so that it can get to know them better and make better recommendations.

This is how Stitch Fix works. After a customer signs up at Stitch Fix, they fill out a style profile with information about their size, style preferences, price range, and so on. Based on this, the Stitch Fix algorithms make recommendations. A Stitch Fix stylist then handpicks pieces to fit the customer's tastes, needs and budget. This is mailed to the customer at a predetermined date. Each box contains a curated selection of five clothing and accessory items; it is customized to fit the individual's preferences and needs. After trying out the items, the customer can keep the ones they like and send the rest back in a prepaid United States Postal Service (USPS) envelope. There is no membership or shipping fee. Customers pay only for the items they keep. There is an upfront $20 styling fee which is applied as a credit toward anything the customer buys.

---

[107] "Stitch Fix's CEO on Selling Personal Style to the Mass Market," Harvard Business Review, May-June 2018. https://hbr.org/2018/05/stitch-fixs-ceo-on-selling-personal-style-to-the-mass-market

Stitch Fix has an inventory-led model. According to Lake: "Using data to better understand what people want enables us to turn over inventory faster than many conventional retailers do, because we can buy the right things and get them to the right people. Selling inventory fast enough to pay vendors with cash from clients turns out to be a very capital-efficient model." The service is available for now only in the U.S. though there are plans to expand to other countries. Stitch Fix was launched in 2011 and went public in November 2017 at a valuation of $1.6 billion. In October 2019, its valuation was $2.2 billion. The company carries more than 700 brands and has some 2 million active users in the U.S.

Sergio Rossi

Like Stitch Fix, Italian luxury shoe brand Sergio Rossi is taking personalization to the masses. But its route is different. Apart from offering personalization on its website, this shoe maker's strategy is to target customers in China via a WeChat mini-program, a separate mobile app within WeChat, China's popular multipurpose messaging, mobile payment and social media app. Sergio Rossi in September 2018 launched the personalization service to woo China's large and digitally-savvy market through WeChat, which has some one billion active monthly users. The WeChat mini-program for Sergio Rossi demonstrates how customers can design a shoe, enables them to design their shoes and then shows them a 360-degree digital preview of their creation. Once they are satisfied with it, customers can buy it through the app. Like Nike, Sergio Rossi lets customers choose from a variety of options relating to material, color and other elements of the shoe. With every element they choose, the customer gets to see how the shoe looks and also how the price of the shoe changes.

> With every element they choose, customers can see how the shoe looks and its price.

Automotive

Mercedes Benz

Like most high-end automakers, Mercedes Benz allows you to build your own vehicles. You can do this online. Once you chose the model you want from the company's fleet of sedans, wagons, coupes, SUVs, convertibles, roadsters, electric and hybrid vehicles, you can choose the elements comprising the vehicle's exterior, interior, entertainment and convenience, and performance and safety features from a range of options. So for the exterior, for instance, you can choose from a range of colors, wheel types, wheel inserts, license plate frames, and so on. For the interior, you can choose the kind and color of upholstery you want, you can choose to add on ventilated front seats, heated rear seats, heated steering wheel, ambient lighting and illuminated window sills, rear side window shades. When it comes to entertainment and convenience, you can choose from packages that include a navigation device, blind spot assist, or voice control features. Then there are additional features like three-zone climate control and rear-seat entertainment. In accessories, you could opt for things like iPad docking station and safety case for tablets. Like some of the other examples in this chapter, you can customize the vehicle you choose on a platform that Mercedes Benz provides.

> Like most high-end automakers, Mercedes Benz allows you to build your own vehicles.

Ducati

Ducati, an Italian motorcycle company owned by Germany's Audi Group, is an example of how a company is building its brand through an "ownership experience." It gives its customers the option to configure their bikes—you can get a range of accessories like side panniers, heated grips, LED turn indicators, silencers, mudguards and so on. You can also buy Ducati apparel including jackets, shirts, sweatshirts, t-shirts, leather trousers, caps, or scarves. And then, it goes a step further. The company offers customers a visit to its factory and the Ducati Museum, has dedicated Ducati grandstands at races and hosts events like the World Ducati Week to give its customers a sense of "belonging to the family." The different models from the premium motorcycle-maker include Diavel, Hypermotard, Monster, Multistrada, Superbike, SuperSport and Scrambler.

Health Care & Wellness

IBM's Watson

IBM's AI platform Watson is driving hyper-personalization in health care. Trained by oncologists at Memorial Sloan Kettering Cancer Center (MSK) in New York City, Watson can understand key data associated with a patient including results from

> IBM's Watson combines data with medical literature to derive its recommended diagnosis and treatment.

blood tests, pathology, imaging reports and the presence of genetic mutations. Combining patient data with vast amounts of medical literature—Watson browses through publications in all languages – it comes up with its recommended diagnosis and treatment for each case. According to an article in The ASCO Post (American Society of Clinical Oncology) titled *How Watson for Oncology Is Advancing Personalized Patient Care*, "using natural language processing software to understand written language and probabilistic algorithms, Watson is able to read and understand millions of pages of text to zero in on information relevant to clinicians' queries and generate multiple possibilities for use in making treatment decisions."[108]

In a study conducted on 638 patients with breast cancer at the Manipal Comprehensive Cancer Center in India, it was found

---

[108] "How Watson for Oncology Is Advancing Personalized Patient Care," The ASCO Post, June 25, 2017. https://ascopost.com/issues/june-25-2017/how-watson-for-oncology-is-advancing-personalized-patient-care/

that 90% of Watson recommendations were concordant with the treatments recommended by the cancer center's tumor board. What's more, while it took physicians an average of 12 to 40 minutes to give their treatment recommendations, it took Watson just 40 seconds. It is expected that as Watson trains with more patients, it will get better at creating personalized treatment plans. Watson, of course, does not replace the physicians. It is an interactive system and the final recommendation to the patients is made by the physicians.

According to Mark G. Kris, MD, lead physician of the Memorial Sloan Kettering–IBM Watson Collaboration, while the initial use of Watson is to "provide a platform to show the different treatment choices for a specific patient and use that information in the treatment decision-making process," what he is really excited about is that "they have built into Watson the ability to create a total care plan for patients with breast cancer that includes not just the treatment the oncologist is planning today, but what may be needed in the future, such as surgery, radiation therapy, or hormonal therapy, so the patient knows what to expect in both the short and long-term."[109]

Novartis

The Novartis-Microsoft alliance takes on the next wave of challenges in medicine.

In October 2019, Swiss multinational pharmaceutical firm Novartis joined hands with Microsoft to set up an AI innovation lab. This strategic alliance, considered to be one of the most expansive between big pharma and big-tech, has two key objectives: AI empowerment and AI exploration. The lab will bring together Microsoft's advanced AI solutions and Novartis vast datasets to create new AI models and applications. This is expected to enable Novartis take on the next

---

[109] "How Watson for Oncology Is Advancing Personalized Patient Care," The ASCO Post, June 25, 2017. https://ascopost.com/issues/june-25-2017/how-watson-for-oncology-is-advancing-personalized-patient-care/

wave of challenges in medicine. The lab will also use AI to solve some of the toughest computational challenges within life sciences like generative chemistry. In an article in *Financial Times*, Novartis CEO Vasant (Vas) Narasimhan said that by applying AI methods to its data sets, Novartis expected "to identify the 'super-responding' patient populations, or patient populations that uniquely respond to different medicines, which then could lead to further testing." Narasimhan indicated that this could result in more personalized medicines in the future.[110]

Penn Medicine

Penn Medicine, the University of Pennsylvania's health system, is at the forefront of immunotherapy — i.e. enabling and empowering an individual's own immune system to fight a disease. CAR-T cell therapy, a form of immunotherapy developed by Penn Medicine, genetically retrains an individual's healthy cells to hunt down and eliminate cancer cells in their body. These engineered cells continue in the individual's body even after the cancer is eliminated and act as permanent protection against the disease. Though these are early days still, CAR-T is believed to represent a turning point in the history of human medicine. Penn Medicine calls this the 'ImmunoRevolution'.

> Cancer treatment vaccines are sometimes made with cells from the patient's own tumor.

Penn Medicine has also developed other personalized immunotherapy such as vaccine therapy for cancer treatment. How does this work? Well, when a body is under attack by an outside organism such as a bacteria or a virus, its immune system responds and attacks the foreign body. But the immune system does not recognize cancer cells as being outsiders. Therefore, it does not mount

---

[110] "Novartis and Microsoft Join Forces to Develop Drugs Using AI," Financial Times, October 1, 2019. https://www.ft.com/content/93e532ee-e3a5-11e9-b112-9624ec9edc59

an immune response against them. Cancer vaccines stimulate the immune system to recognize the cancer cells as foreign and to attack them. Cancer treatment vaccines are sometimes made with cells from the patient's own tumor. These cells are modified in the lab and then put back in the patient's body where they destroy or delay the cancer's growth.

Moderna Therapeutics

Startups like Moderna Therapeutics, Quentis Therapeutics, Tempest Therapeutics are also working on cancer immunotherapies. They are creating next-generation therapies such as messenger ribonucleic acid (mRNA) medicines, personalized vaccines and immune-stimulating gut microbes. The Massachusetts-based Moderna, for instance, is developing mRNA medicines. The mRNA is a single-stranded molecule that carries genetic code from DNA in a cell's nucleus to ribosomes, the cell's protein-making machine. mRNA medicines are sets of instructions that instruct a patient's cells to produce proteins that could prevent, treat, or cure a disease. Moderna believes that using mRNA, it can develop a new generation of transformative medicines for patients.

> Moderna plans to use mRNA to develop a new generation of transformative medicines.

Novo Nordisk and Glooko

In January 2017, NovoNordisk, the global health care provider known for its diabetes care, and Glooko, the California- based diabetes data management platform, entered into a collaboration to develop digital health solutions for people with diabetes. Their first jointly developed product Cornerstones4Care (C4C), a mobile app for personalized diabetes management, was introduced in July 2017. The C4C app combines Novo Nordisk's knowledge of diabetes and personalized patient support with Glooko's expertise in data analytics and its digital platform. NovoNordisk and Glooko say that the four cornerstones of the C4C app are healthy eating, being active, medicine, and tracking, and that it "delivers content that's built around you and where you are in your diabetes journey."

The app uses Glooko's technology to sync a user's blood glucose and activity data from diabetes and exercise devices, and also identifies trends that impact blood glucose levels. The C4C enables people with diabetes to easily measure and track their blood glucose level, activity and meals all in one place – their mobile phones. At the time of the launch, Rick Altinger, then CEO of Glooko, said in a press statement, "More people than ever are using mobile apps for chronic disease management, and the apps, like the new C4C app, go beyond data capture or tracking to provide insights and recommendations based on that data."[111]

> **Novo Nordisk is working with Glooko to strengthen its digital health platform.**

Novo Nordisk is also working with Glooko to strengthen its digital health platform. Being developed along with IBM Watson Health, this is a diabetes management system which stores and analyzes data and delivers real-time feedback to people with diabetes. Novo Nordisk expects that over time, this will enable it to provide more specific and more personalized guidance to patients.

Nestle

Nestlé, the world's largest food company, is using people's DNA to create personalized diets. This is expected to keep customers healthy and add years to their lives. An August 2018 article in *Bloomberg* reports that Nestlé has launched a wellness program called the Nestlé

---

[111] PR newswire press release, July 12, 2017. https://www.prnewswire.com/news-releases/novo-nordisk-and-glooko-advance-their-digital-health-collaboration-with-launch-of-unique-integrated-app-for-improved-diabetes-management-300487023.html

Wellness Ambassador in Japan in which more than 100,000 people have enrolled. Nestlé sends these people a home DNA collection kit and also encourages them to share pictures of what they eat. After analyzing the data that it gets from an individual's DNA and insights from the photos, Nestlé sends them specially formulated food supplements and also suggests lifestyle changes. The program costs some $600 a year for capsules that make nutrient-rich teas, smoothies and other products such as vitamin-fortified snacks.[112]

Nestlé is looking at wellness as a significant growth category in line with the growing consumer interest in this area and expects nutritional drinks and supplements to grow into a nearly $1 billion business within a decade. In his book *Nutrition for a Better Life* published in 2016, former Nestlé CEO Peter Brabeck-Letmathe says personalized diet and health programs are the future of nutrition.

Consumer Packaged Goods

Coca-Cola

Vending machines and soda fountains have been around for years but the beverage giant, The Coca-Cola Company, has transformed them to give customers a new experience. Coca-Cola's new-age soda fountain called 'Freestyle' allows customers to not only order from the featured beverages, but also create their own drinks. The touchscreen-operated dispenser was first introduced in 2009 and since then has been upgraded with features such as a mobile app and Bluetooth connectivity. Unlike a traditional soda fountain that

> **Coca-Cola's new-age soda fountain called 'Freestyle' lets customers create their own drinks.**

---

112 "Nestle Wants Your DNA," Bloomberg, August 30, 2018. https://www.bloomberg.com/news/articles/2018-08-29/nestle-wants-your-dna-and-foodie-pics-to-sell-you-supplements

typically offers only six to eight options, the Freestyle has nearly 200 drink options – including 117 low/no-calorie beverages. These include varieties which are not available anywhere else. Customers can also create their own drinks using the ingredients. Once you order from the existing options or create your personal drink, you can save your preferences on the app for future use. You can also share it on social media. No prizes for guessing why.

Coca-Cola's Freestyle dispensers offer more variety to the customers, while allowing what the company believes is an engaging and personal experience. The tech-smart dispensing machine and the app offer a ton of customer data including geographical locations, choice of beverages, volume of consumption, time of consumption and so on. It also helps Coca-Cola understand how customers respond to promotions, discounts and other offers. This allows for more relevant, personalized and targeted promotions that offer greater value to customers and drive loyalty.

> **A disruptive innovation of 2009 has become a billion-dollar business for the beverage maker.**

According to Coca-Cola, more than 50,000 Freestyle units pour 14 million drinks a day in various locations such as cinemas, restaurants and convenience stores across the United States and some other countries. A disruptive innovation of 2009 has now become a billion-dollar business for the beverage maker. Chris Hellmann, global vice president and general manager, Coca-Cola Freestyle, says in an article on the company website: "Choice and customization are not fads – they're here to stay. So we're focused on making sure the Coca-Cola Freestyle platform stays current and contemporary and that we continue to offer more beverages people want."[113]

---

[113] "Coca-Cola Freestyle Unveils Next-Gen Fountain Dispenser, New Operating System and More," The Coca-Cola Company website, May 18, 2018. https://www.coca-colacompany.com/news/freestyle-unveils-new-dispenser-and-more

Paper Boat

In India, Hector Beverages, the maker of ethnic beverage brand Paper Boat, which sells around a dozen products across 50 SKUs, is customizing some of its products to cater to regional tastes. Take its buttermilk, for instance. The company sells this drink in four southern states of India. In Karnataka the buttermilk is infused with curry leaves, while in Tamil Nadu it is flavored with green chillies, and in Andhra Pradesh and Telangana with ginger. For its mango-based drink Aam Panna, the company uses the local variety of mangoes in different states.

Neeraj Kakkar, co-founder and CEO of Hector Beverages, says the company uses its proprietary customer feedback analytics platform and modifies its recipes based on this. "Today, with the use of technology we can get granular data on customer preferences and we can make economies of scale possible without trading off on customization. To make these changes, all we have to do is to change the recipes online. This is done on computers and takes just two to three minutes." Kakkar adds that he considers this kind of personalization is crucial for premium products like Paper Boat to gain scale. "As we penetrate deeper into the market, the changes that we make to cater to local taste add more value for our customers and drive sales."

Nomige

Belgium-based personal care company Nomige, founded in October 2017 by Dr. Barbara Geusens, a biomedical engineer with a doctorate in dermatological sciences, offers personalized skin care to customers. So what does this entail? Well, typically, skincare products are categorized in four skin types: dry skin, oily skin, mixed skin and sensitive skin. Unlike these off-the-shelf offerings, Nomige's products are tailored to an individual's DNA and lifestyle. The thinking behind this is that a person's skin and the way it ages is unique and significantly influenced by DNA and lifestyle and that the analysis of a person's genes offers insights that cannot be discovered in any other way.

At Nomige, once a customer buys the "Nomige package" (which can be done online), they have to fill an online form sharing details of their lifestyle. After this, they receive a DNA test kit from the company (by mail) along with instructions on how to do a DNA swab. The customer has to send the DNA swab back to the company, which then analyzes the DNA in a certified genetic lab. Based on the information it obtains from mapping the customer's DNA along with the lifestyle information, Nomige can determine their genetic skin profile. For instance, it can determine if the customer is inherently prone to dry skin, or if that is the result of that individual's lifestyle and habits. Following this assessment, Nomige formulates a personalized skin care package for the customer using specific ingredients so that their skin gets exactly what it requires. Each package consists of four products: a day serum, a day/lifestyle cream, a night cream and a night serum. Each product has a specific target and focuses on compensating the 'defects' in the individual's biological processes of skin aging. Geusens says Nomige is General Data Protection Regulation (GDPR) compliant; the customer's DNA is destroyed after analysis and all data is handled anonymously.

> **Nomige's personal care products are tailored to an individual's DNA and lifestyle.**

Given its nature of service and products, Nomige follows an 'on-demand' process. This means every order is processed individually. So far, the company has some 600 customers, primarily from Europe and a few from Dubai, India and Singapore, but Geusens has plans to take it global. She says initially she will try to coordinate as much as possible from Belgium. When volumes rise, she will probably need to set up operations locally for a more efficient flow. In the U.K. and Poland, Nomige is expanding via exclusivity contracts with skin clinics or DNA clinics. Geusens says that given the nature of her business, scaling has its own challenges but technology like CRM systems, automation, chatbots and faster DNA analysis can play a significant role. Geusens adds: "Personalization is very labor-intensive. We make tailor-made products like a tailored suit. Good and personal customer support is key." According to Geusens, Nomige has a 65% loyalty rate.

Media

ByteDance—Jinri Toutiao

In China, ByteDance, a startup founded in 2012, offers personalized news streams to its users via an app called Jinri Toutiao which in Chinese means "today's headlines." The news app first collects articles and videos from third-party providers like traditional media, government organizations, private companies, small publishers and individual content creators. Then, using AI algorithms it personalizes content for its users. The AI basically learns by tracking a user's behavior on the app. For instance, the AI tracks what stories a user dismisses and which ones they read and for how long, at what point do they switch to another post, what stories they read at different times of the day, what is their physical location, and so on. It then personalizes a user's feed accordingly. In April 2017, Toutiao added a social section where people can post short updates.

> **ByteDance offers personalized news streams to its users via AI, which tracks user behavior.**

Toutiao's revenues are primarily from advertisements. According to market estimates Toutiao is installed on more than 240 million unique devices and has some 120 million daily users, which makes it one of China's leading news aggregators. Its parent ByteDance is considered one of the most successful startups not only in China, but globally. According to media reports, in October 2018 ByteDance raised funding at a valuation of $75 billion.[114]

---

[114] "ByteDance Is Said to Secure Funding at Record $75 Billion Value," Bloomberg, October 26, 2018. https://www.bloomberg.com/news/articles/2018-10-26/bytedance-is-said-to-secure-funding-at-record-75-billion-value

ByteDance also owns TikTok, the short-form mobile video app. With this app, users can create and share short, snappy videos of any and every activity—be it dancing, playing, eating, applying makeup, or what have you. In early 2019, this app, fast becoming a strong rival to Facebook and Instagram, crossed one billion downloads. By November 2019, this number was reported to have crossed 1.5 billion. During the COVID-19 pandemic, TikTok saw a huge increase. According to mobile app market intelligence firm Sensor Tower, in Q1 2020, TikTok had more than 315 million installs across Apple App Store and Google Play Store – this was the highest number in a quarter ever for any app *(See Exhibit 6)*.

EXHIBIT 6

TikTok Growth During the Pandemic

The pandemic has lead to a huge increase in the use of digital communication, games, entertainment, and collaboration apps. For example, TikTok is thriving during the global pandemic. As of April, 29, 2020, the social media platform has been downloaded more than 2 billion times globally. It was downloaded 315 million times in the first quarter of 2020 in the App Store and Google Play combined. Notably, these app download figures don't account for third-party app stores that are popular in China. Sensor Tower says India, China, and the U.S. are the countries that account for the most downloads. It's also important to note that downloads don't indicate active users.

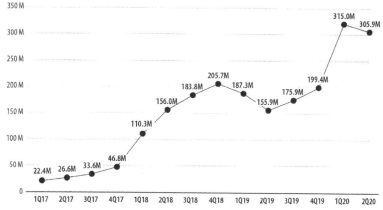

TikTok Global Downloads by Quarter

Source: Sensor Tower Store Intelligence. April 29, 2020.

We see TikTok as a great example of the power of user-generated content. One big challenge for TikTok however involves concerns from lawmakers over its content moderation policies—how does it decide what its users can and can't say and do. In response to this, in March 2020, TikTok set up a Content Advisory Council comprising technology and safety experts to help it shape its policies for the present and the future.

Editorji

In India, startup Editorji Technologies founded by journalist Vikram Chandra, is doing something similar. In September 2018, the startup launched Editorji, a video news app that offers personalized video news feeds to its viewers. Once users sign up for Editorji they have the option to share information about what kind of news they would like to see. The app asks them to tap once on a category that they like, two for a category they love and three for the ones that they dislike. The options include local, national and international news, sports, business, lifestyle, politics, technology, etc. Viewers can also indicate the preferred duration of each story—from 5 minutes to 15 minutes. In addition, the app allows viewers to post their comments on a story, add these to the newscast and share it. Chandra says this feature enables users to create their "own news channel." Editorji is backed by telecom firm Bharti Telecom and newspaper publisher HT Media. Going ahead, possible revenue models for Editorji include advertising, branded content, premium services and content partnerships.[115]

> Possible revenue models for Editorji include advertising, branded content, premium services and content partnerships.

---

[115] "AI-Based News App Editorji Launched," livemint, September 26, 2018. https://www.livemint.com/Consumer/cNkVLUjbW2q18t9gkIabJK/AIbased-news-app-Editor-ji-launched.html

Make Your Data Policies GDPR Compliant

We would like to add a note of caution here. As you go about your efforts at personalization, remember the big issue of data privacy. The critical question is who owns the data. Our position on this is straightforward. We think the European standards and the GDPR are setting a benchmark for what is going to happen to the rest of the world; that the data is owned by the users and unless you have express user permission to use their data, you shouldn't be able to access it or do anything with it. We are increasingly seeing that companies worldwide prefer the GDPR regulation and the changes they are making around their data privacy policies are GDPR compliant. Interestingly, research by various organizations indicates that if consumers perceive that they are getting value in exchange for their personal data, they are open to sharing data. Jean-Francois Gasc, managing director, insurance strategy—EALA at Accenture, wrote in a blog in May 2016: "Our research shows that 82% of insurance customers are prepared to provide their insurers with information about their behavior if it can help them optimize their cover. Furthermore, 78% are willing to allow their insurers to use such information if it gives them access to personalized offers."[116]

> Users own their data, and without their permission, you shouldn't be able to access it.

To assess how aligned you and your organization are with the principle and the ideas and examples discussed in this chapter, we would encourage you to consider the questions listed below.

---

[116] Credit: Jean-François Gasc, Hyper-Personalization Lets Insurers Get Close To Customers To Deliver Great Experiences And Additional Products And Services, 25 May 2016. Used by permission

Ask Yourself:

1. Do you use the traditional approach to offer your products, services and experience to your customers or do you use data to offer personalization?

2. Are you speeding up your digital transformation and digital architecture to offer personalization at scale?

3. Are you aware of the different strategies for personalization?

4. Do you design customized offerings for customers?

5. Do you have platforms that allow customers to customize their purchase?

6. Are you leveraging technologies such as artificial intelligence, data analytics, geo-fencing, facial, voice and emotional recognition, visual search, virtual—augmented—and mixed reality to achieve personalization at scale?

7. Are you using social media for personalization?

8. Do you have a single view of the customer?

9. Have you developed an integrated data strategy?

10. Do you use customer data to offer real benefits to the data owners?

11. Do you incentivize your customers to give you permission to use their data?

12. Are your data policies GDPR compliant?

Chapter 4

Principle 4: Reinvent Your Talent Strategy and Embrace Open Innovation and Open Talent

The best, fastest and most cost-effective innovations may not always come from within your own teams. Open up your innovation process and strategies and harness the wisdom and power of the crowd.

What comes to mind when you think of the premier U.S. space agency, the National Aeronautics and Space Administration or **NASA** as it is popularly known? Cutting-edge research. Outstanding innovation. Unveiling the unknown. Breaking barriers. The best

> **NASA decided to open its innovation process and look for solution providers outside its walls.**

minds at work. One could go on .... But did you know that answers to some of NASA's toughest problems come from people outside the agency, and what's more, from people who have no experience of space travel at all?

Take a problem that NASA scientists were struggling with for years—the prediction of solar storms or solar flares. These are large explosions in the sun's atmosphere. They can disrupt the earth's magnetic field, which in turn can disable satellites and telecommunications networks and cause havoc to a space mission. The best brains and world-class systems at NASA (all costing millions and billions of dollars) could predict a flare just one to two hours in advance and only with 50% accuracy. This was a very small window for the astronauts to get to safety. NASA wanted to predict the storms more reliably and in a more timely way. The solution finally came not from within NASA, but from a retired radio engineer in rural New Hampshire who had previously worked with a cell phone company. This engineer built an algorithm for NASA that could predict solar flares eight hours in advance, with an accuracy of 75%. He did this within 90 days for the chance of winning prize money of $30,000 from NASA.

> **Companies are realizing that the best solution providers may be outside their organizations.**

So how did NASA think of this particular engineer who was outside its domain and network? How did it find him – a retired cell phone employee in rural New Hampshire? Well, it happened because NASA made a conscious decision to open up its innovation process and look for solution providers outside its own walls. NASA posted this problem as an open challenge on Massachusetts-based crowdsourcing platform InnoCentive with award money of $30,000. At that time, InnoCentive, which is an open and free platform for anyone to join, had a crowd of around 200,000 (the number at present is around 400,000). Innocentive posted this challenge from NASA to its community of users that was interested in solving hard technical problems.

NASA is not alone in opening up its innovation process. Apple (technology), Proctor & Gamble (consumer goods), Eli Lilly (pharmaceuticals), Lego (toys).... in sector after sector, companies are realizing that the best solution providers may not necessarily always be within their own organizations or even in their own industries. What's more, they don't even need to be. InnoCentive, an early entrant in this space, has found that the further the discipline of the problem solver from the discipline of the problem, the higher the chance of success. In their study titled *Marginality and Problem Solving Effectiveness in Broadcast Search*, Lars Bo Jeppesen, a professor of innovation management at Copenhagen Business School, and Karim R. Lakhani, professor of business administration at the Harvard Business School, noted that 70% of successful challenge solutions are solved by individuals outside the challenge's specific technical domain and 75% of successful solvers already knew the solution to the problem.[117]

For a medical problem, for example, it is often non-medical experts who come up with a solution. It was probably always true that a company doesn't necessarily have the best talent only within its own ranks. But now, with digital technologies, it is easier than ever to work with outside resources. What is required for a company is the ability to tap these external experts and integrate them with its own internal innovation process. For all those of you who have not yet embraced open innovation, the coronavirus crisis is a good opportunity to build a new talent strategy. Instead of relying only on internal talent, you could consider having a small core team of full-time employees and augment it with the best talent from outside the organization.

Let us also understand that open innovation is not the same as outsourcing, which is an established concept and practice. Simply put, outsourcing is what you do when you contract out some parts of your business to a defined and identified set of external parties. Open innovation, on the other hand, is when you open up your innovation process and invite suggestions and ideas and solutions from whoever may have them.

> **The coronavirus crisis is a good opportunity to build a new talent strategy.**

Why You Need to Open Up

Is this something that you are doing in your company? Have you opened up your innovation process? Are you leveraging the power of open innovation in whatever you are doing? If you haven't as yet,

---

[117] "Marginality and Problem-Solving Effectiveness in Broadcast Search, " Lars Bo Jeppesen and Katim R. Lakhani, Organization Science, February 22, 2010. https://pubsonline.informs.org/doi/pdf/10.1287/orsc.1090.0491

we strongly recommend that you start at the earliest. Otherwise, you could be in danger of being left behind.

Why do we say this? Well, unlike in the past, when you had the luxury to come up with innovations and solutions and new products and new services at your own pace, today's fast-moving ultra-competitive environment is far more demanding. Consumers want the best quality experience, at the most competitive price, and they want it now. In this context, we believe that open innovation is a powerful paradigm. Opening up your innovation process allows you to access the best talent from anywhere in the world and from any discipline. It enables you to augment your internal capabilities with external experts and come up with fresh insights and perspectives and the best possible solutions *(see Exhibit 1)*.

EXHIBIT 1

The Rationale

The Beginning of the Open Innovation Movement

A *NEW YORK TIMES* BUSINESS BESTSELLER

"As entertaining and thought-provoking as *The Tipping Point* by Malcolm Gladwell. . . . *The Wisdom of Crowds* ranges far and wide."
—*The Boston Globe*

THE WISDOM
OF CROWDS
JAMES
SUROWIECKI

WITH A NEW AFTERWORD BY THE AUTHOR

"It has become increasingly recognized that the average opinions of groups is frequently more accurate than most individuals in the group. The author has written a most interesting survey of the many studies in this area and discussed the limits as well as the achievements of self-organization."

—Kenneth Arrow, winner of the Nobel Prize in Economics and Professor of Economics (Emeritus), Stanford University

Book cover, The Wisdom of Crowds by James Surowiecki, 2004. Used by permission of Random House, Inc.

Indeed, it is possible that someone out there may have already solved the problem that you are struggling to solve, perhaps not in the same field but in a totally different one. Or, they could use their knowledge from another field to solve your problem. For instance, when the **Department of Homeland Security (DHS)** in the U.S. wanted a more accurate algorithm to predict security risks at airports, a winning solution came from a game designer—a freshman from Berkley. This game designer was able to develop a better machine-learning algorithm by using his game development skills to create lifelike 3D images of people (some with weapons) that he could use to train his algorithm to be more accurate. The game learned what to look for (in this case the weapons) and came up with a solution that was one of the best. The end result for DHS was a set of algorithms that could detect these weapons with 98% accuracy.

> **Opening up your innovation process lets you access the best talent from anywhere.**

This unlimited and on-demand access to talent also enables you to do things faster and cheaper than if you do them in-house. Not only do you have many more high-quality or better quality resources working on your project which obviously speeds it up, unlike with employees you have to pay these external resources only for the results and not for their time or efforts. Further, you can have an asset-light operation and can scale up or down depending on your requirements, without worrying that your employees don't have the skills required for the new economy.

Here are some numbers from the 2018 State of Crowdsourcing Report by Open Assembly, a Colorado-based strategy and innovation consultancy and the crowdsourcing firm Topcoder, which illustrate the tangible economic benefits of open innovation. When Harvard Medical School wanted to speed up the process of standard DNA sequencing (this is critical for making high-precision, high-throughput readouts of the immune system), contestants from Topcoder reduced the speed from 260.4 minutes to 16 seconds. This was done in just two weeks and for prize money of $20,000. In the DHS example mentioned earlier (where DHS needed to find a more accurate algorithm for predicting security risks at airport security checkpoints), the winning algorithm that delivered 98% prediction accuracy was approximately 30% higher than the current DHS scanning technology and it was the best $2.5 million that DHS had spent in a long time. The Open Assembly report also notes that NASA has done more than 40 challenges on crowdsourcing marketplace Freelancer.com and on average saved eight to 10 times the amount it would have cost as compared to traditional methods.[118] John Winsor, founder and CEO of Open Assembly, (Winsor was also founder of the crowdsourcing advertising agency Victors & Spoils), says that a study of some 1,000 open innovation projects reveals that on average, companies can get "the same or better quality results, four to five times faster and 10 times cheaper." *(See Exhibit 2).*

EXHIBIT 2

Benefits of Open Innovation

The two key benefits of open innovation are innovation velocity and cost effectiveness. The selection of a specific open innovation engagement model – competition (as used by NASA for example), aggregators (such as Top Coder or Innocentive), develop your own developer network (as done by Apple for example) or some combination of these approaches. The selection of the right approach depends on the unique needs of the firm and expected benefits of the various open innovation models.

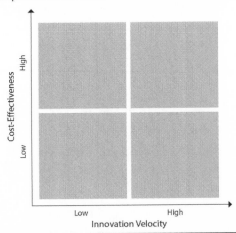

---

[118] "Open Assembly Quarterly State of Crowdsourcing Report: Co-Creating The Future of Work, "Open Assembly, Top Coder, 2018.

One of the best examples of open innovation is in software development. The difference between an average programmer and a top coder is well documented at 10x. Interestingly, most of the top coders do not want to work for a regular company unless it is one of the more glamorous organizations that changes the world. This is increasingly true not just for software coders, but for professionals across different streams. The Open Assembly report observes that the best talent is migrating to the gig economy because of the independence, range and flexibility it offers. The crowdsourcing platforms that match workers to a global market of demand offer a new stability and reliability of work. Today 20% to 30% of workers take part in the gig economy and this number is expected to grow to 60% by 2025. (The gig economy is a temporary work system based on a short-term relationship between workers and companies.) "We believe that companies need to create a "human cloud" around their traditional organizations," says Winsor. This human cloud, he explains, comprises internal crowds, external crowds and individual freelancers *(See Exhibit 3).*

EXHIBIT 3

Shaping the Language for Open Models

A consistent language framework is needed to unify communication about open models. Defining a standard set of terms will support understanding and adoption of new philosophies and practices. Here are Open Assembly's definitions of the terminology associated with crowdsourcing.

OPEN ▸ The mindset or philosophy

CO-CREATION ▸ The process

CROWDSOURCING ▸ The tool

PLATFORM ▸ An organization that digitally hosts a crowd community that is available to help solve problems through crowdsourcing

FREELANCER ▸ A person who earns money through temporary contract work

GIG ECONOMY ▸ A labor market of temporary contract workers

CROWD ▸ A group of people who engage together to solve problems

HUMAN CLOUD ▸ The resource of workers available through digital platforms

Source: Open Assembly Quarterly Report, Fall 2018.

Different Ways to Access Talent

Let's now look at ways you can access external talent. There are a number of different models. In Chapter 2, we spoke about how Apple's growing and vibrant network of 23 million developers (as opposed to hiring them as employees) allows it to offer thousands of valuable apps on its app store. This is something that Apple would never be able to do using only its internal resources. We also spoke about

> Through open innovation, companies can get "the same or better quality results."

how companies like Mphasis are co-creating with their customers and how companies like IBM have set up accelerator programs to tap into the startup ecosystem.

When it comes to crowdsourcing, you can use platforms and marketplaces like InnoCentive, Topcoder, Freelancer and Toptal that aggregate talent. Or, you can reach out to crowds directly, or even use a hybrid model in which you access some talent through platforms/ marketplaces and others directly. The engagement models can range from bids and partnerships, (multiple people offer solutions for your project and you choose and partner with the best one), to competitions (multiple people compete to solve a problem), collaborations (multiple people work together on the same problem), distributed (multiple people work on different aspects of the same project) and so on. Public hackathons also are a form of open innovation. We are seeing a massive adoption of hackathons—from recruitment, to competitive bidding of contracts (companies are using hackathons to pick vendors), to problem-solving, and so on. The compensation to contributors in an open innovation engagement can range from a winner-takes-all model to a sharing platform where contributors get a share of the reward. Internal crowdsourcing, which involves accessing employee innovation across organizational silos, is a good way to get started.

Consider what **Mphasis** is trying out. It calls this new talent model – at present in pilot stage—the 'uberization of workforce'. What does this mean? Simply put, it is a mechanism by which managers within Mphasis can have access to people and skills across the company. Mphasis engineers, irrespective of their locations, their business units, their roles, etc. can be engaged on a part-time basis on projects outside their specified responsibilities. The uberized workforce was born out of the COVID-19 crisis—the company could not remotely onboard new employees at short notice—and now it is becoming part of its post-crisis playbook.

So let's say you are a manager at Mphasis and you have a project for which you need more people or skills that are currently not available in your own team. You—the "consumer"—can put it up as an 'Uber' project on a special platform called 'Pool Next' that Mphasis has developed for

> **The engagement models can range from bids and partnerships, to competitions and collaborations.**

this purpose. You need to give specific details of your requirements in terms of skills, capabilities, timelines and so on. Interested employees can apply to work on this project. If the employees meet your requirements you can sign them on.

Employees who contribute to the Uber projects are expected to do so during their spare time—i.e., without compromising their assigned-billable projects. They get compensated for their deliverables, based on the complexity of the tasks and efforts needed and not on the hours or effort they spend. A dedicated group called the 'Uber Geeks' coordinates between the managers and consumers who post the project on Pool Next and the employees who sign up for delivering the projects. This group defines and guides the project teams and employees on how to go about the process.

Mphasis believes that this model is ideal for projects that can be broken down into logical independent tasks and which don't require much domain dependence. This reduces the dependency on functional knowledge. While there is no limit on the duration of an uberized project, it is recommended that each task be in the range of

20 to40 hours. A longer task will take more than a month to complete and hence have to be tracked closely to ensure timely completion.

The model is expected to benefit all stakeholders. The requesting manager has access to a wider pool of talent, can manage spillover tasks without overburdening the incumbent team, and has the advantage of cross-pollination of best practices from other projects. The employees get exposure to a wider variety of technologies, experience of working with multiple clients, and can develop a wider network among peers. The sharing manager (the manager under whom the employee is working on a full-time basis) gets the advantage of cost-sharing with the uberized project, cross-skilling of the project team, insights into best practices from other projects, and reward points for sharing the resource.

Here are two examples—proof of concept—where Mphasis has used this uberized model. The first example is of a Fortune 500 company where 2,000 servers were down because of a cyber attack. The company's existing IT services vendor said it would take 45 days and $5 million to restore the servers. The company then came to Mphasis. Using the uberized workforce concept, Mphasis was able to have the servers up and running in 13 days and for less than $250,000. By posting it as an Uber project on the Pool Next platform, Mphasis could get 200 engineers from across the organization to work on it in their free time. The second example is of automating test cases for an existing Mphasis client. Fourteen Mphasis engineers from various business units, locations and accounts came together realizing a margin of 60% on the proof of concept. Further to this pilot, Mphasis is gearing up to scale this organization-wide. It could even be extended to the outside world as a platform.

> **Mphasis is trying out a new talent model – the 'Uberization of workforce'.**

Consider London-based, idea management firm **Wazoku**. Founded in 2011, Wazoku has taken a forward-thinking approach to open innovation and talent. Open Assembly's Winsor refers to this as 'Open

Talent 2.0.' In collaboration with InnoCentive, Wazoku has developed a platform and a set of associated services to help efficiently match people and ideas to innovation or business change challenges. The company combines internal crowdsourcing and idea management, open innovation and talent (it offers access to a proven crowd of almost 500,000 innovation experts), and also a unique marketplace of more than 30,000 innovations. Using natural language processing and machine learning technology, global companies can access these when running their innovation calls and potentially uncover a solution in seconds. A proprietary 'Spotlight. ai' algorithm searches the solutions marketplace and returns any potential match to a targeted search. It also recommends the best people to approach for help in solving the specific challenge (*See Exhibit 4*).

EXHIBIT 4

Open Innovation 2.0

Wazoku, in collaboration with InnoCentive, has developed a platform and a set of associated services to help efficiently match people and ideas with business challenges.

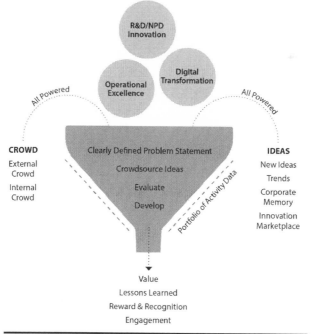

Source: Wazoku Limited, June 2020. www.Wazoku.com

According to Wazoku founder and CEO Simon Hill, a number of global clients including Novartis, HSBC, and various government departments are already benefiting from taking an inside-in, inside-out and outside-in approach to their open innovation approaches, and becoming more agile and more able to respond to new trends and opportunities as they emerge. Take the collaboration between Wazoku and the global law firm Allen & Overy (A&O). In a *Forbes* article titled *Collaboration By Design: How One Global Law Firm Is Tapping The Power Of The Crowd To Innovate,* Winsor notes that the A&O Idea Spotlight platform powered by Wazoku helped break up the silos within the law firm and enabled innovation to be embedded across the organization. Using this platform, everyone at A&O can suggest new approaches to solving legal and client challenges through technology. One project helped paralegals improve their efficiency by about 70% while inserting, cite-checking or correcting footnotes on manuscripts. Keep in mind that these manuscripts can run into hundreds of pages. Two other challenges crowdsourced 30 product, service, and efficiency ideas. In just three weeks, these ideas were added to the innovation pipeline after being evaluated by senior stakeholders.[119]

The Uberization of workforce is ideal for projects with logical independent tasks.

Keep in mind that there is no one right way for adopting open innovation. If you have the scale and resources like Apple to build your own developer network, then that's great. But most companies are not able to do this and using aggregators or a hybrid model are good options. You don't need to take an either/or approach. Each model has its own advantages. Study them well, see what suits your problem best, what model you can manage best, and if required

---

[119] "Collaboration By Design: How One Global Law Firm Is Tapping The Power Of The Crowd To Innovate, " Forbes, June 10, 2019. https://www.forbes.com/sites/johnwinsor/2019/06/10/collaboration-by-design-how-one-global-law-firm-is-tapping-the-power-of-the-crowd-to-innovate/#502a4decbeb8

use multiple approaches. Similarly, depending on the nature of the problem, the complexity, the deadlines, and the costs, decide on the best option between bids, competitions, collaborations, distributed models and so on. You can also start with a competition and use that to identify potential partners. What is important is that you must be able to manage the network of open innovation effectively. The key to doing this is deciding how to reimburse and reward the members of the network. The reward provides a strong incentive to the right people and groups to participate.

Overcoming Obstacles

We would like to add a word of caution here. Be aware that opening up your innovation process is not an easy ride. Many executives have difficulty with this concept because they believe they may lose control. The internal innovation and research and development teams see it as a threat to their roles within the

Wazoku has a platform and associated services to help match people and ideas to innovation.

organization. Their roles identify them as the experts, as problem solvers. They are embarrassed and apprehensive when solutions come from outside. There could also be a clash of cultures between the internal and external resources. Then there are concerns over the loss of intellectual property (IP). Companies think of their IPs as their secret sauce. They worry that if they open up their IPs to crowdsource better solutions, what secret sauce will they be left with? How can they protect their IPs? How do they control the destiny of IP? How do they prevent it from being misused or even used against themselves?

Some of these concerns are related to the mindset and some are business realities. But don't let them become a bottleneck. There are ways to get around these problems. When it comes to IP, for instance, you can put in confidentiality clauses and make the candidates sign non-disclosure agreements. You can open source the foundational elements but retain control over the end implementation stage. You can break a major task into components, use open innovation to develop the components and use internal employees for the integration. See how **Boeing** deals with this issue in terms of outsourcing. The aircraft manufacturer uses only employees for the design of the critical parts of the plane, like the wings, and for the integration. All other parts are designed and produced by thousands of companies around the world.

When it comes to the mindset, one way to overcome internal resistance is to make the internal experts see themselves as solution providers and solution seekers and not necessarily only as problem solvers. Involve the internal teams early on in open innovation projects and make sure they understand its positive implications, the value and benefits that it can bring to the organization and therefore also to them. See what talent you have or need internally and what you can seek from outside, and then organize yourselves with open innovation as part of the solution. Always keep in mind that for open innovation to succeed, it must be integrated with your internal innovation process.

You may find that often it's the mental blocks and cultural clashes that are more difficult to overcome. Crowdsourcing advertising agency **Victors & Spoils** is a good example. When the agency was set up in 2009, it was considered revolutionary. It promised to reinvent the advertising world with its new model of inviting creative ideas from a wide pool of people from outside the organization. The agency was successful and built an impressive portfolio of clients which included Harley Davidson, Chipotle, Coca-Cola, Converse, Crocs, Discovery Channel, GAP, General Mills, Levi's, Mercedes Benz and others. It soon caught the attention of Havas, one of the world's largest global communications

> **There is no one right way for adopting open innovation.**

groups from France, and got acquired by it in 2012. At the time of acquisition, Victors & Spoils had more than 7,000 creatives in its network. "The idea was to create, in an organization of 20,000 people, a digital platform that allowed the best minds to solve the most interesting problems," says Winsor. But in 2018, Havas closed down Victors & Spoils. According to media reports, a Havas spokesperson explained that in line with the quickly changing needs of CMOs, the agency was rapidly increasing its investment in innovation and in areas such as Blockchain, AI and conversational commerce "to be the core of our offering in North America and globally," and that it was "reducing the V&S footprint and reallocating any continuing clients to our Havas Chicago office." Winsor, however, believes that Victors & Spoils' radical approach "threatened Havas' organizational structure." Other factors that went against Winsor were that he was an outsider, he had no political standing inside the company, and he did not speak French. "When David [David Jones, who was the global CEO of Havas at that time], hired me, he told me to shake up things. But the more I shook things up, the more I was seen as a threat. Maybe if someone from the inside had been given charge of this new approach, others would not have felt so threatened," says Winsor.[120]

> **Each model has its own advantages.**

What other lessons can one learn from the Havas-Victors & Spoils experience? Winsor points out that innovators tend to be vocal. They talk of disruption and transformation. This threatens the others. Here is Winsor's advice: "Once you know the open innovation model works, you need to make it seem boring and ordinary for it to be accepted inside the company."

---

[120] "Crowdsourcing Bites the Dust: Havas Closes Victors & Spoils to Make Way for Blockchain and AI, " More About Advertising, August 10, 2018. https://www.moreaboutadvertising.com/2018/08/crowdsourcing-bites-the-dust-havas-closes-victors-spoils-to-make-way-for-blockchain-and-ai/

In addition to the sense of fear that comes with change, inertia poses another problem. How do you deal with this? How do you overcome the need of the majority to continue with the status quo? How do you make people comfortable with the new paradigm? Here is a possible solution: Look at introducing open innovation like introducing any other change within your organization. It comes with all the challenges of change management. Look back at how you managed some of the other changes. Look at what worked and what didn't. There may be some important lessons there that you can use here. We believe that once the team recognizes that the company is not blindly adopting open innovation and that it offers enormous benefits, they will be ready to embrace it. As we pointed out earlier, the pandemic crisis offers a great opportunity to introduce open innovation to your teams. If you were already using this approach before the pandemic, you could increase it further now *(See Exhibit 5)*.

EXHIBIT 5

Overcoming Various Obstacles to Open Innovation

Acknowledge and address the various obstacles to open innovation that you may face within your organization.

OBSTACLES:	AMBIGUITY Why do we need this?	FEAR Will we lose control of our IP?	INERTIA I like the way things are and don't want to change.
Illustrative strategies to overcome the obstacles:	• Set clear goals • Provide strategic justification • Build a business case and show the ROI	• Put the employees in charge as solution seekers • Include IP protection clauses • Clarify how the benefits outweigh potential costs • Set clear rewards	• Introduce open innovation like any other change • Apply learnings from past change management effort • Use the pandemic crisis as an opportunity to introduce the change

As you will see from the companies mentioned earlier in this chapter and others that we will soon discuss, it doesn't matter which industry you are in or what the size of your company is, opening up your innovation process is a *must*. It enables you to respond faster and better to consumer expectations. Further, open innovation must apply to all the decisions and offerings of your company and not only to new products and service development.

Let's now consider how organizations in different sectors have adopted open innovation. Study them in detail and see if there are any lessons for you here. Think about what could suit your organization the best, how you can build on it, and how you can take it forward. Importantly, see how open innovation is not limited to any one area of an organization. It can be applied to several areas and used to address different challenges.

NASA

We began this chapter with an example from NASA. Let's look a little more at what NASA is doing on this front. The premier space agency has what it calls a 'one-stop-shop' website named NASA Solve, where it lists all its open innovation

> **Many executives have difficulty with open innovation because they believe they may lose control.**

initiatives *(See Exhibit 6)*. These are opportunities that are available for anyone who wants to participate. NASA says it is keen to engage with the public at large because it recognizes that "good ideas can come from anywhere," and that NASA Solve is its "gateway to involving more people" in its work. In a May 2017 interview at the Crowdsourcing Week Summit in Washington D.C., Amy Kaminski, NASA's program executive for prizes and challenges, said: "Crowdsourcing has become a tool for innovation at NASA in an organic fashion. No single office, organization, or individual at NASA can claim to have started its use within the space agency. NASA program managers and public outreach specialists as well as NASA-funded researchers across each of our locations and fields of interest have independently 'discovered' crowdsourcing to address their R&D and outreach needs." [121]

EXHIBIT 6

Welcome to NASA Solve!

NASA Solve is an initiative by NASA that lists all their open innovation projects and invites the public to participate in them.

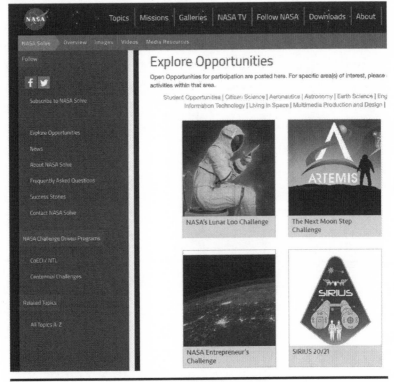

Source: https://www.nasa.gov/solve/index.html. June 2020.

NASA's open innovation initiative includes programs such as the Centennial Challenges and the NASA Tournament Lab (NTL). The Centennial Challenges program is from the Space Technology

---

[121] "Crowdsourcing Innovation: Amy Kaminski, NASA's Program Executive For Prizes & Challenges," Crowd Sourcing Week, May, 10, 2017. https:// crowdsourcingweek.com/blog/crowdsourcing-innovation-nasa-amy-kaminski-prizes-challenges/

Mission Directorate at NASA. This program engages directly with the public. The NASA Tournament Lab, on the other hand, uses crowdsourcing via various platforms such as Topcoder, InnoCentive, Kaggle, Freelancer.com and others.

Here are some examples of problems that NASA has opened up to the public by way of contests:

The Graphic Gateway Challenge was open for around two weeks toward the end of 2018. Through this challenge, NASA was looking for an appropriate graphic to represent a small spaceship that will orbit the moon and will be a temporary home and office for astronauts. The prize money for the selected graphic was $300.

The Recycling in Space: Waste Handling in a Microgravity Environment, as the name suggests, was a challenge through which NASA was looking for technologies and systems that can make it possible to store and transfer logistical mission waste to a thermal processing unit for decomposition. This challenge was open for three months and carried prize money of $15,000.

The 3D Printed Habitat Challenge was looking for solutions to build a 3D printed habitat for deep space exploration, including the agency's journey to Mars. This is a Centennial Challenge and was held in three phases. Phase I was completed in 2015, phase 2 was completed in 2017 and Phase 3 was completed in May 2019. More than 60 teams participated in this challenge and NASA awarded prize money of around $2 million.

> **Often, the mental blocks and cultural clashes are difficult to overcome.**

International Space Apps Challenge is an annual international hackathon that takes place in different cities around the world over a 48-hour period. Various teams engage with NASA's free and open data to solve problems related to earth and outer space. Space Apps 2018 included some 18,000 participants at more than 200 events in 75 countries. Space Apps 2019 which was held on October 18-20,

2019 included some 29,000 participants in more than 230 events held across 80 countries.

As these examples above show, NASA's open innovation projects span a wide range in terms of complexity of the problems that the agency is trying to solve, the model of engagement, and the resources it is willing to commit.

Topcoder

> **Introduce open innovation like any other change within your organization.**

When Jack Hughes set up Topcoder in 2001, it was with a simple thought: Is it possible for a company to hire software developers as and when required instead of having them on the payroll? And, how would one know how to hire the best developers? Hughes, an avid chess player, was familiar with the game's ranking method. He wondered if a ranking system could be created for the developers. Well, what started as that stray thought, went on to become a community for coders and is now a global network of talent and a leading crowdsourcing company.

Topcoder in 2020 has more than 1.5 million members— software designers, programmers, developers, data scientists and technologists—in some 190 countries on its platform with expertise that spans the software development life cycle. It connects enterprises with these individuals on-demand, who in turn help enterprises to solve their problems and accelerate their innovation. This is typically done via competitions that Topcoder hosts and manages. Once a company comes to Topcoder with a problem it needs to solve, Topcoder manages the entire crowdsourcing logistics. The company pays only for the outcome – the winning solution.

Since its inception, Topcoder has held more than 22,000 competitions and awarded more than $80 million as prize money to its members. Topcoder also helps companies engage in a hybrid model—i.e., a problem can be divided between the Topcoder pool and the company's internal resources. The firm has an impressive client list that includes marquee names such as IBM, GE, Harvard Medical School and eBay. Its revenues come from the fees that its customers pay for using its platform and for having access to its community. Members on the Topcoder platform are also ranked according to their skills. This helps companies if they want to recruit them.

General Electric

Despite General Electric's (GE) current problems, we can learn from the initiatives they developed. For instance, in 2013, GE launched an open innovation initiative called GeniusLink. Meant for GE teams and external clients, GeniusLink described its mission as crowd-powering the business by connecting with experts at the right time. Three years later, in 2016, as part of GeniusLink, GE launched Fuse, an open crowdsourcing platform connected to a network of "microfactories" that were capable of rapid design and prototyping. Through Fuse and other crowdsourcing platforms such as Upwork, 10EQS, Topcoder and Fulcra, GeniusLink connected solution seekers to a pool of more than 21 million experts outside GE. It also had a pool of some 115,000 experts within GE. These were all business, operations and technology experts who were spread over 195 countries and across various industries.

NASA engages with the public because it recognizes that "good ideas can come from anywhere."

In an interview in 2017 at the crowdsourcing event Crowdsourcing Week Summit in Washington D.C., Dyan Finkhousen, the then director of open innovation and advanced manufacturing at GE, managing director of GeniusLink and president of GE Fuse, said: "GeniusLink was incubated in GE Corporate under the direction of GE vice-chair Beth Comstock. This was a strategic experiment to see how and if open innovation and crowdsourcing techniques could be applied at GE and how GE could harness the power of the crowd to augment quality, accessibility of information and speed to market. In a shift to scale, GE Global Operations assumed responsibility of GeniusLink, further expanding the boundaries of how the crowd can fluidly provide resource and intellectual firepower." [122]

Teams within GE and their customers could leverage GeniusLink for a range of services. These included professional services like marketing, consulting and advisory services, experts-on-demand; product and technology development services like ideation, prototyping, design and small batch manufacturing; data and analytical services like market research predictive modeling, pricing analytics, and so on. GeniusLink worked on more than 700 engagements. It would start by working with the teams to identify and determine which problems/projects were fit for crowd-powering and then manage them till the final delivery. The format was typically by way of posting challenges. Awards included cash prizes, co-development opportunities, licensing opportunities, scholarships, internships, and so on.

> GeniusLink's mission was crowd-powering the business by connecting with experts at the right time.

By 2019, the combined work Finkhousen's crowdsourcing program supported drove a positive impact of more than $6 billion for the company. According to Finkhousen, this impact was the result of the time saved by accelerating the lifespan of projects, generating organizational productivity through the projects, and the additional revenue generated by the projects.

When GE restructured its corporate operations in 2018 and 2019, GeniusLink was among the many corporate operations that

---

[122] "Open Innovation at GE: The Power of the Global Crowd [Q&A], "Crowdsourcing Week, June 27, 2017. https://crowdsourcingweek.com/blog/open-innovation-at-general-electric/

were either discontinued, outsourced, or shifted into GE business unit operations. GeniusLink's corporate operations were dissolved in June 2019 while the vendor relationships and some of the ongoing programs were embedded into the operations of GE tier-one business units. In some cases, the business units that were divested by GE also regained some of the GeniusLink legacy programs and vendor relationships.

GE GeniusLink was a global operations management consulting business which educated enterprise teams about the capabilities and resources available in expert marketplaces and platform operations. After GeniusLink was dissolved, Finkhousen moved out of GE and launched Shoshin Works, a management consulting business that addresses the same need for a much broader client community, and provides similar services to enterprise organizations.

> **Finkhousen's crowdsourcing program drove a combined positive impact of more than $6 billion.**

Procter & Gamble

In 2000, A. G. Lafley, the then newly appointed CEO at Procter & Gamble (P&G), decided that the company needed to reinvent its innovation model. His reasoning was that the firm's innovation success rate—the percentage of new products that fulfilled their financial objectives—was stagnating at about 35%. Lafley mandated that 50% of P&G's innovations must come from outside the company. Lafley was not suggesting cutting down the R&D team but leveraging them better. He wanted half of the new products to come from the in-house labs and the rest *through* them by partnering with innovative minds outside the company and building on their IP to augment internal innovation. In response to this directive from its new CEO, the company set up an open innovation initiative called Connect + Develop to "engage with innovators and patent-holders" to meet the company's needs for products, technology, in-store, e-commerce and the supply chain. Lafley's target was met by 2005. External collaboration became part of everyone's daily work, not just the job of a specialized department. Over the years, the win-win nature of P&G's C+D partnerships has been demonstrated quantitatively: C+D enabled projects have delivered 70% higher than average NPV, and some 40% of partners have multiple deals with the company.

P&G posts specific requirements on the Connect + Develop portal and invites potential partners to submit their innovations. For example, in early 2019, for its oral care business, the company was looking for compounds or devices in the form of paste, rinse, or tooth strip that can provide breakthrough whitening benefits with a daily use safety profile. It also sought non-prescription-based products, technologies or ingredients that could relieve or prevent any kind of oral pain or discomfort or provide oral healing. Particular areas of pain relief included dentinal hypersensitivity and canker sores. In its effort to solve the consumer pain point of inadequate sleep, the company is looking for technologies that can create better sleep environments through the control of environmental factors such as air flow, air quality, scent, light, air temperature, humidity, and sound levels. Here, the company has listed that it would be open to looking at technologies that could be standalone products and/or integrated into a single sleep enhancement product.

> CEO A.G. Lafley mandated that 50% of P&G's innovations must come from outside the company.

P&G also recognizes that there may be breakthrough solutions out there for problems or ideas that it had not even identified so far, and therefore it also invites innovations that may not be related to any particular posts in its identified categories.

Apart from specific dos and don'ts for each product or technology requirement posted on Connect + Develop, there is also a defined set of criteria for accepting any submission. For instance, it should be an innovative technology, ready-to-go product, unique expertise, or commercial opportunity; it should address an unmet need for P&G

customers, and it must include protectable intellectual property. Each submission is first reviewed by a Connect + Develop team member, who then sends it to relevant business and/or technical persons within the company to evaluate its technical merit or strategic business fit. If a submission is accepted, it could result in a licensing or supplier agreement or other types of collaborations. The Connect+Develop program encompasses relationships across the world with universities, national laboratories, multinational corporations, small businesses, startups and NGOs. Collaboration types range from simple engineering service agreements, to 1:1 research collaborations, to public/private consortia with multiple parties, to launches of new companies with startup partners.

Target Corporation

The Minneapolis-based retailer launched its first accelerator program in Bangalore, India's tech capital, in December 2013. This program gives startups a platform to develop, scale and test their products in a live retail environment. They also get access to Target mentors in India and the U.S. As of early 2019, 36 startups have graduated from this program and have worked with Target teams in India and Minneapolis across stores, marketing, finance, legal, merchandising, mobile and digital. Each batch of startups that is selected for this program undergoes a four-month intensive program. They work on developing transformative and innovative retail solutions using emerging technologies such as artificial intelligence, machine learning and analytics. Some startups that have participated in the Target Accelerator Program, include Kenome (uses artificial intelligence to help enterprises make sense of dark data using cutting-edge deep learning, natural language processing and knowledge graphs), Point105-AR (provides a holistic 3D asset management solution

Target's accelerator program with Indian startups lets it leverage the industry's best minds.

for augmented reality experiences) and StyleDod (provides a tool that automatically converts floorplans into 3D designed rooms, fully furnished with merchandisable products.) A July 2018 article in *YourStory.com*, reported Rakesh Mishra, vice president of marketing at Target India, as indicating that India is a key driver of innovation in the retail sector globally and Target's accelerator program with Indian startups allows it to leverage some of the industry's best minds.[123]

Target's other programs with startups include Target Takeoff and Target Incubator. Target Takeoff describes itself as an "abbreviated accelerator with a product-centric focus." Target launched this initiative in 2017 with a focus on "better-for-you" products like PiperWai (natural deodorant) and Think.Eat.Live (foods made with natural superfoods). For the 2018 and 2019 programs Target selected startups in the beauty products space. Some of these like Girl+Hair, Yuni Beauty, Oars + Alps have already made it to Target's online and physical stores.

Target Incubator started in 2018 is a part virtual, part Minneapolis-based four-month program focused on the next generation of entrepreneurs who care about the impact their business has on people and the planet. Target says it is interested in these entrepreneurs because "they see the world differently, and therefore recognize solutions to problems differently." The 2019 cohort of eight startups includes Washington, D.C.-based KnoNap, a socially-driven company that has developed a cocktail napkin capable of testing for specific date rape drug presence (to check if the drink is spiked with date rape drug, one simply has to place a few drops of the drink on a designated part of the napkin. If

> **Target Takeoff is an "abbreviated accelerator with a product-centric focus."**

---

[123] "Target selects 6 startups in India for its accelerator programme, " YourStory, July 14, 2018. https://yourstory.com/2018/07/target-selects-6-startups-india-accelerator-programme

the drug is present the color around the saturated area will change), and New York-based Mickey's Mission which produces 3D custom dolls made to represent children who are not represented in the doll industry.

Mofilm

"Many voices are better than one." This is the tenet that Mofilm, a London-based crowdsourcing platform that specializes in video content, lives by. Mofilm's premise is that it is becoming increasingly important for brands consistently to create locally relevant and locally authentic content. But doing this at scale for fragmented audiences can be tough, slow and expensive. To overcome these hurdles and deliver relevant video content cheaper and faster than traditional agency models, Mofilm has built a crowd of more than 10,000 filmmakers and creative people from across 180 countries, from different backgrounds and cultures. Mofilm's internal team of curators manages these filmmakers.

> Mofilm has built a crowd of some 10,000 filmmakers and creative people from 180 countries.

For instance, Mofilm has created a five-part set of films for Bose depicting what music means in people's lives. The website claims that "with over 20 million views, the films are the most viewed Bose content of all time." For Emirates Airlines, the agency's community created a 17-part drone series showing aerial footage of the airline's key destinations. Mofilm's website says this series, called "View from Above" has "had over 6 million views to date and counting."

Typically, when Mofilm gets a project from a client, its internal team first works with the client to develop an appropriate brief and then shares the brief with talent from its global community of filmmakers for ideas. Once the client selects the best responses, the Mofilm team works with the filmmakers to further develop their ideas and also to execute them. The production funds vary according to the project.

Mofilm reaches out to its crowd with other kinds of engagements also. For instance, if the client wants to see finished content, Mofilm runs contests and the winning submission from the crowd gets a prize. If the client is looking only for ideas rather than finished video content, the filmmakers who submit ideas are reimbursed if their ideas are selected.

Rebecca Sykes, CEO of Mofilm, describes the company's core proposition as "the democratization of creativity." When she took over as CEO in April 2018, Sykes said: "Mofilm and its core proposition—the democratization of creativity—is even more relevant today than it was when we founded the business. We are living in a time when technology has the power to cross borders and raise voices. We need to embrace diversity in our storytelling and smart brands are recognizing that." [124] Mofilm's list of clients includes Coca-Cola, Lux, Chevrolet, Reebox, Cornetto and others. The company was founded in 2007 by Andy Baker, Ralph Cochrane and Jeffrey Merrihue. In 2016, it was acquired by brandtech firm You & Mr Jones.

> **Mofilm's core proposition is the "democratization of creativity."**

Mofilm believes that in these times of the coronavirus crisis, its model makes more sense than ever before. For instance, during lockdown, Mofilm's community of filmmakers has been shooting in and around their own homes using their own personal equipment without fear of catching infection. They have been producing content of various kinds including new product launches for their clients. Mofilm is also leveraging its animators and illustrators across the world to build bespoke virtual studios for its clients to help them create content like stills and gifs etc. without needing to shoot. The access to local crews that Mofilm provides is expected to help companies

---

[124] "Rebecca Sykes Named CEO of MoFilm, The World's Leading People – Powered Marketing Company", You & Mr Jones, April 17, 2018. http://youandmrjones.com/assets/2018-04_Rebecca_Sykes_named_CEO_of_MOFILM.pdf

overcome travel limitations that they are likely to face in the months ahead.

BBDO—Flare Studio

In 2016, marketing agency BBDO, which is part of Omnicom Group, an interconnected global network of marketing communications companies, launched Flare Studio, a new-age agency which crowdsources content from individuals and production houses. But unlike Mofilm, which is open to all brands, Flare Studio just services brands that are clients of its parent group. One could say it's like an in-house crowdsourcing arm of Omnicom to enable it to offer the best talent to the group's portfolio of more than 5,000 brands worldwide.

Flare Studio has a three-tier model: Open Studio, Studio Plus and Studio Pro. The categories differ in terms of the nature of the engagement a brand wants, and also on the experience of members who are signed up on the platform. Open Studio, for example, is the entry-level tier and is open to all creative members. All briefs that are posted in this category are competition-based and any member can participate. The creatives have to submit finished content and the concerned

> **Flare Studio lets Omnicom crowdsource talent for more than 5,000 brands.**

brand selects the winners. For briefs that are posted in Studio Plus, the creatives have to make pitches. If a brand likes the pitch, the creative gets a production budget to make the film. Studio Plus is open for creatives who have some degree of experience. Studio Pro, the top-most category, comprises larger projects with bigger budgets. The selection process is more refined than Studio Plus. The client selects multiple ideas against one brief. These ideas then have to be further developed by the respective creatives. Following this, the client makes a final selection which is then awarded the full commission. Studio Pro is open to the top-level creatives and production companies enlisted as members on Flare Studio. Based on a member's track record on the platform, it can upgrade them to a higher category.

When Flare Studio was launched, Nick Price, head of content at AMV BBDO and founder of Flare, said: "Flare Studio is a bold undertaking—bringing the benefits of the crowd but also injecting it with the right amount of agency know-how to make sure the work reflects an understanding of our brands and can work for them within the crowdsource model. That's a very different approach from anything else in the market." [125]

Eli Lilly

At the American pharmaceutical firm Eli Lilly, open innovation focuses on collaboration. The company's goal is to discover molecules with the potential to become medicines and its Open Innovation Drug Discovery (OIDD) program gives outsiders access to the same tools and expertise that are available to its own scientists. The OIDD program is open to investigators at eligible research universities, research institutes and small biotechnology companies. The "eligibility" refers to the agreement that the organizations need to enter with Eli Lilly to become affiliated with the program. Researchers from affiliated institutions can use offerings from Eli Lilly in various ways. For instance, they can use Eli Lilly's molecules to test their own biology hypotheses; use the pharma company's computational design tools to generate their own structures; submit compounds for screening in Lilly's and Elanco's assay modules; have their chemical scaffolds considered for inclusion in the Lilly compound collection, and so on. If Eli Lilly's scientists

> At the U.S. pharmaceutical firm Eli Lilly, open innovation focuses on collaboration.

---

[125] "BBDO Worldwide Launches Flare Studio: A Whole New Way To Meet Clients' Increased Demand For Video Content," Omnicom Group, October 9, 2016.

find the results that emerge from the OIDD program interesting, the company invites the relevant organization for further collaboration with a Lilly Discovery team. This can be by way of short-term collaborations based on research plans, or acquisitions of chemical compounds, or licensing agreements and so on. Eli Lilly was an early user of Innocentive.

Quirky

Quirky, a community-led invention platform, sources innovative product ideas from whoever wants to share them and brings them to fruition through partnerships with product designers and manufacturing companies. The company operates under a licensing business model. The licensees or designated distribution partners manufacture the products which come off the Quirky platform and in turn sell those

> **Quirky runs competitions for companies that are looking for product ideas.**

products to retailers under the Quirky brand name. These partners pay Quirky a product royalty for the rights to manufacture the product and brand royalty to use the Quirky name. Quirky pays the members from whom the idea first originated and also others on the platform who may have helped to refine that particular idea. These members get royalty on every item that is sold.

So how does Quirky decide to go ahead with any idea that its members submit? To begin with, it looks at how unique the idea is, if it is patentable, if there is a market for the product, the competitive landscape, how viable it is to manufacture, and so on. Quirky also conducts a survey on its own platform to gage what the other members think of any particular idea. If it feels the idea could be a winner, it accepts the idea. This then goes through the development phase of designing, prototyping, testing, sourcing materials and so. If all of this passes muster, the idea moves to the production phase after which it is launched. (The products are also available on the Quirky e-shop.)

Quirky's manufacturing partners are involved in the product development process from the very start. In an interview with *Entrepreneur.com* in September 2017, Gina Waldhorn, the company's president at that time, said: "They talk to us day in and day out about gaps in the market, trends, new technologies and potential materials. We *begin* our process by talking to them, so we know what they're looking for."[126] Apart from taking the ideas from its members to companies, Quirky also runs competitions for companies that are looking for product ideas. These competitions are posted on Quirky. com and interested members can participate in it. According to the company website, Quirky has more than 1.3 million members, has created 321,000 inventions and so far has paid royalty of over $11 million.

Entrepreneur Ben Kaufman launched Quirky in 2009. Its first major breakthrough was in 2010 when one of its members came up with an idea for a flexible surge protecting power strip. The product called Pivot Power was a bestseller; it reportedly got its inventor and other community members who contributed to the design, more than $2 million in royalty. A few years later, the company ran into trouble and in 2015 it filed for bankruptcy. It was acquired by Q Holdings and is now trying to get back on its feet.

Smart India Hackathon

The Smart India Hackathon (SIH) is one of the world's biggest open innovation models. A 36-hour software and hardware hackathon held in multiple locations across the country,

The SIH crowdsources innovative ideas from students across India for solutions to pressing problems.

---

[126] "Good News, Inventors! Quirky Has ' Reinvented' Itself, Pursuing Licensing Deals for Inventors," Entrepreneur India, September 27, 2017. https://www.entrepreneur.com/article/300900

the SIH aims to crowdsource innovative ideas from technology students from across India for solutions to some of the most pressing problems facing the country. At the same time, it also hopes to foster an innovation culture among the students. India's ministry of human resources launched the SIH in 2017 and it has now become an annual event. In 2017, more than 45,000 students participated in the SIH. In 2018, this number went up to over 100,000 and in 2019, it crossed 200,000. The number of participating agencies seeking solutions increased six times from 29 in 2017 to 169 in 2019, and the ideas received against problem statements in 2019 increased some 6.5 times as compared to 2017.

The problem statements for the hackathon are identified and posted by leading public and private organizations, union ministries and NGOs. The SIH2019 had more than 500 problem statements across themes such as health care, smart vehicles, food technology, waste management, clean water and so on. For example, it asked students for ideas for building an app similar to that of Uber for an ambulance service in order to provide a fast and reliable ambulance service; a low-cost prediction solution to locate faults in power distribution networks to enable better maintenance; a portal that could provide rich, real-time data and status on how an epidemic is spreading for better management of the epidemic. For every problem that is posted on the SIH portal, one winning team is selected and awarded a cash prize. The prize money depends on the complexity level of a problem statement. For SIH2019, it started from Rs. 50,000 (approximately $700 @ $1= Rs. 70) for the most simple problems, Rs. 75,000 ($1,000) for complicated problems and Rs. 100,000 ($1,400) for complex problems. Participating teams are required to have six members with at least one female member. The ideas are evaluated on the basis of criteria such as feasibility, practicability, sustainability, scale of impact, user experience and potential for future work progression. Addressing the grand finale of the 2018 SIH, India's Prime Minister Narendra Modi noted that governments can't bring about change by themselves and that change requires participative governance. [127]

Lego Group

In 2018, the Denmark-based toy production firm Lego completed 10 years of crowdsourcing and co-creation with its fans. Lego's crowdsourcing platform is called Lego Ideas and is open to anyone above the age of 13 years. Members can submit ideas for new Lego products and/or vote for ideas of other members. Any idea that receives more than 10,000 votes from members has a chance of being selected to become part of the company's portfolio. To submit their product idea, members need to build it with either Lego bricks or through the Lego digital designer. They then have to take a photograph or render their digital images. After this they have to write a clear description and then submit their idea. If the submission meets all the required guidelines, it is published on the website. If 10,000 other members like an idea and so does the Lego Ideas review board, it could go into production. The owner of the idea gets mentioned as its "fan designer" and also a royalty payment. Members can also participate in contests that are posted on the platform. The contests could be for building Lego models, or for creating videos or posters. Some contests are decided by votes and others by judges. The winners of contests get prizes such as shopping sprees, signed Lego sets or even trips. To see some examples, go to https://ideas.lego.com/.

Lego began this crowdsourcing initiative in 2008 in Japan as a pilot with Cuusoo Systems, a Tokyo-based crowdsourcing platform. The pilot was called Lego Cuusoo, and was available only in Japanese. Seeing potential in this concept, in 2011 the company launched an international version of Lego Cuusoo. In 2014, the Lego Cuusoo Beta became Lego Ideas. In the past 10 years, this platform has grown to

---

[127] "PM Modi Pitches for ' Participative Governance', "Business Standard, March 30, 2018. https://www.business-standard.com/article/news-ani/pm-modi-pitches-for-participative-governance-118033000918_1.html

more than a million members and has received 26,000 product ideas. Of these 26,000 ideas, 166 got votes from 10,000 plus supporters. And of these, 23 products have become part of Lego's portfolio. These include the Lego Ideas Pop-Up Book, Lego Ideas Voltron, Lego Ideas TRON: Legacy and many more.

Celebrating the 10th anniversary of the company's crowdsourcing initiative, Daiva Staneikaite Naldal, head of Lego Ideas, said in a company statement that the initiative proves "that the collective opinion of this creative crowd not only identify great products, but also yield authentic and engaging stories about people and their passions."

Consider how Lego has engaged with its members during the coronavirus crisis to come up with new ideas. During the pandemic, video platforms such as Microsoft Teams and Zoom have become highly popular across the world. Alongside, people have started using custom backgrounds on these platforms. Spotting an opportunity to build a Lego experience, Lego invited its members to create Lego brick-built backgrounds for video calls. While this was not part of a contest, the incentive for the members was that the best entries might be published on Lego's social media platforms.

> **The idea's owner becomes its "fan designer" and gets a royalty payment.**

Open Assembly

Earlier in the chapter, we spoke about Colorado-based strategy and innovation consultancy Open Assembly. The company was founded in 2017 by John Winsor, an entrepreneur and thought leader in open innovation. (As mentioned earlier, Winsor co-founded the crowdsourcing agency Victors & Spoils in 2009.) Winsor believes that open methodologies, collaborative business models, tools and technologies can play a critical role in helping incumbent organizations to transform themselves and remain relevant. He set up Open

Assembly in alignment with the Laboratory for Innovation Science at Harvard (LISH) and research pioneered by Karim Lakhani and Michael Tushman, professors of business administration at Harvard Business School.

LISH is a Harvard-wide research program on innovation. One of its major streams of research is open innovation. Based on key insights from LISH, Open Assembly develops new ways of working using open strategies. The company's main areas of focus are to help incumbent organizations transform themselves and stay relevant through new ways of working; help open system platforms to develop best practices and build scalable open methodologies; and create content and publish reports on the future of work. Another area of interest at Open Assembly is to help bring about a cultural shift that will enable freelancers and gig workers to get the same benefits as full-time employees.

"The big question is can organizations make this shift to open innovation before they get bought out or they die," says Winsor. According to him, many companies are "just not ready to make this shift." At the same time, he observes that in some industries, like advertising for instance, companies are beginning to change. Some of the companies and platforms that Open Assembly has worked/works with include GE, Microsoft, Deloitte and Accenture.

We believe that the creation of companies such as Open Assembly that help other companies build open innovation capabilities, the increase in the number of aggregators like Topcoders and the number of people who join them, and developers networks like the Apple and Google networks are an indication of the increased demand for open innovation.

To assess how aligned you and your organization are with the principle and the ideas and examples discussed in this chapter, we would encourage you to consider the questions listed below.

Ask Yourself:

1. Are you using the COVID-19 crisis as an opportunity to upgrade your talent by reinventing your talent strategy?

2. Do you have the right mix of internal and external talent?

3. Have you opened up your innovation process and strategies to harness the wisdom and power of the crowd from across the world?

4. Are you scaling your teams up or down depending on your requirements?

5. Are you innovating faster and cheaper by using open innovation?

6. Do you know the different ways of accessing talent? Are you accessing open innovation directly and/or through external platforms? Are you using different approaches like via bids, competitions or collaborations?

7. Are you paying your people for results or for efforts?

8. Are you ensuring that your model is rewarding for all participants?

9. Are you overcoming internal resistance to open innovation by explaining its value and benefits to your internal teams?

10. Are you involving your internal talent early on in open innovation projects and leveraging them to implement strategies and to lead change?

11. Are you integrating the external innovations with your own internal innovations?

12. Are you safeguarding your IP?

Chapter 5

Principle 5: Seize the Need for Speed and Design for Agility, Adjacencies and Adaptability

Consumers are unwilling to wait. Equip yourself to quickly introduce new and better products and services, promptly identify and understand new developments, and swiftly change tracks as required. In times of crisis, this is even more important.

I want the works.

I want the whole works.

Presents and prizes,

And sweets and surprises

Of all shapes and sizes.

And now.

Don't care how, I want it now.

Don't care how, I want it noooooooooooooow.

Digital native companies have changed the paradigm of customer experience

That was Veruca Salt, the spoiled brat, back in the 1971 American musical fantasy film *Willy Wonka and the Chocolate Factory*. It pretty much sums up the attitude of most consumers today. They want it all. And they want it now.

As we have been discussing, digital native companies have changed the paradigm of customer experience. And the heightened experience that these legacy-free companies are providing has reset consumer behavior and expectations, not just in their own markets but across segments. Because consumers don't think in silos or in terms of verticals, they now expect, indeed demand, the same level of relevant, real-time, personalized value and experience from every company with which they interact. Building on this, we saw why it was imperative for companies to recast their mental, business and revenue models, undertake customer-centric digital transformation, co-create with all relevant stakeholders, open up their innovation process, and design for personalization at scale if they want to survive and win against the disruptors.

> The themes of speed, agility, adaptability, and adjacencies are closely knit and tend to overlap.

Here is another key aspect that we must focus on: The need for speed and designing for agility, adjacencies and adaptability. The COVID-19 pandemic and the way it has disrupted our lives underscores why it is critical to be agile, to have the ability to adapt, and to leverage adjacencies. We have seen how the pandemic has impacted everyone—individuals, small and big businesses, and countries as a whole. In many places across the globe, there have been disruptions in supply chains, travel restrictions, shutdown of offices, educational institutions, theaters and shopping places. The stock markets have taken a beating and uncertainty looms large. At the time of writing, the full impact of COVID-19 on the world economy is yet to be assessed. While no one could have predicted this pandemic, it would be good to reflect how prepared you and your company were in responding to such a crisis.

Think about what we discussed earlier: During the pandemic, work-from-home became the norm for most companies; education moved online on a scale not seen earlier; creative art museums and cultural institutions like the Metropolitan Opera, the Met, the Barnes Foundation, the Getty and others began creating innovative digital programing that engages their traditional audiences and new global audiences; our social and business communication became digital. What about you? Were you quick to sense the potential impact of the coronavirus? Were you able to minimize the damage? How well could you adapt to the new environment? What new areas could you leverage? There are valuable lessons for all of us in how we respond to such crises.

In this chapter, we will discuss the why and how of designing for agility, adaptability and adjacencies. Some of what we may discuss here may seem familiar from earlier chapters. But this is not by chance or mere repetition; it is by design. The different principles that we are proposing for companies to remain relevant, competitive, and successful, are tightly integrated. All of them are linked to the global truths (listed in Chapter 2) which start and end with the end-consumer, and with which every business has to contend.

> **A feature of agile development is that large projects are broken into smaller chunks.**

As we talk about any one aspect, we need to keep going back and forth to the others. In this chapter, you will find that the themes of speed, agility, adaptability and adjacencies are closely knit and tend to overlap *(See Exhibit 1)*.

EXHIBIT 1

The 3 A's for Sustainable Competitive Advantage

Growth is easiest if focused on adjacencies and is most likely to succeed if the enterprise is agile and adaptable.

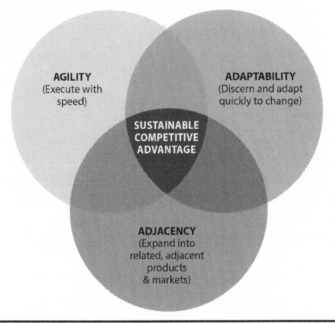

AGILITY
(Execute with speed)

ADAPTABILITY
(Discern and adapt quickly to change)

SUSTAINABLE COMPETITIVE ADVANTAGE

ADJACENCY
(Expand into related, adjacent products & markets)

Why is Agility Important?

Let's begin with agility. What does it mean when we say you need to be agile? Well, one aspect, of course, is speed. You need to be fast. You need to always be on top gear. Look at the media industry. Look at Netflix or Amazon Prime Video. The velocity with which content is getting released is probably an order of maybe 10 to 15 times higher than the pace at which content was released say five or 10 years ago. Or take the software industry. We are seeing a 100 to 150 times increase in the velocity at which new software code is released.

Agile, in fact, started in IT as a method for developing software. Previously, it was standard to begin a software development cycle only after having a detailed requirements document. But now, we develop the minimum functionality required and launch the minimum viable product. The rest of it is led by market feedback. This means that functionalities are added *after* we launch the product based on the live feedback from consumers. This approach is now gaining traction in various sectors. [The traditional Waterfall model—also known as linear sequential life cycle model—is a linear approach. It follows the sequential order i.e. a project development team moves to the next phase of development or testing only after the previous step has been completed successfully.]

One key feature of successful agile development is that large projects are broken down into smaller chunks. A key rule for dividing a project is that each unit must end with an output (product/service/solution/experience) in which consumers see value, and for which they are willing to pay. If used effectively, this can result in the particular output moving from "concept-to-cash" in eight weeks. This is an approach underlying many accelerators. Also, keep in mind that being agile applies to all the interactions a company has with its consumers, and this includes customer service. One of the challenges here is slow automated response systems. But advances in voice recognition and AI promise improvement in these areas as well.

With customers unwilling to wait for years for a new product or service, you simply don't have the luxury of doing market research spread over months, followed by months of product or service design, and then months of testing, before you finally launch it. That ship has sailed. Instead of adopting a Ready, Aim, Fire approach and launching a perfect product, you should adopt a Ready, Fire, Aim approach and launch a minimum viable product, i.e. a product with minimum, basic features. Make sure that it has enough value that customers are willing to buy it and enough future benefits to retain early adapters. You should then closely monitor customer feedback and launch the next version of the product

> **Customers are unwilling to wait for years for a new product or service.**

with the necessary adjustments. This is not a one-time process but a continuous one. You must create feedback loops and the whole process must become iterative in the way you build your product and services. Think of a mobile app, for instance. You first define the minimum functionality required to launch the app. Once it is ready you launch it, and then, based on the response from your users, you continuously enhance it by adding new functionality and features.

Consider this example from the financial sector. In mid-2014, when the financial services giant **Charles Schwab** decided to launch its own robo-advisory services to take on disruptors such as Betterment and Wealthfront, it decided that it would build and launch something fast and then keep improving it. The team working on this product assumed the mindset of a young and nimble company rather than that of a huge financial institution which would do things in a bureaucratic way. Schwab launched its Intelligent Portfolios in March 2015. In an interview in November 2016 Eliel Johnson, vice president and head of user experience design and research at Schwab, told business magazine *Fast Company* that the company's Intelligent Portfolios "felt real from its earliest stage, in a way that helped the people working on it make a better product." Johnson said: "You know the proverbial 'A picture's worth a thousand words?' Well, a prototype is worth 10,000 words." It took Schwab five months to develop and launch the first offering of its Intelligent Portfolios and it took the company two months to get the first 1,000 customers for this offering.[128] As of August 2019, Schwab Intelligent Portfolios had 350,000 customers and $38 billion in assets under management.

> **Assume the mindset of a young, nimble company rather than that of a large organization.**

---

[128] "How Charles Schwab Fought Back Against the Robo-Adviser Startup Invasion," *Fast Company*, May 11, 2016. https://www.fastcompany.com/3059565/how-charles-schwab-fought-back-against-the-robo-adviser-startups

That compares to $15 billion for Betterment and $12 billion for Wealthfront.

Another approach to agility involves what is called "fast prototyping." Unlike in the minimum viable product approach, which gives the consumer a real working product, fast prototyping gives the users a concrete visualization of the end product. This, in turn, helps to speed up product development. Whatever be your approach, keep in mind that when we think about speed, it is important that we also have a metric to measure it, like break-even-time, for instance. Break-even-time or BET is defined as the time from the start of investment until product profits equal the investment in development. In other words, BET is the time it takes a product or service to earn back the money invested in creating it. This metric was introduced by Hewlett Packard years ago. Think of metrics that you can use in your line of business.

> **Fast prototyping helps users of the end-product, which helps speed up product development.**

Mphasis' Autocode.AI, a deep learning-based framework which applies AI across multiple stages of the software development process, is an example of how AI can be deployed to speed up things. Developed by Mphasis NEXT Labs, Autocode.AI is used by software engineering teams for rapid prototyping and to accelerate the process of software development. This includes new code creation based on unstructured inputs and code fix for a range of issues including testing and vulnerabilities assessment. The framework leverages a variety of deep learning methods that improve efficiency, speed and productivity through automating the entire prototyping to design and development process.

An example of the use of AutoCode.AI is to search using natural language. AutoCode.AI uses deep learning methods to look up relevant portions of code from large codebases. Say you want to set up a simple web page. Typically it takes a couple of hours to do this. Using Autocode.AI, it can be done in a minute. All you need to do is sketch out what you want, take a picture or scan the sketch and upload it to Autocode.AI, which then takes over and delivers your web page.

Autocode.AI has two core modules which handle images and natural languages. One module converts the images to code. The other module takes natural language queries as input and then does a code search and code generation using deep learning techniques. Both modules are hosted on internal servers and made available to the organization through an intuitive and easy-to-use interface. As users keep using the platform, the usability data, the wireframes uploaded, and the natural language queries which they input, are all logged. This data is then tagged and used again to retrain and fine-tune the models.

> **Agility is about being better, more effective, and strategic.**

Mphasis developed AutoCode.AI as a key initiative in applying AI and machine learning to create service differentiation. Mphasis uses Autocode.AI in design workshops and for creating initial prototypes in NEXT Labs. It is also working with a client to convert their standard visual designs into code. Autocode.AI is best leveraged for rapid prototyping in every engagement. And now with the COVID-19 crisis triggering digital acceleration, the company can use Autocode.AI to accelerate prototyping wherever it is required *(See Exhibit 2)*.

EXHIBIT 2

Autocode.AI - Leveraging AI to Automate & Accelerate Coding

Autocode.AI from Mphasis Ltd. leverages AI technologies like deep learning to automate code development and code fixing and reduce the time and cost of development by up to 50%. The flowchart shown here is an example for generating an HTML code from a wireframe. An example application is when people generate such hand-drawn prototypes in a design workshop. Autocode.AI can then be used to generate and host the initial version of the website in a few minutes or hours. Thus, people are able to see this working and make modifications to the design immediately, instead of having to wait for a few days to see the first version of the website.

Deep Learning-based Design & Coding Module

Details for Design

Text, Voice Image, Workflow Parsing

Image Generator → Template Designer → Code Generator

Input to Cloud Architecture Configuration → Architecture on recommended Cloud Template → Containerize

Business Benefits

✔ Go directly from whiteboards to code - in days or hours

✔ Rapidly prototype applications to generate hyper-personalized designs

✔ Accelerate the development time by automating repetitive/ standard code blocks

✔ Reduce cost of product development across the software development lifecycle

Source: Mphasis Ltd., June 2020

Think Beyond Just Speed

Agility is not just about shortening your product cycle. It is not just about rapidly introducing new products and services. It's about being better, more effective, and strategic. It's about the agility of the strategy, the agility and ability to flip models and offerings. This new way of working has a significant bearing on how you actually plan your business. Take R&D budgets, for instance. You may still have the same budget, but it has to be spread across multiple launches versus one launch. Or, take data management. We all know how bombarded we are with an avalanche of data, especially in terms of consumer behavior and consumer purchase behavior, so much so that a lot of managers are almost paralyzed because of the amount of information. To deal with this real-time data (not just historical data), in real-time—because when we talk about speed in the current context it's about working in real-time—you need to completely change the paradigm of how you deal with data. This in turn, will lead to more experimentation since it provides real-time insights on the causal impact of the initiatives with which you are experimenting. (We will discuss this experimentation aspect in detail in Chapter 6.)

Keep in mind that agile is an approach which embraces uncertainty. The traditional way of working relied on planning because the assumption was that we knew what the future holds. But given the current state of flux and unpredictability, and how customer expectations are driving what companies need to do, it's hard for organizations to have a clear idea of how rolling out a product, or a functionality or a service will pan out. So, along with being fast, agility means that an organization needs to put the customer ahead of everything else, and you need to have an iterative process that continuously captures customer feedback. You need to be flexible. You need to be responsive. You need to be proactive. You need to see better. You need to have a strong "peripheral vision" that can catch and interpret weak signals around you, as propounded by experts and authors George S. Day and Paul J. H. Schoemaker. You need to have the ability to sense and spot new opportunities, identify and understand and act on new developments, pivot and correct your course if needed, quickly change tracks when required, and successfully steer yourself in a new direction *(See Exhibit 3).*

> **Agile is an approach that embraces uncertainty.**

EXHIBIT 3

Leveraging Agile Principles Across Your Organization

Enterprises can use the agile development approach, used in software development, within any business project or initiative. With agile, you break down large initiatives into smaller chunks and focus on quickly implementing these in the form of sprints and advance the projects in manageable, achievable increments, while deriving greater value.

The Old Way

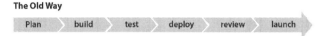

The Agile Way

An article titled *The drumbeat of digital: How winning teams play* by Jacques Bughin, Tanguy Catlin, and Laura LaBerge in the June 2019 *McKinsey Quarterly* notes that while business leaders are aware that their companies must adjust and accelerate, they are not clear "how much and how fast to adapt their business rhythms." The authors say that their research shows that digital leaders "appear to keep up a drumbeat in their businesses that can be four times faster, and twice as powerful, as those of their peers." They go on to add that "strategic power and rapid pace are mutually reinforcing. When digital leaders launch initiatives at a greater rate than peers do, they create opportunities to collect data, analyze them, and learn faster than other companies. That learning about the evolution of markets, consumer attitudes, and behavior, in turn, sets those companies up to make bigger, better, faster acquisition and capital expenditure decisions — which, in turn, fuel new initiatives and more learning."[129]

Consider this approach developed by Deloitte in relation to advertising. In July 2019, Heat, the advertising agency owned by Deloitte, launched a new practice called Heat AI. This leverages artificial intelligence and machine learning to predict with 70% accuracy which online trends and conversations would grow in popularity 72 hours *before* they peak. Using proprietary technology and patented algorithms, Heat AI captures, aggregates and analyzes 100 million posts a day from 50,000 sources like social media, news sites and blogs. These insights are then used to develop real-time and impactful content and to reach the right audience at the right time. Heat applied this principle to a number of brands successfully. Deloitte suggests that an agile organization requires four interrelated decisions:

1. A predictive AI model for early identification of cultural trends and their likely endurance for 72 hours a week.

2. An agile content development system that allows the development of real-time content that addresses the identified cultural trends and customizing it for both the strategy and positioning of the brand, and the needs of the individual customers or segments.

3. An agile content distribution system that can distribute the generated content in real-time to the selected persona and segments.

4. An agile infrastructure that enables the above three in real-time.

---

[129] "The Drumbeat of Digital: How Winning Teams Play," McKinsey Digital, June 27, 2019. https://www.mckinsey.com/business-functions/mckinsey-digital/our-insights/the-drumbeat-of-digital-how-winning-teams-play

When you think of agility in this broader context, you will realize that becoming agile has implications for practically every component of your organizational architecture. You need to revisit everything and you need to orchestrate the entire architecture of your organization to embrace agility. (In Chapter 8 we will discuss in detail the creation of an agile organizational architecture and network orchestration.)

Even as you do all this, even as you move toward becoming agile, remember to be stable and consistent. Don't let your need for agility result in a lack of focus, which in turn could lead to chaos. Keep in mind that agility is not an end in itself but a means to an end. Ensure that everyone understands why it is important to be agile and what's at stake if you don't embrace it.

According to a 2017 global survey by McKinsey, "81% of respondents in agile units report a moderate or significant increase in overall performance since their transformations began. And on average, respondents in agile units are 1.5 times more likely than others to report financial outperformance relative to peers, and 1.7 times more likely to report outperforming their peers on non-financial measures." (Financial measures included aspects such as revenue, growth, profitability, cost efficiency and so on. Non-financial measures included the

> **Have a strong peripheral vision, which can catch and interpret weak signals around you.**

development and innovation of the performance unit, how responsive it was to customer needs, its productivity, time-to-market, etc.) This survey had 2,546 participants from across regions, industries, company sizes, functional specialties and tenure.[130]

A March 2020 McKinsey article titled *Enterprise agility: Buzz or business impact?* says an analysis of 22 organizations that have

---

[130] "How to Create an Agile Organization," McKinsey & Co., October 2, 2017. https://www.mckinsey.com/business-functions/organization/our-insights/how-to-create-an-agile-organization

undergone agile transformations showed three main outcomes: 10 points to 30 points improvement in customer-satisfaction, 20 points to 30 points improvement in employee-engagement, and 30% to 50% improvement in operational performance. The article says these three benefits are mutually reinforcing and together produce a fourth outcome: 20% to 30% improved financial performance. The 22 organizations that were analyzed were across the six sectors of financial institutions, telecom, health care and pharmaceuticals, public sector, advanced industries, and mining, oil and gas.[131]

Leveraging Adjacencies: Beyond the Obvious

> Becoming agile has implications for practically every component of your organizational architecture.

Let's now move to adjacencies. When it comes to new opportunities, companies typically look at leveraging adjacencies. These are low-hanging fruit, and they are the easiest ones to try to leverage strategically because you already have a foothold in the segment. An adjacency could mean introducing a new offering to your current market, expanding your current product offering to a new segment, reaching either your current or new segment via new distribution, using your current distribution to reach new segments or offering new products. Usually, when leveraging adjacencies, companies tend to think only in terms of products and markets. We recommend that you look at it in a broader context. Look at opportunities to leverage your competencies, resources and networks. Think of adjacencies also in terms of distribution systems. But that too is not enough. To become truly successful you must not only go into products, markets, and distribution areas that are new to you, you must also look at those that are *new to the world*, the ones which

---

[131] "Enterprise Agility: Buzz or Business Impact?," McKinsey & Co., March 20, 2020. https://www.mckinsey.com/business-functions/organization/our-insights/enterprise-agility-buzz-or-business-impact

have not yet been discovered. As we suggested above, you need to develop sharp peripheral vision to spot weak signals and identify new opportunities. So, think beyond the traditional view of adjacencies. Keep in mind that adjacencies are important expansion and growth opportunities but it is imperative to go beyond the immediate and obvious ones *(See Exhibit 4).*

EXHIBIT 4

Looking at Adjacency Beyond the Core

Enterprises can evaluate and create many adjacent growth opportunities.

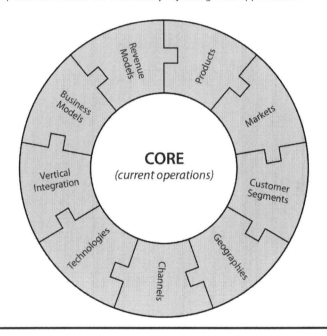

CORE
(current operations)

Revenue Models

Products

Business Models

Markets

Vertical Integration

Customer Segments

Technologies

Geographies

Channels

Here is another way to look at adjacencies. Let's go back to using the yardstick of how well you know your customer – i.e. how much are you increasing your share of the customer's wallet. As we discussed earlier, Amazon Prime is not just a free shipping model; it is Amazon's way to understand what else can be positioned and sold to the consumer. The reason why Amazon is able to launch one product after the next, or one service after the next, is because they have found the model of how to milk their knowledge of their customers.

During the pandemic, when many companies were cutting down on their workforce, Amazon saw a surge in its business and hired more than 175,000 new full-time and part-time employees to service the needs of its customers. According to a May 2020 *Bloomberg* article, Amazon also began reallocating engineers to find better solutions to tackle the operational challenges thrown up by the crisis. For instance, robotics engineers turned their focus to making company's warehouses more suitable for social distancing norms. These warehouses were originally designed for optimizing efficiency.[132]

We have earlier spoken how **Uber** started off as a cab-hailing company and then expanded into other modes of transportation like bikes and air-taxis. Uber then leveraged its learning and capabilities into completely different areas like food delivery and others. During the pandemic crisis in order to focus on its services of cab-hailing and food delivery, Uber quickly took decisions like moving its bike-sharing business to scooter and bike-sharing startup Lime in which Uber led a $170 million investment. While Uber customers will continue to have access to bikes and scooters in both Uber as well as Lime apps, this will be managed by Lime.[133] Uber also closed Uber Works, its temp staffing app.

> Look at products, markets, and distribution areas that are new to the world.

Look at Indian food-tech company **Zomato**. It started in 2008 as an online restaurant discovery firm and then a few years later it

---

132 "Amazon Wants to Innovate Its Way Out of the Pandemic," Bloomberg, May 18, 2020. https://www.bloomberg.com/news/articles/2020-05-18/amazon-wants-to-innovate-its-way-out-of-the-pandemic

133 "Uber Leads $170 Million Investment in Bike-Sharing Startup Lime," Economic Times, May 7, 2020. https://tech.economictimes.indiatimes.com/news/startups/uber-leads-170m-investment-in-bike-sharing-startup-lime/75604046

moved into food delivery. As co-founder and CEO Deepinder Goyal explained in a media interview, Zomato's move into food delivery was based on the ability to cross-sell. Goyal said: "We believe that a standalone (food)-delivery business doesn't make economic sense. Our customer acquisition cost is lower than that of others due to the advertising/listings business. We keep getting traffic there and that translates into food delivery very often."[134] In August 2018, Zomato added yet another line of business called Hyperpure—supplying ingredients like vegetables, fruits, groceries, dairy, seafood, chicken and meat to restaurants. A blog by Goyal in March 2019 says that within three months, Hyperpure was servicing 350 restaurants in Bangalore and by March 2019 this had shot up to 1,000 restaurants.[135] In another blog in October 2019, Goel wrote: "We set up Hyperpure to not only provide fresh and clean ingredients to our restaurant partners, but to also reduce wastage and inefficiencies in the supply chain. In the past six months, we have successfully executed over 65,000 orders for 2,200 restaurants across Delhi and Bengaluru. On an average, restaurants place five to seven orders every month, with an average order value of $100. Our revenue from Hyperpure for H1 (first half of the year) stands at $6.5 million (compared to zero in H1 FY19) with a hearty FY20 projection (10x growth)."[136]

> **Look at how much are you increasing your share of the customer's wallet.**

In December 2018, Zomato expanded again: this time into the events space. One of its first events was "Zomaland", a multi-city

---

[134] "Zomato's Full-Course Strategy: From Supply to Delivery and More," Economic Times, November 16, 2018. https://economictimes.indiatimes.com/small-biz/startups/newsbuzz/zomatos-full-course-strategy-from-supply-to-delivery-and-more/articleshow/66645881.cms

[135] "Hyperpure v0.2—Now Set to Supply 2500+ Restaurants Every Day in Bangalore," Zomato, March 1, 2019. https://www.zomato.com/blog/hyperpure

[136] Zomato H1 FY2020 Report. https://www.zomato.com/blog/h1-fy2020-report

food carnival with street performances, pop-up restaurants and food exhibitions, etc. In a media interview, Gaurav Gupta, chief operating officer at Zomato, explained that the company now thinks of itself "as a food company, and not just a food-tech company." The idea behind doing events, he said, is that "if there is a food experience that needs to be brought to the user, even if it's an offline one, we should be the ones bringing it to the consumer."[137]

In April 2020, capitalizing on the opportunity provided by the pandemic lockdown, Zomato launched a grocery delivery service. This serves multiple purposes. One, it is a new business stream for Zomato. Two, it builds an instant connection with customers; through its grocery delivery, Zomato was able to fulfill an immediate and basic customer need. Three, with people not able to dine out during the lockdown and also apprehensive about ordering outside food especially during the initial days of the pandemic, the new grocery delivery business helped Zomato mitigate the slowdown in its restaurant search and food deliveries. The company also launched food delivery in a new geography – Turkey; it launched 'takeaway' in Australia, New Zealand and Portugal; and signed up with more than 25,000 restaurants globally for providing 'contactless dining' features such as scanning a menu card through a QR code, ordering and paying through an app *(See Exhibit 5)*. In a May 2020 blog post, Goel said that the Zomato's product

> Zomato's move into food delivery was based on the ability to cross-sell.

and engineering team got the contactless dining product ready in "just a matter of weeks." According to Goel, given the uncertainty caused by the pandemic especially in the restaurant business, his strategy is to "make a complete shift toward being a transactions first company,

137 "Zomato Enters the Events Space; Set to Launch Multi-City Food Carnival Zomaland," The Economic Times, December 10, 2018. https://economictimes. indiatimes.com/small-biz/startups/newsbuzz/zomato-enters-the-events-space-set-to-launch-multi-city-food-carnival-zomaland/articleshow/67016027.cms

focusing heavily on a small number of large market opportunities in the food value chain."[138]

EXHIBIT 5

Contactless Dining in the Pandemic Era

In this pandemic era, food tech companies like Zomato continue to deliver food, while focusing heavily on safety – e.g. contactless delivery, rider temperature checks, restaurant safety certifications, rider safety certifications, etc. They have also introduced contactless dining to make the in-dining experience safer.

Source: https://www.zomato.com/blog/contactless-dining. June 2020.

---

[138] "A More Focused Zomato," Zomato, May 15, 2020. https://www.zomato.com/blog/focused

In July 2018, 82-year-old U.S. doughnut and coffee chain **Krispy Kreme**, which has some 1,400 outlets around the world, bought a majority stake in **Insomnia Cookies**. Founded in 2003 in a dorm room at the University of Pennsylvania, Insomnia Cookies, with its menu of cookies, cakes, ice cream, brownies and milk, has more than 150 outlets across the U.S. Insomnia Cookies outlets are mostly near college campuses, are open (and also do deliveries) till 3 a.m., and are extremely popular, especially with the student community. This move by Krispy Kreme is expected to help it piggyback on Insomnia's late-night deliveries and also expand its reach. During the pandemic, keeping safety precautions in mind, Insomnia introduced features such as contact-free delivery and curbside pickup. (Incidentally, Krispy Kreme was acquired by the Luxembourg-based JAB Holdings in 2013. JAB has been extending its presence in the food and beverage space with acquisitions such as Panera Bread, Peet's Coffee, Einstein Bros. Bagels, Keurig Dr Pepper, and Caribou Coffee.)

Coca-Cola and **PepsiCo** are also cases in point. These companies realize that their traditional products are under threat. Driven by an understanding of, and being responsive to, how customer tastes and behavior are evolving, they have changed their product portfolios to include lifestyle products, sporting products, and health and nutrition products. Here are some examples. Take Gatorade, Pepsi's popular sports drink. In 2016, Pepsi introduced an organic version of Gatorade, and in 2018 it introduced a sugarless version of the drink. In March 2020, Pepsi announced that it was acquiring Rockstar Energy for $3.85 billion. In January 2020, Coca-Cola launched its first energy drink under the Coca-Cola brand in the U.S. Called Coca-Cola Energy, this comes in four variants: Coca-Cola Energy, Coca-Cola Energy Cherry and their zero-calorie counterparts. Other non-cola additions in Coca-Cola's product portfolio are Aquarius Glucocharge, an enhanced rehydration drink, and Minute Maid Vitingo, a powder beverage that tackles malnutrition *(See Exhibit*

> **Coca-Cola and PepsiCo are trying to modernize their product portfolio based on consumer trends.**

6). Both these were launched in India in May 2018. Speaking at the launch, T. Krishnakumar, President, Coca-Cola India and South-West Asia, said, "These enhanced and nutritious beverage options have been developed specifically for the Indian consumers to suit their needs of enhanced and nutritious hydration."[139]

EXHIBIT 6

Illustrative Adaptability Strategy (Acquarius)

Aquarius Glucocharge is an example of the adaptability strategy used by Coca-Cola to tailor an existing product – hydration beverage Acquarius – for a specific market like India.

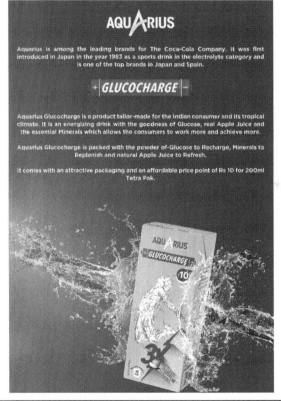

Source: https://www.coca-colaindia.com/brands/know-aquarius-glucocharge-apple March 2020.

---

[139] "Coca-Cola India Sets Foot Into New Categories of Enhanced Hydration and Nutritious Dilutables," Coca-Cola website, May 3, 2018. https://www.coca-colaindia.com/newsroom/coca-cola-india-sets-foot-into-new-categories-of-enhanced-hydrat

These cola companies are also adding items such as coffee-based drinks and sparkling water to their menu cards. This again is a different take on the traditional notion of adjacencies because Coca-Cola and PepsiCo are trying to modernize their product portfolio based on consumer trends.

Another example is **Anheuser-Busch InBev (AB InBev)**, the world's largest beer company with more than 500 beer brands. In January 2020, looking at the growing popularity of hard seltzer (seltzer with alcohol—these are mostly fruit-flavored sparkling waters that are fermented like beer), AB InBev launched its third hard seltzer but this time under its top-selling light beer brand Bud Light. The Bud Light Seltzer has 5% alcohol and comes in four flavors—black cherry, lemon-lime, strawberry and mango. AB InBev calls it an easy-drinking, light and bubbly seltzer for any occasion. Hard seltzer is estimated to be $1 billion-plus a year industry and expected to grow three-fold by 2021. By launching its new hard seltzer under the popular Bud Light brand InBev is hoping to cash in on this new consumer trend.

Consider sportswear firm **Adidas'** new way of reaching out to its customers —through Snapchat, the multimedia messaging app. Adidas produced an 8-bit baseball game called *Baseball's Next Level* in partnership with AvatarLabs, a Los Angeles-based digital agency. *Baseball's Next Level* is a home run derby and allows players to play as some of Adidas' major league baseball athletes. The company then partnered with Snapchat to enable Snapchat users to play this game on the app and to buy Adidas' 8-bit themed baseball cleats from within the app itself.

> In the future, Airbnb will focus more on longer-term stays.

Look at **Airbnb's** moves. In mid-2019, the company introduced a new fee structure to attract more hotels to its platform. In its traditional model, both the hosts and the guests on its platform were charged a fee. Under the new structure, independent hotels and hospitality companies pay a "host-only" fee; guests are not charged anything. This helps Airbnb compete with firms like Booking.com and other online travel providers who do not charge any fee to consumers. These changes were in line with Airbnb's plans to position itself as an end-to-end travel provider with services such as experiences, as well as flights and car bookings. And, as we noted in Ch. 1, Airbnb had expanded its offerings to include more luxurious properties and also unique local experiences.

The COVID-19 pandemic has brought a new focus at the company. While the coronavirus pandemic has given a massive blow to the travel and hospitality industry, Brian Chesky, CEO of Airbnb says he is confident that in the post-pandemic world people will continue to travel. Talking to *Business Insider* in May 2020, Chesky pointed out that the desire to travel and explore is intrinsic to human nature and that this would always remain.

> **Balance your forays into adjacencies with legacy businesses and with innovative, new-to-the-world experiments.**

According to him, while travel may be on pause during the pandemic it would come back, though in different ways. For instance, he expects that people will now travel more for leisure than for work and going ahead Airbnb will focus more on longer-term stays.[140] In a note to Airbnb employees in May 2020, Chesky added that in the coming times travelers will want choices that are "closer to home, safer, and

---

[140] "Airbnb CEO Brian Chesky Predicts a Wildly Different Future of Travel and Living, And It Sounds Pretty Great," Business Insider, May 13, 2020. https://www.businessinsider.in/retail/news/airbnb-ceo-brian-chesky-predicts-a-wildly-different-future-of-travel-and-living-and-it-sounds-pretty-great/articleshow/75719752.cms

more affordable" and that Airbnb will plan its future moves around these consumer trends.[141]

So, think of adjacency not just as the next complementary product or service. Think of it as extending your consumer knowledge, of extending your "single view" of the customers and using that as a channel for distribution of new products and services. This can be extremely powerful for identifying new growth opportunities. Further, instead of measuring only market share, look at measuring the share you have of your customers' wallet. Use your customer knowledge to cross-sell to them and increase the wallet share that you have.

> **Build the capability to quickly mold yourself to flourish in any environment.**

A word of caution here before we move on. In line with what we said about agility going hand-in-hand with stability and consistency, we would urge all companies to keep in mind that even as you look at adjacencies, you need to balance it with both legacy businesses and also with truly innovative, new-to-the-world experiments.

Adapt and Innovate

And now to the third A—adaptability. One could say that companies have always had to adapt. Indeed, while talking about adaptability of living organisms, one could go as far back as Darwin's theory of evolution. But, as we have seen throughout this book, in a dynamically changing environment, this becomes even more critical. You need to build the capability to quickly mold yourself to flourish in any environment *(See Exhibit 7)*.

---

[141] "May 5: An Important Update from Airbnb," Airbnb Resource Center, May 5, 2020. https://www.airbnb.co.in/resources/hosting-homes/a/may-5-an-important-update-from-airbnb-188

EXHIBIT 7

Adaptability Considerations

Enterprises have to adapt their products and services to changes in their business environment.

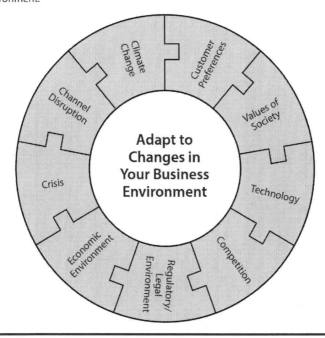

Take **IKEA.** The Swedish furniture retailer opened its first store in India in August 2018 in the city of Hyderabad. A year later, in August 2019, IKEA launched its e-commerce presence in Mumbai, expanded this to cities of Hyderabad and Pune, with Bangalore and Delhi/National Capital Region (NCR) to follow.

To cater to the needs of Indian consumers who usually have their furniture custom-built and assembled by local carpenters, IKEA has adapted the way it sells its furniture. Instead of its typical do-it-yourself model that is popular globally, in India IKEA offers assembling of furniture as an after-sales service. And instead of its typical large format stores which are located away from the city centers, in India where weak public transport and bad roads make long distances a strong deterrent, IKEA is looking at a combination of formats. An IKEA India spokesperson says: "Along with big format stores, we will build stores in city centers and also have an online presence. Our retail plans are evolving to have much more digital capabilities to meet the many customers where they are and when they want to meet us. The aim is to reach 100 million people in India by 2022 with a multichannel approach." In another move, IKEA is testing renting out its furniture in a few markets like the Netherlands, Poland, Switzerland and Sweden.

> **Amazon introduced a cash-on-delivery option in India, the first of its kind in the world.**

Or consider how **Amazon** adapted its strategy to the Indian market. In 2013 when it entered the country, one of the fastest-growing e-commerce markets, Amazon found that one of the biggest constraints in online shopping in the country was that Indian consumers were not comfortable with online payment. To overcome this obstacle, it introduced a cash-on-delivery option. This was a first-of-its-kind for Amazon globally, and it was then introduced to other countries. Over the years, with its initiatives such as introducing same day/next day deliveries, partnering with local mom-and-pop shops for deliveries and pick-ups, enabling Indian consumers to buy products sold on its U.S. website while paying in Indian currency, Amazon has been a strong driver of e-commerce growth in India. Incidentally, Uber too, lets its customers in India pay by cash.

Look at how **Yum China** has added Crayfish burgers, lotus leaf-wrapped rice and chicken burgers topped with *kimchi* to its menu to boost sales at its KFC and Pizza Hut outlets in the country. Or how, **Beyond Meat and Impossible Foods**, California-headquartered plant-based meat substitute companies are catering to the changing tastes of consumers. These are examples of how adaptation to cultural changes is giving rise to new industries. With many people becoming vegan or vegetarian because of environmental and health concerns, both Beyond Meat and Impossible Foods are coming up with a new generation of products mimicking the taste, texture and smell of real meat.

Their strategy seems to have found traction. Beyond Meat has seen phenomenal growth, with total revenues increasing more than five times from $16.2 million in 2016 to $87.9 million in 2018. An August 2019 article in Forbes reports that Beyond Meat is one of the fastest-growing food companies in the U.S. and its revenue is expected to increase another four times from $87.9 million in 2018 to $358 million in 2020.[142] The company went public in May 2019 raising $241 million at $25 a share. In July 2019 with its stock price crossing the $200 mark, Beyond Meat had a market cap of $12 billion.[143] A

> **Plant-based meat substitute companies are catering to the changing tastes of consumers.**

May 2019 article in Financial Times notes that investors were paying for "a future in which the $1.4 trillion global meat market has been replaced by engineered products that satisfy even the most ardent of carnivores."[144]

Popular fast-food chains are also getting into the act. An August 2019 article in *The Verge* reports "Burger King rolled out its Impossible Whopper to all of its U.S. stores, and Subway announced plans to test the Beyond Meatball Marinara in 685 restaurants in the US and

---

[142] "What is Driving a 4X Jump in Beyond Meat's Revenue by 2020?," Forbes, August 28, 2019. https://www.forbes.com/sites/greatspeculations/2019/08/28/what-is-driving-a-4x-jump-in-beyond-meats-revenue-by-2020/#c69e7e4496d3

[143] "Beyond Meat Extends Its Post-IPO Surge to 734%, Breaking the $200-a-Share Threshold for the First Time," Business Insider, July 23, 2019. https://www.businessinsider.in/Beyond-Meat-extends-its-post-IPO-surge-to-734-breaking-the-200-a-share-threshold-for-the-first-time/articleshow/70350575.cms

[144] "Why Beyond Meat's Valuation Is Hard to Swallow," Financial Times, May 28, 2019. https://www.ft.com/content/50d88aa0-809a-11e9-9935-ad75bb96c849

Canada. Carl's Jr. now sells a meatless burger made by Beyond Meat, and White Castle is offering the Impossible Slider."[145]

In Israel, companies like **Aleph Farms** and **Future Meat** Technologies are working on cultured meat—meat produced directly from animal cells without the need to raise and slaughter animals. In October 2019, Future Meat announced that it would be opening what it termed the world's first cultured meat pilot production plant south of Tel Aviv in 2020. In a press statement the company said that it aims to introduce hybrid products. These will combine plant proteins (to provide texture) and cultured fats (to give the aroma and flavor of meat). Yaakov Nahmias, the company's founder and chief scientist, said: "The worldwide demand for protein is growing exponentially, and the only way to meet this demand is by fundamentally reinventing animal agriculture."[146]

Consider how streaming video startup **Quibi** founded by former movie mogul Jeffrey Katzenberg and former chairman of Hewlett Packard Meg Whitman has brought out an entirely new format by adapting to changing customer behavior. The name Quibi is a contraction of 'Quick bites' and refers to short programs made especially for the mobile screen. Launched in April 2020, Quibi videos include long-form narratives distributed in short chapters, daily news programs, documentaries, food shows, reality programs and so on. There are new episodes every day, each spanning

> **As you bend to adjust to new situations, remember to lead with breakthrough innovations.**

---

[145] "Beyond Meat and KFC Partner to Test Fried Plant-Based 'Chicken'," The Verge, August 26, 2019. https://www.theverge.com/2019/8/26/20833145/beyond-meat-kfc-fried-chicken-test-plant-based-sample-date

[146] "Future Meat Technologies Raises $14 Million in Series A Funding, Announces Pilot Production Facility," Future Meat press release, October 10, 2019. https://www.prnewswire.com/il/news-releases/future-meat-technologies-raises-14-million-in-series-a-funding-announces-pilot-production-facility-300936425.html

10 minutes or less. Viewers can watch it online or offline. Quibi's premise is that given the short attention span of today's millennials, they would not be interested in lengthy programs. Advertisers are also showing interest in this format and are willing to put their weight behind it. For instance, P&G and nine other advertisers have pledged $150 million in advertising purchases. Quibi had announced funding of $1.4 billion as of January 2020. Investors include Walt Disney Co. and WarnerMedia. In a sign that just raising capital from top media brands may not be enough to ensure success, Quibi has struggled to reach the size of audience it had expected. A July 2020 article in *Vulture* magazine was titled, "Is Anyone Watching Quibi?"[147]

A key point in regard to adaptability is the importance of real-time monitoring in order to identify the need for change – this could be, say, a decline in sales or changing market conditions. Throughout the book, we have been highlighting the need to offer real-time personalized experiences. This clearly requires continuous adaptability. Let's also remember here the example of the retailer and its communications agency that we discussed in CALL TO ACTION. Recall how the agency used predictive AI to identify and predict likely cultural trends based on influential conversations on social networks and how it then linked these to the retailer's products and created real-time advertising and marketing

> **Don't just adapt, you also have to impact the environment.**

content. What's more, it distributed the content in quick time. See how adaptability comes into play here. And, of course, keep in mind that you have to not only adapt to the environment, you have to also impact the environment. And, importantly, even as you bend yourself to adjust to new situations, remember to also lead with breakthrough innovations.

---

[147] "Is Anyone Watching Quibi," Vulture, July 6, 2020. https://www.vulture.com/2020/07/is-anyone-watching-quibi.html

Let us now look at how different companies are becoming agile, or embracing adjacencies, or adapting to new ways of working. You will see that while some examples demonstrate one or two of the three aspects of agility, adjacencies and adaptability, some others demonstrate all three. This goes to show that the three can be closely intertwined. As you go through each of these examples, we encourage you to reflect on which of the three aspects are at work in the particular example and how the remaining ones can be added. Think also about how you can perhaps adopt a similar approach in your company, keeping in mind of course your unique business reality.

SEI Investments—IMS Division: Firing on All Cylinders

The investment manager services (IMS) division at Pennsylvania-based wealth management technology firm SEI illustrates how an organization has leveraged all the three AAAs. SEI IMS provides investment organizations of all types with advanced operating infrastructure. When Steve Meyer, executive vice president and head of global wealth management services joined SEI in 1992, IMS was the smallest unit within SEI. Its revenue was $10 million and margins were around 12%. Under Meyer's leadership, IMS has grown to $450 million in 2020 with margins at over 35% *(See Exhibit 8)*.

> **SEI IMS proposed a solution to address their clients' present problems and long-term goals.**

EXHIBIT 8

The Growth Path of SEI's IMS Business Unit

A great example for growth driven by anticipating market needs, developing innovative solutions, and expanding to new markets.

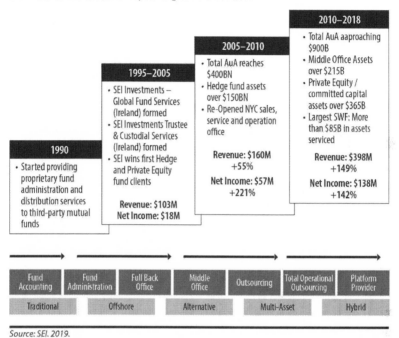

2010–2018
- Total AuA aaproaching $900B
- Middle Office Assets over $215B
- Private Equity / committed capital assets over $365B
- Largest SWF: More than $85B in assets serviced

Revenue: $398M
+149%

Net Income: $138M
+142%

2005–2010
- Total AuA reaches $400BN
- Hedge fund assets over $150BN
- Re-Opened NYC sales, service and operation office

Revenue: $160M
+55%

Net Income: $57M
+221%

1995–2005
- SEI Investments – Global Fund Services (Ireland) formed
- SEI Investments Trustee & Custodial Services (Ireland) formed
- SEI wins first Hedge and Private Equity fund clients

Revenue: $103M
Net Income: $18M

1990
- Started providing proprietary fund administration and distribution services to third-party mutual funds

| Fund Accounting | Fund Administration | Full Back Office | Middle Office | Outsourcing | Total Operational Outsourcing | Platform Provider |

| Traditional | Offshore | Alternative | Multi-Asset | Hybrid |

Source: SEI. 2019.

Let's see how IMS achieved this. SEI was founded in 1968 and in its early days, the company's business was based on TRUST 3000, its flagship processing and accounting system for banks. In the 1980s, when banks started offering mutual funds to customers, but could not distribute their own products due to regulatory constraints, SEI became a distributor for these mutual funds. Also, SEI did fund accounting for these bank-sponsored mutual funds. This was a commoditized business and SEI realized that this was a losing proposition. The value that SEI was offering was to provide a distribution and marketing service to these banks to primarily sell within the banks' own channel. Once regulations allowed banks to distribute their own products,

SEI would be left with only the commoditized fund accounting—something for which banks would not be willing to pay a lot of money. Indeed, that is just what happened. Around this time, SEI founder Al West decided to reinvent the company and since IMS didn't seem to have a good offering, there was talk of selling off the IMS division.

> **IMS's value proposition was based on dealing with the pain points of managers.**

Meyer, however, felt that the IMS model was ripe for disruption. "I and a couple of others felt that this might be akin to doing dirty laundry, but it's important to people. If we did it really well and provide value to our customers, we could differentiate ourselves," says Meyer. Instead of looking at solving only one piece of the puzzle, SEI decided to take a holistic look at the needs of the clients and the markets and see how IMS could differentiate itself. With this in mind, Meyer decided that instead of doing only one service (fund accounting) for one market (banks), IMS should expand its offering and the markets it was servicing.

In the mid 1990s, IMS expanded into the traditional investment manager marketplace in the U.S. Its first clients included Turner Investment Partners and Pilgrim Baxter Investment Partners. These firms wanted someone who could manage their entire back-office work so that they themselves could focus on their core investment products and their clients. To cater to the needs of its new clients, IMS expanded its solution from fund accounting to cover the complete back-office administration. What's more, when these new clients (and also some of IMS' banking clients) were looking to sell their products globally and wanted a full back-office infrastructure in locations like Cayman Islands and Dublin, IMS decided to expand geographically. It set up operations in Dublin, Ireland and added an office in the Cayman. Further, it grew its Dublin operations to service not only the U.S. investment managers expanding internationally, but also other international investment managers.

Meyer didn't stop at this. When hedge funds emerged as a new asset class, he decided to go after it. Meyer recounts that when IMS won its first hedge fund client, his team was not at all familiar with the workings of hedge funds. In fact, after winning the first contract, the head of sales at IMS asked Meyer: "What is a hedge fund?" Meyer replied: "I don't know but we will find out." Meyer says he was confident that they could learn and deliver. With alternate investment becoming popular, IMS also expanded to the private equity space. Alongside, it kept expanding its solution breadth to cater to the demands of these new markets.

IMS' value proposition was based on solving the pain points of the managers and the needs of the end-investors and it found good traction. However, it was considered a boutique player. It did not get invited to the RFP process of the big funds. As Meyer points out, it needed "one big institutional player to give SEI a chance and that would give it institutional quality and legitimacy." This break came in 2005. A leading global investment banking firm was looking to outsource all its back-office operations and thanks to some focused outreach contacts, Meyer's team got invited to the RFP process though they were told that "there was less than a 1% chance" that they would win it. They were considered too small and not well-known enough. Meyer didn't let this dissuade him. They went after it aggressively. He was convinced that the only way to bag the deal was to change the game. Instead of looking only at the present-day pain points of the investment bank's managers, the solution SEI IMS proposed promised to also address their future problems and help them to achieve their long-term goals. Importantly, IMS proposed that all of it would be on a data-driven holistic platform, with a focus on supporting the end-client experience for their managers. "We knew it was a game-changer. No one else was talking like this," says Meyer.

> **IMS is focused on supporting the end-client experience.**

Meyer's confidence was well placed. His team won the contract. But it came with its own share of implementation challenges. To deliver on his promise, Meyer had to take tough decisions such as pulling out *all* IMS salespeople from the field and making them part of the implementation team and service team for almost a year. This meant no new business for IMS and slowed down the unit's growth. But this courageous move brought rich dividends for IMS. Winning this big contract and implementing it successfully put SEI IMS in the big boys' league. It opened up the upper-end of the market for them and there has been no looking back.

In 2019, capitalizing on the firm's continuous evolution, drive for growth and passionate focus on the evolving needs of clients, SEI realized that IMS' market—manufacturers of financial service products and services—and the market of SEI's private banking unit—banks and other financial intermediaries—were converging. SEI, therefore, merged the two units under Meyer's leadership and created a new meta platform called 'One SEI'. This allows them to customize a platform offering for each client based on the best elements of the underlying platforms. Initial results have been extremely encouraging, and despite the recent coronavirus and the civil unrest crises, the combined unit continues to grow. Much of this growth can be attributed to SEI's customer-centric values, agility and leadership.

Here is Meyer's list of what he thinks SEI IMS did right:

1. They kept expanding into new markets and also expanded and adapted their solutions.

2. Their goal was not just to grow and expand the market, but to disrupt it.

3. They looked to solve the problems that kept the managers awake at night.

4. They focused on the emerging needs of the manager, not just the present-day needs.

5. They were open to leveraging outside partners for building their solutions. This also brought in fresh perspective and also made them agile and nimble in terms of delivery mechanism.

6. They believed in their strategy.

7. They did not take no for an answer – Persistence!!

8. They did not fear failure – they made plenty of mistakes, but used them as learning opportunities and fuel to drive further!!

We think SEI's IMS division is a great example of adopting agility, adjacencies and adaptability. They recognized emerging markets. They adapted and equipped themselves to leverage new opportunities. They brought in new partners so that they could be agile and nimble. IMS' journey also reinforces the theme of our book – the need to be customer-centric. Further, it exemplifies the need to have courageous leadership. Look at how they got into areas they knew nothing about. They pulled people off the sales field and were willing to sacrifice growth to deliver on their promise. They went against the corporate culture of building everything in-house. They believed in themselves when not many people did.

General Electric—On Startup Mode

As we mentioned in Chapter 4, while General Electric (GE) has been going through major changes in recent times, some of the approaches they introduced over the years were successful at their time and are great examples that we can learn from. For instance, in 2013, the then GE Chairman and CEO Jeffrey Immelt introduced a new concept called FastWorks within the corporation. Based on the Lean Startup principles, FastWorks was a responsive and speedy product development initiative and was developed by GE and Eric Ries, author of the bestselling book *The Lean Startup*. It combined the flexible and transparent characteristics of a startup with GE's size and resources.

As part of this initiative, employees were trained to refocus and retool their workflow, and encouraged to bring customers in earlier and try out things.

The initial FastWorks team comprised Ries and a few others. They trained a number of coaches on FastWorks and these coaches in turn taught Lean Startup principles to around 3,000 GE executives. In the first year, 100 FastWorks projects were launched within GE in the U.S., Europe, China, Russia, and Latin America. The projects ranged from building disruptive healthcare solutions to co-creating a new solution for flow metering in multiphase oil wells.

FastWorks wasn't only about being fast or simple. It was about discovering, understanding and validating what clients really need and value. In the FastWorks process, GE teams posed questions to customers to understand the problems that they want to solve and the desired outcomes. The team working on any issue developed a hypothesis that also included certain assumptions. It then tested those assumptions and got them validated by the customer. For instance, it broke down the problem into smaller pieces or used the minimum viable product approach. The idea was to test and learn and then make changes based on those findings. To ensure quick decision-making, instead of large teams, only the main stakeholders on a project were involved.

> **FastWorks was about discovering, understanding, and validating what clients need and value.**

Interestingly, while a lot of time was spent on customer discovery, the FastWorks approach delivered better outcomes faster because it was based on data, on customer validation and on rapid learning cycles. This approach empowered GE employees to adopt an entrepreneurial mindset and gave them space to make small mistakes, learn from these mistakes, iterate based on data and feedback and keep moving forward *(See Exhibit 9).*

EXHIBIT 9

GE's 'FastWorks' - A Startups-Inspired Framework

GE Power used GE FastWorks (a 'startups-inspired' approach that they used across their organization), to make multiple improvements to a popular gas turbine by shaving off 25% off the standard development time.

Source: GE, https://www.ge.com/news/reports/startup-power-plant-adapting-silicon-valley-methods-building-turbines. June 2020.

Here is an example of a FastWorks initiative. When GE Power wanted to upgrade one of its most popular gas turbines, instead of first making the changes and then taking the new turbine to its customers, the team first took inputs from 11 customers. Instead of choosing from within the various customer inputs, the GE team decided to incorporate all the requests. They streamlined the process and approvals, empowered engineers down the line to take decisions, consulted with experts when required, released models as soon as they were ready so that parts could be cast and machines, ensured that different groups could work in parallel, and so on. All this enabled the team to respond to any obstacles and new information quickly.

Using the FastWorks approach, GE Power was able to reduce the gas turbine's development time by 25%, from four years to three years (it was launched in March 2017), while at the same time meeting all the customer requirements. It proved to be a great test case for combining GE's size and resources with the fast and flexible culture of a startup.[148]

As is often the case with any change, FastWorks had its share of skeptics within and outside the organization. However, while GE discontinued FastWorks as a separate initiative, many of the themes of Fastworks like customer focus, continuous improvement and feedback loops are alive at GE through its focus on Lean. Though agile was originally promoted and propagated through the efforts of a seasoned corporate team, it was gradually absorbed into the operating culture of the enterprise at large, having evolved into a new way of thinking and a new way of working for teams around the world.

ING Group – Banking on Agile

In June 2015, inspired by Spotify, one of the first companies to innovate its organizational design, and other technology companies, the Dutch banking group ING introduced the agile way of working. The rationale for doing this was simple: It wanted to develop an omnichannel strategy and give its customers a seamless and high-quality service across different channels. For instance, a customer may want to visit a branch for getting investment advice but then make the investment online or over the phone. ING realized that to make this possible, it needed to have an agile way of working.

In an interview with McKinsey in 2016 about its journey to become agile, Bart Schlatmann, then chief operating officer of ING Netherlands, and Peter Jacobs, the chief information officer,

---

[148] "The Startup Power Plant: These Engineers Are Building Turbines the Silicon Valley Way," GE website, May 3, 2017. https://www.ge.com/news/reports/startup-power-plant-adapting-silicon-valley-methods-building-turbines

said that inspired by what it saw at various technology companies, ING decided to reorganize itself to work in multidisciplinary teams, or "squads," which included experts in data analysis, marketing, user experience design, product and commercial specialists, and IT engineers.[149] The focus of each squad (having nine members) was on solving a specific client-related issue. It had end-to-end responsibility for the concerned issue and a common definition of success. So each squad had to write down the purpose of what it was working on, agree on a way of measuring the impact it had on clients, and decide how to manage its daily activities.

> ING introduced the agile way of working to develop an omnichannel strategy.

Schlatmann and Jacobs said that ING is "progressing well" in their objectives of being quick to market, lowering impediments, increasing employee-engagement, and enhancing client experience. ING is doing software releases on a "two- to three-week basis rather than five to six times a year," and its customer-satisfaction and employee-engagement scores are up "multiple points."

The four main elements of ING's transformation are: the agile way of working (in squads, constantly testing new offerings without being constrained by managers regulating the handovers and slowing down teamwork); having a suitable and transparent organizational structure; the approach to DevOps (collaborative or shared approach to the tasks performed by a company's application development and IT operations teams) and continuous delivery in IT (frequent releases); and a new people model.

Sharing their experience, Jacobs said that while it's fine to start small with agile, what one should not do is "cherry-pick from the different building blocks." He observed that some people officially

---

[149] "ING's Agile Transformation," McKinsey Quarterly, January 10, 2017. https://www.mckinsey.com/industries/financial-services/our-insights/ings-agile-transformation

welcome the agile work style, but continue with the existing organizational structure and governance. This, he said, "defeats the whole purpose and only creates more frustration." He added that "leadership and determination are the keys to making it happen." An article titled *One Bank's Agile Team Experiment* in the March – April 2018 issue of *Harvard Business Review* noted: "More than two years in," Ralph Hamers, CEO of ING Group, "considers the talent experiment a big success. Customer-satisfaction and employee-engagement are both up, and ING is quicker to market with new products. So the bank has started to roll out this new way of working to roughly 40,000 employees outside its home country."[150]

Sony Pictures Entertainment—Using Cloud & Automation

California-based Sony Pictures Entertainment operates in multiple areas. These include production, acquisition and distribution of motion pictures and television content; television networks; creation and distribution of digital content; operation of studio facilities; and development of new entertainment products, services and technologies. When the Digital Media Group (DMG) of Sony Pictures Technologies was developing the next generation of software system to manage entertainment assets, it ran into a "last-mile" challenge, i.e., delivering the software system to users after development is complete. ('Users' were employees at Sony Entertainment who were responsible for managing the TV shows, movies, etc. that the end-customers were watching.) Typically, the last mile is bogged down by manual processes and other constraints; the software is delivered to the users only months after development is completed. Sony Pictures' DMG wanted to offer its users increased agility and deliver new features and

---

[150] "One Team's Agile Team Experiment," Harvard Business Review, March-April 2018. https://hbr.org/2018/03/the-new-rules-of-talent-management#one-banks-agile-team-experiment

changes along with infrastructure updates and, at the same time, also reduce infrastructure and delivery costs.

This is how DMG achieved its objective: It partnered with Stelligent Systems, a Virginia-based firm (now owned by Mphasis) that specializes in helping companies accelerate their software development cycle using automation on the Amazon Web Services (AWS) infrastructure. Stelligent created a fully-automated deployment pipeline for Sony's DMG in which the complete software system including the application code, configuration, infrastructure and data is built and tested with every change. Releasing software is built into the development process. It is an always-releasable software for the B2B audience. This continuous delivery model empowers any authorized team member from development to operations to make the required changes without being bogged down by organizational bureaucracy.

DMG's executive director Charles Cole says, "With this fully-automated approach, we can be more adaptive and responsive to our customers by releasing new features and changes based on business needs in a matter of minutes rather than a multi-month release process." There are other advantages too. With software release happening at the click of a button, DMG's developers can now focus on adding new features instead of spending time and effort on releasing the software. And because it is deploying cloud-based infrastructure, DMG needs to pay only for software that is used rather than for unutilized hardware, thereby reducing costs significantly.

Warby Parker: Leveraging Pop-up Stores

Eyeglass retailer Warby Parker, which started as an online operation in 2010, was among the first etailers to open brick-and-mortar stores in order to connect better with its customers. It opened its first physical store in 2013 in New York and as of March 2020 has over 100 stores in the U.S. Another interesting way that Warby Parker, which positions itself as a retailer of high-quality affordable eyewear, reaches out to its customers is through pop-up shops.

Warby Parker has set up pop-up shops in a decked-up yellow school bus which went on a cross-country retail tour called The Warby Parker Class Trip, at kiosks in hotels, as yurts (tents on collapsible frameworks), as newsstands, and so on. Its pop-up stores allow Warby Parker to not only showcase its wares to a new audience, it also helps it quickly gather consumer feedback and speedily apply the lessons.

In a conversation with Thomas Robertson, academic director of the Baker Retailing Center at the Wharton School, Warby Parker's co-founder Dave Gilboa compared his company's pop-up strategy to the "agile" approach to software development. Gilboa said: "With every pop-up, we want to give people a reason to come in. Sure, we want to generate sales, but we also want to ensure we're able to gather enough data points to generate meaningful learning."[151] For instance, the pop-ups are a great way for Warby Parker to quickly determine the best locations to set up its permanent stores. Pop-ups are also part of the trend of showrooming where consumers visit physical stores to get a touch and feel of the product before actually buying it online.

> **Pop-ups are an effective way to determine the best locations to set up permanent store.**

In his opinion piece, Robertson lists others like Warby Parker who use pop-ups. These include luxury fashion houses like Prada, startups like Of Mercer (workwear), online home goods retailer Snowe, and footwear brand Allbirds. Robertson said: "Many retailers are treating their pop-up stores as a way to test, learn and iterate on new ideas. To some, it's about testing a hypothesis or validating a new concept. To others, it's about evaluating new markets, studying consumer behavior or collecting actionable data to inform marketing strategy,

---

[151] Credit: Thomas S. Robertson, The Pop-Up Has Grown Up, June 19, 2018, Business of Fashion. Used by permission

R&D and business decisions. But for most, it's still about building brand recognition, engaging new and loyal customers, and igniting social media and PR buzz."[152]

For the post-COVID-19 scenario, Warby Parker, like other retailers, mall operators and indeed all organizations, has redesigned its customer experience to incorporate COVID-19 protocols like social distancing, contactless shopping features, enhanced sanitization, and so on.

Simon Property Group: More than Just Malls

Malls operators too have been getting into the pop-up space. The **Simon Property Group**, one of the largest mall operators in the U.S., has earmarked a permanent space for pop-up shops in its Roosevelt Field mall in New York. Simon Property calls this platform the edit@ Roosevelt Field and describes it as "a curated space for revolving brands, products & trends." According to Zach Beloff, national director of business development at Simon, they want to build a new avenue that would enable brands to come to physical retail early in their life cycle. Talking to *CNBC*, Beloff said: "Brands are looking for the ability to scale, and to scale quickly, and Simon is looking for ways to partner with brands to facilitate that ability to scale."[153]

Malls have also been expanding from retail stores to add experience lifestyle spaces like movie theaters, restaurants, exhibitions, spas, gaming arcades, live performances and so on. In China, for instance, many of the new vertical malls include parking, food shopping, retail, entertainment like movie theaters and gaming arcades, personal care like spas and hair dressers, hotels, and even apartments. Property developers are also now coming up with more integrated developments

---

[152] Credit: Thomas S. Robertson, The Pop-Up Has Grown Up, June 19, 2018, Business of Fashion. Used by permission

[153] "Pop-up Shops Find a Permanent Home at the Mall," CNBC, October 16, 2017. https://www.cnbc.com/2017/10/16/pop-up-shops-find-a-permanent-home-at-the-mall.html

comprising different elements like residential, corporate, hospitality, hospitals, schools and malls.

The approach to shopping mall development and how developers need to be continuously alert to changing the allocation of space to assure that malls have the right mix, illustrates both agility and adaptability. Further, focusing on adjacencies driven by consumer buying behavior can result in the correct selection of specific tenants.

Harman: Moving Up with Connected Devices

In September 2018, Connecticut-based Harman International, a fully-owned subsidiary of Samsung Electronics, which is well-known for audio products and infotainment systems, introduced a device that can convert almost any car into a state-of-the-art connected car. Called the Harman Spark, the device pairs with a smartphone app. It is available through telecom service provider AT&T and works with most car models from 1996 onwards. The Spark comes with a host of features, services and a payment platform. The consumer simply needs to download the app from the App Store or Google Play and plug the Spark into the vehicle's diagnostic port under the steering wheel. While there is a fixed price for the device, AT&T offers different rate plans.

The Harman Spark can convert any car into a state-of-the-art connected car.

The Spark provides features and services such as a Wi-Fi hot spot (this connects up to eight devices allowing passengers to stream videos, listen to music, or play games), emergency crash assistance, roadside assistance, vehicle diagnostics, location information, and parking reservations, among other features. Harman Spark is an example of how you can quickly move an older version (in this case, a car) to a new version with an intermediary intervention without needing to totally overhaul the older system. It shows agility and adaptability on part of Harman *(See Exhibit 10).*

EXHIBIT 10

Harman Spark: Upgrading Your Car Instantly

Harman Spark is a device that instantly upgrades a car to a state-of-the-art connected vehicle. It has features and services such as a wi-fi hot spot which allows passengers to stream videos, listen to music, or play games, driving feedback, trip analysis, emergency crash assistance, roadside assistance, vehicle diagnostics and so on.

SAME CAR. WHOLE NEW RIDE.

Source: https://car.harman.com/solutions/smart-auto/harman-spark. June 2020.

In a press statement, Sanjay Dhawan, Chief Technology Officer at Harman and president of Harman Connected Services, said: "Consumers today are looking for simple devices that make their lives efficient and seamless. Harman Spark allows them to easily and affordably transform older vehicles into smart cars of the future with connected applications."[154] In addition to leveraging its deep expertise in hardware and connected services, Harman plans to continue partnering with innovative brands like AT&T and develop industry-first technologies that advance connectivity across automotive, consumer and enterprise markets.

Spotify—Betting on New Opportunities

Spotify, the leading music streaming service which was launched in 2008, has a catalog of more than 40 million tracks and some 200 million users (of which over 100 million are premium users). The company is looking at new ways, beyond music, to engage with users. Its vision is to become the world's leading audio platform. In the past two years, it has been taking big strides in the podcasting space and, according to its founder and CEO Daniel Ek, it is now the second-largest podcasting platform after Apple's iTunes. In a February 2019 blog post, Ek says: "With the world focused on trying to reduce screen time, it opens up a massive audio opportunity. This opportunity starts with the next phase of growth in audio — podcasting. The format is really evolving and while podcasting is still a relatively small business today, I see incredible growth potential for the space and for Spotify in particular."[155] Ek expects, based on radio industry data, that over time, more than 20% of all Spotify listening will be non-music content. According to media reports, Spotify is also testing a new feature that will allow its users to create podcasts easily.[156]

Spotify made three acquisitions in early 2019 in the podcast space – Gimlet Media, Anchor and Parcast—for around $400 million.

---

[154] "AT&T and HARMAN Launch Advanced Connected Car Device," press release on Harman website, September 24, 2018. https://news.harman.com/releases/at-t-and-harman-launch-advanced-connected-car-device

[155] "The Path Ahead: Audio-First," Spotify website, February 6, 2019. https://newsroom.spotify.com/2019-02-06/audio-first/

[156] "New Spotify Feature Could Make Creating a Podcast Much Easier," Silicon Republic, August 29, 2019. https://www.siliconrepublic.com/companies/spotify-create-podcast-feature

Gimlet is an independent producer of podcast content, Anchor is a leader in podcast creation, publishing, and monetization services, and Parcast is a podcast studio that focuses specifically on story-based series across genres like mystery and crime. These acquisitions are expected to help Spotify become both the premier producer of podcasts and the leading platform for podcast creators. In its 2018 Q4 shareholder letter, Spotify said: "Growing podcast listening on Spotify is an important strategy for driving top of funnel growth, increased user engagement, lower churn, faster revenue growth, and higher margins." It also stated that it wanted to make more acquisitions in the podcast space and that it had "line-of-sight on total spend of $400 million to $500 million on multiple acquisitions in 2019."[157]

Spotify's push into podcasts also helps it develop a new channel for consumption of its core music business. In a conversation with *TechCrunch*, Courtney Holt, the head of Spotify Studios, explained that an expanded podcast offering and better user experience was resulting in people spending more time on the platform overall, including listening to more music.[158]

A 2018 Wall Street Journal article notes that according to consumer and market research firm Edison Research, "monthly podcast listenership in the U.S. has more than doubled over the past five years." If executed well, podcasting will not only expand Spotify's audience base by bringing in a newer audience and more of their time and wallet, it will also allow the company to improve profit margins since podcasts cost less than music.[159]

---

[157] Spotify shareholder letter Q4 2018. https://s22.q4cdn.com/540910603/files/doc_financials/quarterly/2018/q4/Shareholder-Letter-Q4-2018.pdf

[158] "Spotify Buys Gimlet and Anchor in Podcast Push, Earmarks $500 Million for More Deals," TechCrunch, February 6, 2019. https://techcrunch.com/2019/02/06/spotify-doubles-down-on-podcasts/

[159] "Spotify, Pandora Turn to Podcasts for Listeners, Profits," The Wall Street Journal, November 18, 2018. https://www.wsj.com/articles/spotify-pandora-turn-to-podcasts-for-listeners-profits-1542553200?mod=hp_lead_pos10

Spotify now wants to enter another area: hardware. According to a January 2019 *Financial Times* news report, the company is planning to roll out a voice-controlled in-car music player. Spotify's users typically listen on smartphones and connected speakers from players such as Apple, Google and Amazon. Spotify's device, which is likely to cost around $100, is expected to use Bluetooth to sync to car stereos. It will also have preset buttons corresponding to Spotify playlists. With tech firms pushing their own streaming services, Spotify wants to build a direct connection to consumers.[160]

Amazon: From the Everything Store to More

We have earlier discussed how Amazon is able to continuously expand its portfolio of products and services thanks to its deep knowledge of its customers. Let's now look at one more adjacent area that it has been moving into—delivery/package management. To make sure that customers can access their Amazon deliveries safely and reliably at their own convenience, in 2017 Amazon introduced a service called Amazon Hub. This comprises lockers for residential and other complexes. Of course, lockers are not a new concept for Amazon. In 2011, it had launched 'Amazon Lockers' at public places like grocery stores, gyms and convenience stores. Customers simply have to locate a locker close to them, mention the locker location as their delivery address and use a code (sent by Amazon) to unlock the locker and take delivery of their products within three days. If the item is not picked up within the specified time, Amazon takes it back.

The Amazon Hub, however, has an important difference from the Amazon Lockers—it is not restricted only to Amazon packages. It accepts deliveries from all carriers and retailers. By doing this, the Hub not only cuts down the time and cost of its own deliveries, which is very important especially for improving its margins for its

---

[160] "Spotify to Release Voice-Controlled Music Player for Cars," Financial Times, January 18, 2019. https://www.ft.com/content/bcc9b71a-1b33-11e9-b93e-f4351a53f1c3

Prime service (which offers free and quick shipping), and solves an important pain point for customers (of easily picking up products at their convenience), it is also a new line of revenue for the company. Further, it enables Amazon to collect purchase information about consumers—for instance, which other retailers they shop from, how frequently they order, the size of the orders, what time of the year they shop the most, and so on. And data, as we all know, is the new lifeline for companies. Of course, Amazon-branded hubs across buildings give the company great visibility.

Amazon is also partnering with residential apartments to offer a service called "Easier with Amazon." This includes one-year free membership of Amazon Prime, a free Alexa device and locker services for every apartment in the building. According to news reports, Amazon is exploring the possibility of extending the locker service to single and multi-family homes.

In its effort to improve its logistics and delivery capabilities, Amazon has been experimenting with delivering packages via drones and delivering the packages to the trunks of their customers' cars. It is now looking at leveraging autonomous vehicles. In February 2019, it invested in an autonomous driving startup called Aurora which was founded in 2016 by Chris Urmson, one of the core members of Google's self-driving car project, Sterling Anderson, formerly autopilot chief at Tesla, and robotics professor Drew Bagnell, a co-founder of Uber's self-driving car unit.

> **Amazon Hub enables Amazon to collect information about consumers.**

WeWork—From Co-working to Co-living

In 2020, co-working space company WeWork, has been in the news for all the wrong reasons. Its biggest investor SoftBank gave it a valuation of $2.9 billion as of March 31, 2020. In 2019, the company's private valuation before its failed IPO was $47 billion. But it's still an interesting company to consider.

WeWork, which was founded in 2010, transformed the way people work—in friendly and trendy co-work spaces with a strong sense of community, instead of the traditional formal offices. In January 2019, it rebranded itself as the We Company—a clear signal that the company had big ambitions beyond leasing out shared working spaces. Co-founders Adam Neumann and Miguel McKelvey were looking to transform how people live. Announcing the new identity of the company, Neumann, the company's chief executive at that time, said that the We Company would have three divisions— WeWork, which runs co-working, serviced offices across the world; WeLive, its co-living residences; and WeGrow, the education business run by Neumann's wife, Rebekah Paltrow.

WeWork expanded into the co-living space in 2016. WeLive offers fully furnished shared apartments for both short as well as long stays. These come with furniture, bedding, towels, utensils, Wi-Fi, television and what have you. Other amenities include round-the-clock housekeeping teams and concierge service, personal kitchens as well as common eating places and other shared community spaces. As of May 2020, there are two WeLive locations in operation, both in the U.S. One is in New York City and the other is in Crystal City in Washington D.C. In a 2018 interview with Wired, Neuman had pointed out that reinventing the way people live is tougher than changing the way they work. At the same time though, he was bullish. "WeLive," he said, "is going to be a bigger business than WeWork. You can write that."[161]

The COVID-19 pandemic has raised questions about the model of WeWork itself. With social distancing and work-from-home becoming the new normal, is there a future for co-working spaces? Sandeep Mathrani, who took over as CEO in February 2020, believes

[161] "How WeWork Became the Most Hyped Startup in the World," Wired, June 6, 2018. https://www.wired.co.uk/article/we-work-startup-valuation-adam-neumann-interview

that social distancing will actually spur the demand for co-working spaces. In an interview with *CNBC* in May 2020, Mathrani said in order to maintain the required social distancing, companies will need more space. WeWork facilities, he added, can not only provide this space, by design they also have the flexibility to configure any kind of seating. They also have the advantage of being geographically distributed within cities and around the world and this, he said, can cater to the needs of a distributed workforce.

While the future will show how this actually pans out, what is interesting to note is how the company is thinking of capitalizing on the opportunities that could arise out of the pandemic.

To assess how aligned you and your organization are with the ideas and examples discussed in this chapter, we would encourage you to consider the questions listed below.

Ask Yourself:

1. **Have you capitalized on the opportunities that the pandemic has provided with agility and adaptability? Did you leverage adjacencies during the crisis?**

2. **Are you quick in thinking and doing? Are you always in top gear?**

3. **Have you developed an iterative process? Have you adopted approaches like fast-prototyping or introducing minimum viable outputs?**

4. **Do you also think beyond speed?**

5. **Do you have a strong peripheral vision? Can you sense and spot new opportunities quickly and swiftly change tracks as required?**

6. **As you prepare to introduce new and better products, services, solutions and experiences, do you continuously analyze and re-evaluate your strategy?**

7. Do you leverage adjacencies beyond the immediate and the obvious? Along with products, markets, and distribution areas that are new to you, have you looked at areas that have not yet been discovered?

8. Do you use your customer knowledge to cross-sell and increase your share of the customer's wallet?

9. In a dynamically changing environment, can you adapt rapidly? Do you have the capability to flourish in any environment?

10. Even as you adapt, do you also innovate?

11. Do you balance speed and agility with consistency and stability? And do you balance adjacencies and adaptability with both legacy businesses and also with the truly innovative new to the world experiments?

Chapter 6

Principle 6: Innovate Then Experiment, Experiment, Experiment

To come up with a winning strategy, we must understand causality, i.e. the link between what we do and its outcome. Only experimentation allows us to understand this. Especially in times of

> **Crises offer a unique opportunity to keep trying out new things.**

crisis, it is critical to have the discipline to design new initiatives as experiments. Crises also offer a unique opportunity to learn from natural experiments.

"One area where I think we are especially distinctive is failure. I believe we are the best place in the world to fail (we have plenty of practice!), and failure and invention are inseparable twins. To invent you have to experiment, and if you know in advance that it's going to work, it's not an experiment. Most large organizations embrace the idea of invention, but are not willing to suffer the string of failed experiments necessary to get there. .... We all know that if you swing for the fences, you're going to strike out a lot, but you're also going to hit some home runs. The difference between baseball and business, however, is that baseball has a truncated outcome distribution. When you swing, no matter how well you connect with the ball, the most runs you can get is four. In business,

every once in a while, when you step up to the plate, you can score 1,000 runs. This long-tailed distribution of returns is why it's important to be bold. Big winners pay for so many experiments. "[162]

The above statement is from **Amazon** founder and CEO Jeff Bezos' 2015 letter to the shareholders. You may want to double click on it. It contains some valuable lessons regarding what we are discussing in this chapter: the need for adaptive experimentation.

Before we go deeper into this, let us also consider natural experiments and what we can learn from them. Crises, in particular, offer a unique opportunity for this because given the sheer magnitude of change at such times, we have no option but to keep trying out new things. We simply cannot continue in the pre-crisis mode. If we want to navigate a crisis successfully, we must see what can work and then keep improving on our efforts. If we are open to it, we will see that crises throw up new opportunities for us to explore.

> **Experiments meet the critical conditions of causality.**

We have spoken earlier about innovative initiatives by The Met, the Barnes Foundation and the Getty to creatively engage their audiences online and attract new ones during the pandemic. Consider the innovative virtual At-Home Gala by The Met in April 2020. More than 40 leading artists from across the world performed from their homes in a live stream. This has lessons for not only other cultural institutions but also every organization: instead of canceling an event, turn it into a virtual one! Look at Apple. In May 2020, Apple announced that it would host its annual Worldwide Developers Conference virtually this year in the Apple Developer app and on the Apple Developer website. Given that Apple has a global developer community of some 23 million developers, this is a big move.

---

[162] "Jeff Bezos Letter to Shareholders, 2015, "Amazon. https://drive.google.com/file/d/0BzVmPBUYS4gaVE9Cc2tualVLMjA/view

Even as you try out new things, keep in mind that for maximum learning and the best results, you must have the discipline to design any new crisis-related initiatives as experiments. Before we discuss adaptive experimentation and its benefits, let us first understand what it means and how it differs from other activities and initiatives or the usual research approaches.

What is Adaptive Experimentation?

Traditional ways of working typically result in throwing up correlations but not necessarily causality, or the link between what we do and the outcome. Experiments, on the other hand, meet the condition of causality, which is that Event A has to precede Event B, and that when A happens, B happens as well.

> **Only experimentation tells you exactly which strategy worked best and what to do next.**

They rule out all other possible explanations for the results you get. Whenever you enter a new market, the approach you now use in your current market is the control and the new approach is the test.

Take the example of your advertising activities. Whatever be your product or services, you are probably spending a lot of money on advertising and at the end of the year you get some results – it could be better sales, better market share, or better brand recall. In your traditional route, however, because you have only one strategy in play, you have no way of knowing the *exact* impact of your advertising spends. For instance, you don't really know how much of the improved sales was due to the advertising spends and how much was because of other factors like, say, an improved distribution system or change in packing or pricing. The results that you get don't tell you whether you should increase advertising, keep it at the same level or reduce it. On the other hand, if you design experiments across multiple strategies, you will get conclusive results that can guide you to take the next steps. For example, in some markets you spend X amount in advertising, in some markets you spend double the amount, and some other markets you quadruple the amount. At the end of a specified period and using controlled parameters, you compare the results and based on the different outcomes, you can make an informed decision on what to do next. Your decisions are free from biases, intuition or gut instinct. They are also independent of the decision-maker's position in the organizational hierarchy.

In a nutshell, when you engage in only a single strategy, regardless of the results, you don't have any conclusive information on what to do next. Only experimentation tells you exactly which strategy worked best and what to do next. Adaptive experimentation involves the creation and implementation of continuous and iterative experiments to improve your strategies over time. By pursuing several approaches, you will be able to better identify strategies for the next level of experimentation, yielding results that improve with each step. The whole idea of adaptive experimentation is that based on the results we get, we modify what we are doing. No other research methods allow you to do this.

> **Experiments showed Microsoft that its users found fewer but larger ads acceptable.**

And remember, you can use adaptive experimentation for every decision you make—be it around developing new products and services, positioning, pricing, messaging, marketing, distribution, related to operations, talent acquisition, logistics, increasing revenues, building trust, or creating a better customer experience. Basically, every important decision should be subject to experimentation.

Take **Microsoft**. A few years ago, when advertisers on its search-engine Bing wanted larger space for their ads so that they could add more information, the company wasn't sure what to do. It was possible that larger ads could result in dissatisfaction among Bing users. Faced with this uncertainty, Microsoft decided to run a series of tests.

For instance, it showed larger ads from its advertisers but without increasing the total space devoted to ads. This meant fewer ads in a given space as compared to the previous format. The results from its experiments showed Microsoft that this could work; fewer but larger ads were acceptable to its users. Microsoft went ahead with the move, and in the process increased its revenue by more than $50 million annually, according to a 2017 *Harvard Business Review* article titled *The Surprising Power of Online Experiments*, by Ron Kohavi, general manager of the analysis and experimentation team at Microsoft, and Stefan Thomke, professor of business administration at Harvard Business School.

In this *Harvard Business Review* article, Kohavi, and Thomke point out that an "experiment-with-everything" approach has helped Bing "identify dozens of revenue-related changes to make each month— improvements that have collectively increased revenue per search by 10% to 25% each year." The authors say that these improvements, along with many other alterations that enhance user satisfaction, are the "major reason that Bing is profitable and that its share of U.S. searches conducted on personal computers has risen to 23%, up from 8% in 2009, the year it was launched."[163]

Amazon arrived at the placement of credit card offers through a series of experiments.

Kohavi and Thomke also point to **Amazon**'s simple move of placing credit card offers on the shopping-cart page instead of the home page. This has resulted in adding tens of millions of dollars annually to Amazon's bottom line. How did the company arrive at this placement of credit card offers? Through a series of experiments, of course. A *Fast Company* article in 2016 titled *Why These Tech Companies Keep Running Thousands Of Failed Experiments* lists

---

[163] Credit: Ron Kohavi and Stefan Thomke, The Surprising Power of Online Experiments, September–October 2017 Issue, Harvard Business Review. Used by permission

Amazon Web Services (AWS), Kindle, Prime, Echo and Amazon's third-party sellers as some of the "multibillion-dollar" experiments "that have all paid off in the long run" at Amazon. The article adds that at the time of writing, AWS was "the fastest-growing B2B company in history."[164]

"At **Google**, experimentation is practically a mantra," says a company report titled *Overlapping Experiment Infrastructure: More, Better, Faster Experimentation* by Diane Tang, Ashish Agarwal, Deirdre O'Brien and Mike Meyer. The authors say: "We evaluate almost every change that potentially affects what our users experience. Such changes include not only obvious user-visible changes such as modifications to a user interface, but also more subtle changes such as different machine learning algorithms that might affect ranking or content selection. Our insatiable appetite for experimentation has led us to tackle the problems of how to run more experiments, how to run experiments that produce better decisions, and how to run them faster."[165]

> The direct mail industry was one of the earliest adopters of experimentation.

Experimentation is not a new concept. One of the earliest adopters was the direct mail industry. Every player in this industry knew that there was no way they could go with just one format and hope to succeed. They saw that by simply tweaking the layout a little, changing the font type or size, or adding a visual here or there, they could get major results. Through adaptive experimentation, they could take the most effective decisions regarding every variable in their direct mailers. Think about the opportunities that we have today

---

[164] "Why these Tech Companies Keep Running Thousands of Failed Experiments, "Fast Company, September 21, 2019. https://www.fastcompany.com/3063846/why-these-tech-companies-keep-running-thousands-of-failed

[165] "Overlapping Experiment Infrastructure: More, Better, Faster Experimentation, " Diane Tang, Ashish Agarwal, Deirdre O'Brien, Mike Meyer, Google Inc. 2010.

in terms of accessing large samples of customer data; they give us a better window to experiment than ever before.

A/B Testing

One of the simplest ways of experimenting is A/B testing. An A/B test enables you to test how much a particular variable affects your audience's reaction. In this, you set up two variations of the same offering – say a webpage, or a product, or an advertisement. One version—Version A—is the current version that your users are experiencing at present. This is what is called the controlled version. The second version – Version B – is the modified version, the one with the new feature you want to test. You send Version A to half your sample and Version B to the rest (users are assigned the versions randomly). You then compare their reactions, compute the key metrics and determine which version performed better. In the next step, the more effective of the two versions becomes the controlled version and you can have a new modified version. You can continue with this as many times as you like.

Several digital experimentation platforms like Optimizely, Monetate, Unbounce, Mixpanel, VWO, HubSpot, Omniconvert, Crazy Egg, Convert, and others have emerged that facilitate A/B testing and fast experimentation. Look at how their customers are using these platforms. For instance, one of the largest nonprofit scientific and educational institutions in the world, the National Geographic Society, used Monetate to boost both the subscription base for all of its publications, as well as its Society membership registration program. Or see how, in 2012, as part of President Barack Obama's fundraising campaign, the Obama Digital team used Optimizely. One of the tests was for a promotion for supporters to win dinner with the President. The team tested a text version of the form against one

> An A/B test lets you test how much a variable affects your audience's reaction.

with the photo of the President. The result: adding Obama's photo produced a 6.9% increase in donations to enter the sweepstakes *(See Exhibit 1)*.

EXHIBIT 1

Experimentation Gives 2012 Obama Campaign a Boost in Donations

In 2012, as part of President Barack Obama's fundraising campaign, the Obama Digital team was able to iteratively increase donation conversions by 49% and sign-up conversions by 161% by drawing on a deep understanding of their users' motivations, desires, and behavioral quirks. For instance, in one promotion which offered supporters an opportunity to win dinner with the President, adding his photo produced a 6.9% lift in donations to enter the sweepstakes.

Source: Public domain - https://www.obamalibrary.gov/photos-videos

Once you are comfortable with A/B testing and start seeing results from your experiments, you can begin more complex forms of experimentation if required. There is no limit to the number of variables and levels with which you can experiment. Each variable (positioning, price, distribution outlets, advertising, etc.) can come in any number of levels (different positioning, different advertising messages, different levels of advertising spend, etc.). There are lots of experimental designs out there and there is a very rich literature in the area of experimentation.

Why is Adaptive Experimentation Important?

Let's look at the benefits of adaptive experimentation *(See Exhibit 2).*

EXHIBIT 2

Benefits of Adaptive Experimentation

Here are the reasons why you need to adopt adaptive experimentation:

1. It helps understand the causal impact of any activity and facilitates data-driven decisions.

2. It provides the incentive to develop truly innovative initiatives and encourages bold experiments.

3. It forces measuring of results.

4. It requires continuous monitoring of the business environment.

5. It creates an innovative corporate culture resulting in breakthrough ideas.

6. It helps attract the best talent.

7. It creates a compelling competitive advantage.

---

1. **It helps us understand the causal impact of any activity and therefore enables and empowers us to make better decisions**. As we have been discussing in previous chapters, the world is changing at an unprecedented pace. The need of the hour is to be agile, quickly change course when required and make decisions in real-time. If we use only traditional marketing research, which relies on historical data, we will never get the answers that enable us to stay ahead. Small-scale experiments can be used as pre-tests before deciding on a strategy, but you can also design your entire strategy as a series of experiments. For example, you can allocate 80% of your budget to your preferred strategy but use 20% to experiment with other innovative strategies. In this case the results of your experiments are in real-time.

2. **It provides the incentive to develop truly innovative initiatives and encourages us to go with bold experiments.** Why is this? Because it simply doesn't make sense to experiment with slight variations on a strategy since it won't result in any great learning. The focus has to be on bold, innovative strategies.

3. **It forces you to measure the results.** Experimentation requires measurement. The challenge today is that many organizations do not know the ROI of many of their initiatives. Experimentation requires you to determine the measures that you will use to determine success or failure and develop a measurement system.

4. **It requires continuous monitoring of the business environment.** If you conduct field experiments, it is important to continuously monitor the business environment to identify if there are any new conditions that can affect one of the experimental groups and not the others—such as a strike in a specific city, or snowstorm in some market. Knowing if these events occur, allows the researcher to control for their effect as covariates in the analysis.

5. **It creates an innovative corporate culture resulting in breakthrough ideas.** How does it do this? Well, everyone knows that not every experiment will succeed. By promoting continuous experimentation, we send a message to the entire organization that it is okay to fail. We are in effect saying that one must challenge the status quo and take risks. We acknowledge that failure is an integral part of the journey to success and that we must celebrate lessons from failure.

6. **It offers the ability to attract the best talent.** In previous chapters, we spoke about the competition for talent. We discussed how innovative people usually don't want to work with organizations that are risk-averse and not open to

innovation. Think about that here. By the mere fact that you are communicating to everyone that experimentation is at the core of everything you do, that you encourage experimentation with bold innovative ideas, you will be way ahead of your peers in being able to attract the best minds, the best resources.

7. **It creates a compelling competitive advantage.** You not only learn faster, hire better talent, and come up with innovative strategies, you thoroughly confuse the competition. Because you are experimenting continuously, your competitors can't discern your master experimental design. So, while they see your activities in the marketplace, they are not able to relate the results to the activities. They are clueless about your thinking and what your next steps are likely to be. The more complex and the more continuous your experiments, the more you confuse the competition. Think for yourself what this means in the highly competitive times that we are in at present.

These of course are benefits of any experiment. The adaptive experimentation process—which implies continuous experimentation in real-time—adds the dimension that these benefits are in real-time and encompass the entire organization. This leads to a more agile organization with evidence-based decision processes and a higher likelihood of becoming an innovative organization, an early adopter of predictive analytics, and other advances.

If you have any doubt about the importance of adaptive experimentation, just dig around a little. You will find that the best companies, be it Amazon, Microsoft, Apple, Google, Facebook, Uber, Netflix, Airbnb and others, don't make any decision unless they experiment. They continuously run a series of experiments; they run thousands of experiments. We will look at some of these later in the chapter. For those of you who are interested in knowing more about experimentation and how it helps in making data-driven decisions, *The Power of Experiments* by Harvard Business School professors Michael Luca and Max H. Bazerman is a great resource with examples of experimentations by various companies such as eBay, Alibaba and StubHub.

Implementing Adaptive Experimentation

Once we understand what adaptive experimentation is and the benefits it confers, we need to see how best we can implement it in our organizations.

Here are some key action steps for adaptive experimentation developed by one of us (Wind) and listed in the Wharton School's Nano Tools for Leaders. Keep in mind that adaptive experimentation is a continuous and iterative process rather than a linear process. It is a way of thinking involving continuous, iterative experiments. The learning that takes place in step 5 informs the refinement and determination of the next objectives in step 1, meaning that outcomes improve over time.

1. **Determine your objectives:** What achievement(s) is worth the time, effort, and resources needed to run an adaptive experiment?

2. **Create a culture of innovation:** Involve your organization's architectural processes and structures, including technology, reward systems, and incentives. To get buy-in from everyone involved and encourage innovation, assure them that if the results in their experimental areas are not successful, their individual (and group) reward and compensation will not be impacted. Compensate the experimental team if the results of the control are better than those of the test. This reduces the resistance to change.

3. **Design the experiment:** For any innovative strategy, develop full executions, including a selection of markets in

which to implement them. Strategies should be innovative, involving significantly different alternative approaches for resolving a challenge or taking advantage of an opportunity. It is critical that all experiments follow the ethical standards of doing no harm to the participants.

4. **Implement the experiment in a controlled and regulated manner:** A critical aspect of every experiment is the random assignment of respondents to the test and control groups. In medical research it is known as Randomized Control Trial (RTC). An ongoing measurement system must be in place to evaluate your efforts as well as to monitor markets and control for external effects. The monitoring of any changes in the environment is important and the findings (for example a strike, an unusual storm, a change in government policy, etc.) can be used in the analysis as covariate (using ANCOVA – analysis of covariance to analyze the results of the experiment.)

5. **Analyze your results, and use lessons** about what worked and what didn't to develop your next series of experiments. It is important to understand the context in which the experiments are done and its impact on the generalizability of the results. Further, while interpreting the results, search for theories that explain *why* you achieved the results you did.[166]

Funding Adaptive Experimentation

When it comes to funding the adaptive experimentation, the control – the strategy that is considered to be the best—could receive 80% to 90% of the resources, but at least 10% to 20% of the resources could

---

[166] "Adaptive Experimentation: Nano Tools for Leaders," Wharton, 2011. https://executiveeducation.wharton.upenn.edu/thought-leadership/wharton-at-work/2011/06/adaptive-experimentation/

be devoted to experimentation. Here is what you could do: Say your budget for an initiative is $10 million. If you are fully confident that option A is the best option, allocate $8 million to strategy A. Use the other $2 million to experiment with a variety of things in real-time, in a manner that you can get results within two weeks. At the end of two weeks, you will know the exact response that the other strategies B, C, D, etc. have garnered. Then, if strategy C, for example, gave better results than A, you could increase the spend on the winning strategy and continue experimenting with other strategies. This is a continuous process of learning, making decisions, and improving what you are doing. And with this process, you are moving to as much as real-time management as possible, as opposed to relying on historical data.

We believe that most legacy organizations are by and large inefficient. Over time, they have added lots of unnecessary functions, processes and systems. If they were to do a careful analysis of their way of functioning and eliminate things that are redundant and adopt more efficient ways of working (like opening up their innovation process, for instance), they can easily save 20% of their costs. This money can be used for experimentation. The key is to adopt a strategy focused on "doing the right thing right". This goes back to the quality movement of the 1980s and is especially critical for legacy organizations.

> **Adaptive experimentation helps us understand the causal impact of any activity.**

Challenges in Adopting Adaptive Experimentation

Of course, as with any change, adopting the adaptive experimentation approach comes with its own challenges *(See Exhibit 3)*.

EXHIBIT 3

Obstacles to Adopting Adaptive Experimentation

Obstacles one needs to overcome to successfully implement adaptive experimentation:

- Risk-averse mindset
- Fear of failure
- Believing that experimentation is more expensive
- Short-term orientation
- Not including it as part of every strategic plan and budget
- Lack of needed experimental skills
- Inability to measure the results

One key challenge is the risk-averse mental model of the company's leaders, a mindset that is afraid to experiment and wants to maintain the status quo. You may recall that we discussed in Chapter 1 how traditional mental models are in danger of becoming outdated and leaving your business vulnerable to disruptors. Think about that here in the context of what we have just discussed about adaptive experimentation. Realize that by simply continuing to do what you have been doing all along is not allowing you to learn, because you have failed to establish a causal link between what you are doing and the results. Most of the time, you are at best establishing correlation. That doesn't empower you to make the best decisions. This is why it is important to have control group(s). It establishes causality and allows us to draw specific conclusions. Without a control, one does not have an experiment but only an initiative that does not allow knowing the lift the experimental variable causes. Adaptive experimentation forces you to challenge your assumptions. It makes you come up with new strategies. So, be ready to think differently. Recast your mental model.

A related challenge is the fear of failure. Every company that promotes the status quo is essentially telling its employees: "Don't make mistakes. If you make a mistake, you are out." In such an organization, no one will have the courage or the interest to experiment because they will be afraid to fail. Just like a culture of experimentation is a great way of sending the message that failure is permitted, if you have a risk-averse culture that penalizes people for failure, no one will have the courage to experiment. And if you simply pay lip service to experimentation, your employees will at best do minor experiments. They won't take any big bold risks and in turn, the company will miss the big opportunities. As we listed above in our action points, make sure that you don't penalize people for failure. In fact, we would recommend that you develop a whole set of processes and incentives for "lessons from failures" and highlight and celebrate these learnings.

> **Adaptive experimentation enables and empowers us to make better decisions.**

Startups do this in an interesting way. In most startups, the original idea is not what brings them their success. They test the original idea, they learn from it, and based on their learning they pivot to something else. And they keep pivoting until they come up with the winning idea. YouTube, for example, was originally a dating site. Twitter began life as Odeo, a platform for discovering and subscribing to podcasts. Shopify started as an online storefront for selling snowboarding gear. And Flickr began as an online video game. In the startup world, pivoting is not seen as failure; it is seen as learning from something that did not work as expected. Think about it. Pivoting is basically sequential experimentation. This is not a very efficient way of experimentation, but that's the way startups typically develop. As opposed to sequential experimentation, adaptive experimentation is concurrent pivoting. Here, too, the lessons need to be celebrated.

Another challenge is the myth that experimentation is more expensive. People think if they focus on only one initiative, one strategy, they have to spend only on that one thing, but that developing material for multiple versions – A, B, C – be it multiple commercials, marketing plans, pricing, distribution, and so on, will cost them more. Well, sure, it will cost a little more, but at the same time, the benefits are enormous because this is the only way you will know which of these strategies are most effective. And, if one of the new approaches is even 10% or 20% more effective than the current ones, then you would have recovered the entire cost of experimentation and also given your customers a better experience. As Bezos said, big winners pay for a lot of experiments.

Companies sometimes fall short of following ethical standards of doing no harm to the participants. As Hannah Fry, professor at University College London's Centre for Advanced Spatial Analysis, notes in her article titled *Big-Tech Is Testing You*, they must be held accountable to "reasonable ethical standards" or it could result in manipulation.[167]

Some publicly traded companies may have another challenge: balancing the investments required for experimentation with the myopic quarter-on-quarter expectations of shareholders. Here are some ways of addressing this. One way is to highlight the cost-benefit aspect. Two, create a portfolio of experiments. Some can be short-term experiments that are aimed at improving what you are doing in the here and now, while others can be more long-term. We will discuss this in more detail in our next chapter. Three, be more active in selecting the company shareholders; focus on shareholders who have long-term perspectives.

The In-House Advantage

You can approach experimentation in different ways. For instance, you could adopt a centralized model (a central team of data scientists carries out experiments for different business units), a decentralized

> The adaptive experimentation process leads to a more agile organization.

---

167 "Big Tech Is Testing You," The New Yorker, February 24, 2020. https://www. newyorker.com/magazine/2020/03/02/big-tech-is-testing-you

model (different business units have their own data experts), a center of excellence model (this can be either in a centralized structure or in a decentralized structure). There is no right or wrong model, and you don't have to restrict yourself to any approach. What is important is that you figure out what works best for your organization.

We believe that one of the best investments you can make as you start on the journey of adaptive experimentation is to hire someone, maybe even a junior person with a Master's degree in statistics or experimental design or experimental psychology, basically someone who understands experimentation and can implement it. This function should preferably be an in-house function and should be an integral and key part of the firm's operations. Keep in mind that it's a great way to develop your knowledge base. Think of the enormous data that your various experiments will generate and how, based on the results of your experiments, you can start developing empirical generalizations. It could form the core of the knowledge base, the management information system, the knowledge sharing system in your company.

As we have mentioned earlier, getting the buy-in of the relevant people within the organization is critical for the adaptive experimentation approach to be successful. If you are an established organization and this is something you are doing for the first time, you could start small, showcase the results, demonstrate the value, get the relevant people on board, get more teams enthused and involved, and gradually scale it up. But

> **Adaptive experimentation is a continuous and iterative process rather than a linear one.**

if you have new leadership in the company, and if the new leadership believes in experimentation, you can start right away with large-scale experiments and not necessarily with the little ones. What is critical is that every experiment should be a *good* experiment. It should not be just an activity or an initiative. It must have the right kind of control variables and must allow us to draw specific conclusions. It must show causality.

Choosing the Right Experiments and Preparing for Empirical Generalizations

How does one pick and choose which experiments to run in any given area? Here is one effective way: Encourage everyone in the organization to submit their ideas for experimentation. But also tell them that it is not enough for them to just give an idea. They must structure each idea in terms of an experiment with innovative tests, appropriate controls and

A minimum of 10% to 20% of resources could be devoted to experimentation.

meaningful measures. It must have specific yardsticks for measuring impact. The yardstick could be anything. For instance, how will it help to differentiate from the competitors, by how much will it increase the share of wallet of the target consumer, is it synergistic with the overall corporate strategy, how many new customers will it help attract, and so on. Once you have the ideas in the form of suggested experiments, you need to put them through a screening process and evaluate them. Check if it is really innovative, is it practical, is it implementable, is it scalable, what would be the cost of running the experiment, what is the likely return, what is the cost-benefit of the idea, and so on. Then come up with a portfolio of experiments with which to move forward.

The portfolio should include experiments with improved current operations as well as innovative new initiatives preparing the company for the future. In a crisis environment for instance, one should focus on both experiments of how to improve current operations (like improving the engagement and reach of their online initiatives for universities or cultural institutions, or online sales for corporations) as well as innovative experiments combining their old pre-crisis approaches with the lessons from their experience during the crisis (like how to change the definition of work and the workplace given the successful experience with work-from-home.) Every company has to develop its own set of criteria for evaluating potential ideas for experimentation. A good rule is that it must be in line with the unit's or company's business goals and also with its vision and mission.

> **One challenge to adopting adaptive experimentation is the risk-averse mental model of the company's leaders.**

Meta-analysis of various experiments and other data the company has, including natural experiments, are other important aspects to keep in mind. Meta-analysis is very powerful because it establishes convergence validity of results and allows us to identify empirical generalizations. As mentioned earlier, it is also critical to understand the context in which experiments are done in analyzing and interpreting the results and assessing their generalizability. Replication is another important way of validating results.

And how do you know if the experiment has yielded valuable insights? Kohavi and Thomke put it succinctly in their 2017 *Harvard Business Review* article *The Surprising Power of Online Experiments*: "If you really want to understand the value of an experiment, look at the difference between its expected outcome and its actual result. If you thought something was going to happen and it happened, then you haven't learned much. If you thought something was going to happen and it didn't, then you've learned something important. And if you thought something minor was going to happen, and the results are a major surprise and lead to a breakthrough, you've learned something highly valuable."[168]

Earlier in the chapter we saw some experiments that were run by Microsoft and Amazon and others. Here are some more examples of how companies are using experimentation.

---

[168] Credit: Ron Kohavi and Stefan Thomke, The Surprising Power of Online Experiments, September–October 2017 Issue, Harvard Business Review. Used by permission

Microsoft

Let's look at Microsoft again as described in the *Harvard Business Review* article *The Surprising Power of Online Experiments by Ron Kohavi and Stefan Thomke*. Microsoft's analysis and experimentation team of more than 80 people runs hundreds of online controlled experiments on various Microsoft products like Office, Windows, Bing, Cortana, and Skype. Here is a test by Microsoft that resulted in a new, regular feature not just on its own website, but for others too.

Formerly, in line with the way most websites opened links, when users clicked on the Hotmail link on the MSN home page, it would open in the same tab. In 2008, a Microsoft employee in the U.K. suggested opening the Hotmail link in a new tab. The company ran a test with about 900,000 users in the U.K and was impressed with

> **Adaptive experimentation forces you to challenge your assumptions.**

the results. While most changes to engagement have an effect smaller than 1%, the engagement of users who opened Hotmail increased by an 8.9%!

Microsoft decided to go ahead with this new version, but because it was still a new idea, the company decided to release it only in the U.K. In June 2010, Microsoft ran the test in the U.S. with 2.7 million users. Finding similar results, the company decided to release this change worldwide. It then went a step ahead. It decided to see the impact of this—opening the link in a new tab—in another area. It ran a test on more than 12 million users in the U.S. who initiated a search on MSN. The result: clicks per user increased by 5%. *The Surprising Power of Online Experiments* notes that "opening links in new tabs is one of the best ways to increase user engagement that Microsoft has ever introduced, and all it required was changing a few lines of code."[169]

---

[169] Credit: Ron Kohavi and Stefan Thomke, The Surprising Power of Online Experiments, September–October 2017 Issue, Harvard Business Review. Used by permission

> **Do not penalize people for failure.**

In another instance, Microsoft was looking at reducing the time it took Bing to display search results. Before going ahead with this activity, it wanted to ascertain how much it should invest in a potential improvement, how many people it should put on the job. It conducted a series of A/B tests in which artificial delays were added to study the effects of minute differences in loading speed. Kohavi and Thomke point out that the tests showed that every 100-millisecond difference in performance had a 0.6% impact on revenue. They say: "With Bing's yearly revenue surpassing $3 billion, a 100-millisecond speedup is worth $18 million in annual incremental revenue—enough to fund a sizable team. The test results also helped Bing make important trade-offs, specifically about features that might improve the relevance of search results but slow the software's response time." They go on to add: "At Microsoft as a whole, one-third (of the experiments) prove effective, one-third have neutral results, and one-third have negative results. All this goes to show that companies need to kiss a lot of frogs (that is, perform a massive number of experiments) to find a prince."[170]

Uber

At Uber, at any given time there are more than 1,000 experiments running on its experimentation platform which supports experiments across its portfolio of apps for drivers, riders, Uber Eats, and Uber Freight and enables the company to launch new ideas. In a blog post in August 2018 titled *Under the Hood of Uber's Experimentation Platform*, the authors Anirban Deb, Suman Bhattacharya, Jeremy Gu, Tianxia Zhou, Eva Feng, and Mandie Liu write, "Experimentation is at the core of how Uber improves the customer experience. Uber

---

[170] Credit: Ron Kohavi and Stefan Thomke, The Surprising Power of Online Experiments, September–October 2017 Issue, Harvard Business Review. Used by permission

applies several experimental methodologies to use cases as diverse as testing out a new feature to enhancing our app design."[171]

Below are some charts outlining the types of experimentation methodologies that Uber's experimentation platform team uses (*See Exhibit 4*).

EXHIBIT 4

Methodologies Used by Uber's Experimentation Team

Experimentation is at the core of how Uber improves the customer experience. Uber applies several experimental methodologies to use cases as diverse as testing out a new feature to enhancing their app design.

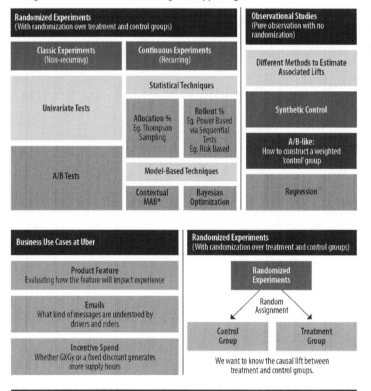

Source: Under the Hood of Uber's Experimentation Platform. https://eng.uber.com/xp. August 28, 2018.
*MAB: Multi-armed bandit (MAB)-based continuous experiments.

---

[171] "Under the Hood of Uber's Experimentation Platform,"Anirban Deb, Suman Bhattacharya, Jeremy Gu, Tianxia Zou, Eva Feng and Mandie Liu, Uber, 2018. https://eng.uber.com/xp/

A November 2018 *Harvard Business Review* article by Jeff Fossett, Duncan Gilchrist and Michael Luca titled *Using Experiments to Launch New Products*, describes how Uber rolled out its Express Pool service in 2018. Here is an extract from the article: "One simple and often overlooked way for larger companies to experiment is to randomize the introduction of new products across a set of markets. To see how this can be valuable, consider how Uber rolled out its Express Pool service in 2018.[172] At the time, the company was already running UberPool, a service that allows passengers heading in the same direction to share rides and costs. With UberPool, passengers are picked up and dropped off wherever they like, as with other Uber services. But with the Express Pool service, which costs even less than UberPool, passengers are generally asked to walk short distances to meet their rides and to reach their destinations. In 2018, in the run-up to the launch of Express Pool, Uber tasked one of us (Duncan, who manages a group of economists and data scientists within the company) with assessing how likely it was to succeed. How many riders would opt-in, and how would the service affect the broader—and more complex—Uber ecosystem?

> **Big winners pay for a lot of experiments.**

"To answer those questions, Duncan and his team conducted an experiment, launching Express Pool in six large markets and then comparing metrics in the launch cities with those in others. Leveraging recent advances in experimental methods—especially a statistical method that allowed Uber to use a weighted combination of other cities to form a more-suitable "synthetic" control group—the team was able to tease out the ways in which the rollout was influencing Uber usage. Unsurprisingly, Express Pool created new kinds of trip

---

[172] Credit: Jeff Fossett, Duncan Gilchrist, Michael Luca, Using Experiments to Launch New Products, November 05, 2018. Harvard Business Review. Used by permission

matches. But the experiment also accounted for the effect that Express Pool had on existing Uber products and made clear that launching it would make good business sense. As a result, Uber was able to confidently introduce Express Pool to many of its major markets. This confidence, and the finding that inspired it, would not have been possible without the experiment."[173]

Airbnb

In a 2014 post in *Medium.com*, an online publishing platform, Jan Overgoor, then data scientist at Airbnb, notes that the company uses controlled experiments to "learn and make decisions at every step of product development, from design to algorithms." Controlled experiments, Overgoor adds, "are equally important in shaping the user experience."

Airbnb has built its own testing framework to run experiments. Overgoor explains why: the complex nature of the company's business, he says, means that experimentation is "more involved than a regular change of a button color." He lists the complexities: Airbnb users can browse the site without signing up and logging in. This makes it more difficult to tie a user to actions. Users often switch devices while booking. For instance, they could start the process on a laptop, but then move to a mobile phone. Also, typically bookings take a few days to confirm, and they are dependent on external factors like responsiveness of hosts. On top of all this, the booking flow is complex. It begins with users searching for accommodation. Once they shortlist a place, they either contact the host, or in some cases, can make an instant booking. If they are required to contact the host, the host has to accept an inquiry and

Every experiment should be a good experiment.

---

[173] Credit: Jeff Fossett, Duncan Gilchrist, Michael Luca, Using Experiments to Launch New Products, November 05, 2018. Harvard Business Review. Used by permission

then the guest has to make the booking. But, whatever be the flow, a critical metric for Airbnb is the overall conversion rate between searching and booking.

The most common way that a user engages with Airbnb is through its website. So an important metric for the team is that when someone is searching for accommodation, Airbnb should be the first result to pop on their search-engine. They must find it quickly and easily. An 2018 article titled *Experimentation & Measurement for Search-Engine Optimization by Brian de Luna, data scientist at Airbnb* says that in late 2017, the company created a new landing page, which they internally called the "Magic Carpet." The new page featured a large header with an image and search box, along with reviews and listing. Its content was clearer than the earlier page and it took less time to load because of its lighter code structure. It had some other improvements too. Airbnb's hypothesis was that the features of the new landing page would increase its relevance, and therefore would result in a higher ranking on search-engine results. This in turn would drive more traffic to its website.[174] The *Harvard Business Review* article *Using Experiments to Launch New Products* notes: "To run the experiment, Airbnb exploited the fact that it had landing pages with different URLs for different markets (San Francisco, Boston, New York, etc.). This meant that they could randomize the different URLs to include the new design or not, thereby isolating the design's effect on search-engine traffic. And by doing that they were able to show that the new design was a success: the new landing page, it turned out, was driving a ~3.5% increase in search traffic, an improvement

> Experiments must be in line with the company's goals and with its vision and mission.

---

[174] "Experimentation & Measurement for Search Engine Optimization: Leveraging a Market-Level Approach to Measure Landing Page Effectiveness on Airbnb," Brian De Luna, Airbnb, 2018. https://medium.com/airbnb-engineering/experimentation-measurement-for-search-engine-optimization-b64136629760

corresponding to tens of millions of incremental visitors per day for the platform. Based on these findings, Airbnb launched the new design for all markets." [175]

In his post Groover notes that when Airbnb wanted to see the impact of changing the maximum value of the price filter on the search page, it ran tests to see the impact of changing the maximum value from $300 to $1000. The experiment ended up neutral. However, the company did in fact launch the increased max price filter. This was because it was found that certain users like the ability to search for high-end places and since there was no dip in the metrics by adding this feature, it decided to accommodate them. Another feature that Airbnb team tested was a new way to select what prices users want to see on the search page. However, tests showed that users preferred the old filter. Therefore, the company did not launch the new feature. [176]

In a 2017 post titled *4 Principles for Making Experimentation Count,* Lindsay M Pettingill, data scientist at Airbnb, summarizes four key principles that underlie experimentation at the company:

1. Product experimentation should be hypothesis-driven,

2. Defining the proper 'exposed population' is paramount,

3. Understanding power is essential, and

4. Failure is an opportunity.

In the post Pettingill writes that when she joined Airbnb in 2015, the company was doing less than 100 experiments in any given week. By 2017, this number had increased to 700. [177]

---

[175] Credit: https://hbr.org/2018/11/using-experiments-to-launch-new-products, Harvard Business Review. Used by permission

[176] "Experiments at Airbnb, "Jan Overgoor, Airbnb, 2014. https://medium.com/ airbnb-engineering/experiments-at-airbnb-e2db3abf39e7

[177] "4 Principles for Making Experimentation Count, "Lindsay M. Pettingil, Airbnb, 2017.
https://medium.com/airbnb-engineering/4-principles-for-making-experimentation-count-7a5f1a5268a

Netflix

> Every product change at Netflix goes through A/B testing.

At Netflix, only members get to see the full range of content that the streaming service offers. Non-members don't have access to this. What non-members see is a screen that offers them a free 30-day trial. If they sign up, they can watch all content on Netflix absolutely free for 30 days. They can watch it anywhere, on any device. And this free trial comes with no strings attached. If they like the service, they can choose a payment plan that suits them and continue to watch beyond the trial period. If not, they can just cancel and leave at any point in time. In the background of the Netflix home page viewers can see a few movie posters, but no other details regarding the contents.

Now, common sense suggests that if non-members could see the full range of content that Netflix has to offer, the likelihood of their signing up for the service would be higher. In fact, according to a survey that Netflix did about *the one thing* that the respondents would like to know about Netflix *before* signing up, 46% said they would like to be able to see what kind of content the service has. Netflix therefore decided to test different options they could present to non-members to preview the available titles. Netflix ran this test five times. To their surprise, every time the original screen (without the browsing option) emerged as the preferred choice.

And here is the reason why: showing and telling is not the same as experiencing. Simply seeing Netflix's full content portfolio didn't give the non-members any sense of the experience that Netflix had to offer. For instance, the ability to pick up watching exactly from where you left, the ability to watch seamlessly on multiple devices, recommendations made especially for them, and so on. As opposed to this, the low barrier to entry, which is the free month – all that the user has to do is to give Netflix their payment details with the guarantee that they won't be charged if they decide to not continue—

surpasses the need to know the complete content before signing up. In exchange for this very minimal commitment, the user gets to have the full and best experience that Netflix has to offer. And this in fact results in a higher conversion rate. As Anna Blaylock, a product designer at Netflix and who was one of the prime drivers of running the above tests, said in a presentation: "The test may have failed five times, but we got smart five times."

In a 2016 blog post titled It's All A/Bout Testing: The Netflix Experimentation Platform, the authors Steve Urban, Rangarajan Sreenivasan, and Vineet Kannan write that "every product change" at Netflix—be it adaptive screening, the UI layout, the title artworks, personalized home page, etc., goes through "a rigorous A/B testing process before becoming the default user experience.... Even the images associated with many titles are A/B tested, sometimes resulting in 20% to 30% more viewing for that title." The authors go on to say: "Results like these highlight why we are so obsessed with A/B testing. By following an empirical approach, we ensure that product changes are not driven by the most opinionated and vocal Netflix employees, but instead by actual data, allowing our members themselves to guide us toward the experiences they love."[178]

> **Uber always has more than 1,000 experiments running on its experimentation platform.**

HP

At HP Inc., the experimentation journey started in 2015. At that time, it was running some infrequent and isolated A/B tests. Today, those fragmented pockets of A/B testing have grown into a formal center of excellence that promotes A/B testing throughout the company. In a

---

[178] "It's All A/Bout Testing: The Netflix Experimentation Platform," Netflix, April 29, 2016. https://netflixtechblog.com/its-all-a-bout-testing-the-netflix-experimentation-platform-4e1ca458c15

webinar on Optimizely, Neville Davey, experimentation manager—worldwide lead at HP, and Anmeen Leong, experimentation manager—Americas, share the story of this journey. The company's business, they point out, is seeing a transformation by way of how customers are interacting and how they browse and shop, and experimentation is an integral part of how the company is gearing up for this.

The experimentation team, which now has 12 members, started out with one business unit—the U.S. direct-to-consumer online store. The team decided on this particular unit because of its high traffic and high order volume which ensured a sizable testing sample size. They started with simple experiments and introduced campaigns that had a meaningful business impact by way of increasing the conversion rate and average revenue per visitor. Some quick wins helped the team to establish credibility. They then went on to HP's B2C stores in other geographies and also areas like the business-to-business store, the customer support sections on its websites, and the brand and marketing pages on HP.com.

Over the years, the center of excellence has created different assets to help introduce new internal stakeholders to A/B testing. For instance, a playbook maps out the key activities of managing an experimentation program for a business unit. Apart from the center of excellence, HP also has a testing council for those stakeholders who need more hands-on help with the day-to-day testing activities. According to Davey, the experimentation team has succeeded in getting new business units across all major regions to adopt A/B testing and is supporting campaigns in over 10 countries. The volume of campaigns has doubled year-over-year and there has been a three-fold increase in the associated revenues.

> **Airbnb has built its own testing framework to run experiments.**

In 2017, HP felt that its Black Friday sale page was not optimized for speed and customer experience and that it needed to enhance it. The experimentation team developed a new single-page application and tested it against the current classic webpage version. As far as the users were concerned it looked just the same. The change was in the back-end. The team carried out this test on the pre-Black Friday sale page. There was an improvement of some 40% in page load time and 15% in conversion. The company then rolled out the single page application for the actual Black Friday and Cyber Monday sales pages. This contributed to double-digit year-over-year sales growth for that business unit over this period.

Leong attributes the growth and success of experimentation at HP to three pillars: solid program management, good technology and data, and evangelizing the program. Going forward, the team's goal is to continue the expansion of stakeholder involvement and to grow campaigns by a further 50% year-over-year.

McKinsey & Company

In September 2019, in a first-of-its-kind move, consulting firm McKinsey opened a retail store of its own. By testing the effectiveness of new technologies in real-life scenarios, McKinsey expects to improve its own understanding and

Shoppers can try products in augmented reality mirrors.

provide better insights to its retail clients on how they can create the winning in-store consumer experience. Called the Modern Retail Collective, McKinsey's store is around 5,000 square feet in size and retails products such as underwear, makeup and jewelry. It is located in the Mall of America in Bloomington in Minnesota, the country's largest retail and entertainment center, and is a collaborative venture between McKinsey, Mall of America, retail brands and technology providers like Microsoft, Zebra, Square, and Smartrac.

In this store, retailers can test the latest technologies with real customers. For instance, shoppers can try out products virtually in augmented reality mirrors, access product information from their phones by scanning near field communication (NFC) tags, check out quickly through a portable point-of-sale device, and so on. A post on McKinsey's website says: "Every four months, a new set of brands will be featured in the Collective with a new use case to test. Examples could include looking at the impact of in-store technology on conversion, sales-associate productivity, inventory automation, post-purchase engagement, and more. By analyzing data from in-store technologies, the team can stitch together and understand customer journeys to unlock unprecedented insights for improving engagement and operational efficiency." Through this store, McKinsey is creating the ability to continuously experiment.[179]

To assess how aligned you and your organization are with the principle and the ideas and examples discussed in this chapter, we would encourage you to consider the questions listed below.

Ask Yourself:

1. **Do you understand the importance of experimenting during a crisis and the value of learning from natural experiments?**

2. **Is adaptive experimentation an intrinsic part of your management philosophy?**

3. **Do you use experimentation for every decision, whether it involves tactical changes or transformational efforts?**

4. **Does your entire organizational architecture support adaptive experimentation?**

5. **Have you developed processes and incentives for lessons from failures and do you highlight and celebrate these learnings?**

---

[179] Credit: Excerpted from "An inside look at the McKinsey store revitalizing brick-and-mortar business", McKinsey & Company, www.mckinsey.com. Copyright (c) 2020 McKinsey & Company. All rights reserved. Reprinted by permission.

6. Have you developed a portfolio of experiments? Are these in line with your company's business goals and its vision and mission?

7. Is every experiment you do a good one, with the right kind of control variables? Does it show causality?

8. Do you learn from your experiments and do you apply these lessons to create a sustainable advantage and build long-term value?

Chapter 7

Principle 7: Redraw Your Timelines and Build a Portfolio of Initiatives Across All Innovation Horizons

Your battle is not only for today. You need to plan concurrently across horizons for experiments and initiatives that can help you offer new valuable experiences and also address new markets in both the short and long-term. In times of crisis, this is even more critical. You need to address the current crisis, create opportunities it offers, and prepare for the next crisis.

Every crisis contains many opportunities. In the face of any crisis, we need to ask ourselves how can we cope with the current crisis, what opportunities does this crisis create, how can we respond quickly and effectively, and what can we do to anticipate and prepare for any crises in the future? The answers to these questions lie in looking beyond the present and building a portfolio of initiatives across all innovation horizons. This principle applies to other times also, after the crisis has abated.

Here are some examples. When should we start planning for our children's college education? When should we start planning for our retirement? When should we start planning for our old age?

> **Look beyond the present and build a portfolio of initiatives across all innovation horizons.**

There are no prizes for the right answer. After all, it's a no-brainer. We need to plan for these life events way before they actually happen. We need to look into the future and plan for these stages of our lives *even as we manage our current expenses.* We cannot wait for the children to finish their schooling and *then* figure out how to fund their higher studies. We cannot retire and *then* look around to see how to fund our sunset years. We cannot let the concerns of our present-day activities blind us to what *we need to do in the current* to secure our future. Right?

> **While you focus on current operations, look at other markets and solutions.**

Well, the same goes for businesses. In order to create a successful and sustainable business, we need to operate and manage the current or the short-term, and also build for the medium and long-term. Now, you may say that's obvious and it is what you do all the time. But think about it again. Are you really allocating your resources effectively across different horizons and building a portfolio of offerings to make yourself future-proof? It may be worthwhile to do a quick review of your activities on this front.

Our experience shows that most companies tend to focus only on current operations. They live in the here and now, and they are most comfortable doing the tried and tested. We believe that all companies, irrespective of their size, industry and maturity, need to allocate their resources to build a portfolio of continuous experiments and initiatives in three innovation horizons.

Innovation Horizons

What do we mean by this? Simply that even as you are experimenting with your current operations and improving and optimizing them, and ensuring that you are profitable and competitive, you need to look two steps ahead. You need to start exploring and considering the next generation of growth opportunities. And, you need to start sowing the seeds of transformational opportunities within your own industries or even beyond them.

You need to explore adjacent markets and solutions that are being used by others but not your own firm. These could be by way of geographies, product categories, business models, or technologies. One way of assessing their viability is by answering a simple question: "Will they help me increase my share of wallet with my current customers?" At the same time, you need to start looking at new markets and solutions – these are areas that others are not addressing, or even exploring, at present. Again, what is important is that even as you are focusing on your current operations (which is horizon 1), you need to look at other existing markets and solutions (horizon 2) and totally new to the world markets and solutions (horizon 3).

> **What we do today to build our tomorrow will determine our growth trajectory.**

The diagram below, which is our modified version based on the framework presented in the book *Innovation Tournaments* by Christian Terwiesch and Karl Ulrich[180], illustrates our thinking *(See Exhibit 1)*.

---

[180] https://wsp.wharton.upenn.edu/book/innovation-tournaments/

EXHIBIT 1

Innovation Horizons

Regardless of who you are, every company has to focus not only on 'now' but, plan and prepare for horizons 2 and 3.

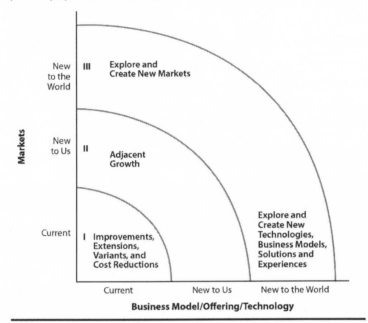

When you think in terms of these horizons and what others are doing, remember that your competitors are not only those in your industry. The competition is for the consumer's time and attention and engagement and it goes beyond traditional industry boundaries.

So, if you are a bank, and you are not offering mobile banking to your customers and have no plans to do so in the near future, you are setting yourself up for failure. Mobile banking is already here and that is where the industry is moving. It is imperative that you start exploring some initiatives in mobile banking that you can offer to your customers sooner than later. That would be your horizon 2. Simultaneously, think of what you could do with Blockchain or predictive AI that could transform your sector and also put you ahead of the others. That would be your horizon 3.

Planning for the future has always been important. So why are we talking about it here? Well, because as we have been highlighting throughout the book, the forces and pace of change that we are witnessing now are unprecedented. And therefore, we must *act now* to create the future. What we do today to build our tomorrow will determine our growth trajectory. And increasingly, growth is not going to come from simply taking market share from others but from spotting and creating new opportunities.

> **The three horizons are not necessarily earmarked by time.**

The Horizons Are Dynamic, Not Static

Keep in mind that these three horizons are not static but dynamic. Experiments and initiatives in horizons 2 and 3 that show promise can be adopted as full-fledged activities to become part of your current portfolio, i.e. horizon 1. In fact, one could even say that the three horizons are not necessarily earmarked by time. Combining a current day (horizon 1) technology with a transformative (horizon 3) business model can result in a disruptive product or service today. We saw this with **Uber**, when we discussed how a new way of looking at an existing problem resulted in a totally new business that has disrupted not just the taxi industry but the entire mobility sector, and even beyond.

If you look back at the various examples that we have been discussing across the different chapters, you will find that many of those companies are in fact allocating their resources across different innovation horizons. We will look at some of them again as we go along, but for now look at **Google/Alphabet's experimental X, (The Moonshot Factory)**. Many of the Alphabet's "moonshot" projects—Waymo (self-driving cars), Chronicle (cybersecurity) and Verily (life sciences), Dandelion (geothermal energy), Loon (Internet balloons) and Wing (delivery drones)—have been spun off as independent businesses. These are great examples of Google's bets that have moved across different horizons.

From being highly futuristic projects, these have moved to horizon 2 and to the present. Consider Wing. In October 2019, in a first-of-its-kind partnership, Wing and U.S. retailer Walgreens launched a pilot program to test on-demand, door-to-door drone delivery service of select items in some categories such health and wellness and food and beverages in Christiansburg, Virginia. Meanwhile, Israeli drone delivery company Flytrex which was started in 2013 by Yariv Bash and Amit Regev and launched its first experiment in Reykjavik in collaboration with AHA, Iceland's largest e-commerce platform, is currently expanding its operations to North Carolina, USA *(See Exhibit 2)*.

EXHIBIT 2

Drone Delivery is Here

Flytrex is an Israeli drone delivery company started in 2013 by Yariv Bash and Amit Regev to provide fast deliveries specially to places that are difficult to access. The Tel Aviv-based company launched its first experiment in Reykjavik in collaboration with AHA, Iceland's largest ecommerce platform. It is currently expanding its operations to North Carolina, USA. Flytrex's Bash also co-founded SpaceL, which developed the Israeli spacecraft Beresheet.

Source: https://flytrex.com. June 2020.

Going back to our retirement example could also be useful here. When we are young, and in our middle-years, retirement is horizon 2 or horizon 3 for us. When we reach retirement age, it becomes our horizon 1. And then, we have to plan for the next stages of our lives, the next horizons.

It's also important to understand that what is horizon 2 and 3 for you could be horizon 1 for someone else, like say, your competitor. Take **Amazon** and **Walmart**. For Amazon, online retail was horizon 1. It was their existing business. Adding brick-and-mortar stores was horizon 2. It was the opposite for Walmart, which started with physical stores and then moved online. Fully-automated, cashier-less stores would be their horizon 3. Or look

> **Combining a current technology with a transformative business model can result in a disruptive product.**

at the electric car market. At the time the electric car was the current business for **Tesla**, its horizon 1, for most other automobile firms it was more in the future. And for Tesla itself, making electric cars affordable for the masses, and exploring driverless cars is its horizon 2/horizon 3. How companies are allocating resources for innovations in the mobility space – be it electric cars, electric bikes, electric scooters, driverless cars—are examples of investing concurrently in different horizons. We will look at some of this in detail later in this chapter.

Let's also look at different innovation horizons in times of crisis *(See Exhibit 3)*. Horizon 1 is all about addressing the crisis. For instance, this could be by way of increasing the effectiveness of our virtual communication in engaging our customers and other stakeholders. Horizon 2 is about identifying new opportunities and designing experiments to start exploring them and preparing ourselves for the post-crisis new reality. Say, reconfiguring work and the workplace to incorporate the pre-crisis patterns with the lessons we have learned about working from home during the crisis. Horizon 3 comprises preparing for the next crisis. Imagine another wave of the coronavirus or the next BIG crisis of global climate change. Do we have the early warning systems to forecast when it is likely to happen? What contingency plans can we prepare to try to prevent it? And if we cannot prevent the crisis, how can we assure the speed and success of our response?

EXHIBIT 3

Strategic Horizons in a Crisis

Even in time of crisis we have to think about the future.

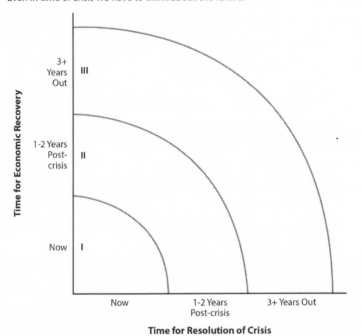

The Allocation Dilemma

One dilemma that leaders often wrestle with is deciding how to allocate resources to each of the three horizons. Well, current operations certainly need to get most of the resources since that is what is bringing in the money. Depending on your mindset you could look at a 90:7:3 or 80:12:8 ratio. So, if you are highly risk-averse, you could allocate 90% for your current operations, 7% for other existing markets and solutions and only 3% for the speculative, new to the world experiments and initiatives. If you are more open-minded, you could look at allocating 80% of your resources to your current operations, 12% for other existing markets and solutions and 8% to the unknown. We believe there should be no hard and fast rules here. It depends on what you, as a company and as a leader, are comfortable with. Some factors that could come into play are, what are the new ideas you have identified for the future? How much will it cost to develop experiments and initiatives around these new ideas? How successful are your current strategies? Can you spend less on your current strategies and operations than what you are doing today and divert the savings to get ready for the future? The allocation also depends on the state of your business. If your offering has become a commodity, or faces severe competition, or relies on obsolete technology which is likely to be replaced in the short-term by new and better technology, you may decide to allocate a much smaller part of your resources to current operations.

The allocation of resources among the three innovation horizons depends also on what you expect might happen. For example, take the speed of recovery in terms of health risks and in terms of the economy during the pandemic crisis of 2020. One must create at the minimum three scenarios and for each of these, we need different resource allocations. For instance, one scenario could be a prolonged downturn where the speed of health and economic recovery both are slow. A second scenario could be where recovery is very fast on both health and economic fronts. A third scenario could be mixed recovery. We spoke about this in CALL TO ACTION.

We have found that often when executives are asked to look at new initiatives, their first response is "Give me the money for it." While this is a natural inclination, we believe it's the wrong approach. As we pointed out in Chapter 6 on the need for experimentation, most established organizations do many things simply out of habit and not for the value they get. If these organizations were to adopt more efficient ways of working, if they were to

What is horizon 2 and 3 for you could be horizon 1 for your competitor.

reimagine and reinvent their operations, they could save up to 20% of what they are spending at present.

This money can be invested in activities in horizons 2 and 3. As an organization, you need to stop doing things simply because you are used to doing them. You need to get rid of non-value producing activities and be willing to allocate resources on initiatives where the return on investment is not certain. In Chapter 4, we highlighted the benefits of open innovation. We discussed how moving some activities to open innovation can save you money even while providing better and faster results. Think about that when you are looking at how to fund new experiments and initiatives.

> **Allocation of resources depends on what you, as a company, are comfortable with.**

Every company has its own unique situations and characteristics. So, identify where you are in your journey, stop doing things that have no value any more, recognize your risk-taking ability, and decide how much you want to allocate for the different horizons. The key point is you simply cannot focus only on your current business. You must *proactively* allocate some resources for horizons 2 and 3. If you want to continue to lead, you must *proactively* budget for the medium and the long-term.

A February 2019 McKinsey article titled *Bias busters: Pruning projects proactively* suggests two ways of deciding whether or not to continue investing in any existing asset. One, every year a company's corporate planning team must identify 3% to 5% of assets that are underperforming and could be divested. The onus then is on the business unit to prove that these assets can be turned around and are worth continuing. Two, categorize existing businesses into groups such as grow, maintain or dispose, and have clear investment rules for each group. Executives must explain why existing businesses should be grown or maintained rather than discarded.[181]

---

[181] "Bias Busters: Pruning Projects Proactively, "McKinsey, February 6, 2019. https://www.mckinsey.com/business-functions/strategy-and-corporate-finance/ our-insights/bias-busters-pruning-projects-proactively

When it comes to choosing experiments and initiatives across the horizons, this depends on your company's situation. You should set priorities based on market needs, opportunities, competition, the cost of developing the new ideas, the cost of delaying them, and the risks involved.

The Capabilities Checklist

Let us now look at the capabilities required to build a portfolio across the innovation horizons. Broadly speaking, you need management capability on the one hand and technical and executional expertise on the other. Management capability is having the ability to understand the need to go beyond the status quo and having the courage and willingness to embrace the unknown. Technical expertise consists of understanding experimental design and having the ability to implement new ideas. Here, the executional capabilities depend on the different areas with which you are dealing.

> Stop doing things simply because you are used to doing them.

Let's say you are a company (in any area) and there are huge developments in technology such as artificial intelligence or Blockchain in your industry. Clearly, this is something you can't ignore. The technology is already here. Or, maybe you are a bank and not active in mobile payments. Or, you are a pharma company and not looking at gene therapy, or immunotherapy. If you are not already doing something as part of your ongoing operations in these new technologies, it is critical that you have some experiments in these areas because that is where your industry is moving. It's not only about new technologies, though. It could be related to say, marketing. We have spoken earlier about how consumers are increasingly becoming skeptical and empowered. If marketing teams continue with traditional ways of reaching out to consumers, there could be a huge disconnect. Companies must be willing to try out new things in the marketing domain. Similarly, in every area, you must be willing to test what is untested for you and also what is untested for the world.

Of course, embarking on this route has its own challenges. As is the case with trying to do anything new, you need to have the courage to bet on the unknown. And, given the pace of change around us, you need to do it fast; you cannot put it on the back burner. So if you, as the leader, believe that you don't have the mental makeup for driving experiments and initiatives across the three horizons, if you can't champion this, then you need to empower your team members to do it. Let the heads of the different business units or different brands take charge of it.

A question that may arise is whether you need to have different teams working on the different horizons. As with the allocation ratios, here too we would say it depends on your situation. For instance, at the overall corporate level or in your various business units or your different brands, if you have enough people with the skills and capabilities and the bandwidth to work across the three horizons, you don't really need separate teams. But, if you find that your current structure can't stretch beyond the current horizon, then by all means put together new units and/or new and dedicated teams for horizons 2 and 3. New markets and new offerings are often outside the boundaries of existing business units and current brands. In such a scenario, you may need a corporate unit to focus on the development of new offerings for new markets. See what works best for you and decide accordingly.

> **If you want to lead, you must proactively budget for the medium and long term.**

You must be willing and able to take the necessary steps to build or acquire the required capabilities. If you don't have the capabilities within the organization to design and execute experiments and initiatives across the different horizons, you must have the courage to go out and bring in new talent. You could forge strategic partnerships, you could look at acquisitions, you could open up your innovation process, you could think in terms of establishing accelerators. Alongside, look at building and leveraging networks. Look at the networks that you have, see how you can orchestrate and manage them most effectively. Wherever needed, you must also have the courage to fire employees who are not able or willing to acquire new skills. We have spoken about these measures in our previous chapters. See how well it ties up here.

We have also discussed the need to change the organizational architecture in order to be a winner in the new world. We spoke about the need to change processes, the need to bridge the silos between various departments, leverage initiative and resources across them, eliminate duplication of effort, and offer an integrated experience to the consumers, to build a culture that encourages and rewards innovative thinking, to rework the incentive structures, reexamine the performance measures, and so on. Remember what we said earlier about moving to a more sophisticated and more effective measure such as increasing your share of the consumer's wallet instead of simply looking at increasing your market share. All those elements are relevant here. In the next chapter we will look at all this in greater detail. In Chapter 5 we spoke of the need to be an agile organization. Think of how important that is in the context of looking across horizons. With the environment being as dynamic and as competitive as it is, you need to be quick and agile in terms of coming up with new initiatives and new experiments to stay ahead of the game.

> **Have the courage to test what is untested for you and for the world.**

Momentum in Mobility

Let us go back to the mobility space. As we saw in our previous chapters, there is a huge buzz around electric and driverless vehicles. Huge investments are being made, new models being planned, partnerships and acquisitions being forged, and so on. Here is a task for you. Look at the different activities in the mobility space in the context of the different horizons, and try and see for yourself how different players are making their moves in different horizons and also how these moves are shifting from horizon 3 to 2 to 1. If you are from this industry, ask yourself if you are on track like your competitors. If you are from another industry, reflect on what similar developments you can envision in your industry and what you should be doing to participate in these trends.

Electric Cars

From Premium to Affordable

Let us consider what's happening in the electric vehicle space. Take **Tesla,** the most high-profile player in this area. When Tesla was founded in 2003, its immediate goal (horizon 1) was producing electric vehicles that would be better, quicker and more fun to drive than gasoline cars.

> Be willing to take the steps to build or acquire the required capabilities.

Tesla's vision for the future, its medium and long-term plan (horizons 2 & 3) was to make its electric vehicles not only better than gasoline cars, but also make them affordable *(See Exhibit 4).* In a post in 2006, Tesla co-founder and CEO Elon Musk said that the "overarching purpose" of the company was "to help expedite the move from a mine-and-burn hydrocarbon economy toward a solar electric economy," and that Tesla's strategy was "to enter at the high-end of the market, where customers are prepared to pay a premium, and then drive down market as fast as possible to higher unit volume and lower prices with each successive model." [182]

---

[182] "The Secret Tesla Motors Master Plan (Just between You and Me),"Tesla, August 2, 2006. https://www.tesla.com/blog/secret-tesla-motors-master-plan-just-between-you-and-me

Tesla launched its first electric car, the Roadster, in 2008. This was a sports car. It then went on to launch Model S, a premium all-electric sedan in 2012. In 2015, Tesla expanded its product line with Model X, a sport-utility vehicle. The following year, in 2016, the company introduced Model 3, a low-priced, high-volume, mass-market electric vehicle. Interestingly, when Tesla announced Model 3 for $35,000, it spurred tens of thousands of people to put down $1,000 deposits long before production started in 2017. The company's latest Model Y, a midsize SUV is expected to be available by fall of 2020. As of the end of May 2020, Tesla's website showed an eight to 12 weeks' delivery timeline for this model.

EXHIBIT 4

Illustrative Example of 3 Horizon Strategies – Tesla

Concurrent portfolio of all 3 horizons – Tesla.

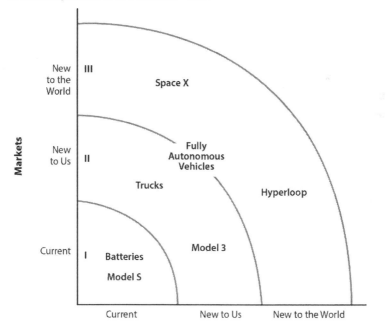

Meanwhile, German automobile manufacturer **Porsche**, a Volkswagen company, unveiled its first electric car, the Taycan, in September 2019. Taycan comes in two versions—the 751 horsepower Taycan Turbo S priced at around $185,000 and the 670 horsepower Taycan Turbo for around $151,000. The base version of the car is expected to be priced at less than $100,000.

In keeping with its goal of creating a sustainable energy ecosystem, Tesla also makes energy solutions like solar panels, solar roofs, and power packs for homeowners, businesses, and utilities to manage renewable energy generation, storage, and consumption. In order to significantly

> **Be open to changing the organizational architecture.**

reduce battery cell costs, Tesla has an in-house cell production facility called the Gigafactory. This supports both its automotive and energy products.

And where do Musk's plans to transport people in hyper-loops, and his space exploration activities, fit in? It was in 2013 that Musk first spoke about a futuristic transportation system. His Boring Company set up in December 2013 is working on hyper-loop tunnels. Musk has used open innovation competition to develop innovative designs for the hyper-loop. If Musk's thinking bears fruit, it might be possible to travel from say Washington D.C. to New York City in half an hour. On the space exploration front, Musk's SpaceX, started in 2002, designs, manufactures and launches advanced rockets and spacecraft. Musk wants to revolutionize space technology and his ultimate goal is to enable people to live on other planets. We would say these are Musk's horizon 3.

Aerospace group **Boeing's** $20 million investment announced in October 2019 into Richard Branson's space tourism firm Virgin Galactic is another example of a horizon 3 investment. **Virgin Galactic** has already completed two crewed flights of its vehicle into space and prior to the pandemic was anticipating a commercial launch in 2020. This will now depend on how the pandemic unfolds. In February

2020, the company announced its 'One Small Step' initiative as part of its re-opening of spaceflight ticket sales (it had stopped new ticket sales after its first space flight in December 2018) whereby people can register for seats on payment of a fully refundable deposit of $1000 and be front of line when the tickets are made available. According to a company statement in May 2020, 400 people from across 44 countries had registered under this program. On full ticket payment this could translate to over $100 million in revenue. (Prior to the One Small Step, the company had 600 customers with reservations on its spaceflights.) Virgin Galactic's former CEO George Whitesides said that the company's strategic goals and its plans for commercial launch continued to be areas of focus.

Partnering for Growth

Here are a few other developments in the electric vehicle space. In April 2019, Ford announced an investment of $500 million in **Rivian**, a Michigan-based electric vehicle startup which has developed a battery-powered pickup truck (expected to be available in late 2020) and an electric sport-utility vehicle (expected to be available in 2021). Rivian is considered a potential rival to Tesla. This partnership is expected to help Ford catch up with rivals in the new technology and accelerate its efforts to come up with its own electric vehicles. In February 2019, Amazon led a $700 million funding round in Rivian.[183] In Chapter 5, we discussed Amazon's investment in autonomous driving startup Aurora as part of its strategy to improve its logistics and delivery capability. Think about it here. See how these different pieces are forward-thinking moves by

> There is a huge buzz around electric and driverless vehicles.

---

[183] "Electric Truck Start-Up Rivian Announces $700 Million Investment Round Led by Amazon, "February 15, 2019.
https://www.cnbc.com/2019/02/15/rivian-announces-700-million-investment-round-led-by-amazon.html

Amazon to leverage next-generation technologies to transform the way it operates and thereby emerge stronger.

Meanwhile, American supermarket chain **Kroger** has been making significant inroads on this route. After a successful pilot in Arizona in 2018 with robotics firm Nuro, a California-based startup working on a self-driving vehicle to transport local goods, in April 2019, Kroger launched its autonomous grocery delivery service in Houston, Texas. The service uses a fleet of manual and self-driving Toyota Prius cars and Kroger will be adding the next generation of Nuro's driverless vehicles to its fleet *(See Exhibit 5)*.

EXHIBIT 5

Kroger's Grocery Autonomous Delivery Vehicle

The Kroger Co. (NYSE: KR) and Nuro announced a partnership to redefine the grocery customer experience for Americans by piloting an on-road, fully autonomous delivery experience. Kroger and Nuro launched their autonomous delivery service in spring of 2019. Houston is the second market for Kroger and Nuro's delivery service, after their first pilot market in Scottsdale, AZ.

Credit: Kroger and Nuro Press Release, June 28, 2018, Nuro. Used by permission.

Nuro was founded in 2016 by Dave Ferguson and Jiajun Zhu, who were formerly with Google's self-driving car project. In a 2018 press statement at the launch of the unmanned service in Scottsdale, Ferguson said: "Nuro envisions a world without errands, where everything is on-demand and can be delivered affordably. Operating a delivery service using our custom unmanned vehicles is an important first step toward that goal."

We will talk more about autonomous vehicles below. But first, let's see some more developments in the electric vehicle space. In April 2019, German automaker **Daimler** paid $100 million and picked up a 10% stake in Sila Nanotechnologies, a California-based battery materials startup co-founded by Gene Berdichevsky, a former Tesla employee. This is one of the first tech unicorns (valuation of more than $1 billion) in the area of enhancing battery chemistry. The next-generation battery know-how is expected to reduce the cost and increase the range of electric vehicles. In an April 2019 *Financial Times* article, Berdichevsky pointed out that a car is now defined by its chemistry. He said: "The range, the cost, the acceleration and the recharge time are all a function of the chemical materials going into the cell." [184] Look at how Daimler's stake in Sila is in line with its target of wanting 25% of its fleet to be electric cars by 2025. Meanwhile Volkswagen and BMW (along with Goldman Sachs, IKEA and others) are backing Swedish battery maker Northvolt, started by former Tesla executives.

> **Musk wants to revolutionize space technology to let people live on other planets.**

Building New Concepts

Volkswagen is betting big on its modular electrification toolkit (MEB), an underlying chassis or platform designed specifically for electric vehicles. The automaker has been working on the MEB since

---

[184] "Daimler invests $100m in Californian battery start-up, "Financial Times, April 2019. https://www.ft.com/content/f18add04-6033-11e9-b285-3acd5d43599e

2015 and it is expected to be the building block for some 30 models across the Group's brands by 2025. So far, Volkswagen has presented three e-concept vehicles based on the MEB. It plans to start series production of a compact car based on the MEB in 2020. An article in the Volkswagen magazine describes the MEB as "an investment in mobility of the future."

Volkswagen is opening up the MEB to third parties too. Germany-based electric vehicle startup e.GO Mobile AG has signed up as its first partner. Volkswagen is also talking to other potential collaborators. This could well be a significant shift in the way the automobile industry works. In what way? Well, typically, automakers develop their own powertrains (comprising the engine, transmission and drive shafts, etc.) and traditionally their powertrains distinguish their vehicles from those of their competitors. But in this digital age, users are increasingly becoming more interested in the electronic and infotainment features of the vehicles. So, if an automaker decides to go with Volkswagen's MEB, it doesn't need to worry about the powertrain. Instead, it can sharpen its focus on what matters more to today's consumers. For Volkswagen, it is a way of not only recovering the costs it has incurred on developing the MEB, but it could also result in new business and revenue models. If its electric chassis becomes the industry standard, Volkswagen could dominate the after-market for maintenance. See the long-term innovative thinking at play here.

> Users are increasingly interested in the vehicles' electronic and infotainment features.

Meanwhile, German startup **Lilium**, the maker of a five-seater electric jet, wants to revolutionize urban transportation by drastically reducing travel time. The company's vision is of "a world where anyone can fly anywhere, anytime." Lilium was founded in 2015. In 2017, the company successfully flight-tested a two-seater prototype, and in May 2019, the five-seater Lilium Jet had its maiden flight over Germany. The Lilium Jet is powered by 36 all-electric engines and is capable of traveling up to 300 kilometers in 60 minutes *(See Exhibit 6)*. Lilium plans to start an app-based on-demand air taxi service from 2025. Since inception, Lilium has received funding of more than $100 million from investors such as Atomico, Tencent, LGT, Freigeist and Obvious Ventures. The company employs some 300 people.

EXHIBIT 6

Lilium's Air Taxi

Lilium was named as one of the top innovative companies in Europe, in 2020, by Fast Company. The company says it has successfully completed more than a hundred tests of the vehicle flying at speeds of up to 62 mph. The Lilium Jet has an intrinsically simple design. With 36 single-stage electric motors providing near-instantaneous thrust in almost any direction, control surfaces, such as rudders, ailerons or a tail, aren't required. Neither are the oil circuits and gearboxes you would find in a typical aircraft. This contributes to the Lilium Jet having around the same number of individual parts as a family car, or 1,000 times fewer than a traditional jetliner. As well as making the aircraft simpler and faster to design, it also means less maintenance and less cost once in operation.

Credit: Lilium, GmbH. https://lilium.com/ March 10, 2020. © 2020 Lilium GmbH. All rights reserved.

Going Driverless

Let's go back to the autonomous cars arena. Just a few years ago, the idea of autonomous cars was just that, an idea. Any car company that was doing anything on this front was on horizon 3. Today, autonomous cars are a reality. They are now horizon 2 for some companies. And, soon, they could be horizon 1.

Waymo

> Automakers do not necessarily need to offer full-fledged level 5 features.

Look at **Waymo**'s journey. It began as Google's self-driving car project in 2009. In 2012, Google employees started testing the technology on highways. In 2015, a custom-built prototype vehicle named Firefly took to public roads and Steve Mahan, a legally blind person and a non-Google employee took the world's first fully public self-driving ride on public rides in Austin, Texas in the Firefly. In 2016, this self-driving car project was spun off as a separate self-driving technology company under Alphabet. In 2017, Waymo invited residents in Phoenix, AZ to join in the first public trial of self-driving vehicles. The company is using their feedback to shape its technology, service, and customer experience. The same year, Waymo's fully self-driving vehicles started test-driving on public roads without anyone in the driver's seat. In 2018, Waymo launched Waymo One, a commercial self-driving service (with trained drivers who serve as backup), in the Metro Phoenix area in Arizona. The company plans gradually to expand the service to other areas.

In April 2019, Waymo announced that it was setting up the world's first factory dedicated to the mass-production of Level 4 autonomous vehicles in Detroit. (Level 4 automation is defined as a car that can drive itself almost all the time without any human input but might be programmed not to drive in unmapped areas or during severe weather. This is a car you could sleep in. Level 5 automation means full automation in all conditions. Automakers don't necessarily need to wait to offer full-fledged level 5 features. They can start with offering partial solutions of value.) Waymo is also testing self-driving trucks.

Acquisitions and Partnerships

In March 2019, **Daimler Trucks**, the world's largest truck manufacturer and a division of the Daimler Group, acquired a majority stake in U.S.-based **Torc Robotics**, a self-driving technology startup that develops software for fully autonomous vehicles. Torc has its genesis in the Virginia Tech university team that entered the 2004 DARPA Grand Challenge, the driverless car contest sponsored by the U.S. Defense Advanced Research Projects Agency. (Incidentally, Google's self-driving project also goes back to a 2005 DARPA Grand Challenge.)

Other auto majors have also been going the acquisition or partnering route to accelerate their autonomous journeys. In 2016, General Motors acquired San Francisco-based Cruise Automation reportedly for more than $1 billion. The following year it announced that it plans to add more than 1,100 new jobs and invest $14 million in a new research and development facility for Cruise Automation over a five-year period. In 2018, General Motors partnered with the SoftBank Vision Fund for a $2.25 billion investment and with Honda for $2.75 billion investment in Cruise. General Motors itself also put in an additional $1.1 billion. Then, in May 2019, Cruise got a fresh infusion of funds of $1.15 billion from asset management firm T Rowe Price and its existing investors General Motors, SoftBank's Vision Fund, and Honda.[185] In 2017, Ford made a $1 billion investment

---

[185] "GM's Cruise Gets $1.15 billion New Cash From T. Rowe Price, SoftBank, " Reuters, May 7, 2019.
   https://in.reuters.com/article/gm-autonomous-cruise-investment/gms-cruise-gets-1-15-billion-new-cash-from-t-rowe-price-softbank-idINKCN1SD1Z3

in Pittsburgh-based Argo AI as part of its plans to start a robotaxi service.[186]

> Uber's investments in self-driving cars, bikes, and food delivery are part of a risk-mitigation strategy.

In June 2019, Fiat Chrysler Automobiles entered into a partnership with autonomous driving startup Aurora to develop and deploy self-driving commercial vehicles. The same month Hyundai Motor Group, which includes Hyundai Motor Company and Kia Motors Corporation, also invested in Aurora in a series-B financing round. Hyundai and Kia have been working together since 2018 to develop the Aurora Driver's integration into Hyundai's fuel cell vehicle Nexo.

In April 2019, Toyota took a minority stake in Uber's Advanced Technologies Group, the unit that is working on self-driving vehicles. (Uber spun off its ATG as a separate entity just weeks before it filed for an IPO and Toyota, which had already made an investment of $500 million in Uber in August 2018, decided to take a stake in the new entity.[187] Softbank's Vison Fund and the Japanese auto parts supplier Denso have also invested in Uber's ATG.)

Uber's strong focus on autonomous cars, spinning off the ATG, getting funding for it, is part of its strategy to future-proof itself. The cab-hailing market is picking up globally and getting increasingly competitive. It is not just other popular cab-hailing competitors like Lyft and Ola that Uber has to contend with, but also other players with new models that are threatening to disrupt the space. Take Here

---

[186] "Ford Invests $1 Billion in Pittsburgh – based Argo AI to Build Self-Driving Cars by 2021, "TECH Crunch, February 18, 2017. https://techcrunch.com/2017/02/18/ford-invests-in-pittsburgh-based-argo-ai-to-build-self-driving-cars-by-2021/

[187] "Toyota to Invest $500 Million in Uber For Self Driving Cars, "Reuters, August 28, 2018.
https://www.reuters.com/article/us-uber-toyota/toyota-to-invest-500-million-in-uber-for-self-driving-cars-idUSKCN1LC203

Technologies, a Germany-based location technology company. In January 2019, Here Technologies launched a new transportation app called SoMo (short for social mobility). This app adds a social layer to mobility. It aggregates all available transportation options in real-time and also leverages social networks and connects people based on their mobility needs. So, while today Uber is the leader in the cab-hailing segment, its leadership knows that they must make more bets to stay ahead. And then there is of course the threat of autonomous cars disrupting the very business model of all cab-hailing firms. Uber's investments in self-driving cars, and bikes, and food delivery are all a part of this risk-mitigation strategy.

> **Companies in autonomous driving have been allocating resources to make it a reality.**

In November 2019, Hyundai and Chinese autonomous driving technology startup **Pony.ai** launched BotRide, a shared, on-demand, autonomous vehicle service in Irvine, California. Users can hail an autonomous Hyundai vehicle directly from their smartphone using the BotRide app. The app directs passengers to nearby stops for pick up and drop off. Pony.ai has been testing its robotaxi pilot service in China since late 2018.

Chinese firms seem to have some advantage on the autonomous driving track. China has designated some places for testing autonomous vehicles. Streets in these designated places have facilities such as digital lane markers that can switch parts of the road to AV-only on demand and sensors to guide cars. There are also rules about how humans can move around in these designated areas. This support from the government makes it easier for Chinese firms like Baidu, Pony.ai and WeRide to test out their technologies and also limits their legal liabilities in case of accidents.

We can see from these examples how companies in a space that once seemed so far off in the future have been allocating their resources to make it a reality. Going by various statements (in the pre-corona crisis days), the early 2020s seem to be when most automakers are looking to come up with their Level 4 self-driving vehicles. An increased focus on the required infrastructure and standards supporting regulations, including vehicle-to-everything (V2X) regulations—where self-driving cars could talk to one another, to traffic lights, and to other elements in the environment—could speed up the development. But after the crisis, automakers will also need to assess the demand for self-driving vehicles. According to a *New York Times* article titled *Who Will Own the Cars That Drive Themselves?*, a survey of auto owners in 2019 showed that 31% were excited about developments in autonomous cars. In May 2020, in a poll of 400 active car shoppers, this number was 22%. While the samples were different, it does suggest a potential decline in interest. Concerns regarding shared rides and vehicles used by others also need to be considered in the post-COVID-19 era.[188]

Let's move on to what some companies in other industries are doing.

Making Inroads Into New Areas

In October 2018, U.S.–based **Mastercard and Grab**, the Singapore-based ride-hailing company, which is fast expanding into other areas such as food delivery and mobile payments, entered into a partnership to launch Grab Pay, a prepaid card *(See Exhibit 7)*. This was launched in Singapore in December 2019. Next on the card are Philippines and other places in the region. Why is this important for the two companies? Well, 200 million people are expected to enter the middle class in this region by 2030. This

The Mastercard-Grab partnership can give both companies significant insights regarding consumer trends.

---

[188] "Who Will Own the Cars That Will Drive Themselves?" The New York Times, May 29, 2020.
https://www.nytimes.com/2020/05/29/business/ownership-autonomous-cars-coronavirus.html

partnership can give significant insights regarding consumer trends to both Mastercard and Grab and help them plan their future strategies and create more relevant products and services.

EXHIBIT 7

Grab-Mastercard Launch Asia's First Numberless Cards

Grab Launches Asia's First Numberless Card in partnership with Mastercard. The GrabPay Card has no numbers on the physical card, offering users exceptional security when they transact. The GrabPay digital and physical card vastly expands Grab's offline and online merchant ecosystem, allowing users, regardless of whether they have a bank account, to transact securely and easily online or offline, at nearly 53 million merchants worldwide that accept Mastercard cards.

Source: https://newsroom.mastercard.com/asia-pacific/press-releases/grab-launches-asias-first-number-less-card. December 5, 2019.

According to Grab's co-founder Anthony Tan, key targets for the company are to expand its financial services business and become south-east Asia's top food delivery service. In June 2019, Grab received funding of $300 million from U.S. investor manager Invesco, taking

Invesco's total investment in the company to $703 million.[189] Grab's other investors include Softbank, Toyota and Microsoft. **Microsoft** has also invested in Uber as well as Ola, the ride-hailing business in India. Microsoft recognizes the emerging ride-hailing sector as fast-growing and these partnerships are a way to strengthen its share of business in this industry. In a media statement, Peggy Johnson, executive vice president at Microsoft, said: "Our partnership with Grab opens up new opportunities to innovate in both a rapidly evolving industry and growth region."[190]

In earlier chapters, we discussed some other strategies of Microsoft like its acquisition of LinkedIn and Github. We saw how over the past decade Microsoft has moved Office from a set of productivity tools to a cloud service across any platform and device. We also discussed how **IBM** is transforming itself for the digital age. We spoke about how this 107-year-old company moved from being a hardware manufacturer to a consulting and services firm and is now betting big on its cloud and AI platform. We saw how tech giant **Apple** is reinventing itself and building new business models and new revenue streams with new services such as the Apple TV+ (entertainment/video streaming), Apple News + (news), Apple Arcade (gaming) and Apple Card (credit card). Recall what Apple's CEO Tim Cook indicated in January 2019 about the future of the company. Cook said that he believed that Apple's biggest contribution would be in health care. Apple is creating its future, now. [191]

---

[189] "Grab raises $300m from Invesco to move beyond ride-hailing", Financial Times, June 2019. https://www.ft.com/content/bc6feca6-98d5-11e9-8cfb-30c211dcd229

[190] "Grab forges strategic cloud partnership with Microsoft to drive innovation and adoption of digital services across Southeast Asia, "Cision PR Newswire, October 9, 2018. https://www.prnewswire.com/in/news-releases/grab-forges-strategic-cloud-partnership-with-microsoft-to-drive-innovation-and-adoption-of-digital-services-across-southeast-asia-696016251.html

[191] "Tim Cook: Apple's greatest contribution will be 'about health', "CNBC, January 8, 2019.
https://www.cnbc.com/2019/01/08/tim-cook-teases-new-apple-services-tied-to-health-care.html

Do keep in mind that these things don't happen overnight. These examples show how these companies are thinking for the long-term and have been allocating their resources across different innovation horizons. As we said earlier, when you look at the examples we discussed earlier in the book across different contexts like that of recasting your mental, business and revenue models, or opening up your innovation process, or designing for agility, adjacencies and adaptability, you will see how many of them illustrate what we are advocating here. This shows how the principles we are proposing are intertwined.

Take **Disney** and the video-on-demand space. When Netflix started its on-demand video streaming service, for other players in the entertainment space, like Disney for instance, video streaming was probably a horizon 2 activity. It was something new that others (like Netflix) were doing, but Disney itself was not. However, Disney was ready to change. Once Disney realized this was a growing space, it decided to step into it and has been gradually increasing its presence. As we noted earlier, in 2016 it bought a 33% stake in BAMTech, a leading player in direct-to-consumer streaming technology and increased this to a majority stake the following year. In 2018, it launched its first streaming service, the sports-related ESPN+. The same year Disney also acquired 21ˢᵗ Century Fox and its blockbuster context and streaming service Hulu. In November 2019, Disney launched a second streaming service. Called Disney+, this offers a portfolio of Disney titles, original series, content from Marvel and Star War franchises, etc. Disney+ is priced at $7 a month in the U.S, lower than Netflix. Clearly, on-demand streaming is now top priority for Disney. It is going all out to make it work. We would say, it's now at horizon 1 for Disney.

> **Once Disney realized that video streaming was growing, it decided to gradually increase its presence.**

Karl Ulrich, author of the *Innovation Tournaments*, spoke in a *Knowledge@Wharton* interview about **Pixar Animation Studios**, which is a subsidiary of Disney. Pointing out that Pixar is "quite disciplined on evaluating several hundred storylines for movies before they decide what to do," Ulrich noted: "So what we see as consumers at the end of the process is really the result of very careful and structured process of evaluating ideas and developing ideas in order to identify those that are really going to work well."[192]

In a 2008 Harvard Business Review article titled *How Pixar Fosters Collective Creativity*, Ed Catmull, who co-founded Pixar along with Steve Jobs and John Lasseter, shared key aspects that led to Pixar's success and how one can build a sustainable creative organization. Catmull wrote that their absolute commitment to certain principles and practices played a central role. Pixar, he noted, is "a community in the true sense of the word. We think that lasting relationships matter, and we share some basic beliefs: Talent is rare. Management's job is not to prevent risk but to build the capability to recover when failures occur. It must be safe to tell the truth. We must constantly challenge all of our assumptions and search for the flaws that could destroy our culture." According to Catmull, "If you want to be original, you have to accept the uncertainty, even when it's uncomfortable, and have the capability to recover when your organization takes a big risk and fails."[193] In his 2014 book titled *Creativity, Inc.: Overcoming the Unseen Forces That Stand in the Way of True Inspiration,* Catmull talks in detail about Pixar's journey over the years. [194]You may want to take some pointers from there.

If we go back to the innovations that we discussed in health care – the work that **Penn Medicine** or startups like **Moderna Therapeutics, Quentis Therapeutics, Tempest Therapeutics** are

---

[192] "Wharton's Karl Ulrich Analyzes the Strategies of Today's Most Successfully Innovative Companies, "Knowledge @ Wharton, February 20, 2012. https://knowledge.wharton.upenn.edu/article/whartons-karl-ulrich-analyzes-the-strategies-of-todays-most-successfully-innovative-companies/

[193] "How Pixar Fosters Collective Creativity, "Ed Catmull, Harvard Business Review, 2008. https://hbr.org/2008/09/how-pixar-fosters-collective-creativity

[194] Ed Catmull, Creativity, Inc.: Overcoming the Unseen Forces That Stand in the Way of True Inspiration, Transworld Publishers, 2014. https://www.creativityincbook.com/about/

doing in immunotherapy – we will find that while earlier we spoke about them in the context of personalization, all of them are in fact also placing calculated bets on the future. They are working at creating next-generation and new to the world treatments.

Nestle is exploring new horizons with its investments in developing DNA-based personalized nutrition. Nestlé's bread and butter today is its regular food and beverages and nutrition business, but concurrently it is also getting ready for the future where it expects personalized nutrition to be big business. In April 2019, Nestlé made a new investment in the future. It announced the creation of the Nestlé R&D Accelerator. To be based in Lausanne, Switzerland, the accelerator will bring together Nestlé scientists, students and startups. As the name suggests, the idea is to accelerate the development of innovative products and systems. In a media statement, Stefan Palzer, executive vice president and CTO of Nestlé S.A. said: "We have taken a number of steps to accelerate innovation, including our enhanced prototyping capabilities and the funding of fast-track projects.

> **Nestle is getting ready for a future where personalized nutrition will be big business.**

With the Nestlé R&D Accelerator and its proximity to our R&D and business teams, we will bring open innovation to a new level. Combining our internal expertise and the deep knowledge of our academic and industrial partners with the external entrepreneurial creativity is a unique approach and will create an innovation powerhouse. It will accelerate the translation of innovative ideas and concepts into tangible prototypes and products."[195]

We could go on with more examples. But suffice to say that if we were to look at any thriving business, any disruptor or successful

---

[195] Credit: Vevey, Switzerland, Launch of Nestlé R&D Accelerator to boost innovation and speed-to-market, Apr 10, 2019. https://www.nestle.com/media/pressreleases/AllPressReleases/nestle-research-and-development-accelerator-launch. Used by permission

defender, it is certain that one of their key success factors would be their willingness and ability to allocate resources across different innovation horizons.

To assess how aligned you and your organization are with the principle and the ideas and examples discussed in this chapter, we would encourage you to consider the questions listed below.

Ask Yourself:

1. Do you have the capability to address the current crisis, create opportunities it offers, and prepare for the next crisis?

2. Do you plan continuously and concurrently for the future even as you manage your current day-to-day business?

3. Do you continuously identify new and transformative growth areas?

4. Do you carry out experiments and initiatives across all innovation horizons?

5. Do you review all operations regularly and systematically and discard activities that do not contribute value?

6. Do you regularly identify your horizons 1, 2 and 3 investments?

7. Do you proactively allocate resources for activities across the different horizons based on the unique situation of your company?

8. Do you assess the distribution of your resources among the 3 horizons? Do you have at least 10% in horizons 2 and 3?

9. If you do not have any investments in horizon 3, do you reflect on what these could be?

10. Do you have the courage to quickly do what is untried and untested?

Chapter 8

Principle 8: Deploy Idealized Design, Recreate Your Organizational Architecture and Network Orchestration

---

Does your organizational vision, architecture, and network orchestration support your disruptive strategies? To capture opportunities in times of crisis and disruption, you may have to change your vision, objectives and strategy. This would require a new idealized design as well as redesigning the organizational architecture and network orchestration.

During times of crisis, opportunities often arise for mergers and acquisitions (M&A). These target M&A candidates are attractive because, beaten by the crisis, they are available at alluring prices. However, before rushing to capitalize on these "bargains," it is prudent to first go through an idealized design exercise and explore at least two scenarios: a post-crisis scenario with the acquired company and one without it. One can also expand the scenarios to reflect the expected time of recovery, more than two M&A conditions, and so on. Going through such an exercise is a useful addition to the traditional due diligence process, and can help assure that the new acquisition leads to the desired outcome.

The AOL-Time Warner merger failed because the organizational architecture could not deliver the integrated strategy.

Undertake idealized design to determine the ideal vision, mission, objectives and strategies for your company.

Failures teach many lessons. For Steve Case, the founding CEO of AOL, a big takeaway from the Time Warner acquisition was what Thomas Edison said a century earlier—that "vision without execution is hallucination." [196] (Case shared this in an October 2015 podcast with Business Insider) [197]. When Case's new-world media company AOL bought old-world media firm Time Warner in 2000 for a whopping $165 billion, it created the world's largest media conglomerate. It was heralded as the merger of the century; the combined entity AOL-Time Warner was expected to be a winning combination of old and new. But it failed to fulfill its promise. In 2005 when Case left the merged entity he said it was an unsustainable partnership. In 2009, AOL and Time Warner split into two separate companies.[198]

In an interview with CNBC in 2019, Case said that AOL and Time Warner had issues with "culture" and too much "short-term orientation." Some people in the combined entity were not enthusiastic about its digital path. "They tended to play defense, trying to protect what already existed as opposed to playing offense and try to create

---

[196] "Billionaire investor Steve Case says the failure of the 2000 AOL Time Warner mega merger taught him a crucial lesson about execution," Business Insider, October 13, 2018. https://www.businessinsider.in/Billionaire-investor-Steve-Case-says-the-failure-of-the-2000-AOL-Time-Warner-mega-merger-taught-him-a-crucial-lesson-about-execution/articleshow/66197365.cms

[197] "Billionaire AOL cofounder Steve Case says we're at the start of the internet's third wave, and he's laying the groundwork to benefit from it,"Business Insider, October 5, 2018. https://www.businessinsider.in/Billionaire-AOL-cofounder-Steve-Case-says-were-at-the-start-the-internets-third-wave-and-hes-laying-the-groundwork-to-benefit-from-it/articleshow/66089500.cms?utm_source=contentofinterest&utm_medium=text&utm_campaign=cppst

[198] "It's Time to Take it Apart, "Washington Post, December 11, 2015. https://www.washingtonpost.com/wp-dyn/content/article/2005/12/10/AR2005121000099.html

what the future would be." [199] Talking to Business Insider again in 2018, Case explained that while ideas were important, executing them well was even more so. The AOL-Time Warner merger failed to get that part right, he added.[200] The team was unable to establish the trust required to make the combined company thrive.

The coming together of AOL and Time Warner was a brilliant strategy that failed because the organizational architecture was not capable of delivering the new integrated strategy. As we come toward the end of our book, we would like you to think about your organizational architecture and how ready it is for the challenges you have to gear up for and the strategies on which you have to deliver.

In previous chapters we have described how every industry and business is going through massive upheavals. The changes are complex, and they occur on multiple fronts. We have suggested various strategic principles for you to not

> **Achieving your objective by doing what you do now is not a stretch goal.**

only defend yourself against disruptors but also become successful disruptors yourself and capture opportunities in times of crisis. We have spoken about the need to challenge our mental, business and revenue models, the need for creative destruction, for building a customer-centric front-to-back digital architecture, of leveraging the cloud and the cognitive technologies, of co-creating with customers, offering personalized experiences, being agile, adopting open innovation, continuously experimenting, allocating resources across different innovation horizons, and so on.

---

[199] "Steve Case to AT&T: Learn from my AOL-Time Warner failures,"CNBC, June 13, 2018. https://www.cnbc.com/2018/06/13/steve-case-to-att-learn-from-my-aol-time-warner-failures.html

[200] "Billionaire investor Steve Case says the failure of the 2000 AOL Time Warner mega merger taught him a crucial lesson about execution, " Business Insider, October 13, 2018.. https://www.businessinsider.in/Billionaire-investor-Steve-Case-says-the-failure-of-the-2000-AOL-Time-Warner-mega-merger-taught-him-a-crucial-lesson-about-execution/articleshow/66197365.cms

The Importance of Idealized Design

All these principles will enable you to deliver relevant and real-time value and experience to your customers. But to ensure that you can *execute* on all these principles, you need to take some critical steps. To begin with, you need to undertake an idealized design process to determine the ideal vision, mission and objectives and strategies that you want for your company. What do we mean by this? 'Idealized design' is a concept propounded by Russell Ackoff, Wharton professor of management science and a pioneer in the field of operations research, systems thinking and management science. Most people and most organizations first look at where they are at present and then, based on that, they try to figure out how they can reach a desired outcome. In idealized design, the idea is to first envision the ideal state and then work backward to the current state. Instead of simply improving the different parts, you first design the whole and then design the required parts.

> Examine every component of your organizational architecture and network orchestration.

In their book *Idealized Design: Creating an Organization's Future Today,* Ackoff and his co-authors Jason Magidson and Herbert J. Addison state: "The way to get to the best outcome is to imagine what the ideal solution would be and then work backward to where you are today." [201] This is important because it prevents you from creating boundaries and barriers before you even know what you want to achieve. For instance, consider a stretch objective such as landing on the moon in a defined time frame or developing fully autonomous cars or flying cars. When you have such stretch objectives, you have to start by designing the future and then, using backward planning, ask yourself questions on how to get there. How do you know if an objective is a stretch objective or not? It's a simple test. If you can achieve the objective by continuing to do what you currently do, it is not a stretch objective.

---

[201] Russell Lincoln Ackoff, Jason Magidson and Herbert J. Addison, "Idealized Design: Creating an Organization's Future," Wharton School, 2006. https://books.google.co.in/books/about/Idealized_Design.html?id=KBiKQgAACAAJ&redir_esc=y

The **Zero Hunger | Zero Waste** initiative by U.S.-based leading food retailer Kroger is a great example of a stretch objective. More than 40% of the food produced in the U.S. each year is estimated to be wasted, while one in eight people remain hungry. Kroger has envisioned a world without waste and hunger. In 2017, Kroger announced that by 2025 it would end hunger in the communities it is present in and also eliminate food waste across the company. Rodney McMullen, Kroger's chairman and CEO calls this Kroger's "moonshot".

Zero Hunger | Zero Waste is a seven-point plan *(See Exhibit 1).*

EXHIBIT 1

Kroger's Zero Hunger | Zero Waste Plan

The Zero Hunger | Zero Waste initiative by U.S.-based leading food retailer Kroger is a great example for inspirational vision and stretch objective. As more than 40% of the food produced in the U.S. each year is estimated to be wasted, while one in eight people remains hungry, Kroger aims to end hunger in the communities it is present in and also eliminate food waste across the company by 2025.

Source: Kroger website, June 2020.

Kroger knew that it could not achieve this objective on its own. It decided to crowdsource for solutions, asking communities, partners and other stakeholders to help provide ideas, feedback and best practices as the effort evolved. It also developed transparent metrics to track its progress. The progress card below is from the company's 2019 Sustainability Report *(See Exhibit 2)*.

EXHIBIT 2

Kroger's Zero Hunger | Zero Waste Progress Card

Kroger publishes progress reports tracking the success of it's Zero Hunger | Zero Waste initiative. Below is an excerpt from their 2019 sustainability report.

Goal: Establish $10 million Innovation Fund
Target Year: 2020
Progress:
- Established The Kroger Co. Zero Hunger | Zero Waste Foundation to advance our mission.
- Introduced the Zero Hunger | Zero Waste Innovation Fund to help fill the gap in philanthropic funding to end food waste. First open call resulted in nearly 400 funding requests for $1 million in grants.

Goal: Accelerate food donations to give 1 billion meals by 2020; 3 billion by 2025
Target Years: 2020 and 2025
Progress:
2020: • Rescued 100 million pounds of food company-wide in 2018 through Zero Hunger | Zero Waste Food Rescue, a 10% increase from 2017.
2025: • Achieved 2018 store participation goals: 83% of stores donate food consistently every month, and 51% of stores rescue food from all five fresh departments.
    • With food and funds combined, Kroger and The Kroger Co. Foundation have directed nearly 650 million meals in two years toward our three-year, 1-billion-meal goal.

Goal: Donate not just more food, more balanced meals
Target Years: 2025
Progress:
- Tested programs to expand Zero Hunger | Zero Waste Food Rescue to include additional items for higher nutrition. Examples include: 1) fresh, never-frozen seafood; 2) select Deli fresh prepared foods; and 3) excess raw milk captured for processing.

Goal: Advocate for public policy solutions
Target Year: 2025
Progress:
- Convened and joined multi-stakeholder discussions about hunger and waste at national and local levels.
- Worked with states to expand items that can be safely donated; supported recycling infrastructure development where needed.

Source: Kroger Sustainability Report, 2019. http://sustainability.kroger.com/Kroger-2019-ESG-Report.pdf

---

Kroger was founded in 1883. As of September 2019, it operated some 2,800 grocery retail stores in different formats like supermarkets, seamless digital shopping options, price-impact warehouse stores, and multi-department stores. It also operates around 35 food production or manufacturing facilities and has 44 distribution centers. Kroger has identified its purpose as: 'To feed the human spirit.' The company says: "We believe our world is hungry for uplift. It's a universal need, as powerful as our need for food or fuel. That's why, with caring as our currency, we feed the human spirit." **Zero Hunger | Zero Waste** was inspired by this purpose. It came about when McMullen challenged the company's corporate affairs team to define a vision for who Kroger is in the community. Kroger believes that Zero Hunger | Zero Waste has the power and potential to help it live its purpose and fulfill it and is an integral part of its strategy.

Zero Hunger | Zero Waste is Kroger's moonshot. What is *yours*? Can you identify what is your moonshot? To help you create an idealized design, we have developed a tool for you. You will find this in the next chapter.

Organizational Architecture and Network Orchestration

Once you have the idealized design in place, you need to examine every component of your organizational architecture and network orchestration and see to what extent they allow you to execute on the principles we have recommended. Keep in mind that organizational architecture and network orchestration are closely linked. For example, to enable the operations of an Uber network or Airbnb network you need a technology platform and creative business model.

> Redesign your organizational architecture in a way that lets you implement your new strategies effectively.

What are the components of the organizational architecture and network orchestration that will allow us to successfully design and implement our strategies? It's the usual suspects. We have touched upon them in previous chapters. They include organizational values and culture; business and revenue models; the processes—both the value-creating and supporting processes; the organizational structure; governance and leadership; employees and the talent we have access to outside the organization; performance measures and incentives; the technology we use; resources by way of funds, but increasingly also the data we have, our customer networks, our distributor networks; the physical spaces around the globe; the design and implementation of a network orchestration involving either creating a network (think Apple Developer network, Facebook network, Uber network of drivers and customers, etc.) or joining various networks and designing the ideal ecosystem that will allow the firm to achieve its vision and objectives *(See Exhibit 3).*

EXHIBIT 3

Key Components of Organizational Architecture

Having the right organizational architecture and network orchestration is critical for successful implementation of the strategies that will accomplish our objectives and vision. The key components of the organizational architecture and network orchestration are listed below.

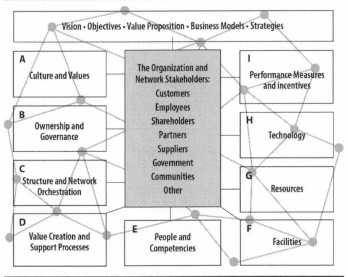

Source: Adapted from diagram in the book titled Driving Change by Jerry Wind and Jeremy Main.

You need to adopt an all-encompassing and holistic approach toward your organizational architecture and redesign it in a manner that you can implement all your new strategies effectively and deliver a seamless customer experience. Ask yourself: If you have to move toward offering "real-time and personalized experience," is your organization and network ready to deliver it? The organizational architecture must be geared to equip you for the new reality. Let's also keep in mind here that the agility, flexibility, speed, etc. that we spoke about in Chapter 5 on the need for an agile organization, relates to every element of the organizational architecture.

Remember that redesigning your internal organizational architecture is not enough. You also need to open up your innovation strategies and build strong networks. Ask yourself if you have the right network orchestration to bring about open innovation and all the benefits it brings. When you are reinventing your organizational architecture, redesign your external network also. We firmly believe that only with this holistic approach can you get optimum results.

The Need for Courage

Planning and executing the necessary changes in all these and other elements of organizational architecture and moving from the current state to the idealized state involves massive change management. These changes are likely to lead to resistance, to disruption, to resentment, to difficult decisions involving firing of loyal employees, and closing of unprofitable lines. These are difficult decisions for most executives.

> **Everyone in a key position within the organization must be bold to bring about change.**

The solution is not procrastination but decisiveness. This requires courage and determination from the top leadership. And, remember, it is not only the CEO who needs to have courage. Everyone in a key position within the organization must be bold to bring about change.

This is especially important in times of crisis because speed of action and decisiveness, while at the same time being compassionate, is critical. As we have been reiterating, every crisis offers an opportunity for change. We have discussed the forced changes brought about by the coronavirus—the changes caused by social distancing, work-from-home, closing of classrooms, museums, cultural institutions, sports activities, retailing, among several others. The leaders of these institutions had no choice; they had to change. But, after the crisis, will they have the courage to resist just going back to the pre-crisis patterns? Will they be willing to make the needed change taking into account the lessons from the crisis?

Why are we emphasizing this point about courage? Well, because any change can be frightening. Most people, and this applies also to the top management in organizations, are afraid of introducing major changes because of their possible repercussions. They prefer to maintain the status quo. Think about it. Say the CEO has just a few years before he retires. What is his mindset likely to be? In all probability he will think: "Why should I rock the boat? Let my successor worry about it." This is true for people down the chain too. Everyone is worried about the impact any kind of change will have on their jobs and roles. So they prefer to keep doing the same things.

We mentioned earlier that a key challenge for legacy firms is to maintain and grow their current business even as they launch new strategies and businesses. At the same time, wherever required they need to be ready to cannibalize their existing business to make way for the new. A company that has been a poster child for cannibalizing its business is **Intel** *(See Exhibit 4)*. New models that Intel introduces cannibalize previous models. But again, most companies are afraid of cannibalizing their current sales and so they are afraid of introducing new solutions that could potentially cannibalize what they are doing. This lack of courage leads to a fear of any kind of change and results in an anti-change, anti-innovation mindset. And this is a sure path to becoming redundant.

> **Lack of courage results in an anti-change, anti-innovation mindset.**

A prime example is **Kodak**, which was afraid to lose its film-based business and missed becoming a leader in digital photography, though it invented that technology.

EXHIBIT 4

Have the Courage to Cannibalize and Innovate

To be on the leading edge of technology and market leadership, companies have to continuously innovate and have the courage to cannibalize their existing products.

Getting back to the components of organizational architecture, let us look at how you can redesign them to make them more effective in helping you achieve your goals.

Culture

Your company's culture is critical. Culture includes the underlying shared beliefs, attitudes, assumptions, values, and ways of interacting that lead to your organization's unique environment. Our stated values allow us to communicate important issues. For example, "do not harm" as a value will increase the likelihood of striving for a "win-win" relationship with everyone, be it consumers, employees, or partners. A value like 'transparency' will encourage the development of transparency in all operations. A value like "always be fair and inclusive" will ensure that there is no discrimination on any grounds be it race, gender, or religion. It will send a strong message and make everyone in the organization realize that any unfair practice or discrimination is unacceptable and will not tolerated by the management.

Our values must also respond to what's happening around us. At Pennsylvania-based wealth management technology firm SEI Investments, for instance, during the Black Lives Matter upsurge in mid-2020 in the U.S., the company put out a strong and clearly articulated corporate statement on its website. SEI made it clear that racism had no place in society and that it would fight systemic racism and social injustice and would work toward becoming a force for change.

> Ensure that you are leveraging technologies that enable you to make real-time decisions.

So, to begin with, formulate a clear strategic vision. This sets the company's direction. Then, effectively communicate the value of the culture and ensure that *everybody* in the organization from the highest to the lowest employee across all functions and departments understands the values that are intrinsic to you.

An important part of a company's culture is resilience. In good times, it helps companies to perform better than their peers. In tough times, in times of complete uncertainty like the COVID-19 pandemic, it helps companies to survive. A meta-analysis published by consulting firm Gallup in May 2020 shows that an important factor in making organizations resilient is employee-engagement. According to Gallup, five elements that differentiate resilient business unit cultures from others during a crisis are as follows: Employees have clarity from their managers about what is expected of them; they have the right resources to get the work done; they get opportunities to leverage their strengths; they see a connection between their work and a larger purpose of the organization, and they have committed co-workers they can respect and on whom they can depend.

Here are some key aspects of culture and values that we believe are required for the success of the strategies we are advocating:

- Have a sense of urgency toward everything.
- Do the right things right.
- Be inclusive, fair and compassionate.
- For every price point, ensure the highest possible quality.
- Balance the short-term and long-term orientation.
- Encourage creativity and innovation.
- Adopt an experimental philosophy.
- Be collaborative and encourage bridging silos.
- Be accountable. Behave as an owner.
- Be customer-centric.
- Create win-win strategies for all stakeholders.
- Be transparent.

Processes

Look at your organization's processes. Like all organizations, in yours too some processes are service functions while others are value-creating functions. Some processes deal with fundamental questions: For example, how do we get new clients? How do we serve our clients better? How do we manage portfolios? Or, what is the process for dealing with complaints? How you approach each process can have a huge impact. For example, you can look at the processes for dealing with customer complaints as a necessary evil or you can look at them as an opportunity for engaging with customers, understanding them better, strengthening your relationship with them and thereby serving them better. Consider call centers. If you are an organization with a call center, the odds are that you have outsourced it probably to India or other low-wage countries. Yet, what if you looked at a call center not as a cost center with the objective of minimizing cost but as a process to improve customer engagement and experience and potentially generate new revenues? Or, take your accounting functions, including the pricing process, negotiations with vendors, or sending out invoices. Reexamine anything that touches the customer and ensure that they meet your objectives for fostering "win-win" relationships with the customers. In effect, you can turn any interaction with the customer into an engagement with the customer and a value-creating function. You just need to make sure that every one of them is in sync with your larger goal.

Another key point is that organizations tend to cling to, and in fact even cherish, old and familiar processes. But given the huge advances in automation and technologies such as AI and cognitive computing and the enormous changes in the business environment, we need to regularly examine all current processes and keep assessing whether different processes are needed. It is imperative to reexamine the appropriateness of all old processes and assess if they are still needed to fulfill new demands.

This is especially true in times of crisis when many earlier processes simply cannot be followed. This is in fact a great opportunity for bringing about change. For example, from traditional sales process involving face-to-face meetings to a digital sales process; from requiring physical signatures on documents to allowing digital signatures; from traditional check deposit in banks to electronic deposit; from checks to electronic transfer of funds or mobile payments; from fixed work hours to flexible hours, from work at the office to a virtual organization with a mixture of work-from-home and office presence,

> **Check if the current structure allows you to implement our eight principles.**

and so on. In times of crisis when there is forced social distancing and availability of transportation is restricted, for example, companies have no choice but to reexamine and change many processes *(See Exhibit 5)*.

EXHIBIT 5

Illustrative Shifts in the Ways of Working

Processes at the workplace need to change and keep pace with the new ways of working.

FROM	TO
Fixed work hours	Flexible work hours
Working at office premises	Working from anywhere
Face-to-face internal meetings	Virtual meetings
Face-to-face client/sales meetings	Hybrid including digital selling
Physical signatures on documents	Digital signatures
Traditional check deposits in banks	Electronic deposit
In-branch check deposits	Check images uploaded via app
Mostly local teams	Global teams
Mostly full time employees (FTE)	Mix of FTE and open talent

When it comes to decision-making processes, ensure that you are leveraging real-time data, real-time and mobile dynamic dashboards, predictive analytics, and other technologies (including augmented reality using fashionable glasses as display devices) that enable you to make real-time decisions. Think in terms of "choice architecture" or the different ways in which choices can be presented and how that impacts decision-making. For example, consider the choice of offering opting-in versus opting-out as part of a customer acquisition or engagement process. The organ donation example shows that while you get very few volunteers when it is opt-in you get a huge response when it is opt-out.

Structure

Similarly, examine your organizational structure. What is the reporting structure? How does information flow within your organization? What is the basis for making decisions? What is the basis for operations, for development, for marketing? Is your organization structured by way of business divisions, or market segments or functions? Is it a flat organization? Is it a hierarchical organization? Is it a network organization? Check if the current structure allows you to implement the principles we have discussed in the previous chapters. If it doesn't, then make the appropriate changes.

For example, given our emphasis on customer focus, we recommend that the organizational structure should be by homogenous markets (or clusters of similar markets). A B2B market structure can include account-based strategies with profit and loss for each account and focusing on maximizing the share of wallet of each account. Structural and other organization architecture solutions are needed to encourage bridging the silos and leveraging resources across the organization. Often, structure dictates the profit and loss reporting units of organizations. It therefore has to be augmented with processes, measures, incentives and other components of the organizational architecture that will facilitate bridging the profit and loss silos and also allow the creation of integrated (across silos) solutions and seamless customer experience. Ensure that whatever be the structure, it allows you to keep your customers at the center while leveraging your resources and assuring efficient and effective operations.

> **Examine if you have what it takes to create a multi-locational and virtual organization.**

Virtual Organization

Examine if you have what it takes to create a multi-locational and virtual organization where teams across the world across different time zones are working on the same projects. Take the setting up of R&D centers of excellence, for instance. You could have one center in the U.S., one in Bangalore and one in Israel and in each location you can have a team working on the same project. Given the time difference between the locations, this allows you to have a 24/7 R&D operation around the globe which significantly reduces the time of development. Importantly, with different teams bringing in diverse expertise, if managed well, this model can result in better output. And, since costs vary in different parts of the world, it can also be more cost-effective. One challenge here is that since the team members know each other only virtually they may not have the personal rapport that is essential for effective teamwork. To overcome this obstacle, in the initial stages of the project you could get the teams to meet in person and spend some time together.

Consider **Stelligent,** an Mphasis company that specializes in development and operation (dev-ops) automation on Amazon Web Services. Stelligent has around 50 scrum teams with members working at remote locations across the U.S. The teams use open and transparent collaboration platforms to work together

> **Create an organization that can accommodate open innovation and flexible working hours.**

seamlessly. The Stelligent scrum teams also have weekly virtual sessions known as 'sharing and caring' every Friday. During these sessions, team members update each other and share new ideas on how to take their projects forward. In addition, the Stelligent teams meet in person once a year at AWS's annual conference Reinvent which is held in Las Vegas.

Apart from all this, it is important to create an organization that can accommodate open innovation and flexible working hours to accommodate the needs of key employees. This is especially critical for women with young children or for those who are major caregivers for other dependents.

People

Look at your people-related issues. Do you have the right people for the job? Are you able to attract the best talent? Are you able to develop it? Are you able to retain it?

We firmly believe that your people policies must be fully inclusive and non-discriminatory and consistent with your stated vision. Inclusion is key to the success of every organization. Many companies are in fact institutionalizing 'blind hiring' in which the gender, race, ethnicity, age, etc. of candidates is being masked to ensure absolute meritocracy. In some cases, organizations have seen that more than 68% of candidates selected through blind hiring were women as against previous averages which were 50% of this number. The best example for blind hiring is symphony orchestras that years ago started blind auditions, and as a result had more women musicians. (The lead study in this area was by Claudia Golden and Cecilia Rouse in 2000). Keep in mind that diversity should not be limited to age, race and gender. It is critical to include diversity of thought and disciplinary expertise. Diversity brings in diverse perspectives and views and disciplinary expertise that may otherwise not have been brought to the table.

Open innovation is also a must. Any plans for getting talent must include not just direct hiring to build the internal team but also strong access to external talent. The best brains may prefer to work at their own time and remotely from home or from other places. They may not necessarily want to come to a physical location, a physical office. They may not want to work full-time with you. The challenge here is (a) what specific talent to look for externally and how to get it and (b) what are the implications for the type of talent you need internally. We believe that you need designers/architects who can design the assignments for the open innovation talent and you need the integrators who can take the external and internal work and create the type of output—product, service, solution and experience—that the consumers are looking for and value.

> **Make your people policies fully inclusive and non-discriminatory and consistent with your vision.**

When it comes to internal talent, the challenge is first identifying what are the skills and competencies that the organization requires, then identifying the talent that has these traits, recruiting this talent, nurturing and growing it with training and development, and then finally, retaining it. Keep in mind that if the present talent does not have the required competencies and is also not able to develop the competencies despite all training and reskilling efforts, then you must take the required action to replace these team members, however hard the decision may be.

Ask yourself if your people strategies empower you to get the best talent to work with you? Do you have the resources within your organization to enable it? Are your incentives and performance measures the right ones for your new outlook? Are you able to match people's passions and competencies with the job requirements? Are you paying more for effort or for results? Are you reskilling your people? Do you have the courage to let go of employees who are no longer adding value? All through your people engagements, keep in mind that any group of people whether customers or employees is heterogeneous. Generation Z and millennials are different from baby boomers. It is critical to understand the needs and wants and objectives of people while creating the internal and external workforce. This is as critical as dealing with customers. A key challenge is how to align people's passions with the job requirements. Google, for example, allows its engineers to select projects on which they want to work.

> **Understand people's needs, wants and objectives while creating the internal and external workforce.**

An important aspect of talent for the new world is the leadership. The new business environment mandates a co-creating leadership style that values "win-win" solutions for all involved. In addition, the leadership must believe in and advocate the values that we outlined above regarding the culture of an organization. It must be able to inspire and motivate internal and external constituencies and provide stretch objectives and inspirational leadership. It must be able to generate trust and be trusted. And it should be perceived as being fair and competent. Further, as in times of war, in times of crisis it is critical that leaders are not only decisive and competent but also compassionate.

Networks

> **No company can succeed without strong network orchestration.**

We also increasingly see the need for leveraging networks. The stronger your networks, the more value they add to your business. Of course, networks have always been important. But now, they are critical. In companies such as Facebook, Uber, Airbnb, LinkedIn and others, we can see how digital technologies have increased manifold the value that networks can bring to an organization. In their 2016 book *The Network Imperative*, authors Barry Libert, Megan Beck and Yoram (Jerry) Wind, point out that the growth, profit and scaling advantages of network orchestrators result in "unprecedented market valuations." According to the authors, when they "examined companies in terms of price (market value) to revenue ratio, which we call a company's *multiplier,*" they found that "the average network orchestrator has a multiplier of 8x, compared with 5x, 3x and 2x for technology creators, service providers, and asset builders, respectively." [202]While these numbers are from the pre-corona crisis years, the benefits of networks will certainly be even more important in the post-crisis era.

We believe that in the current networked and interdependent era, no company can succeed alone without strong network orchestration. In previous chapters, we spoke about how networks

---

[202] Barry Libert, Megan Beck and Yoram (Jerry) Wind, The Network Imperative: How to Survive and Grow in the Age of Digital Business Models, Harvard Business Review Press, 2016. https://hbr.org/product/the-network-imperative-how-to-survive-and-grow-in-the-age-of-digital-business-models/10062-HBK-ENG

can be around talent, around customers, partners, suppliers, distributors, investors, influencers and others. Look at the role networks play in your organization and in your business. Ask yourself if your organization is geared to embrace and leverage the potential that networks offer. Move from being company-centric to being network-centric. Competition today is not firm-against-firm but network-against-network. Take Uber and Airbnb. for instance. It is the strong networks that they created which help them to compete successfully with others in their segments. In times of crisis, there is an opportunity for most firms to establish closer and more engaged relationships with their customers and create a network supporting one another. Some nonprofit organizations like the Barnes Foundations are creating a valuable audience network with daily programs to engage their audiences.

Technology

In CALL TO ACTION we discussed how every business today is a digital business. We saw how the role of technology has changed from being an "enabler" (something that companies use to get things done), to becoming a strong

> **Leverage technology to create differentiation and competitive advantage.**

"differentiator." The key is how well you leverage technology to create a sense of differentiation and competitive advantage. The COVID-19 crisis has clearly demonstrated the critical role of digital technology and the urgent need to speed up digital transformation.

Here are some questions you could ask yourselves: Are you using new digital technologies to understand and predict what your customers want? Do you have a customer-centric front-to-back model? Are you designing your back-end operations in a manner that you can offer your customers personalized, relevant and timely products, services and experiences? In Chapter 2 we had suggested that you could do this by introducing an intelligent intermediary layer (comprising cloud and cognitive technologies) to connect your company's front-end (i.e. the customer engagement layer) with your back-end systems, instead of replacing the entire core systems of your organization, which would be a costly and time-consuming affair. Think of how well this can work for you.

We have also seen how the use of technology is critical to achieving personalization at scale. Examine how well you are leveraging the latest developments in AI. How efficiently are you developing an integrated data strategy? Are technologies such as geo-fencing, facial recognition, voice recognition, emotional recognition, visual search, virtual reality, augmented reality and gesture controls part of your technology portfolio? To what extent is your company using them? Are you optimizing technologies such as mobile, cloud, Blockchain and others? To what extent do you augment your decision capabilities with an AI cognitive assistant such as Watson? (Remember the discussion we had in Chapter 3 of how the Memorial Sloan Kettering Cancer Center uses Watson to help diagnose and decide on treatment.)

Look also at the opportunity offered by automation to increase the efficiency of processes. Further, understand the implications of technology on the skills required by people. What are the new skills that people need to acquire to make the most effective use of the latest technologies?

Facilities

The forced work-from-home and the need for social distancing because of the COVID-19 pandemic has major implications for facilities. As companies reassess the traditional concepts of work, it will lead to a redesign of the workplace. Often, companies overlook the importance of having the right kind of facilities. But physical space is an important element

A good design is one that encourages interdisciplinary collaboration.

of organizational architecture. Offices communicate and facilitate the culture we want to encourage. An open office, for example, sends a message of open communication. It is a strong message to both employees and to the outside world. A good design is one that doesn't isolate each discipline function in its own space, but rather encourages interdisciplinary collaboration. Facilities that allow teams to work together are integral to an organization's success. Consider **Bloomberg**'s headquarters in New York. It uses glass everywhere to communicate transparency and is structured in a way that one cannot take the elevator directly to their floor. To reach their respective workspaces, everyone has to go through a common floor (which offers food and drinks). This encourages interaction across silos. Of course, given the demands and the constraints that the pandemic has imposed, companies will now have to work around this creatively.

The use of art in an organization's facilities can also communicate a strong message. **SEI**, founded by Alfred (Al) West, has art everywhere in its facilities with the purpose of encouraging employees to think as artists and challenging the status quo. The artworks at SEI are from the West Collection collected by West and his daughter over the past three decades and are on long-term loan to SEI. At any given time more than 1,500 works from the West Collection are installed at the SEI Corporate Campus in Oaks, Pennsylvania and also in all of SEI offices around the world. This is part of the unique SEI culture. According to West (as mentioned in a blog on the West Collection website), "The collection's intent is not to aesthetically please, but to make one think."

Resources

At times of crisis, cash is king and cash management has priority. Yet, it is the best time to reassess *all* the resources the company has, can access, and needs. There is no better time than during a crisis and disruption for reassessing the needed resources and courageously experiment with bold reallocation of resources.

It is also the time to reassess the soundness of prior allocation. For example, if digital transformation was a low priority before the crisis, the social distancing and the need to rely on digital communication require management to reallocate their resources and speed things up.

When it comes to resources required to implement our strategy, we need to look beyond the amount of funds we have. As we pointed out in the previous chapter, simply by reimagining and reinventing their operations and working more efficiently, organizations can easily save around 20% of what they are spending at present. This then can be allocated to fund some of the other initiatives. So it's not just how much we have, but how effectively we are using what we have. In this technology-driven world, data and the associated predictive analytics are a key resource. And, as always, talent is one of our biggest resources, as are our networks of customers, distributors, partners, etc.

> **What matters is not how much we have, but how we use what we have.**

In a dynamic and fast-changing world that requires agility, it is crucial to assure flexibility in the allocation of resources. Asset-light strategies like accessing outside talent versus hiring, outsourcing versus building your own factories, and so on enable this way of working. So does having a culture of experimentation and running the business as portfolios of experiments. Further, it is important to leverage resources across silos.

Performance Measures

We can manage only what we can measure. That is why performance measures are an important element of organizational architecture. When it comes to measuring the success of our customer-centric strategy, some important metrics include: share of wallet, repeat buying/loyalty, being in the consideration set of prospects, complaints, net promoter score and so on. Having customers as co-designers and co-promoters is also a strong indication of how engaged we are with our customers. Having easy access to these metrics in real-time—say a dashboard on a mobile platform—empowers us to know where we stand and to make quick decisions.

It is fashionable today to consider oneself as a responsible and fair firm that practices conscious capitalism. Companies like to think of themselves as being environmentally conscious. They believe that they are expanding their objective from maximizing long-term shareholder value to maximizing the value to all stakeholders. However, unless these admirable objectives are translated into specific performance measures, they will have no impact. With socially responsible investing gaining importance, we would encourage you to ensure that you have the right measures to assess your progress toward environment, sustainability and governance (ESG). As we had mentioned in Chapter 1, a 2020 Deloitte report titled *Advancing environmental, social, and governance investing: A holistic approach for investment management firms* estimates that by 2025, ESG-mandated assets in the United States could grow three times as fast as non-ESG-mandated assets and comprise half of all professionally managed investments.

> **Having easy access to real-time performance metrics empowers us to make quick decisions.**

Ensure that you have the right measures for employees, distributors, and all other stakeholders including society. Further, it is important that even in times of crisis we recognize the need for balancing short-term and long-term performance measures – between survival during the crisis *and* preparing for life after the crisis.

Incentives and Compensation

When it comes to incentives and compensation, we need to ensure that these are aligned with corporate objectives as well as the aspirations of employees and network partners. Are they perceived as being fair? Are the incentives structured to make the recipients feel and behave as owners? Do the incentives balance long-term and short-term accomplishments? Do the incentives balance the individual contribution, the contribution of their team and business unit and the overall achievements and performance of the corporation? When recipients truly feel that the incentives and compensation are fair, it motivates them to perform at optimum levels.

Incentives need not be just financial in nature. While financial incentives are important, let's not ignore the power of non-financial incentives such as recognition, title, free time to work on what the person is passionate about, flexible hours and so on. Given the heterogeneity among employees and partners, we need to avoid a one-size-fits-all incentive and compensation system and instead allow for customization. This of course must be perceived as fair. Current practices resulting in women receiving lower compensation than men performing the same job is unacceptable.

> **Align incentives with corporate objectives as well as the aspirations of employees and network partners.**

Reinvent Typical Management Functions

Even as you do all this, there is one more area you need to reexamine and reinvent: the traditional roles of typical management functions. Take the role of marketing, for instance. Traditionally, the four P's of marketing are product, price, place (distribution) and promotion (and advertising). The chief marketing officer (CMO) is supposed to be leading all these. But the reality is that in most organizations the CMO does not have full control over any of these. Product is often the baby of the R&D or product/brand management team; pricing is usually done by the brand manager or president of the business unit in collaboration with finance; distribution is handled by the sales force or is a separate function. The CMO is typically left with some responsibility for the brand and advertising.

We suggest that the role of the marketing head should be changed. CMOs must be experts about consumers and they must be orchestrators of the firm's offerings to address the consumers' needs and expectations. In other words, they must orchestrate the various functions that together can create and deliver the needed customer experience. Increasingly companies are starting to realize this and are creating new positions such as chief customer experience or chief revenue officer whose job is to focus on the integration of various functions required to deliver the consumer experience. Similarly, reexamine all other functions and roles to determine to what extent they impact the customer experience and then shape them in a way that will lead to the needed outcomes.

> **Reexamine and reinvent the traditional roles of typical management functions.**

Let's now look at a few companies and how they have designed some elements of their organizational architecture and network orchestration to help them implement their vision and strategy. These elements include leadership, structure, culture, resource management, processes, use of technology and so on.

The Blackstone Group

Consider investment group Blackstone. What started as a boutique merger-and-acquisition advisory business in 1985 by Stephen Schwarzman and Peter Peterson has grown into the world's largest buyout firm. As of March 2020, it had assets under management (AUM)of $538 billion. This comprises private equity ($175 billion), real estate ($161 billion), credit and insurance ($129 billion) and hedge fund solutions ($ $74 billion). By 2026 Blackstone aims to have $1 trillion in assets under management *(See Exhibit 6).*

EXHIBIT 6

Blackstone Business Group

The Blackstone Group provides "more than just capital" and applies "a bottom-up strategy of transformation" to grow its portfolio companies. Blackstone believes in technology as a business driver to transform organizations and help them become more impactful.

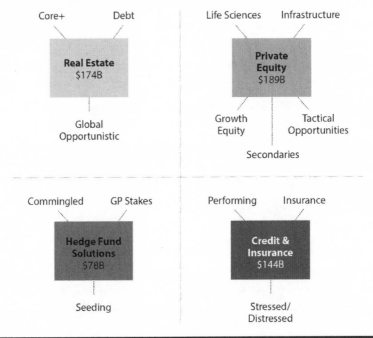

Source: https://www.blackstone.com/the-firm/overview. September 2020.

In its private equity business (as of October 2019), Blackstone had around 100 portfolio companies which have a combined revenue of $77 billion. These companies are spread across the globe and span a wide range of industries like IT services, health care, financial services, auto repair centers, etc. (Disclosure: Mphasis is a Blackstone portfolio company.) Like any private equity player, Blackstone's aim is to increase the valuation of each portfolio company resulting in healthy returns for its investors (pension funds, academic and charitable institutions, governments and other institutions, retail investors, etc.) and for itself at the time of exiting the company. Take Hilton Worldwide. This was Blackstone's largest-ever investment. In 2018 it exited Hilton after 11 years with a $14 billion profit, more than tripling its initial investment.

In a 2017 podcast, Dave Calhoun, who was then Blackstone's head of private equity portfolio operations and a member of Blackstone's management committee, said the company's objective is to grow its operating earnings at twice the rate of the S&P. Describing its investment philosophy, the company's website says "We are patient investors who practice the art of the long view." Further, Blackstone provides "more than just capital" to its portfolio companies and has "a bottom-up strategy of transformation."

The company has a program called Blackstone Advantage which provides an ecosystem to enable the portfolio companies to run themselves more efficiently. The program leverages Blackstone's scale, expertise and network to drive operational efficiencies and growth for its portfolio companies.

> **Blackstone believes in technology as a business driver to help organizations become more impactful.**

Blackstone has a portfolio operations group comprising experts in various areas of operational improvements such as revenue growth, procurement, leadership development, lean process, IT optimization, data science, employee health care and so on. These experts provide strategic guidance to all the portfolio companies. An expert in the U.S. healthcare system, for example, helps all of Blackstone's portfolio companies to design and implement the most appropriate health care practice in their business. An expert in procurement designs and implements the best procurement strategies, and so on.

One of the things that Blackstone believes in strongly is technology as a business driver to help organizations become more impactful. Chairman and CEO Schwarzman has individually contributed about $350 million to Massachusetts Institute of Technology's AI program because he believes that's where the big bet is. Blackstone encourages all its portfolio companies to leverage technology to become future-ready and well-positioned for both short-term and long-term growth.

Blackstone also leverages the advantage of scale that its portfolio provides. For instance, when it comes to indirect purchases that its companies make (like papers and scissors for offices or benches and other things for production facilities, etc.), Blackstone creates contracts that accumulate the volumes of indirect purchases that all its companies make and it then competes for big contracts at significantly reduced prices and higher service levels. Further, it has an e-procurement operation for high-frequency contracting. So instead of say, entering into a contract for three years, it can auction every few months. In his podcast (mentioned earlier) Calhoun says: "Our scale does give us discounts, our scale does give us access to better practices." Reiterating Blackstone's investment philosophy, he adds: "We want to make the investments and the bets and create the disciplines and operating rhythms that are good for that 10-year outcome."

> **Blackstone encourages cross-selling between the portfolio companies and encourages them to leverage one another's strengths.**

Consider Gates Corporation, a global manufacturer of power transmission belts, fluid power products, and other critical components used in diverse industrial and automotive applications. Blackstone acquired Gates in July 2014 for $5.4 billion. During the due diligence process, Blackstone found that achieving operational excellence was not a high priority at Gates so even before they closed the deal, Blackstone put in place a lean roadmap for Gates. At every plant, Blackstone and Gates looked at the various processes and defined the kind of improvements they expected and the resources this would need. This helped Blackstone roll out the lean program at Gates as soon as the deal was closed.

Or consider Service King, one of the largest independent U.S. chains of automobile body repair centers. In July 2014, Blackstone acquired a majority stake in the company. When Service King wanted to expand its centers multifold, Blackstone brought in a non-executive

The first thing Blackstone did after acquiring Mphasis was to bring in new leadership.

chairman at Service King. Interestingly this person came from Panera Bread—an American chain store of bakery-café fast-casual restaurants. While the two industries are totally different, Panera Bread which is present in more than 2000 locations, is one of the most successful companies in the country with a *repeatable model*. That is the expertise that Service King needed.

Blackstone also holds CEO and CXO conferences where senior executives from its portfolio companies can meet and understand from each other and subject matter experts the best practices in their own and other industries. Further, Blackstone encourages cross-selling between the portfolio companies and encourages them to leverage each other's strengths.

According to a June 2019 article in Forbes, Blackstone generally intervenes in a few ways after it takes over a target company. It appoints a leadership team that can drive rapid growth; it ensures that management has access to the data it needs to make decisions, and it concentrates on steady improvements in revenues and profitability. [203]

Beyond all this, values form a core component of Blackstone's approach. In his podcast Calhoun describes what values mean for Blackstone. "It's more important than organization structure. It's more important than the lines in the sand that you draw. It's more important than the procedures that you put in place because it overcomes all of those things. It overcomes boundaries. It creates teamwork and

---

[203] "How Blackstone made India its largest market in Asia,"Forbes India, June 7, 2019. https://www.forbesindia.com/article/boardroom/how-blackstone-made-india-its-largest-market-in-asia/53849/1

it creates camaraderie and a belief system that reinforces everything. Without it, the bigger companies get, the more clumsy they look. Because everyone is looking for things to get solved on org charts and they hardly ever do."

The guiding principles at Blackstone as listed on its website are:

- Accountability
- Excellence
- Integrity
- Teamwork
- Entrepreneurship

Mphasis

Mphasis is one of Blackstone's success stories. The share price when Blackstone acquired Mphasis in September 2017 was Rs. 435 (around $6.24 at the exchange rate of $1=Rs. 69.70). In June 2019, it was about Rs. 1000 ($14.34). That's a growth of 2.5 times in 10 quarters. How was this achieved? Well, the first thing that Blackstone did after acquiring Mphasis was to bring in new leadership. In January 2017, I (Rakesh) joined as CEO. In my first year at Mphasis, we introduced a new customer-centric two-pronged approach comprising front-to-back digital transformation and service transformation driven by IP assets.

We have spoken about the front-to-back digital transformation in Chapter 2. This involves creating an intelligent intermediary layer (comprising the cloud and cognitive technologies) which connects a company's front-end with its back-end systems. Mphasis' service transformation solutions combine people, process, and technology levers to enable enterprises to achieve scalable, digital, future-ready operations. The company has developed a proprietary Intelligent Automation Framework and its integrated approach helps break data silos. The objective is to enable core systems to support and drive an organization's digital imperatives with measurable KPIs and outcomes, deliver quick returns on investments while lowering the overall total cost of ownership.

When I (Rakesh) took over as the CEO of Mphasis, I came without any baggage. Coming from outside, one doesn't look at silos the way people internally would, and nothing is a stupid question when you're looking at things with a fresh pair of eyes. I saw a lot of potential in Mphasis' strong set of service offerings on the digital side. We were doing a great job, but in isolation. We needed to stitch it all together into one service offering to be truly successful, and that's exactly what I did upon taking the mantle.

The new *mantra* at Mphasis is the 'Power of 8'. This refers to eight portfolio areas that Mphasis strategically picked in 2019 to develop world-class expertise.

The eight areas are:

1.   Next-generation application development
2.   Modernization
3.   Enterprise automation
4.   DevOps
5.   Next-generation data technologies
6.   Next-generation application management services
7.   Next-generation infrastructure management services
8.   Cybersecurity

This portfolio of eight services was chosen by Mphasis after a careful analysis of trends in the industry, both in tech services and in the industries in which its clients operate; analysis of the big areas of technology spends, insights from its existing business; and the company's ability to win and execute in any areas it might choose.

In order to develop world-class expertise and execute on these eight services successfully, Mphasis first transformed itself. It adopted an agile approach and pivoted its go-to-market around a portfolio led "tribe and squad" model *(see Exhibit 7)*. This is how it works: Each of the eight service offerings has its own 'tribe' i.e. a cross-functional solutions group comprising people from the company's market-facing solutions teams, its delivery practice teams, from Next Labs, from design thinking and so on. The tribes focus on developing, evolving and building next-gen offerings. Each tribe, in turn, has cross-functional 'squads' that come together on a need basis to focus on specific milestone developments or live deals using agile methodologies. Prior to this approach, Mphasis had several versions of its offerings which were created by teams from various walks of the company. With the tribes in place, Mphasis has standardized its offerings. It has created one master pitch per tribe. Each master pitch is considered as a single source of truth and can be contextualized based on the client's needs. On an average, at least two tribes come together to solve a certain client problem.

EXHIBIT 7

Teaming for Success: The Mphasis Tribe-Squad Model

Mphasis has structured its Go-to-Market approach for its new generation solution portfolio that involves cross-functional teams organized and operationalized into **Tribes** and **Squads** for agility and customer success. **Tribes** are permanent groups responsible for building and evolving solutions while **Squads** are ad hoc groups that come together to work on a sales deal or collaborate on a project to deliver a solution.

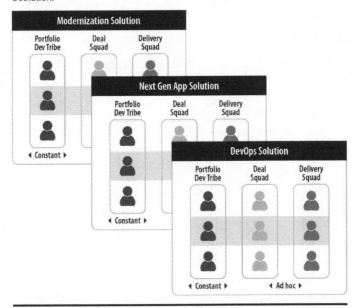

Source: Mphasis Ltd., June 2020.

Mphasis believes that organizing its go-to-market teams around the tribe/squad model has enabled it to offer agility and innovation to its clients. Adopting this model has helped Mphasis in improving accountability, speed of go-to-market, and deal growth. In addition, design thinking workshops, hackathons, proof-of-concept-led engagements and co-innovation have become the new normal at the company.

Here is another example from Mphasis. In 2018, when Mphasis acquired Stelligent, it sent the Stelligent team of 50 members its employee handbook. This had Mphasis guidelines regarding its gun policy, clean desk policy, work-from-home policy, use of email signatures, and so on. The Stelligent team was puzzled. For one, they simply couldn't understand the need for email signatures. They all use Slack, the collaboration software. Email, for them, is "previous generation." The "clean desk" was another puzzle. Stelligent said they are all scrum workers. They don't have desks.

> **The new mantra at Mphasis is the 'Power of 8'.**

They work from anywhere! For Mphasis, the Stelligent acquisition was an important step to acquire new capabilities to make itself more relevant to its customers and stay ahead in the game. So how did Mphasis bridge the gap between the culture, the mindsets and the work styles of the two companies? The then Stelligent CEO Bill Santos pointed out that startups believe in being open and transparent and suggested to Mphasis that it should adopt Slack. Mphasis evaluated Slack as an option, and looked at how to adopt this at scale for its 26,000 employees as well and not limiting it to 50 employees of Stelligent. Mphasis then leveraged "Teams" as the collaboration platform bringing the best of technology, security and collaboration to the two organizations.

Similarly, since most of the information in the employee handbook was more relevant to the team working in physical delivery locations than for scrum teams that worked remotely,

Mphasis' employee handbook was upgraded and updated to be inclusive of scrum workers as well. An acquisition can lead to positive change if the acquiring company is open to innovation and change. And this links back to what we said earlier in the chapter about reinventing your processes to make them more effective.

3G Capital Partners

At Brazilian investment company 3G Capital Partners, the model is one of aggressively cutting jobs and cutting costs at companies it invests in. The firm is known for bold acquisitions, steely determination and meticulous planning. Once it acquires a company, unlike a typical private equity firm, 3G generally owns these positions forever. It usually brings in a fresh and young leadership team, every employee is given clear targets, top performers are promoted quickly, and all expenses are monitored closely. Meritocracy and constant business improvement are popularly used terms within the company. The 3G formula typically results in high profitability at the investee firms and high returns to shareholders. For instance, two years after 3G bought food company H. J. Heinz in 2013, profit margins at Heinz jumped by 58%. Heinz's 28% profit margin was way higher than the average industry margins of around 16% and 3G's approach was considered a wakeup call for the industry. Some of 3G's high-profile investments include quick-service restaurant brands Burger King (in 2010) and Tim Hortons (in 2014) and Popeyes (in 2017), and food firms H. J. Heinz (in 2013) and Kraft Foods (in 2015). In 2015, Heinz and Kraft merged and became the Kraft Heinz Company. 3G Capital started in the beer business more than 30 years ago and created Anheuser-Busch InBev (AB InBev), the largest and most successful beer company in the world.

> 3G Capital Partners is known for bold acquisitions, steely determination, and meticulous planning.

The AB InBev portfolio comprises more than 500 beer brands from around the globe.

Soon, however, 3G came under fire. In February 2019, Kraft Heinz reported a $15.4 billion write-down in assets, a dividend cut and a subpoena from the Securities and Exchange Commission. The news hammered down its shares by 27% and wiped out more than $16 billion in market value. Critics say 3G leans too heavily on cost-cutting and doesn't pay attention to what the consumers want, for instance, by way of healthier and organic options in the case of Kraft Heinz.

> **Kraft Heinz changed its culture to become more consumer-focused.**

An April 2019 *Bloomberg* article reported that at an event ahead of the Brazilian conference at Harvard and MIT, referring to the Kraft Heinz debacle, Jorge Paulo Lemann, co-founder of 3G, told students that the company was changing its culture to become more focused on the consumer. [204]

Chevron Corporation

Chevron Corporation is one of the world's leading integrated energy companies. Headquartered in California, Chevron has more than 52,000 employees worldwide, working across 162 countries. Since 1879, Chevron has grown to explore, produce, and transport crude oil and natural gas and other energy products; produce petrochemical products; generate power; and develop future energy resources.

Speaking at the NASSCOM Technology and Leadership Forum 2019 (Nasscom is an association of India's software and services companies), Sebastian T. Gass, Chevron's general manager

---

[204] "Lemann Says 3G Has to Focus on Consumers After Kraft Heinz Rout," Bloomberg, April 6, 2019.
https://www.bloomberg.com/news/articles/2019-04-05/lemann-says-3g-has-to-focus-on-consumers-after-kraft-heinz-rout

– technology, strategy and services, said that the past five years in the energy industry have been "a wild ride." Commodity prices, for instance, have halved resulting in a reduction in capital budget. At Chevron, the capital budget in 2014 was about $40 billion. In 2019, it was $20 billion. At the same time, there has been a huge shale revolution going on in the world.

> An acquisition can lead to positive change if the buyer is open to innovation.

This has meant shifting from big capital projects that took 10 years to investment cycles of six months. There has also been a major shift in production worldwide to the United States through unconventional shale gas.

According to Gass, Chevron is faced with what he calls "two change vectors" operating at two different speeds. One change vector is energy transition and the second is digital and digital acceleration.

For the 140-year-old company, energy transition is not new. It has seen the transition from wood to coal, coal to oil, oil to gas and now to renewables. Gass pointed out that the pace at which energy transitions happens is "relatively slow, but it's massive at scale" and the best way for companies like Chevron to address such energy transitions is to have a "50-year business plan." But the second vector of change—digital acceleration—demands speed. For Chevron, this means that it needs to "incorporate speed, not only in the way it rolls out its technology, but also from a business model evolution perspective."

The lesson that Chevron has learned in these complex times is what it calls 'Winning in every environment.' This means one can no longer predict the market and you have to be able to succeed independently of market dynamics. According to Gass, "adopting digital, a new way to make decisions, and a culture of innovation" are "key ingredients" that Chevron had adopted to succeed in the current context.

Citing examples of change at Chevron, Gass said the company is transitioning its IT department from a "corporate IT shop to a modern engineering organization." It has reorganized its IT department from "working on applications and projects to a system of digital platforms at the business unit and function level." It is also "radically changing its culture toward more transparency, more self-organization, and more innovation."

Gass lists three key initiatives that Chevron has adopted to encourage a culture of innovation despite being in an industry that requires a lot of forward planning:

1. Chevron has set up a small team that is focused on business workflow iteration and innovation. This team is working toward introducing an innovation culture. This is a culture that is more willing to take risks, more willing to fail fast, and has better and more critical thinking than what Chevron has in its very process-oriented company culture.

2. It has set up a venture capital arm that is active in scanning technologies and continuously brings startups around the world within the Chevron system. The company learns and innovates through these startups.

3. It is working toward a change in its overall culture by setting a different tone top-down that allows different performance management systems, creative thinking, new ways of structuring of projects, and so on.

"I think the combination of those three things will help us to accelerate the culture of innovation," said Gass.

Speaking about what it means for an energy company when data is considered the "new oil," Gass said that data has always been very relevant at Chevron. "We shoot seismic (a method of geophysical prospecting), we interpret what's down in the earth and we model it in order to find all oil, and then we model the reservoir. So we've been this doing all of our life." He added that now however it has taken on "a new dimension" for "opportunistically growing data sources" for training machine learning and for becoming a data-driven enterprise. "We have seen big success in data science. That started out five years ago with very specific data science applications and it is now getting more holistic and integrated with entire supply chains and decision cycles."

FedEx—Microsoft

In May 2020, in the midst of the COVID-19 pandemic, FedEx and Microsoft forged an interesting alliance. The two firms are collaborating to come up with a range of data-driven services for their customers by combining the power of FedEx's global digital and logistics network with Microsoft's cloud computing technology. We see this as a great example of network orchestration. FedEx is opening up the data on its systems as a data platform, with the underlying AI platform from Microsoft. Together, this can result in new data monetization and revenue models.

The first service—which is expected to be rolled out in late 2020—is called FedEx Surround. Using the power of data and analytics, it will allow FedEx and Microsoft customers to see their inventory activities across the globe down to regional and local levels. Why is this more important than ever before? Well, as we all know, during the pandemic one area that has seen tremendous disruption is supply chains. This in turn has resulted in unpredictability of deliveries. If companies can get highly data-driven precise information and insights regarding their inventory and other related factors such as natural disasters, weather conditions, traffic conditions, incorrect addresses and so on, they can get better visibility and intervene early wherever needed and avoid any logistical slowdown.

> The FedEx and Microsoft alliance can result in new data monetization and revenue models.

Think about it. See how a traditional company like FedEx is venturing into the network—gig economy by monetizing data as an asset. FedEx's data platform will become available on a subscription basis to shippers and manufacturers, chargeable based on the "surround" services being consumed. We believe companies like FedEx will continue to pivot their business models to account for more of such "platform-based services" and at some point, may even open up their own operations as a network. For example, you may not have to ship the whole package using FedEx. Instead, you may want to use just their "last-mile" connectivity and tap into their network for the final delivery to consumers. This, in turn, would mean that you will need to pay for consumption of only that part of the network.

As you can see, these companies described above are working on different elements of their organizational architecture and network orchestration in order to stay ahead in the game. We encourage you to also examine every element within your organization and, wherever required, redesign them to support your disruptive strategies.

To assess how aligned you and your organization are with the principle and the ideas and examples discussed in this chapter, we would encourage you to consider the questions listed below.

Ask Yourself:

1. **In order to capture opportunities in times of crisis, an idealized design is a must. Have you developed an idealized design?**

2. **Do you have an appropriate organizational architecture to execute on the principles we have recommended? If not, are you willing to examine each and every component of your organizational architecture and wherever needed redesign them?**

3. As a leader, do you have the courage to make the necessary changes?

4. Is your culture customer-centric, the structure-customer focused, and do all your processes add value to the customer?

5. Have you created a multi-locational and virtual organization? Do your facilities encourage multidisciplinary collaboration?

6. Do you have the right talent for these disruptive times? Do you embrace open innovation and have the right mix of internal and external talent?

7. Do you leverage various networks? Do you experiment with different network orchestration models?

8. Do you deploy technology not just as an enabler, but as a differentiator? Do you use it effectively to achieve personalization at scale?

9. Do you use all your resources, be it cash, or data, or people, effectively?

10. Do your performance measures include share of wallet and engagement (NPS) and speed?

11. Are your compensation and incentives policies aligned with your corporate objectives as well as the aspirations of employees and network partners?

12. Have you reinvented your management functions to bring about the desired customer experience?

Implement Now

Having a great strategy is not enough. The key is how we implement it. Execution is king. Create your implementation framework and forge new tools to build resilience.

The previous chapters have shown that in the face of crisis and unprecedented and exponential forces of change, maintaining the status quo is not feasible. If you don't create opportunities in times of crisis, if you don't defend yourselves against disruptors, and if you don't become disruptors yourselves, you will become irrelevant. You will perish. You also now know the eight principles of transformation in times of crisis that you need to embrace to be successful. In this concluding chapter, we will show you how to put these principles into practice, and how to turn ideas into action

This is critical because simply knowing the principles is not enough;

the key to capturing opportunities in times of crisis and defending against disruptors and ideally becoming a disruptor is to implement these eight principles effectively. We have designed this chapter to be driven by a lot of questions. Your answers will put you on track to implement our principles, help you transform in times of crisis, chart your journey to success, and transform you into **architects of disruption.**

In the Introduction, we showed you how to develop an implementation strategy. We also gave you an overview of the implementation framework and a list of the 10 tools that we have developed to help you implement each of the eight principles and your winning strategy. In this chapter we will go deeper into these. As mentioned in our Introduction, we are working on developing an app that will include all of this.

Implementation Framework

1. Start with the assessment of the COVID-19 pandemic, the George Floyd civil justice crisis in the U.S., other recent crises and other forces of change and their implications.

2. Given that the forces of change and their interdependencies require challenging the current status quo, it requires rethinking and reinventing your mental, business and revenue models to assure that these are consistent with the changing environment. You must ensure that the models address the threats and capitalize on the opportunities during and after the crisis.

3. As part of challenging your current mental, business and revenue models, start implementing the eight principles (which in turn may change the mental, business and revenue models).

4. A key part of the new strategy to create opportunities in times of crisis and defend against disruptors and ideally become a disruptor is the creation of an idealized design to establish an ideal vision, mission, objectives and strategy.

5. As we move to the generation of strategies (to achieve the ideal vision, mission, objectives and strategies) let us rely on various approaches for generating creative options. Keep in mind that there are many different approaches for enhancing creativity.

6. Since any strategy would include the generation of messages and offerings, it is important to assure that in designing these messages and offering, we meet the R.A.V.E.S and M.A.D.E.S criteria and deliver them through all touchpoints. (These are discussed at length later in this chapter.)

7. At the core of our proposed disruptor strategies is the idea of adaptive experimentation.

8. To implement the new strategies, funding is always a concern. Our belief is that no new funding is required. Most legacy companies can reallocate their resources to eliminate waste, redundancies and activities that no longer create value. This will free up resources that you can allocate (at least in the range of 20% of the current budget) to the new initiatives.

9. To implement the proposed strategies, we have to assure that our organizational architecture and network orchestration is designed to implement the new experiments and initiatives. A key aspect of the new architecture is the design of a control dashboard that will allow management to continuously monitor their progress and guide them in making the needed adjustments and changes.

10. Finally, to assure smooth implementation, it is crucial to get the needed buy-in from all internal and external stakeholders.

Implementation Model

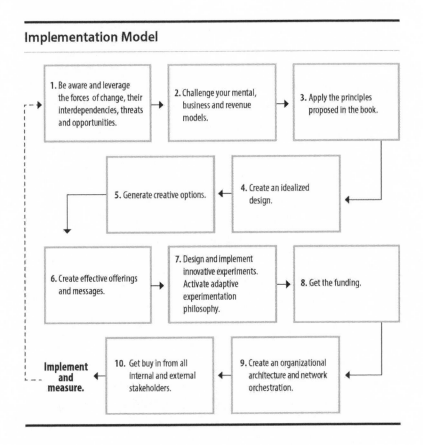

Tool Kit

Before we go into the details of the 10 tools, here is an overview.

Some of the tools are simple questions in text form while others are visual tools. Do keep in mind that these tools are not solutions by themselves; using these tools will help you to arrive at the solutions (i.e. the principles that we have shared with you). They will help you apply the eight principles in a manner that is specific to your organization. Importantly, this need not be a one-time exercise. Using these tools, you will be able to continuously assess your progress and keep identifying and acting on new steps that will ensure that you are *always way ahead in the game.*

There are two self-assessment tools which will help you evaluate:

1. Your awareness of the forces of change and their interdependencies; how ready and willing you are to address their threats and take advantage of the opportunities they offer; your assessment of the impact of the crisis and its implications.

2. Whether you are challenging your mental, business and revenue models.

The remaining tools will help you to:

3. Apply the principles we have proposed in the book.
4. Create an idealized design.
5. Generate creative options.
6. Create effective offerings and messages.
7. Design and implement effective and innovative experiments and an adaptive experimentation philosophy.
8. Get the needed funding.
9. Build a control dashboard to manage the agile transformation process in real-time.
10. Get the needed buy-in from all relevant internal and external stakeholders.

Tool #1: Environmental assessment—monitoring the forces of change and their likely impact

How aware are you of the forces of change and their interdependencies and how ready and willing are you to address their threats and take advantage of the opportunities they offer?

We began this book by highlighting some key forces of change that are disrupting each industry. These include the COVID-19 pandemic; exponential advances in science and technology; dramatic changes in the media landscape; empowered and skeptical consumers; disruptive cultural, social, economic and geo-political environments; and new business and revenue models. We also spoke about how these changes are disrupting every industry.

Ask Yourself:

- If you are reading the book while the COVID-19 crisis is still on, have you developed scenarios regarding the likely time for the end of the health crisis and the economic recovery?

- Do you have an early warning system to alert you to the next black-swan crisis?

- Are you fully aware of the changes happening around you?

- Are you fully cognizant of the impact that the different changes are having/can have on your business?

- Can you catch the signals of change before they envelop you?

- What are the key threats, the headwinds of these forces of change and their interactions with your business?

- What are the major opportunities, the tailwinds these forces of change offer?

- Have you developed plans to address the threats and capitalize on the opportunities?

TOOL 1

The Forces of Change: Addressing Their Threats and Capitalizing on Their Opportunities

Threats vs. Opportunities	Forces of Change					
	Disruptive advances in science and technology	Dramatic changes in the media landscape	Empowered and skeptical consumers	Disruptive forces of nature, cultural, social, economic and geo-political environments	New business and revenue models	Overall (reflecting the interactions of the various forces)
Threats						
1. How much of a threat is this to your current operation?	12345678910	12345678910	12345678910	12345678910	12345678910	12345678910
2. What can you do to address these threats? (specify)						
Opportunities						
3. How much of an opportunity does it provide for reimagining your business?	12345678910	12345678910	12345678910	12345678910	12345678910	12345678910
4. What can you do to capitalize on these opportunities? (specify)						

Tool #2: Assessing mental, business and revenue models

The pandemic crisis and the new business environment demand new thinking. Recognize the need to change, the need to reinvent and to transform yourself, and be ready for the new reality. Understand that maintaining the status quo is equal to death. To evaluate and understand where you stand vis-à-vis your thinking, identify your current mental model, business model and revenue models and see how relevant they are. Check how they have worked for you during the crisis and what you need to change.

Ask Yourself:

- Do you have a new mental model for the new reality which takes advantage of the lessons you and others have learned from your experience during the crisis?

- Are your current mental models and associated business and revenue models consistent with the changing business environment?

- Have any of these models been disrupted in your and other industries? If so, what defense, if any, has been successful and how did it succeed?

- How can you change your current mental, business and revenue models to ensure that they are consistent with the changing environment?

- What are the new mental, business and revenue models which can capitalize on the opportunities thrown up by the crisis and which can help you defend against the disruptors?

- What are the new mental, business and revenue models required to become a disruptor?

- What are the new mental, business and revenue models from other industries and contexts that could be adapted and applied to your situation?

TOOL 2

Challenging Your Mental, Business and Revenue Models

Instructions	Models		
	Mental	Business	Revenue
1. Can your current model address the threats and capitalize on the opportunities offered by the forces of change?	1 2 3 4 5 6 7 8 9 10	1 2 3 4 5 6 7 8 9 10	1 2 3 4 5 6 7 8 9 10
2. If the rating is below 8, what changes do you have to make to your models? What new models would be required? (specify)			
3. What experiments can you design to test the feasibility and validity of the new models?			

Tool #3: Applying our principles

Let us now look at how you can apply our eight principles effectively. To begin, assess the degree to which you are applying our principles. On a scale of 0 to 10, where 0 indicates that you are not applying a principle at all and 10 indicates that you are applying it effectively, figure out where you stand. The distance between the current rating and 10 indicates the areas that require further action. The Spider Web tool below will help you identify the areas on which you need to focus. As mentioned earlier, keep in mind that it's not enough to focus on any one or only on some of the principles. To create opportunities in times of crisis, you have to implement all eight.

TOOL 3

Apply the Eight Principles

Instruction 1: Go over each principle and rate your organization on the degree to which it follows the principle.

Principles	Rating (0-10)
1. Challenge Your Mental Models and Always Stay Ahead	
2. Reimagine and Reinvent Your Approach to Customers and Shareholders	
3. Speed Up Digital Transformation and Design for Personalization at Scale	
4. Reinvent Your Talent Strategy and Embrace Open Innovation and Talent	
5. Seize the Need for Speed and Design for Agility, Adjacencies and Adaptability	
6. Innovate and Experiment, Experiment, Experiment	
7. Re-draw Your Timelines and Build a Portfolio of Initiatives Across All Innovation Horizons	
8. Deploy Idealized Design, Recreate Your Organizational Architecture and Network Orchestration	

TOOL 3

Apply the Eight Principles

Instruction 2: Once the rating (on 0-10) of each of the 8 principles is done connect the 8 and create the spider.

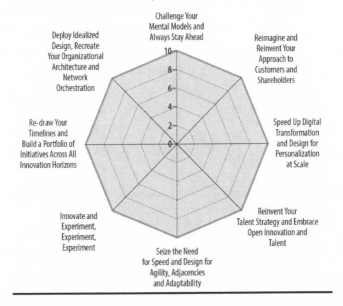

Instruction 3: Given the current situation, identify the key opportunities these principles offer.

Opportunities	

Instruction 4: Prioritize the opportunities and identify the key actions/ experiments that will allow capitalizing of these opportunities.

Key Actions/Experiments	
Key Action 1	
Key Action 2	
Key Action 3	

Tool #4: Creating an idealized design

As discussed in Chapter 8, in idealized design the idea is to first envision the ideal state and then work backward to the current state. Instead of simply improving the different parts, first design the whole and then design the required parts.

To begin, decide if you as the CEO or entrepreneur of a startup want to do it yourself or with a team. If you want to do it as a team, select an interdisciplinary team that includes creative people with diverse experiences and perspectives. Also make sure the team includes a few Internet natives. Do not be constrained by your current talent. Recruit new talent as needed. Once the team is selected, go through the following process:

1. Select an ideal future state. Say, landing on Mars, doubling your stock price in three years; doubling your share of wallet in three years, and so on.

2. Select an award you would like to get for this achievement.

3. Select a media outlet of your choice to announce the award.

4. Select a time period. This should be a specific target date.

5. Write the headline announcing the award.

6. Write the three or five key reasons for getting the award, including what innovative things you had to do to achieve the award.

Once the story is complete, validate its desirability and go through the needed iterations. Then assemble a small team to start a backward planning process to achieve your ideal. If you are part of a legacy organization, create a separate unit headed by a champion whose sole objective and incentive is tied to the achievement of the stretch objective. Make sure to protect the champion since in this role they will violate many of the rules of your current organization. The team will have to develop the vision, objectives, strategy and the needed organizational architecture and network orchestration to achieve the stretch objective.

TOOL 4

Create an Idealized Design

Questions	Answers
1. Select an ideal future state. Say, Zero Hunger | Zero Waste by 2025, doubling your stock price and share of wallet in three years, etc. Make sure you specify a target date.	
2. Select an award you would like to get for this achievement.	
3. Select a media outlet of your choice to announce the award.	
4. Write the headline announcing the award.	
5. Write the three or five key reasons for getting the award, including what innovative things you had to do to achieve the award.	

Tool #5: Generating creative options

"Imagination is more important than knowledge. For knowledge is limited to all we now know and understand, while imagination embraces the entire world, and all there ever will be to know and understand."
—Albert Einstein.

Capturing opportunities in times of crisis, defending against disruptors and becoming disruptors ourselves, require generation and implementation of creative options. Given how important creativity is, approaches that help us generate creative options are essential. While there are many approaches that are available and you may already be familiar with them, we have selected five approaches for you which we believe are of value and easy to implement. These approaches also augment one another.

1. Morphological analysis

This is the most fundamental approach. It requires the identification of an objective and the generation of the key components of a strategy to achieve it. The strategy is decomposed into key factors (such as segments you do and can target, the positioning, etc.) For each factor we have to identify all the current and conceivable elements (strategic options).

Tool 5.1 below illustrates this approach. It starts by identifying an objective—funding a nonprofit organization—and four key elements of a strategy to achieve this objective. These elements are—the segment, positioning, who approaches the segment, and the context of the approach. For each of the four elements, we identify a set of options. Once the structure is complete, we have to start connecting the options of each of the four elements. Each line is thus a potential strategy.

In our figure, the bold line represents **Strategy 1** which focuses on the trustees of the institution approaching them with an educational message. The approach is by the development department in the context of one-on-one meetings. **Strategy 2** represented by the dotted line focuses on the segment of local members with the positioning appeal for developing new ventures and as part of a kick start or other crowd-based campaign using digital strategy. In this manner, you can generate thousands of strategic options which you can then start evaluating on your desired criteria.

The value of the morphological structure is not just in the initial identification of strategic options but also as a way of incorporating in it the results of any other approaches for generating creative options by adding elements and options and editing the initial set of elements and options. For instance, if you are engaging in an idealized design exercise, the outcome can be incorporated as new strategy elements and options.

TOOL 5

Generating Creative Options

Capturing opportunities in times of crisis, defending against other disruptions or becoming a disruptor all require the generation and implementation of creative options. This set of tools is aimed at helping you and your team generate creative options. While there are many tools that you may have used and are familiar with, we selected 5 tools that we found to be of value, and which are easy to implement.

5.1. Structure a Morphologic Analysis

Instruction 1: Identify the objective.

Instruction 2: Identify the key strategies required to achieve the objective (the columns).

Instruction 3: For each strategy area identify as many options as you can (the rows).

Instruction 4: Start connecting elements from the various columns in a way that each line represents a strategic option.

Instruction 5: Evaluate the various strategies (lines) on your evaluation criteria.

Instruction 6: Keep the structure open so that you can add strategies.

Objective: Funding a non-profit organization

Segment	Positioning	Approach by	Context
• Foundations	• Education	• Head of institution	• One on one
• Government	• Building the future	• Trustee	• Dinner
• Trustees	• Capital Campaign	• Development Department	• Breakfast
• Local members	• Endowment	• Friends	• Conferences
• Other prospects	• New Venture	• Crowd	• E-mail
• Crowd		• Celebrities	• Telephone
•	•	•	• Digital Campaign

2. Lessons from benchmarking

The key to successful benchmarking for identifying new creative options lies in expanding its scope beyond that of direct competitors to those of others in the industry and, most critically, to those from other industries. For example, if you are a bank, the comparison could be expanded to other non-bank financial service providers such as insurance companies and mutual fund companies. The most valuable benchmarking, however, will be against companies from other industries that currently do not compete with banks. This is especially critical given that consumers do not compare banks only to other banks but expect the same level of service and convenience they get from the best providers in any industry. For instance, the service level established by Federal Express regarding notification of status of each package is now the expected standard from all companies in all industries.

Tool 5.2 illustrates this approach and its triple scope along with an example. The results of these analyses can provide insights into needed new strategic options (plus data on the success of the various options). It can also be incorporated in the morphological analysis.

5.2. Benchmarking

Instruction 1: Identify your direct competitors and explore what can you learn from them.

Instruction 2: Identify other players in the industry who are not your direct competitors and explore what you can learn from them.

Instruction 3: Identify companies from other industries and especially the new economy firms (such as GAFA). Imagine that they would enter your industry and explore what can you learn from them.

Consider the following banking example:

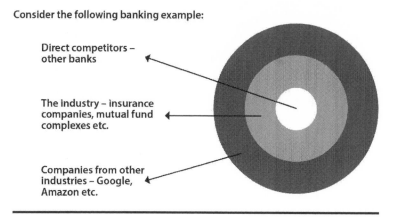

Direct competitors – other banks

The industry – insurance companies, mutual fund complexes etc.

Companies from other industries – Google, Amazon etc.

3. Employ rules

A fourth approach is the use of a variety of rules for generating creative options. Consider for example the two sets of rules – SCAMPER and redesigning principles—outlined in Tool 5.3. These are often used in product and service design.

5.3. Creativity Rules

Scamper:	Redesign principles such as:
Substitute	Eliminate steps
Combine	Eliminate interfaces
Adapt	Minimize detours
Modify	Process in parallel
Put to another use	Increase efficiency
Eliminate	Eliminate bottlenecks
Reverse	Design for quality

The outcomes of such processes can be incorporated in the morphological analysis.

4. Insights from consumer behavior and cultural trends

Insights for the generation of creative options can be derived from changing consumer behavior, especially those linked to cultural trends. This requires continuous and ideally real-time monitoring of consumer behavior including:

- Changes in purchase patterns such as the shift from store-based sales to e-commerce and to seamless shopping experience and purchase online and offline (omnichannel).
- Consumer conversation on social networks.
- Specific stores and websites that continue to attract key consumer segments.
- Social trends as reflected in the mass and social media, movies, videos and music.
- Theories and findings regarding human behavior (in their consumer and non-consumer roles) that includes trends such as:
  - decreased trust in all institutions, including businesses.
  - increased empowerment.

- interest in having a positive social impact—the current focus on purpose-led businesses.

- independence—the growth of the GIG economy and the size of the self-employed and entrepreneurial segment.

- search for happiness (as captured by positive psychology).

- increased heterogeneity of every country – think of the split in the U.S. in its acceptance of President Trump.

- increased complexity and dynamic nature of the consumer journeys.

- consumer use of mobile and other enabling technologies.

These and similar analyses of the changing consumer behavior and social-cultural trends are a *must* for any firm. Given the speed of change as reflected in the speed of adoption of new technologies, this monitoring has to be done in real-time. The outcomes of these analyses provide key insights for new creative options and can be integrated into the morphological analyses.

5.4. Insights From Consumer Behavior and Cultural Trends
What can you learn from the following?

- Change in purchase patterns
- Consumer conversations on social networks
- Specific stores and websites that continue to attract key consumer segments
- Social trends as reflected in the mass and social media, movies, videos and music
- Decreased trust in businesses
- Increased empowerment
- Interest in having a social impact – the current focus on purpose-led businesses
- Independence – the growth of the GIG economy and the size of the self employed and entrepreneurial segment
- Search for happiness (as captured by positive psychology)
- Increased heterogeneity of every country
- Increased complexity and dynamic nature of the consumer journeys
- Consumer use of mobile and other enabling technologies
- The experience economy – search for real time personalized experience
- The sharing economy
- The changing consumer behavior in times of crisis
- Increased concern for social justice and fairness
- Search for more balanced work-life
- Others?

5.5. Lessons From Brainstorming, Suggestion Boxes, Analysis of Consumer Conversations on the Social Networks, Complaints and Other Communication With Consumers and Stakeholders
Lessons from
A. Brainstorming
B. Suggestion boxes
C. Analysis of consumer conversations on the social networks
D. Complaints
E. Other communication with consumers and stakeholders
F. Examining the above are there any emerging patterns and what are their implications?

5. Lessons from analogies

Analogies are helpful for any aspect of the strategy by providing both examples with relevant data on the success of the strategies and motivation to consider them. Consider how BMW is experimenting with an Airbnb model for cars, or how Uber is expanding its scope to other services such as meal delivery using the same platform it invented for passengers. As with other tools for generating creative options, the outcomes of the lessons from analogies can be incorporated in the morphological analysis.

Another example of using lessons from analogies to generate creative options is how California-based IDEO improved the speed and deficiency of an operating room by studying and learning the lessons from the operations of a Formula 1 pit stop.

Tool #6: Creating effective offerings and messages

Once you have your strategy in place, you need to ensure that you are getting your offerings and messages across to all the stakeholders. Examine your current and planned offerings and messages. On a 1-10 point scale assess the degree to which they meet the following three sets of criteria as explained in the book *Beyond Advertising: Creating Value Through All Customer Touchpoints* by authors Yoram (Jerry) Wind and Catherine Findiesen Hays.

1. Multichannel offerings and distribution

Are the physical and digital channels you use consistent with the following:

- 24x7 consumer journeys?
- Omnichannel options available to the target consumers?
- New channel options facilitated by innovative scientific and technological developments?
- All the relevant paid, owned and earned media?

Also check, if in the transition from the pandemic crisis to the new reality, are you assuring the safety of the face-to-face interactions? Are you taking advantage of the lessons learned during the pandemic such as redefining work to include work-from-home, and leveraging digital communication?

2. R.A.V.E.S

Do your current and planned offerings and messages meet the R.A.V.E.S creative effectiveness criteria for the following:

- Relevant and respectful?
- Actionable?
- Valuable—emotionally, cognitively and monetarily?
- Experiential?
- Shareable stories?

Given the enormous number of people impacted by the pandemic, make sure that the 'relevant and respectful' rule includes a compassionate approach and that your message is relevant to the life of the consumers you are trying to reach. This is critically important because the consumer sentiment surveys during the pandemic show intentions to reduce and postpone discretionary purchases, and more fundamentally, reassess the purpose of life. The 'actionable' steps should be taken with special care for the safety of those responsible for them. The 'valuable' needs care addressing all three dimensions of value—emotional, cognitive and monetary —all are of increased importance. 'Experiential' is especially critical for retailers, restaurants and travel destinations, and even cultural institutions. Consumers are getting accustomed to life without them. So why should they, for instance, switch back from e-commerce to retail shopping or from eating at home to going to restaurants? It is only the ability to have a unique and amazing experience that will motivate people to leave their homes.

3. M.A.D.E.S

Is the context in which you present and offer your offerings and messages consistent with the M.A.D.E.S context criteria? These are as follows:

- Multisensory
- Audience characteristics and real-time needs and behavior
- Delivery devices
- Environment—both the editorial context and the external environment (such as climate, location…)
- Synergy—the synergy among the multiple touchpoints

TOOL 6

Creating Effective Offerings and Messages

Let's assess our 'current versus planned' offerings and messages:

1. Multi channel offerings and distribution – Are the physical and digital channels you use consistent with:	Current	Planned
The 24x7 consumer journeys	1 2 3 4 5 6 7 8 9 10	1 2 3 4 5 6 7 8 9 10
The omni channel options available to the target consumers	1 2 3 4 5 6 7 8 9 10	1 2 3 4 5 6 7 8 9 10
The new channel options facilitated by innovative scientific and technological developments	1 2 3 4 5 6 7 8 9 10	1 2 3 4 5 6 7 8 9 10
All the relevant paid, owned and earned media	1 2 3 4 5 6 7 8 9 10	1 2 3 4 5 6 7 8 9 10
The ability to offer seamless experience across all touchpoints	1 2 3 4 5 6 7 8 9 10	1 2 3 4 5 6 7 8 9 10
2. Do your current and planned offerings and messages meet the R.A.V.E.S. creative effectiveness and engagement criteria?	**Current**	**Planned**
Relevant and respectful	1 2 3 4 5 6 7 8 9 10	1 2 3 4 5 6 7 8 9 10
Actionable	1 2 3 4 5 6 7 8 9 10	1 2 3 4 5 6 7 8 9 10
Valuable – emotionally, cognitively and monetarily	1 2 3 4 5 6 7 8 9 10	1 2 3 4 5 6 7 8 9 10
Experiential	1 2 3 4 5 6 7 8 9 10	1 2 3 4 5 6 7 8 9 10
Shareable story	1 2 3 4 5 6 7 8 9 10	1 2 3 4 5 6 7 8 9 10
3. Is the context in which you present and offer your offering and message consistent with the M.A.D.E.S. context criteria?	**Current**	**Planned**
Multi sensory	1 2 3 4 5 6 7 8 9 10	1 2 3 4 5 6 7 8 9 10
Audience characteristics and real time needs and behavior	1 2 3 4 5 6 7 8 9 10	1 2 3 4 5 6 7 8 9 10
Delivery devices	1 2 3 4 5 6 7 8 9 10	1 2 3 4 5 6 7 8 9 10
Environment both the editorial context and the external environment (such as climate, location etc.)	1 2 3 4 5 6 7 8 9 10	1 2 3 4 5 6 7 8 9 10
Synergy – the synergy among the multiple touch points	1 2 3 4 5 6 7 8 9 10	1 2 3 4 5 6 7 8 9 10
4. What 3 things could you do to assure that your planned offerings and messages meet the R.A.V.E.S and M.A.D.E.S. criteria and can be delivered through all touch points?		
Action 1		
Action 2		
Action 3		

Tool #7: Design and implement effective and innovative experiments and an adaptive experimentation philosophy

Experimentation enables us to understand causality and empowers us to devise our next successful strategy using near-real-time data and hard evidence. It helps us to learn faster, build a culture of innovation, attract the best talent, confuse the competition, and create a compelling competitive advantage.

Designing an Effective Innovative Experiment

1. For each of the major strategies to achieve your stretch objectives and idealized design vision, what are the key short- and long-term experiments that could make a big difference? Make sure they differ significantly from your current strategies and that they capture key elements of the idealized strategy including business and revenue models, the offering, the markets, etc.

2. For each of these innovative experiments what will be an appropriate control? If you like your current strategy, you could use it as a control.

3. What are the key metrics you will use to evaluate the experiment? Make sure to develop both the right conceptual and operational metrics. Prepare a compelling graphic presentation of the expected results to assure that the relevant management will be able to act on it.

4. What will it take to implement the experiment? What is the buy-in required? Who is likely to resist it and how can you get their cooperation?

5. How long should the experiment run?

6. What other factors could affect the results of the experiment? Do you have a measurement system in place to capture them? You could use the data as covariates in analyzing the results of the experiments.

7. Do you have the talent to design and analyze the experiments? If not, consider hiring one person with the needed skills.

Designing an Adaptive Experimentation Philosophy, Culture and Processes

1. When you conduct an experiment and the results support the experimental variable, do you have the needed organizational architecture to scale it up as fast as possible?

2. When the results do not support the experimental variable, are you ready to initiate another experiment?

3. Do you have at any given moment of time multiple experiments related to the three innovation horizons?

4. Do you require the inclusion of innovative experiments in any business plan and budget?

5. Do you have the processes and capabilities to conduct ongoing meta-analysis of the results of all your experiments?

6. Do you have the mechanism and culture to share the results of your experiments and meta-analyses throughout the organization to assure continued learning and improvements?

7. Do you have the culture and processes to look for naturally occurring experiments (whether by you or others in any industry)?

8. Do you have a culture, processes and reward and compensation system that rewards lessons from experiments, whether successful or not?

9. Do you use your experimentation culture as a tool to recruit better talent?

Keep in mind that each experiment should not be viewed as a standalone and single initiative but rather as part of a continuous adaptive experimentation approach. The lessons of an experiment should lead to the next series of experiments and so on.

TOOL 7

Design and Implement Effective and Innovative Experiments and an Adaptive Experimentation Philosophy

The only way to successfully manage in today's turbulent and complex environment is by adopting the adaptive experimentation philosophy. To help you design such a system, please answer the following questions:	
1. In designing your experiments are you focusing on truly innovative initiatives, do you utilize effective designs beyond simple A-B testing? Do you have the right control groups? Are the test and control groups randomized? Do you have the right analytics?	
2. When you conduct an experiment and the results support the experimental variable do you have the needed organizational architecture to scale it up as fast as possible?	
3. If the results do not confirm your hypotheses, are you ready to stop the experiment, reflect on the lessons from it and initiate another experiment?	
4. Do you have at any given moment of time multiple experiments related to the three innovation horizons?	
5. Do you require the inclusion of innovative experiment in any business plan and budget?	
6. Do you have the processes and capabilities to conduct ongoing meta-analysis of the results of all your experiments and draw any empirical generalizations?	
7. Do you have the culture and processes to share the results of your experiment (both successes and failures) and meta analysis, throughout the organization to assure continued learning and improvements?	
8. Do you have the culture and processes to look for natural occurring experiments (whether by you or others in any industry)?	
9. Do you have the culture that assures ethical and valuable experiments and the processes, reward and compensation system that rewards for lessons from experiments whether successful or not?	
10. Do you use your experimentation culture as a tool to recruit the needed creative talent?	

Tool #8: Getting the needed funding

Often, even though we realize that change is all around us and we need to future-proof ourselves, we are held back by the fear of additional costs we may incur. Here are some ways to overcome this hurdle. Reexamine and reengineer your current operations in such a manner that you can save at least 20% of your budget. This may sound unrealistic but our research and experience shows that most legacy companies can in fact save as much as 20% of their costs by reexamining their current operations and doing away with things that add no value, or by using measures such as automating or open innovation wherever possible. Another major source of savings is eliminating redundancy and duplication which is common especially when a firm has a number of independent business units each with its own P&L. This 20% savings can be allocated toward undertaking innovative experiments to prepare the company for the future. Challenge yourself to make sure your organization is "doing the right things right." Further, examine if you have the right balance between the internal and external operations. The internal talent can be responsible for design and integration while the external talent can handle the execution. The advantage of this, as we have discussed earlier, is that you have access to a wider pool of talent with the required capabilities plus you need to pay only for the results. Alongside, leverage open innovation and co-create with customers and other partners and move toward the network orchestrator model.

When it comes to external sources of funding, are you leveraging strategic alliances? Apart from traditional sources such as banks and venture capital (in case of startups), are you exploring new avenues such as sharing the cost of development with customers or other stakeholders? Think of how Tesla took $1000 as deposits from each customer so they could 'reserve' Tesla's Model 3 vehicle. The company received around 450,000 reservations. This not only gave the company an idea of the likely demand for the model but also helped fund its development.

To sum up, it is important to do the right things right. Take a deep look at your operations, identify wasteful or redundant activities and use the savings to take on innovative experiments. Once you have learned from your experiments which projects will serve your objectives best, identify internal and external sources of funding and move forward to innovate.

TOOL 8

Get the Needed Funding

In each of your business units and corporate functions, ask the following questions:	
Internal Funding	
1. Are you doing the right things right? What changes are required to achieve this objective?	
2. Which activities/initiatives/departments can you modify or delete without impacting the value created for your customers and other stakeholders?	
3. Given the modified and deleted activities which people can you delete or replace with open innovation or automation?	
4. Are any units/functions duplicating the same efforts? If yes, can any of them be eliminated, or combined?	
5. What is the total cost savings of all the deleted and changed activities and personnel? If the total is less than 20% repeat the above task until you achieve the 20% target?	
6. Can you raise your prices or increase the demand and profitability of your operations to help generate some of the needed funding?	
External Funding	
7. What partnerships/strategic alliances can you form that will cover some of the cost of the needed new initiatives?	

Tool #9: Have the right organizational architecture and network orchestration and build a control dashboard to manage the agile transformation process in real-time.

In Chapter 8, we discussed organizational architecture and network orchestration in detail. Using the tools below, check if your organizational architecture and network is in line with what we have listed. Do you have the various components? Put together a comprehensive statement of your organization's vision, its mission and the objectives.

TOOL 9

Organizational Architecture and Network Orchestration

9.1. Does Your Organizational Architecture Resonate with This One?

Key Components of Organizational Architecture

The key components of the organizational architecture and network orchestration that allow us to successfully design and implement our strategies.

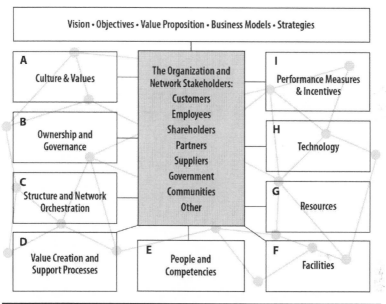

Source: Adapted from diagram in the book titled Driving Change by Jerry Wind and Jeremy Main.

Organization's Vision, Mission, Objectives and Strategy
What is your organization's vision?

What is your organization's mission?

What are your organizational objectives?

What are your key strategies?

Can your organizational architecture implement your strategy and achieve your vision, mission and objectives ?		
Organizational values and culture	Yes	No
Business and revenue models	Yes	No
Value creating and supporting processes	Yes	No
Organizational structure	Yes	No
Governance and leadership	Yes	No
The right internal competencies	Yes	No
Access to outside talent	Yes	No
Performance measures and incentives	Yes	No
Technology	Yes	No
The needed resources	Yes	No
Consumer networks	Yes	No
Distributor networks	Yes	No
Physical spaces across the globe	Yes	No
Network orchestration- created or joined a network/designing	Yes	No
The right ecosystem	Yes	No

Further, building a control dashboard is critical. Our objectives—especially the stretch objectives—can take considerable time. Without a control dashboard we cannot know if we are moving in the right direction. We cannot measure how successful we are in meeting our objectives. And if we cannot measure, we cannot manage the process. A control dashboard gives us a good indication on the progress we have made and what else we need to do to achieve our target.

9.2. Develop a Control Dashboard to Monitor Key Performance Metrics

Below are illustrative metrics. Feel free to modify
and add as needed for your organization

The tool below offers a set of initial areas for consideration. See which of these are relevant for you. Based on your specific and unique business situation, add other metrics that may be significant. Ensure that the control dashboard shows real-time data and has alerts (as an early warning system) to any significant deviation from the plan. It should be designed for a mobile application and should also be simple. We don't need the dashboard of an airplane; we need the dashboard of a car. The key is to identify the right metrics that drive your specific business. For each metric, identify the ideal and then assess how close you are to it.

Some Key Metrics for Any Business Could Be:

- The company's sense of urgency in acting; corporate readiness to address the uncertain environment

- Share of wallet
- Market share
- Net Promoter Score
- Complaints
- Repeat buyers/loss of clients
- Brand equity
- Recurrent revenues
- Critical pipeline
- Results of key experiments
- Changes in consumers' perceptions of the brand(s) and preference for it
- Metrics of the stretch objectives
- Progress on the eight principles (can be as a visual or the spider diagram)

Tool #10: Get the needed buy-in from all relevant internal and external stakeholders

Implementation of any strategy requires meaningful and full buy-in by key internal and external stakeholders. List all the key stakeholders and, for each, assess their likely buy-in and collaboration. If this is low, identify the reasons for the lack of support. To assure that you have the needed buy-in, please answer the following questions:

1. Who are the key internal and external people (stakeholders) whose support is critical for the successful implementation of your strategy and experiments?

2. How likely is each of them to support your strategy and experiment?

3. If not likely, what are the major reasons for their likely resistance?

4. What can be done to overcome their resistance?

5. Are the strategies you envision to overcome their resistance consistent with their objectives and incentives?

6. What can you learn from the resistance to implement that could affect your planned strategy and lead to modifying it?

7. If the internal people required to implement the strategy are not likely to cooperate, are you willing to replace them?

8. If there is resistance, should you consider changing some of your strategy and its implementation plans?

TOOL 10

Get the Needed Buy-In From All Relevant Internal and External Stakeholders

Questions RE Stakeholders	Internal Stakeholders	External Stakeholders
1. Who are the people, groups or organizations most likely to resist implementing the needed changes?		
2. What are the key reasons for their resistance?		
3. What can you do to overcome each of these sources of resistance?		
4. If it is unlikely that you will be able to overcome the resistance what plan B can you design to implement successfully your plans without the resisting stakeholders?		

Conclusion

Having read the book, have you challenged your mental model and crafted a new one for the new reality reflecting the lessons from the crisis? Are you reflecting on the implications of your new mental models on the business and revenue models, on the experiments you need to plan, the metrics you need for the dashboard, and so on?

As we come to the end of this book, we hope you found our journey together helpful and, importantly, that you also enjoyed the process. That you have come this far with us, that you have invested so much of your time on this book, tells us that you agree that clinging to the status quo is not an option.

We hope you will now have the courage to take the next steps. Change, especially of the magnitude that we are suggesting, requires tremendous courage. We hope you will be bold and make the decision to change and have the determination to implement our principles. If you are the CEO, you may find it easier to initiate the needed changes. If you are not the CEO, you still have to challenge the status quo and initiate the needed changes in your area of responsibility and also in collaboration with other internal units and external stakeholders.

We would encourage you to share the book, or the parts relevant for your organization, with your team. It would also be great if you could share your experience with other readers. What worked for you? What were the results you achieved? What challenges did you face? What lessons did you learn? As we mentioned earlier, we plan to create an app and we do have a website, a platform where you can share your experiences. Here is the link: www.transformationintimesofcrisis.com.

We believe that together we can create a network of architects of disruption who can create opportunities in times of crisis, defend themselves against disruptors, and become disruptors themselves. **We hope that our network will flourish and thrive and will achieve both business and personal objectives and those of our key stakeholders, while having a positive social impact.**

Appendix

Principles and Illustrative Quotes from Leading Consulting Firms

The principles that we are offering in this book represent the best practices of leading firms. In the appendix, we have included a few quotes from the websites of some leading consulting and professional services firms. Examination of these ideas and the full range of offerings of these firms provide further support for the validity of the principles.

Principle 1: Challenge Your Mental Models and Always Stay Ahead

Accenture: "Reopening will be more than a restart. It will be the beginning of a new era of business. The rules have changed. Employee and customer behaviors have changed."

Source:

https://www.accenture.com/us-en/about/company/coronavirus-reopen-and-reinvent-your-business

Boston Consulting Group: "In many transformations, companies must also rethink their core business model and reevaluate the value propositions they offer: identifying the right target segments to serve, the products and services to offer, and the model that can maximize revenue and profit from those products and services."

Source:

https://www.bcg.com/en-in/capabilities/transformation/three-part-transformation-framework.aspx

Principle 2: Reimagine and Reinvent Your Approach to Customers and Stakeholders

Deloitte: Amid the uncertainty all humans face today, organizations need to take steps to become more human themselves: this starts with re-evaluating their own values. They need to understand who they are before responding authentically based on a new order of priorities: trust, safety, and connection. Organizations also need to deeply understand those they care most about—their customers, workforce, and partners—in order to Elevate the Human Experience (EHX TM).

Source:

https://www.deloittedigital.com/content/dam/deloittedigital/us/documents/offerings/offering-20200730-double-down-humanity.pdf

https://www2.deloitte.com/us/en/insights/focus/human-capital-trends.html

From massive disruption, organizations have the opportunity to reflect and reimagine what the future holds based on a new order of priorities.

Source:

https://www.deloittedigital.com/content/dam/deloittedigital/us/documents/offerings/offering-20200730-uncertainty-clusters.pdf

IBM: "No industry is immune to the growing shift toward customer-centric business models. Every good business should have a solid understanding of its customers."

Source:

https://www.ibm.com/information-technology/5-ways-spot-customer-centric-business

Slalom: "We are at the beginning of the transformation – from bringing to market what customers say they want to rapidly building physical and digital prototypes to quickly and inexpensively learn what they are willing to pay for and at what level."

Source:

https://www.slalom.com/insights

KPMG: "More informed and skeptical consumers are holding businesses to increasingly higher standards. A company's success in achieving customer-centricity and customer loyalty is no longer a differentiator. It has become a matter of survival. To remain at the forefront, leading companies are transforming their businesses into customer-centric, digitally enabled and connected enterprises capable of responding to customer needs and creating new sources of customer value."

Credit: https://home.kpmg/xx/en/home/insights/2020/01/customer-first-insights.html, KPMG. Used by permission

PricewaterhouseCoopers: "As digitisation continues transforming all aspects of your business, understanding your customers—and exceeding their expectations with your core capabilities—is increasingly important."

Source:

https://www.strategyand.pwc.com/gx/en/functions/customer-strategy.htm

Credit: Reprinted with permission from "Customer strategy: Putting customers first, building value that lasts", Strategy&, PwC's strategy consulting group. © 2019 – 2020 PwC. All rights reserved.

PwC refers to the PwC network and/or one or more of its member firms, each of which is a separate legal entity. Please see www.pwc.com/structure for further details. Translation from the original English text as published by Strategy& arranged by Nitin Rakesh and Jerry Wind.

Principle 3: Speed Up Digital Transformation and Design for Personalization at Scale

Bain & Company: "As products and services become more commoditized, customers expect a seamless, easy experience. Increasingly, companies are using data from a customer's interaction history to personalize their products and services, helping them stand out from competitors."

Credit:

https://www.bain.com/insights/customer-experience-tools-personalized-customer-experience/. "Used with permission from Bain & Company"

Boston Consulting Group: Three Personalization Imperatives During the Crisis. Here are three imperatives for marketers who want to come out of the recovery period at full speed. Activate 'just-in-time' personalization, build the foundation for digital relationships, create emotional connections and drive sales via direct channels.

Source:

https://www.bcg.com/publications/2020/three-personalization-imperatives-during-covid-crisis

Capgemini: "Personalization and recommendations are creating significant impact in terms of the customer engagement and improving the overall lifetime value of your customers."

Source:

https://www.capgemini.com/in-en/service/amazon-personalize/

Deloitte: "The growing use of analytics means that products and service providers are getting better at knowing what their consumers want – and do not want – and are adapting their operations to respond accordingly…. Businesses that embrace personalization have an opportunity to create a differentiated proposition that may command a price premium, and improve efficiency and reduce costs, and offer a path to sustainable growth."

Source:https://www2.deloitte.com/content/dam/Deloitte/ch/ Documents/consumer-business/ch-en-consumer-business-made-to-order-consumer-review.pdf

Slalom: "Companies that invest in digital tools, advanced analytics, and data literacy will not only navigate the COVID-19 pandemic more successfully, they will empower flexible, resilient cultures."

Source: https://www.slalom.com/modern-culture-data

Principle 4: Reinvent Your Talent Strategy and Embrace Open Innovation and Talent

Accenture: "Open innovation (OI) is a vital strategy in times of human existential crisis. Why? Because the complexity of the problems we face means no single organization can survive, nor thrive alone."

Source:https://www.accenture.com/au-en/blogs/insight-driven-health/solving-health-problems-together

Capgemini: "Open Innovation isn't just an opposite paradigm to traditional innovation, crowdsourcing, or the management of internal resources towards innovation."

Source:https://www.capgemini.com/2019/04/building-blocks-of-open-innovation/

Daxue Consulting (China): "In order to implement an effective open innovation strategy in China, companies must balance value created internally through innovation with the value captured through the commercialization of external sources/assets of knowledge."

Source: https://daxueconsulting.com/open-innovation-in-china/

EY (UK): "As disruptive, and at times tragic, as the pandemic has been, it presents an opportunity for companies to rethink and reimagine their workforce for the future of work. By putting humans at the center of their talent strategy, companies can generate long-term value in how they live their culture, deploy their workforce and develop the talent of tomorrow."

Source:https://www.ey.com/en_us/consulting/where-does-employee-centricity-meet-the-future-of-work

McKinsey: Make hybrid work, work. The next normal will see significantly more people working in a hybrid way—sometimes in person with colleagues on-site, sometimes working remotely. This model can unlock significant value, including more satisfied employees and lower real-estate costs. There are other benefits to a hybrid working model, including access to a broader range of talent, greater flexibility, and improved productivity."

Source:https://www.mckinsey.com/business-functions/organization/our-insights/ready-set-go-reinventing-the-organization-for-speed-in-the-post-covid-19-era

PricewaterhouseCoopers: "Work may never be the same. Many organizations accomplished things over the past few months that they didn't think possible, whether it was accelerated decision making, breaking down silos or maintaining productivity while working remotely. How can organizations ensure they don't lose what has been accomplished including:

- Ability "to do more with less"
- Enhancing skills and capabilities (technical and non-technical)

- Making human-centered decisions
- Elevating ways of working
- Determining real estate opportunities
- Launching enabling technologies
- Embedding D&I into ways of working to promote true inclusion and belonging and drive real change
- Doing all this "with" our workforce instead of "to" our workforce so it becomes self-sustaining"

Credit: Reprinted with permission from "Workforce of the Future: Empowered workforce. Energized productivity." © 2020 PwC. All rights reserved. PwC refers to the PwC network and/or one or more of its member firms, each of which is a separate legal entity. Please see www.pwc.com/structure for further details. Translation from the original English text as published by PwC arranged by Nitin Rakesh and Jerry Wind.

Source:

https://www.pwc.com/us/en/library/workforce-of-the-future.html

Principle 5: Seize the Need for Speed and Design for Agility, Adjacencies and Adaptability

Deloitte: "Be agile and flexible. Keep current with the ever-changing environment and your transformation progress."

Source:

https://www2.deloitte.com/us/en/pages/operations/solutions/business-transformation-offering.html

EY (UK): Fast impact. Sustainable results. Whether it's a current crisis or a challenge yet to materialize, companies need the agility to create, preserve or recover value.

Source:

https://www.ey.com/en_us/building-agile-resilient-organization

McKinsey & Company: "No company is immune to the changes brought on by the speed at which our digitally connected and increasingly interconnected world now functions. We all need a new way of working to survive and thrive in this environment .... Agile is a set of principles that allows leaders, teams and entire organizations to anticipate and respond to change.... Whereas "traditional" organizations are static, siloed and hierarchical, agile organizations act as a network of teams operating in rapid learning and fast decision cycles."

Source:

https://www.mckinsey.com/~/media/McKinsey/Business%20 Functions/Organization/Our%20Insights/Harnessing%20agile%20 compendium/Harnessing-Agile-compendium-October-2018.ashx (page 3)

Simon-Kucher (Germany): "Commercial agility – a rare combination of capabilities – is what will separate the winners from the rest as the pandemic persists."

"In short, the ultimate key to surviving this crisis is commercial agility: the ability to make resilient design, sales, cost management, and pricing decisions with unprecedented speed and flexibility – over and over again – until some form of equilibrium returns to your market."

Credit: Mark Billige, Andreas von der Gathen, Surviving The Resurgent COVID-19 Crisis, Simon-Kucher & Partners, May 2020. Used by permission of Mark Billige and Andreas von der Gathen.

Source:

https://www.simon-kucher.com/en/resources/surviving-resurgent-covid-19-crisis

Principle 6: Innovate and Experiment, Experiment, Experiment

Accenture: "The experiment-led approach of Test and Learn is a proven one that gets structured data into your organization. It helps determine the factors that drive results, supporting fast, validated progress with innovation."

Source:

https://www.accenture.com/us-en/accenture-digital-video-test-learn

EY (UK): "Continue to iterate with continuous monitoring, experimentation, evaluation, execution and learning."

Source:

https://www.ey.com/en_us/megatrends/how-megatrends-can-reframe-your-future

Optimizely: "By experimenting everywhere, businesses have a powerful strategy for reorienting towards their customer as the true north, striving to iterate quickly, make improvements, and deliver customer experiences that are delightful and fuel growth."

Source:

https://www.optimizely.com/resources/experimentation-case-studies/ (page 3)

Principle 7: Re-draw Your Timelines and Build a Portfolio of Initiatives Across All Innovation Horizons

Accenture: "To make a Wise Pivot, companies need to reallocate their financial, innovation and talent resources towards businesses of the future, but without neglecting their legacy."

Source:

https://www.accenture.com/_acnmedia/thought-leadership-assets/ pdf/accenture-breaking-through-disruption-embrace-the-power-of-the-wise-pivot.pdf (page 2)

Capgemini: "Incremental innovation can better business performance, but rarely changes the game."

Source:

https://www.capgemini.com/in-en/service/applied-innovation-exchange-2/pillar-1-discover-with-aie-services/applied-innovation-roadmap/

EY (UK): "Starting with your future scenarios, create a multi-horizon strategic map that bridges from the future back to today with a portfolio of initiatives that provide immediate impact — as well as the optionality to test and move into emerging or future markets over time."

Source:

https://www.ey.com/en_us/megatrends/how-megatrends-can-reframe-your-future

McKinsey & Company: "Research shows that agile organizations have a 70 percent chance of being in the top quartile of organizational health, the best indicator of long-term performance. Moreover, such companies simultaneously achieve greater customer centricity, faster time to market, higher revenue growth, lower costs, and a more engaged workforce."

Source:

https://www.mckinsey.com/business-functions/organization/our-insights/the-five-trademarks-of-agile-organizations

Principle 8: Deploy Idealized Design, Recreate Your Organizational Architecture and Network Orchestration

Accenture: Those that can reinvent themselves—their processes, customer experiences, employee and social contracts, and do so in ways that further their purpose—will win.

Source:

https://www.accenture.com/us-en/about/company/coronavirus-reopen-and-reinvent-your-business

EY (UK): "New business models must be sufficiently agile to pivot, shifting rapidly with consumer behavior. A hallmark of success will be timely product and services innovation; however, it cannot be a one-time affair. Companies need to develop an enterprise-wide culture of constant innovation and the organization to support it." (page 1)

Source:

https://www.ey.com/Publication/vwLUAssets/ey-evolving-the-business-model/%24File/ey-evolving-the-business-model.pdf

Deloitte: "Understand your capabilities. Do you have the processes, resources, and talent to achieve the new goals you've set?"

Source:

https://www2.deloitte.com/us/en/pages/operations/solutions/business-transformation-offering.html

IBM: "Companies are re-imagining their business structures and operations to become agile, flexible, and responsive to scale up to cognitive enterprises.

Source:

https://www.ibm.com/blogs/digital-transformation/in-en/blog/companies-must-architect-their-business-for-change/

McKinsey & Company: "Organizational redesign involves the integration of structure, processes, and people to support the implementation of strategy and therefore goes beyond the traditional tinkering with "lines and boxes." Today, it comprises the processes that people follow, the management of individual performance, the recruitment of talent, and the development of employees' skills. When the organizational redesign of a company matches its strategic intentions, everyone will be primed to execute and deliver them. The company's structure, processes, and people will all support the most important outcomes and channel the organization's efforts into achieving them."

Source:

https://www.mckinsey.com/business-functions/organization/our-insights/getting-organizational-redesign-right

Slalom: "Transformation, if done correctly, requires alignment across your entire business—including investment dollars, priorities, measurement and metrics, and a path to execution."

Source:

https://www.slalom.com/insight/five-pillars-digital-transformation-strategy

Slalom: "Culture has proven time and again to be a powerful force that can either accelerate, or topple, the most well thought out corporate strategies."

Source:

https://www.slalom.com/insights/your-organizations-superpower-culture

Index

Note: Page numbers in italics refer to exhibits. Page numbers followed by 'n' indicate a note.

A

B

F

H

I

L

Acknowledgements

In the popular imagination a book often is the product of an author's silent and solitary efforts. While that might be the case for some books, for many of them the reality is the opposite. Most books are collective enterprises – none more so than this one.

The roots of this volume lie in a conference on the "Architecture of Disruption" held in Philadelphia in the fall of 2017. At that event, we discussed preliminary versions of the eight principles with a group of international executives. Encouraged by their response, we decided to collaborate on a book to explore these ideas more fully. Many worthwhile concepts, by their very nature, take a long time to incubate. We re-discovered this reality as we worked on these chapters in 2018 and 2019. By early 2020, we were on the verge of publication when this book about disruption faced its own disruption – and one that comes along once in a century: the global COVID-19 pandemic and the economic crisis. The circumstances forced us to pivot to practice the same principles our book was preaching. We seized the opportunity to rethink. We refocused our attention not just on disruption in general but on helping companies navigate the current crisis, create opportunities and provide lessons that could assist them in the future.

Many people deserve our thanks for turning this book from an idea to the volume you hold in your hands. We would like to thank our academic colleagues who have contributed to the insights in this book. Foremost among them is Philip Kotler, who contributed an outstanding Foreword, which sets the stage. In addition, we thank Blackstone director Harish Manwani for his Foreword, and for his continued coaching and guidance. At the top of our list also are companies – too numerous to name individually here – that have either been disruptors themselves or have successfully fended off challengers through innovation. Their examples inspired us to share their lessons broadly. Special thanks go to our corporate clients and the nonprofit organizations with which we are involved. They provided the opportunity to apply, test and further develop many of the ideas discussed in this book.

We owe profound gratitude to the team that helped us write and produce this book. Deepa Nagraj spearheaded the project as its tireless leader, cheerfully helping us deal with every challenge, large or small. This was in addition to doing her day job of being the global head of communications at Mphasis and the Sparkle Innovation System. Working closely with Deepa and the entire team was Mukul Pandya who was our matchmaker. As the founding editor of Knowledge@Wharton he came up with the idea for our 2017 conference and has been a member of our team ever since. He was key to our ability to pivot rapidly from our original manuscript to the current one and did a superb job editing the final version. Mukul has been involved in all our editorial decisions and as a friend and wise counselor has been with Deepa the recruiter of most of our team and the co-orchestrator of our efforts.

Meenu Shekar, an experienced writer and editor, worked closely with us on crafting the manuscript. Akhila V Kamath and Roshni Bhaumik had a wide range of responsibilities and performed each task with diligence, care and attention to detail. In addition, Rakesh Sreekumar worked with energy and creativity on the exhibits for each chapter. We are grateful to him, as well as to Lara Andrea Taber who worked closely with him to design the exhibits as well as the book cover. We are grateful to Barbara Eberlein for her advice on the book's design, cover and exhibits.

Janet Woods served as the permissions editor and spent countless hours tracking down the rights owners of text as well as visuals for the book. Sanjiv Kumar Sinha prepared the index in record time with care and professionalism. We thank them for their contributions to the book.

Last but not least, we would like to thank you, our readers, for the opportunity to share these ideas with you. We hope that you will use the principles and concepts from this book to conduct experiments and to share your experiences and lessons with us as well as others. We hope to keep in touch through the book's website – https://www.transformationintimesofcrisis.com/– as well as through an app when that is available in the future to help implement the ideas in this book.

– Nitin Rakesh and Jerry Wind

About The Authors

Nitin Rakesh

Nitin Rakesh, a distinguished leader in Technology and Financial services industries, has been CEO of Mphasis since 2017. His career spans over two decades leading large transnational operations, delivering transformative digital solutions to Fortune 500 companies. A computer science engineer at heart, Nitin's lifelong passion for Innovation and Technology is evident throughout his career; with his  deep domain expertise in Banking, Financial Services and Insurance verticals, strong customer orientation and an entrepreneurial mindset, Nitin has been able to bring cutting-edge offerings consistently to accelerate value creation for all stakeholders. This has led to Mphasis' C=X2C²=1™ formula for success, (hyper-personalization; drive n=1 powered by Cloud & Cognitive); driving multi-dimensions of value with an integrated consumer-centric Front2Back™ (F2B) Digital Transformation powered by IP assets. Earlier, as the Founding CEO and Managing Director of Motilal Oswal Asset Management Company, he led the launch of many award-winning innovative investment products, including India's first US equities-based Exchange Traded Fund that tracks the NASDAQ-100 index. His work with companies on advising them on their transformation roadmap with an 'Applied Technology' mindset earned him the Gold Stevie for 'Executive of the Year - Computer Services', under the Management award category. He also won the '2019 American Business Awards & International Business Awards – Gold Stevie' under the 'Tech Innovator of the Year – Services' category. He is one of the first 250 CEOs globally to commit to building an inclusive work environment, end disability inequality through business performance: creating social and economic value of people living with disabilities. Nitin is a founding member of Plaksha University in India, a new model of engineering education and research and founding Trustee of Ashoka University in India.

Jerry Wind

Jerry Wind, an internationally renowned, award-winning academician, is currently Lauder Professor Emeritus and Professor of Marketing at the Wharton School, University of Pennsylvania. He joined Wharton in 1967 with a doctorate from Stanford and took an emeritus status in 2017. His pioneering research on organizational buying behavior, market segmentation, conjoint analysis,  and marketing strategy has resulted in him being one of the most cited authors in marketing. A prolific writer, Jerry has authored and edited 30 books, published over 300 articles and edited top marketing journals. Among his many innovations at Wharton is the development of Wharton Executive MBA, the Lauder Institute and Wharton School Publishing. He also founded and directed for three decades the Wharton Think Tank – the Wharton SEI Center for

Advanced Studies in Management. His contributions in the field of Marketing have earned him numerous awards including the 4 major marketing awards: Buck Weaver, Parlin, Converse, and AMA/Irwin Distinguished Educator Award. He was inducted to the inaugural group of AMA Fellows and is a 2017 inductee into the Marketing Hall of Fame. He was one of the original Legends in Marketing, with an 8-volume anthology published by Sage in 2014. He has consulted with over 100 companies, and is on advisory boards of various companies and nonprofit organizations, and testifies in intellectual property cases. He is a trustee of the Philadelphia Museum of Art, the Curtis Institute of Music and Grounds for Sculpture. He is a co-founder of the first private, non-profit university in Israel, The Interdisciplinary Center (IDC) Herzliya. He is the co-founder of the Purple Project for Democracy and of the Reimagine Education global competition and conference.

Made in the USA
Middletown, DE
19 December 2020